North Florida
& The Florida
Panhandle

North Florida & The Florida Panhandle

Sandra Friend & Kathy Wolf

The Countryman Press ✳ Woodstock, Vermont

FIRST EDITION

DEDICATION

To Sunny, for bringing us together

"If there were no mystery left to explore life would get rather dull, wouldn't it?"
—Sidney Buchman

First Edition

No entries or reviews in this book have been solicited or paid for.

ISBN 978-0-88150-765-2

Maps by Mapping Specialists Ltd., Madison, WI, © The Countryman Press
Text and cover design by Bodenweber Design
Composition by PerfecType, Nashville, TN
Front cover photograph © James Randklev
Interior photographs by the authors unless otherwise indicated

Published by The Countryman Press, P.O. Box 748, Woodstock, Vermont 05091

Distributed by W. W. Norton & Company, Inc., 500 Fifth Avenue, New York, NY 10110

Printed in the United States of America

10 9 8 7 6 5 4 3 2 1

Also by Sandra Friend
50 Hikes in North Florida
50 Hikes in Central Florida
50 Hikes in South Florida
Along the Florida Trail
Florida
The Florida Trail: The Official Hiking Guide
Florida in the Civil War: A State in Turmoil
A Hiker's Guide to the Sunshine State
Sinkholes

Also by Sandra Friend and Kathy Wolf
Orlando and Central Florida: An Explorer's Guide
South Florida: An Explorer's Guide

EXPLORE WITH US!

Welcome to the first edition of *North Florida & the Florida Panhandle: An Explorer's Guide,* the first comprehensive travel guide to this diverse region. All of the attractions, accommodations, restaurants, and shopping have been included on the basis of merit (primarily close personal inspection by your authors) rather than paid advertising. The following points will help you understand how the guide is organized.

WHAT'S WHERE

The book starts out with a thumbnail sketch of the most important things to know about traveling in Florida, from where the waterfalls are (yes, waterfalls!) to which beaches you should head to first. We've included important contact information for state agencies and advice on what to do when you're on the road.

LODGING

All selections for accommodations in this guide are based on merit; most of them were inspected personally or by a reliable source known to one or both of us. No businesses were charged for inclusion in this guide. Many B&Bs do not accept children under 12 or pets, so if there is not a specific mention in their entry, ask them about their policy before you book a room. Some places have a minimum-stay requirement, especially on weekends.

Rates: Rates quoted are for double occupancy, one night, before taxes. When a range of rates is given, it spans the gamut from the lowest of the low season (which varies around the region) to the highest of the high season; a single rate means the proprietor offers only one rate. Rates for hotels and motels are subject to further discount with programs offered through such organizations as AAA and AARP, and may be negotiable depending on occupancy.

RESTAURANTS

The distinction between *Eating Out* and *Dining Out* is based mainly on price, secondarily on atmosphere. Dining in Florida is more casual than anywhere else in the United States—you'll find folks in T-shirts and shorts walking into the dressiest of steak houses. If a restaurant has a dress code, it's noted. Destinations farther from the beach tend to have dressier clientele, especially in city centers.

Smoking is no longer permitted within restaurants in Florida, if the bulk of the business's transactions are in food rather than drink. Many restaurants now provide an outdoor patio for smokers.

KEY TO SYMBOLS

🔱   Special value. The special value symbol appears next to lodgings and restaurants that offer quality not usually enjoyed at the price charged.

✎   Child-friendly. The crayon symbol appears next to places or activities that accept children or appeal to families.

♿ Handicapped access. The wheelchair symbol appears next to lodgings, restaurants, and attractions that provide handicapped access, at a minimum with assistance.

🐾 Pets. The pet symbol appears next to places that accept pets, from B&Bs to bookstores. All lodgings require that you let them know you're bringing your pet; many will charge an additional fee.

⚭ Weddings. The wedding-rings symbol appears beside facilities that frequently serve as venues for weddings.

Your feedback is essential for subsequent editions of this guide. Feel free to write us at Countryman Press, P.O. Box 748, Woodstock, Vermont 05091, or Explorer's Guide, P.O. Box 424, Micanopy, Florida 32667, or e-mail ExploreFLA@aol.com with your opinions and your own treasured finds.

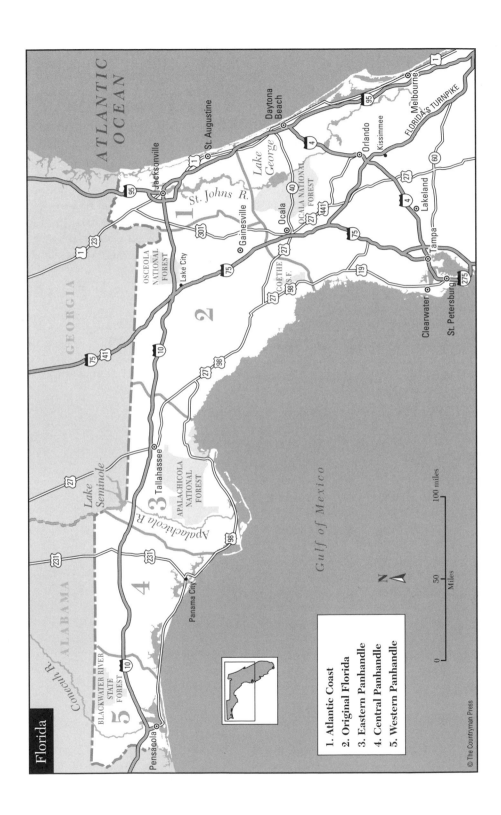

Florida

ATLANTIC OCEAN

GEORGIA

ALABAMA

Gulf of Mexico

1. Atlantic Coast
2. Original Florida
3. Eastern Panhandle
4. Central Panhandle
5. Western Panhandle

Jacksonville
St. Augustine
Daytona Beach
Orlando
Kissimmee
Melbourne
Lakeland
Tampa
Clearwater
St. Petersburg
Gainesville
Lake City
Ocala
Tallahassee
Panama City
Pensacola

St. Johns R.
Lake George
Lake Seminole
Apalachicola R.
Conecuh R.

OSCEOLA NATIONAL FOREST
OCALA NATIONAL FOREST
APALACHICOLA NATIONAL FOREST
BLACKWATER RIVER STATE FOREST
GOETHE S.F.

FLORIDA'S TURNPIKE

N

0   50   100 miles
Miles

© The Countryman Press

CONTENTS

INTRODUCTION

I t's a delight to launch this first edition of *North Florida & the Florida Panhandle: An Explorer's Guide.* As a resident of this region, I've always felt that North Florida and the Panhandle were Florida's best-kept secret, where you can still swim in a spring and hear the frogs croaking from the shore, search for waterfalls along rugged tributaries, glide down a crystalline stream on an inner tube, and in general, have yourself a great time. North Florida feels like the Old South, and it's never more evident in towns like White Springs, Madison, Marianna, and Milton, places that retain vital historic downtowns where people still go to work and sip a cup of coffee. The genteel Old South remains intact: You'll hear a lot of "yes, ma'am" and "no, sir" up here, where live oaks and magnolias thrive and rolling acres of cotton and wheat dance off into the distance. In the early-morning sun, Spanish moss casts shadows on centuries-old antebellum mansions, and a light mist rises from the cotton fields. It is across this swath that Florida's history runs deepest. Spanish missionaries traced trails west from St. Augustine to found missions among the Apalachee in the 1600s. The French, British, and Spanish fought for control of the deep-water port at Pensacola Florida's capital, Tallahassee, was founded in 1824 as a halfway meeting point between the state's only truly populous cities, St. Augustine and Pensacola.

Jacksonville, a modern metropolis both vibrant and historic, anchors the eastern corner of this canvas along with Amelia Island, where the city of Fernandina still shows its Colonial character, and St. Augustine, Florida's oldest European settlement and one of my favorite places to get in touch with art and history. Our coverage follows the languid flow of the St. Johns River upstream to the historic centers of Green Cove Springs and Palatka, and swings across the state to encompass the university city of Gainesville and the laid-back coastal communities of Cedar Key and Steinhatchee.

As you move west, you step back in time—literally. The Central Time Zone begins at the Apalachicola River and extends west to Pensacola. Along the Gulf of Mexico, the shrimpers come in at dawn after a hard night's work harvesting the sea. Time moves slowly here; the farther you stray from the interstate, the more relaxed you'll find the pace. In the Panhandle, agriculture and fishing are still a way of life for many. But tourists now flock to the shore as well, soaking up color along the powdery quartz beaches that extend west from Panama City through South Walton, Destin, Fort Walton, Navarre, and Pensacola.

The Panhandle is a place of natural wonder, where rugged clay cliffs rise high above clear, sand-bottomed rivers; where rhododendron, azalea, and mountain laurel bloom in profusion along streams that seem straight out of the Appalachians; where columbine and trillium add splashes of color to rugged limestone slopes; where vast savannas of pitcher plants shake their draping lemon-yellow blooms in an April breeze.

Welcome to the best that Florida has to offer. Slow down and savor the views.

ACKNOWLEDGMENTS

Building on a fine foundation from the many, many people who helped us pull together our first Florida guide, the one from which this one was born, we'd like to thank the following folks who helped us through the update, including: Adventures Unlimited, Milton; Anita Grove, Apalachicola Bay Chamber of Commerce; Bill Bibby, Macclay Gardens State Park; Harvey Campbell, Original Florida; Janet Chernoff, Wakulla Lodge; Donna Creamer, Pure Water Wilderness; Vernon Compton; Dr. Mack Thetford, and Joshua Wilks, Blackwater River Foundation; Dawn and Kevin Eggleston, Fig Tree Inn; Paulette Goodlin, Columbia County TDC; Christie Gregovich, YPBR; Anita Grove, Apalachicola Bay Chamber of Commerce; Jay Humphreys, St. Augustine, Ponte Vedra & The Beaches VCB; Paul Kayemba, Visit Florida; Sharon Liggett, Tallahassee CVB; Carrie McClean, Jacksonville & the Beaches CVB; Chris Mordi, Amelia Island TDC; Kathy Newby, Santa Rosa County; Linda Patton; Watkins Saunders, Sophia Jane Adams House; Angela Smith, Santa Rosa County; Eve Szymanski, Clay County Tourism; Rob Smith, Jr.; Dawn Taylor, Perry-Taylor County Chamber of Commerce; Jennifer Baybrook, Leah Edwards, Michel Lester and Leanne Vollmer, The Zimmerman Agency; Steve Beck, St. Mary's Fish Camp; Ashley Chisolm and Megan MacPherson, E. W. Bullock Associates, Pensacola; Betsy Couch, Visit Florida; Victoria and Robert Freeman, House on Cherry Street B&B; Carolyn Haney, Amelia Island Tourist; Kathy Harper, Jacksonville & the Beaches CVB; Cassie Henderson, Visit Florida; Stacy Garrett Hopper, Pensacola Bay Area CVB; Tracy Louthain, Beaches of South Walton TDC; Jayna M. Leach, Panama City CVB; Lynn Costin Marshall, Mexico Beach CDC; Paula Ramsey Pickett, Visit Gulf; Sherry Rushing, Emerald Coast CVB; Loretta Shaffer, Beaches of South Walton TDC; Angela Smith, ID Group, Santa Rosa County TDC; Lois A. Walsh, Eglin Air Force Base Armament Museum; Renee Wente-Tallevast, St. Johns River Country; and Louise at the West Nassau Chamber of Commerce.

Kathy would also like to thank her son Jaime Jimino, her daughter Sherri Lemon and her husband, Chris, who kept her car in check, and Terry Myers at her day job, for accommodating her travel schedule.

WHAT'S WHERE IN FLORIDA

ADMISSION FEES If an admission fee is $6 or less, it's simply listed as "fee." Fees greater than $6 are spelled out. Although fees were accurate when this book went to press, keep in mind that yearly increases are likely, especially for the larger attractions and theme parks.

AIR SERVICE Major international airports in the region covered by this book include **Jacksonville International Airport** (904-741-4902). Smaller regional airports served by commuter flights are listed in their respective chapters.

ALLIGATORS No longer an endangered species, the American alligator is a ubiquitous resident of Florida's lakes, rivers, streams, and retention ponds. Most alligators will turn tail and hit the water with a splash when they hear you coming—unless they've been fed or otherwise desensitized to human presence. Do not approach a sunning alligator, and never, ever feed an alligator (it's a felony, and downright dangerous to do) in the wild. Nuisance alligators should be reported to the **Florida Fish and Wildlife Conservation Commission** (352-732-1225; www.floridaconservation .org).

AMTRAK Two daily Amtrak (1-800-USA-RAIL; www.amtrak.com) trains make their way from New York and Washington, DC, to Florida: the **Silver Service/Palmetto,** ending in either Tampa or Miami, and the **AutoTrain,** bringing visitors (and their cars) to Sanford. Stops in North Florida are noted in *Getting There.*

ANTIQUES While **Micanopy** is my favorite North Florida destination for antiques, you won't want to miss the great finds in **Havana, High Springs, Lake City,** and **Monticello,** each worth an afternoon for antiques browsing. **St. Augustine** boasts a don't-miss antiques row on

San Marcos Ave. Since 1985, the free magazine *Antiques & Art Around Florida* (352-475-1336; www.aarf .com) has kept up with the trends throughout the Sunshine State; pick up a copy at one of the antiques stores you visit, or browse their web site to do a little pretrip planning. No matter what you're collecting, it's out there somewhere!

ARCHEOLOGY Florida's archeological treasures date back more than 10,000 years, including temple mound complexes such as those found near Tallahassee at **Leitchworth Mounds** and **Lake Jackson Mounds,** and thousands of middens (prehistoric garbage dumps) of oyster shells found along the state's rivers, streams, and estuaries. Of the middens, the most impressive in size and area are those at **Timucuan Preserve** in Jacksonville, **Mount Royal** in Welaka, and at **Shell Mound** near Cedar Key. More recent archeological finds focus on the many **shipwrecks** found along Florida's coasts and in its rivers, protected by underwater preserves. For information about archeological digs and shipwrecks, contact the **Florida Division of Historical Resources, Bureau of Archeological Research** (www.flheritage.com/archaeology/).

ART GALLERIES Florida is blessed with many creative souls drawing their inspiration from our dramatic landscapes, working in media that range from copper sculpture and driftwood to fine black-and-white photography, giclee, and watercolor. Many artists gravitate into communities, so you'll find clusters of art galleries in places like **Apalachicola, Cedar Key,** and **St. Augustine;** of these, I'd happily drop a bundle in Apalachicola for the beautiful Florida paintings and photography I found there.

ARTS COUNCILS The **Florida Cultural Affairs Division** (www.florida -arts.org/index.asp) offers resources, grants, and programs to support the arts throughout Florida; its Florida Artists Hall of Fame recognizes great achievements in the arts.

BEACHES Where to start? Florida's 2,000-mile coastline means plenty of beaches for every taste, from the busy social scene at **Jacksonville Beach** to the remote serenity of **Dog Island.** In the Panhandle, resorts and condos cluster around the beaches at **Fort Walton–Destin, Pensacola Beach,** and **Panama City Beach;** if you want a quieter experience on the same brilliant sands, seek out Mexico Beach, Cape San Blas, and **St. George Island.** On the peninsula **Amelia Island** offers beautiful strands with luxurious resorts. Public lands are your best places to enjoy pristine dunes and uncluttered beachfronts. My personal favorites in this region include **St. Joseph Peninsula State Park, St. George Island State Park, Little Talbot Island State Park,** and **Anastasia State Park.**

BED & BREAKFASTS Given the sheer number of B&Bs throughout Florida, this book doesn't list every B&B in the regions it covers, but it does give you selections from what I feel are the best I've encountered. There is a mix of historical B&Bs, working ranches, rustic lodges, and easygoing family homes. Some of my choices, but not all, are members of associations such as **Superior Small Lodg-**

ing (www.superiorsmalllodging.com) or the **Florida Bed & Breakfast Inns** (281-499-1374 or 1-800-524-1880; www.florida-inns.com), both of which conduct independent inspections of properties. All of the B&B owners I stayed with were eager to tell their story; most have a great love for the history of their home and their town. I find B&B travel one of the best ways to connect with the real Florida and strongly encourage you to seek out the experiences listed throughout the book. Some motels will offer breakfast so that they can list their establishment as a B&B. I have tried to note this wherever possible, as Internet sites can be misleading.

BICYCLING **Bike Florida** (www .bikeflorida.org) is your gateway to statewide bicycling opportunities. Regional groups have done a great job of establishing and maintaining both on-road bike routes and off-road trails suitable for mountain biking, and information on these routes and trails is listed in the text. Check in with the **Office of Greenways and Trails** (see *Greenways*) for information on rail-trail projects throughout the state.

BIRDING As the home to millions of winter migratory birds, Florida is a prime destination for bird-watching. **The Great Florida Birding Trail** (www.floridabirdingtrail.com), supported by the Florida Fish and Wildlife Conservation Commission, provides guidance to birders on the best overlooks, hiking trails, and waterfront parks to visit and which species you'll find at each location. Sites listed in the regional Great Florida Birding Trail brochures are designated with brown road signs dis-

playing a stylized swallow-tailed kite. Certain sites are designated "Gateways" to the Great Florida Birding Trail, where you can pick up detailed information and speak with a naturalist. In the region covered by this guidebook, these sites include **Fort Clinch State Park** for the East Section, **Paynes Prairie Preserve State Park** for the West Section, and **Big Lagoon State Park** for the Panhandle. The Florida Game and Fresh Water Fish Commission (www.florida conservation.org; 850-414-7929) also has a bird-watching certificate program called Wings Over Florida.

BOAT AND SAILING EXCURSIONS Exploring our watery state by water is part of the fun of visiting, from the blasting speed of an airboat skipping across the marshes to the gentle toss of a schooner as it sails across Matanzas Bay. Many ecotours rely on quiet, electric-motor pontoon boats to guide you down Florida's rivers and up to its first-magnitude springs. I greatly recommend a sail on the schooner *Freedom* in St. Augustine, the narrated cruises at **Wakulla Springs,** and a cruise on **Silver Springs'** classic glass-bottomed boats, but you'll find almost any boat tour you take a delight.

BOOKS To understand Florida, you need to read its authors, and none is more important than **Patrick Smith,** whose *A Land Remembered* is a landmark piece of fiction tracing Florida's history from settlement to development. A good capsule history of Florida's nearly 500 years of European settlement is *A Short History of Florida,* the abbreviated version of the original masterwork by **Michael Gannon.** To see through the eyes of settlers who tried to scratch a living from a harsh land, read the award-winning books of **Marjorie Kinnan Rawlings,** including *The Yearling, Cross Creek,* and *South Moon Under.* For insights into the history of African American culture in Florida, seek out novelist **Zora Neale Hurston;** her works *Their Eyes Were Watching God* and *Jonah's Gourd Vine* touch the soul. For a taste of frontier Florida, try the Cracker western novels of **Lee Gramling,** which draw deeply from Florida's history.

The nonfiction classic *Palmetto Leaves* from **Harriett Beecher Stowe** captures life during Reconstruction along the St. Johns, and to understand Florida culture, read *Palmetto Country* by **Stetson Kennedy,** a Florida icon who worked to compile Florida's folklore with the 1940s WPA project and went on to fight for civil rights throughout the South. For a glimpse of Florida's frenetic development over the past century, *Some Kind of Paradise: A Chronicle of Man and the Land in Florida* by **Mark Derr** and *I Lost It All to Sprawl: How Progress Ate My Cracker Land-scape* by **Bill Belleville** offer serious insights. All visitors to Florida who love the outdoors should read *Travels* by **William Bartram,** a botanist who recorded his adventures along the St. Johns River during the 1700s, as well as the *A Thousand-Mile Walk to the Gulf* by **John Muir** and *A Naturalist in Florida: A Celebration of Eden* by **Archie Carr.** *River of Lakes: A Journey on Florida's St. Johns River* by **Bill Belleville** is a wonderful celebration of our state's mightiest river. When you plan your outdoor activities, don't forget that Florida has more than 2,500 miles of hiking trails—and Sandra walked most of them while compiling her many hiking books, including *50 Hikes in North Florida, The Florida Trail: The Official Hiking Guide,* and *Hiker's Guide to the Sunshine State,* essential for hikers visiting this region.

BUS SERVICE **Greyhound** (1-800-229-9424; www.greyhound.com) covers an extensive list of Florida cities; see their web site for details and the full schedule. Stops are noted in the text under *Getting There.*

CAMPGROUNDS Rates are quoted for single-night double-occupancy stays; all campgrounds offer discounts for club membership as well as weekly, monthly, and resident (six months or more) stays, and often charge more for extra adults. If pets are permitted, keep them leashed. Also see the *Parks* section of each chapter for campgrounds at state and county parks. **Florida State Parks** now uses **Reserve America** (1-800-326-3521) for all campground reservations; a handful of sites are kept open for drop-ins. Ask at the gate.

CHILDREN, ESPECIALLY FOR The crayon symbol ✏ identifies activities and places of special interest to children and families.

CITRUS STANDS, FARMER'S MARKETS, AND U-PICKS Citrus stands associated with active groves are typically open seasonally Nov–Apr. I've listed permanent stands as well as places you're likely to see roadside fruit and vegetable sales (often out of the backs of trucks and vans) from local growers. All U-pick is seasonal, and Florida's growing seasons run year-round with citrus in winter and spring, strawberries in early spring, blueberries in late spring, and cherries in early summer. If you attempt U-pick citrus, bring heavy gloves and wear jeans: Citrus trees have serious thorns. Also, don't pick citrus without permission: It's such a protected crop in Florida that to pluck an orange from a roadside tree is a felony. For a full listing of farmer's markets around the state, visit the **USDA Florida Marketing Services** web site (www.ams.usda.gov/farmersmarkets/States/Florida.htm).

CIVIL WAR As the third state to secede from the Union, Florida has a great deal of Civil War history to explore, particularly in the region covered by this book. Civil War buffs shouldn't miss **Olustee Battlefield,** site of Florida's largest engagement, and should check out **Florida Reenactors Online** (www.floridareenactorsonline.com) for a calendar of reenactments held throughout the state.

CRABS Florida's seafood restaurants can lay claim to some of the freshest crabs anywhere; blue crabs and stone

Sandra Friend

GHOST CRAB

crabs are caught along the Gulf Coast. October is Crab Festival time in **St. Marks,** and you'll find them celebrating the seafood harvest down at **Cedar Key** that month, too. Eat your crab legs with melted butter for optimum effect.

DIVE RESORTS Dive resorts cater to both open-water and cave divers, and feature on-site dive shops. They tend toward utilitarian but worn accommodations—wet gear can trash a room! Lodgings categorized under this header will appeal to divers because of their location, not because of their quality.

DIVING Certification for open-water diving is required for diving in Florida's rivers, lakes, and streams; certification in cave diving is required if you plan to enter the outflow of a spring. Expertise in open-water diving does not translate to cave diving, and many experienced open-water divers have died attempting to explore Florida's springs. Play it safe and stick with what you know. A DIVER DOWN flag is required when diving.

THE DIXIE HIGHWAY Conceptualized in the 1910s by Carl Graham Fisher and the Dixie Highway Association as a grand route for auto touring, the

Dixie Highway had two legs that ran along the East Coast of the United States into Florida, both ending in Miami. Since it ran along both coasts of Florida, you'll find OLD DIXIE HIGHWAY signs on both US 1 and US 17 on the east coast and along US 19, 27, and 41 on the west coast, and even US 441 in the middle—the highway ran through places as diverse as Jacksonville, Tallahassee, and Micanopy.

EMERGENCIES Hospitals with emergency rooms are noted at the beginning of each chapter. Dial **911** to connect to emergency service anywhere in the state. For highway accidents or emergencies, contact the **Florida Highway Patrol** at ✳FHP on your cell phone or 911.

FACTORY OUTLETS You've seen the signs, but are they really a bargain? Several factory outlets offer brand and designer names for less, but you may also get great deals at smaller shops and even the local mall. I've listed some factory outlets that I found particularly fun to shop at that also had a nice selection of eateries and close access to major highways.

FERRIES Florida has few remaining ferryboats; in the region covered by this book, you'll find FL A1A crossing the St. Johns River on the **Mayport Ferry,** and the **Fort Gates Ferry** crossing from the Ocala National Forest to Welaka.

FISH CAMPS Rustic in nature, fish camps are quiet retreats that allow anglers and their families to settle down along a lake or river and put in some quality time fishing. Accommodations listed under this category tend to be older cabins, mobile homes, or

FORT GATE FERRY

Kathy Wolf

concrete block structures, often a little rough around the edges. If the cabins or motel rooms at a fish camp are of superior quality, I list them under those categories.

FISHING The **Florida Fish and Wildlife Conservation Commission** (www.floridaconservation.org) regulates all fishing in Florida, offering both freshwater and saltwater licenses. To obtain a license, visit any sporting goods store or call 1-888-FISH-FLO for an instant license; you can also apply online at www.florida .com, choosing among short-term, annual, five-year, or lifetime options. No fishing license is required if you are on a guided fishing trip, are fishing with a cane pole, are bank fishing along the ocean (varies by county), or are 65 years or older.

FLORIDA TRAIL The **Florida Trail** is a 1,400-mile footpath running from the Big Cypress National Preserve north of Everglades National Park to Fort Pickens at Gulf Islands National Seashore in Pensacola. With its first blaze painted in 1966, it is now one of only eight congressionally designated

National Scenic Trails in the United States and is still under development, but you can follow the orange blazes from one end of the state to the other. The Florida Trail and other trails in state parks and state forests, known as the Florida Trail System, are built and maintained by volunteer members of the nonprofit Florida Trail Association (352-378-8823 or 1-877-HIKE-FLA; www.floridatrail.org), 5415 SW 13th St, Gainesville 32608; the association is your primary source for maps and guidebooks for the trail.

FORESTS, NATIONAL There are three national forests in Florida (Apalachicola, Ocala, and Osceola), all of which are found in the regions covered by this book. These forests are administered by the **USDA Forest Service, National Forests in Florida** (850-523-8500; www.fs.fed.us/r8/florida/) offices in Tallahassee. Established in 1908 by President Theodore Roosevelt, Ocala National Forest is the oldest national forest east of the Mississippi River. A little-known fact is that Choctawhatchee National Forest was established at the same time in Florida's Panhandle. But in the 1940s, the military took it over as a reservation and renamed it Eglin Air Force Base. Recreational users visiting the base have the opportunity to enjoy the old-growth trees preserved by the original National Forest designation.

FORESTS, STATE The Florida Division of Forestry (www.fl-dof.com) administers **Florida State Forests,** encompassing thousands of acres of public lands throughout North Florida; the **Blackwater River State Forest** and **Withlacoochee State Forest** are the state's largest. Each offers an array of outdoor activities

from hiking, biking, trail riding, and camping to fishing, hunting, and even motocross and ATV use. Most (but not all) developed state forest trailheads charge a per-person fee of $2–3 for recreational use. For $30, you can purchase an annual day-use pass good for the driver and up to eight passengers: a real bargain for families! If you're a hiker, get involved with the **Trailwalker** program, in which you tally up miles on hiking trails and receive patches and certificates; a similar program, **Trailtrotter,** is in place for equestrians. Information on both programs can be found at trailhead kiosks or on the Florida State Forests web site.

GAS STATIONS Gas prices fluctuate wildly around the state—and not in proportion to distance from major highways, as you might think. You'll find your best bargains for filling your tank along US 19 in Crystal River; it's always painful to top off the tank in Gainesville. When traveling near the Georgia border it may be worth the drive across to tank up.

GENEALOGICAL RESEARCH In addition to the excellent resources found at the **Florida State Archives** in Tallahassee and **Elmer's Genealogical Library** in Madison, check the Florida GenWeb project (www.rootsweb .com/~flgenweb), for census data, vital records, pioneer families, and links to the state's many historical societies.

GOLF Golfing is a favorite pastime for many Florida retirees, and there are hundreds of courses across the state, impossible for me to list in any detail; a good resource for research is **Play Florida Golf** (www.playfla.com/

pfg/index.cfm), the state's official golf course web site. I've covered courses that are particularly interesting or feature exceptional facilities. Florida is home to both the PGA and LPGA headquarters.

GREENWAYS Florida has one of the nation's most aggressive greenway programs, overseen by the **Office of Greenways and Trails** (850-245-2052 or 1-877-822-5208; www.dep .state.fl.us/gwt/), which administers the state land acquisition program under the Florida Forever Act and works in partnership with the Florida Trail Association, Florida State Parks, water management districts, and regional agencies in identifying crucial habitat corridors for preservation and developing public recreation facilities.

HANDICAPPED ACCESS The wheelchair symbol & identifies lodgings, restaurants, and activities that are, at a minimum, accessible with minor assistance. Many locations and attractions provide or will make modifications for people with disabilities, so call beforehand to see if they can make the necessary accommodations.

HERITAGE SITES If you're in search of history, watch for the brown signs with columns and palm trees that mark official Florida Heritage Sites—everything from historic churches and graveyards to entire historic districts. According to the **Florida Division of Historical Resources** (www.fl heritage.com/services/sites/markers/), to qualify as a Florida Heritage Site a building, structure, or site must be at least 30 years old and have significance in the areas of architecture, archeology, Florida history, or tradi-

tional culture, or be associated with a significant event that took place at least 30 years ago.

HIKING I note the best hiking experiences in each region in the *Hiking* section, and you can find additional walks mentioned under *Green Space*. The most comprehensive hiking guides for this portion of Florida include Sandra Friend's *50 Hikes in North Florida* (Backcountry Guides), *Hiker's Guide to the Sunshine State* (University Press of Florida), and *The Florida Trail: The Official Guide* (Westcliffe Publishing).

HISTORIC SITES With nearly five centuries of European settlement in Florida, historic sites are myriad, so this book's coverage of Florida history is limited to sites of particular interest. For the full details on designated historic sites in Florida, visit the state-administered **Florida's History Through Its Places** web site (www .flheritage.com/facts/reports/places/). Historic sites that belong to the **Florida Trust for Historic Preservation** (850-224-8128; www.florida trust.org), P.O. Box 11206, Tallahassee 32302, honor **Florida's Historic Passport** program, in which your

FORT MATANZAS

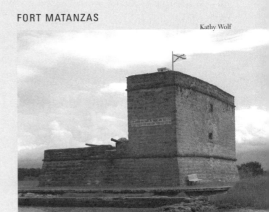
Kathy Wolf

membership of $35 ($50 family) includes a passport that offers special access to member sites—some for free, others for discounted admissions.

HOTELS AND MOTELS In general, chain hotels and motels are not listed in this guide because of their ubiquitous nature. I've included a handful that are either the only lodging options in a particular area or happen to be outstanding places to stay.

HUNTING Hunting is regulated by the **Florida Fish and Wildlife Conservation Commission** (www.florida conservation.org), with general gun season falling between October and February in various parts of the state. Check the web site for specific dates, the wildlife management areas (WMAs) open to hunting, and hunting license regulations.

HURRICANES Hurricane season runs June through November, and when the big winds from Africa start moving across the Atlantic, it pays to pay attention. Follow public announcements on what to do in the event of a tropical storm or hurricane.

INFORMATION Roadside billboards will taunt you to come in for vacation deals. Most are tied to time-shares or are operating in their own interest. True visitors centers will offer information without trying to sell you something. At the beginning of each chapter under *Guidance* I have listed the visitors bureaus and chambers with no commercial affiliation.

INSECTS Florida's irritating insects are myriad, especially at dawn and dusk during summer months. We love our winters when they get chilly enough to kill the little buggers off. If you don't like DEET and you can't stand citronella, you'll spend 99 percent of your time indoors. Flying annoyances include the mosquito (which comes in hundreds of varieties), gnat, and no-see-um; troublesome crawling bugs are the chigger (also known as redbug), a microscopic critter that attaches itself to your ankles to feed; the tick, which you'll find in deeply wooded areas; and red ants, invaders that swarm over your feet leaving painful bites if you dare step in their nest. Bottom line: Use insect repellent, and carry an antihistamine with you to counter any reaction you have to communing with these native residents.

JELLYFISH At almost any time of the year you will find jellyfish in the ocean and washed up on the shore. Take particular care with the blue man o'war jellyfish; the sting from this marine creature is excruciatingly painful. Do not touch the dead ones on the beach; their venom is still potent. Contrary to popular belief, they won't chase you down, but in case you get stung, consider carrying a small bottle of white vinegar in your beach bag; this seems to help alleviate some of the pain. Then seek medical attention. Just as with bee stings, reactions vary.

THE KINGS HIGHWAY Established between 1763 and 1819 to connect coastal communities south from Brunswick through Cow Ford (Jacksonville) and St. Augustine to New Smyrna, this military trail is now approximated by the route of US 1; you will see KINGS HIGHWAY signs on historic sections of the road that are not part of US 1, most notably from Dupont Center south.

MARITIME HERITAGE In a state where many still pull their living from the sea, it's only appropriate that we have a **Florida Maritime Heritage Trail** (www.flheritage.com/archaeology/underwater/maritime/) that ties together the elements of our maritime heritage: working fishing villages such as Cedar Key, Steinhatchee, and Apalachicola; coastal fortresses built to defend Florida from invasion; lighthouses; historic shipwrecks; and our endangered coastal communities such as the coastal pine flatwoods and coastal scrub. Visit the web site for a virtual travel guide.

MUSEUMS Explore our centuries of history: The **Florida Association of Museums** (850-222-6028; www.fla

ST. AUGUSTINE LIGHTHOUSE

Sandra Friend

museums.org) provides a portal to more than 340 museums throughout the state, from the small **Heritage Museum of Northwest Florida** in Valparaiso to the high-tech **Florida Museum of Natural History** in Gainesville. Their web site also provides a calendar of exhibits in museums around the state.

OYSTERS Nowhere in the United States can compare to Apalachicola and its oysters, pulled fresh from the Gulf estuaries along the Panhandle. A lack of industrial pollution and a small population mean the waters are clean and the oysters prime; eat them locally, where the steamed or fried oysters melt like butter in your mouth, and you'll be hooked for life.

PADDLING Canoeing and kayaking are extraordinarily popular activities in Florida, especially during the summer months. A new phenomenon is the appearance of clear-bottomed, Lexan kayaks atop many of the rivers in North Florida that boast beautiful crystalline waters and springs—look straight down and enjoy the view! Most state parks have canoe livery concessions, and private outfitters are mentioned throughout this guide.

PARKS, STATE **Florida State Parks** (850-245-2157; www.floridastate parks.org) is one of the United States' best and most extensive state park systems, encompassing more than 150 parks. All Florida state parks are open 8 AM–sunset daily. If you want to watch the sunrise from a state park beach, you'll have to camp overnight. Camping reservations are centralized through **Reserve America** (1-800-326-3521), 8–8 EST, and can be booked through the Florida State

Kathy Wolf

KAYAKERS

Parks web site. Walk-in visitors are welcome on a first-come, first-served basis. An annual pass is a real deal if you plan to do much in-state traveling: Individual passes are $40 plus tax, and family passes are $80 plus tax, per year. The family pass is good for up to eight people in one vehicle. Vacation passes are also available in seven-day increments for $20 plus tax, covering up to eight people per vehicle. These passes are honored at all state parks except Madison Blue Spring, Homosassa Springs, and the Sunshine Skyway Fishing Pier, where they are good for a 33 percent discount. Pick up a pass at any state park ranger station, or order through the web site.

PETS The dog-paw symbol 🐾 identifies lodgings and activities that accept pets. Always inform the front desk that you are traveling with a pet, and expect to pay a surcharge.

POPULATION According to the 2000 federal census, Florida's population is closing in on 16 million people. What's scary to those of us who live here is that there is a net gain of 800 people moving into Florida *every day*—which means an increasingly serious strain on our already fragile water resources.

RAILROADIANA Florida's railroad history dates back to 1836 with the **St. Joe & Lake Wimico Canal & Railroad Company,** followed shortly by the 1837 opening of the mule-driven **Tallahassee & St. Marks Railroad** bringing supplies from the Gulf of Mexico to the state capital. Railroad commerce shaped many Florida towns, especially along David Yulee's **Florida Railroad** (circa 1850), which connected Fernandina and Cedar Key, and the later grandiose efforts of Henry Plant and the Plant System (later the **Seaboard Air Line**) on the west coast and Henry Flagler's **Atlantic Coast Line** on the east coast. Sites of interest to railroad history buffs are noted throughout the guide under this heading.

RATES The range of rates provided spans the lowest of low season to the highest of high season (which varies from place to place) and does not include taxes or discounts such as those enjoyed by AARP, AAA, and camping club members.

RIVERS For recreation on the Suwannee River and its tributaries, contact the **Suwannee River Water Management District** (386-362-1001; www.srwmd.state.fl.us), 9225 CR 49, Live Oak 32060, for a map that indicates boat ramps; you can also download their recreational guide from their web site. The **St. Johns Water Management District** (386-329-4500; www.sjwmd.com), 4049 Reid St, Palatka 32177, can provide similar information for the St. Johns River and its tributaries, and has an excellent, free guidebook to recreation on their public lands. The **North Florida Water Management District** (850-539-5999; www.nwfwmd.state

.fl.us), 81 Water Management Dr, Havana 32333-4712 oversees major rivers in the Panhandle, such as the Apalachicola and Blackwater.

SCENIC HIGHWAYS The Florida Department of Transportation has designated nine scenic highways throughout the state. In North Florida, enjoy a drive on the **Scenic & Historic A1A Scenic Highway, A1A Ocean Shore Scenic Highway,** and **A1A River & Sea Trail Scenic Highway,** on the First Coast; the **Old Florida Heritage Highway,** which includes 48 miles of back roads around Gainesville; and the **Pensacola Scenic Bluffs Highway.** In addition to these state-level routes, you'll find local designations, such as the **Apalachee Savannahs Scenic Byway,** and county-designated **canopy roads** in places like Tallahassee, Alachua County, and Marion County, where the dense live oak canopy overhead makes for a beautiful drive.

SEASHORES, NATIONAL Encompassing large portions of Santa Rosa Island and Perdido Key, **Gulf Islands National Seashore** provides vast unbroken stretches of white quartz beaches near Pensacola, perfect for sunning and swimming.

SEASONS Florida's temperate winter weather makes it ideal for vacationers, but we do have a very strong tropical delineation of wet and dry seasons, which strengthens the farther south you venture. Winter is generally dry and crisp, with nighttime temperatures falling as low as the 20s in the Panhandle and the 30s in North Florida.

SHARKS Yes, they are in the water. At any given time there are a dozen or more just offshore, but for the most part they will leave you alone. To avoid being bitten, stay out of the water if there is a strong scent of fish oil in the air, which means that fish are already being eaten and you may be bitten by mistake. You will also want to avoid swimming near piers and jetties, which are active feeding zones.

SHRIMP You'll find different types of shrimp fried, broiled, sautéed, and blackened up and down the coast, from Pensacola to Cedar Key. The most sought after are red, white, pink, rock, "brownies," and "hoppers." When you dine, ask for fresh Gulf shrimp and support Florida shrimpers! To learn more about Florida's commercial shrimp species, visit www.wildfloridashrimp.com.

THE SUNSHINE STATE The moniker Sunshine State was an effective 1960s advertising slogan that was also required on motor vehicle tags; it became the state's official nickname in 1970 by a legislative act.

TAXES Florida's base sales tax is 6 percent, with counties adding up to 1.5 percent of discretionary sales tax. In addition, a tourist development tax of up to 10 percent may be levied on hotel accommodations in some cities and counties.

THEME PARKS You could say Florida is the birthplace of the theme park, starting with glass-bottomed boats drawing tourists to enjoy **Silver Springs** in 1878 and to gawk at alligators in the **St. Augustine Alligator Farm** in 1893. But the real heyday came with Dick Pope's water ski and botanical garden wonder called **Cypress Gardens,** circa 1932, soon followed by **Weeki Wachee Springs,** the "Spring of Living Mermaids," in 1947. The 1960s saw an explosion in roadside attractions and zoos like **Gatorland,** and fancier parks like **Rainbow Springs** and **Homosassa Springs** showed off Florida's natural wonders. But when Walt Disney started buying up Osceola County in the 1950s, Florida changed forever. After Walt Disney World opened in 1971, most of the old roadside attractions that made Florida so much fun in the 1960s folded. But Silver Springs and the Alligator Farm are still going strong!

TRAIL RIDING Bringing your own horses? You'll find working ranches and B&Bs with boarding stables listed in this guide, and believe it or not, some hotels will put up your horse— the **Ocala Hilton** (352-854-1400 or 1-877-602-4023; www.ocalahilton .com) currently offers free boarding for your horse with your stay. Remember, under state law, riders utilizing trails on state land must have proof with them of a negative Coggins test for their horses. If you're interested in riding, hook up with one of

the many stables listed in the text. Under state law, equine operators are not responsible for your injuries if you decide to go on a trail ride.

VISIT FLORIDA **Visit Florida** (www .visitflorida.com), the state's official tourism bureau, is a clearinghouse for every tourism question you might have. Their partners cover the full range of destinations, from the sleepy hamlets of the Big Bend to snazzy new hotels along the beach at Destin. Utilize their web site resources to plan your trip, from the interactive map that lets you explore destination possibilities in regions to the vast amount of editorial content that tells the story of each experience.

WATERFALLS Yes, Florida has natural waterfalls! You'll find them flowing into deep sinkholes (such as the ones at **Falling Waters State Park** and **Devils Millhopper Geologic State Park**) or dropping over limestone ledges along creeks and rivers (**Steinhatchee Falls, Falling Creek, Disappearing Creek,** and others). Florida's highest concentration of waterfalls is along the **Suwannee River** and its tributaries, and are best seen along portions of the Florida Trail.

WEATHER Florida's weather is perhaps our greatest attraction. Balmy winters are the norm, with temperatures dropping into the 50s for daytime and 30s at night. When it snows (which is rare), it doesn't stick for long. Our summers are predictably hot and wet, with thunderstorms guaranteed on a daily basis and temperatures soaring up to the 80s in North Florida and the Panhandle. Florida thunderstorms come up fast

TRAIL RIDERS

Sandra Friend

and carry with them some of the world's most violent and dangerous lightning. It's best to get indoors and out of or off the water should you see one coming.

WHERE TO EAT I've limited choices to local favorites and outstanding creative fare, generally avoiding the chains seen everywhere across America. However, several Florida-based chains deserve a mention; you'll enjoy their cuisine when you find them. **Harry's,** a Cajun restaurant found in many cities, delights with tasty seafood and steaks. **Shells,** a family seafood restaurant, serves ample portions for reasonable prices; **R. J. Gators** appeals to the sports-bar crowd. **Too Jays,** a New York–style deli, shines with big breakfasts, stellar sandwiches, and their yummy Mounds Cake. **Woodies** has consis-

tently excellent barbecue at reasonable prices. The **Holiday House** buffets are especially popular with seniors, and you'll find the **Ice Cream Churn,** with 28 flavors of homemade ice cream, tucked away inside convenience stores throughout the state.

WINERIES Florida's wineries run the gamut from small family operations to large production facilities, and some partner to provide a storefront in a high-traffic region while the growing, fermenting, and bottling is done in an area more favorable for agriculture. Native muscadine grapes are the cornerstones of the state's wines. For an overview of Florida wineries, contact the **Florida Grape Growers Association** (941-678-0523; www.fgga.org), 343 W Central Ave, #1, Lake Wales 33853.

The Atlantic Coast

JACKSONVILLE

NASSAU COUNTY

ST. AUGUSTINE, PONTE VEDRA, AND
THE BEACHES

FLAGLER COUNTY

THE ST. JOHNS RIVER

St. Augustine CVB

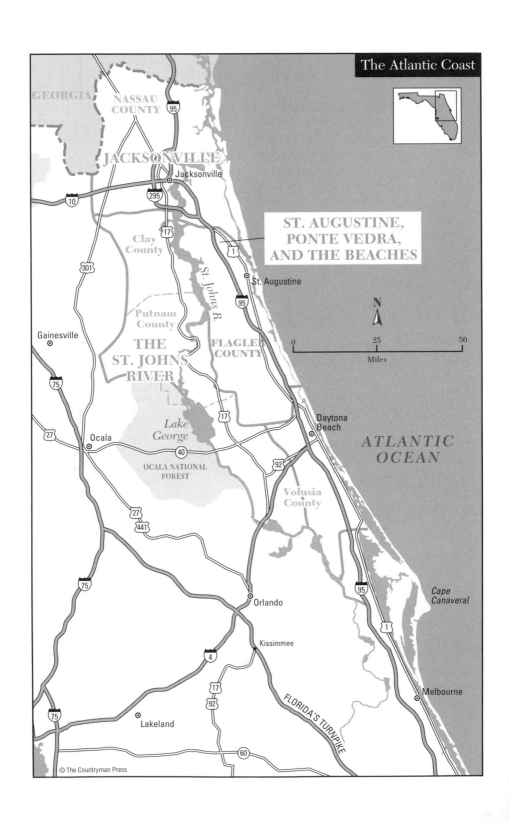

The Atlantic Coast

GEORGIA

NASSAU
COUNTY

95

JACKSONVILLE

Jacksonville

10

295

17

Clay
County

301

St. Johns R.

1

ST. AUGUSTINE,
PONTE VEDRA,
AND THE BEACHES

St. Augustine

95

Putnam
County

Gainesville

THE
ST. JOHNS
RIVER

FLAGLER
COUNTY

N

0   25   50

Miles

75

Lake
George

17

Daytona
Beach

ATLANTIC
OCEAN

27

Ocala

40

92

OCALA NATIONAL
FOREST

Volusia
County

27

441

75

Cape
Canaveral

95

Orlando

1

Kissimmee

4

Melbourne

17

92

FLORIDA'S TURNPIKE

75

Lakeland

60

© The Countryman Press

JACKSONVILLE

The place known as "Cowford" by early Florida settlers who drove their cattle across the shallows of the St. Johns River has grown up into Jacksonville, one of the financial centers of the Southeast. The heart of the region, its lifeblood, has always been the St. Johns River. One of the nation's only north-flowing rivers, it springs from the marshes of Central Florida, its 310-mile length lying only two dozen miles or less west of the Atlantic Ocean's shoreline. By the time it reaches Mandarin Point, Jacksonville's southernmost outpost on the river, it widens to a mighty channel, perfect for commercial shipping.

The earliest human habitation along the river, indicated by the massive shell middens (prehistoric oyster-shell landfills) along the St. Johns, came from the Timucua and their forefathers more than a thousand years before the first Europeans set foot in Florida. On May 1, 1562, three years before the founding of the Spanish colony at St. Augustine, French Huguenots landed along the shores of "The River of May"; their leader, Jean Ribault, claimed this land for France and began a small colony at what is now Fort Caroline. In 1564, more than 200 soldiers, artisans, and civilians settled on the St. Johns' bluff in the protection of the new fort. But just a year later, Pedro Menéndez de Avilés, founder of St. Augustine, marched here with 500 troops and massacred most of the French settlers; the colony was abandoned.

The region stood under many flags. British loyalists settled here during the American Revolution, and American patriots sent them packing. But the Spanish held onto this portion of Florida for nearly 200 years before ceding it to the United States in 1821. "Cowford" was then christened "Jacksonville" in honor of territorial governor General Andrew Jackson in 1822.

A thriving commercial center by the time the state of Florida was established in 1845, Jacksonville saw a great deal of action during the Civil War, with both Union and Confederate forces taking, abandoning, and re-taking the city. When in federal hands, Jacksonville was a launching point for Union raids up the St.

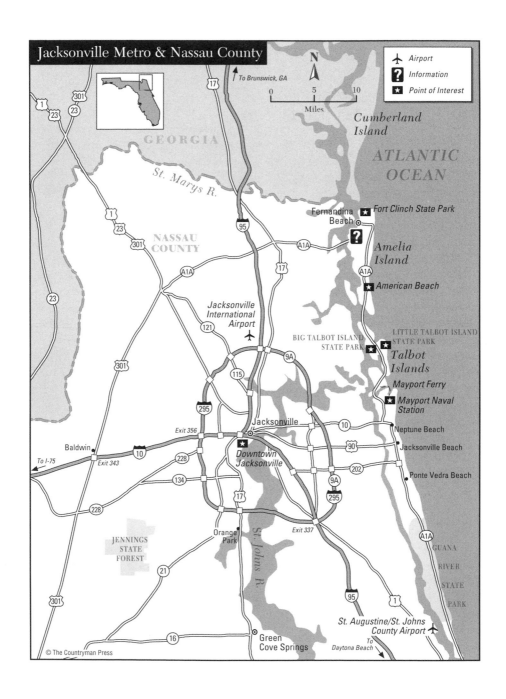

Jacksonville Metro & Nassau County

N

Airport
Information
Point of Interest

To Brunswick, GA

0   5   10
Miles

GEORGIA

Cumberland
Island

ATLANTIC
OCEAN

St. Marys R.

NASSAU
COUNTY

Fernandina
Beach

Fort Clinch State Park

Amelia
Island

American Beach

Jacksonville
International
Airport

BIG TALBOT ISLAND
STATE PARK

LITTLE TALBOT ISLAND
STATE PARK

Talbot
Islands

Mayport Ferry

Mayport Naval
Station

Jacksonville

Neptune Beach

Exit 356

Jacksonville Beach

Baldwin

Downtown
Jacksonville

Ponte Vedra Beach

To I-75

Exit 343

JENNINGS
STATE
FOREST

Orange
Park

Exit 337

St. Johns R.

GUANA

RIVER

STATE

PARK

Green
Cove Springs

St. Augustine/St. Johns
County Airport

To
Daytona Beach

© The Countryman Press

Johns River and along the Florida Railroad west to Olustee. By the late 1800s, the city became a place for Northerners to escape the cold and convalesce. Author Harriet Beecher Stowe once held court on her front porch along the St. Johns River in Mandarin, where passing steamboats would point her house out to passengers and sometimes stop for a visit. Jacksonville Beach blossomed into a turn-of-the-20th-century tourist destination. With bustling business districts on opposite sides of the same street (Atlantic Blvd), Atlantic Beach and Neptune Beach have long been a destination for the region's beach-lovers.

The Great Fire of 1901 marked a turning point. In less than eight hours, it wiped out 2 square miles of wooden buildings, destroying Jacksonville's downtown in what was the largest ever city fire in the South. With 10,000 people homeless and 2,600 buildings gone, the city immediately began to rebuild. More than 20 distinct communities emerged, graced with homes and businesses designed using new architectural styles in stone and brick, not wood. Today, the historic districts highlight classic architecture of the 1920s, '30s, and '40s.

All of Duval County is within the City of Jacksonville's jurisdiction, a point it's tough to believe as you're driving on US 301 on the county's western rural fringe or along the salt marshes paralleling Hecksher Drive north of the St. Johns River. For that reason, destinations within this chapter are broken out under their neighborhood or traditional community names.

GUIDANCE **Jacksonville & The Beaches Convention and Visitors Bureau** (904-798-9111 or 1-800-733-2668; www.visitjacksonville.com), 550 Water St, Suite 1000, Jacksonville 32202. **Jacksonville Chamber of Commerce** (904-366-6600), 3 Independence Dr, Jacksonville 32202. **Beaches of Jacksonville Chamber** (904-249-3868), P.O. Box 50427, Jacksonville Beach 32240. **Beaches Visitor Center** (904-242-0024), 403 Beach Blvd, Jacksonville Beach 32250.

GETTING THERE *By air:* **Jacksonville International Airport** (904-741-4902; www.jaa.aero) is the region's major airport, with regular flights by major carriers.

By bus: **Greyhound** (904-356-9976; www.greyhound.com) takes you into downtown Jacksonville, where transfers to city buses and Skyway are nearby.

SHRIMP BOAT

Jacksonville CVB

By car: **I-95** runs north–south through the heart of Jacksonville. Coming from farther west, take **I-10** to **I-95**. **FL 9** takes you to Neptune and Atlantic beaches.

By train: **Amtrak** (904-766-5110; www.amtrak.com), 3570 Clifford Lane on the north side of Jacksonville, 7 miles from the downtown area.

GETTING AROUND *By public transportation:* **Skyway Express Monorail, Trolley, and City Bus** (904-743-3582 or 904-RIDE-JTA; www.ridejta.org). AirJTA connects the airport with the Rosa L. Parks Transit Station downtown, $3 oneway. The automated Skyway monorail weaves through the downtown area from Kings Ave Garage to the FCCJ campus and the Convention Center on Bay St for only 35¢. Buses take you to the beach or west to Orange Park for 75¢ and up, depending on distance. Exact fares are required, but fare cards can be bought in advance at automated machines. The trolley runs only on weekdays and is free.

By car: There are three main streets that take you from Jacksonville to Jacksonville Beach. To go from downtown to the beaches, take **Atlantic Blvd** or **Beach Blvd** (US 90 east), or from I-95 take **J. Turner Butler (JTB) Blvd** through Southside. **Roosevelt Blvd** (US 17) parallels the west side of the St. Johns River south from downtown past Riverside, Five Points, Avondale, and St. Johns Park to I-295; **San Marco Blvd** (US 13) does the same on the east side of the river from downtown through San Marco and San Jose to Mandarin.

THE SKYWAY

Jacksonville CVB

By boat: **River Taxi** (904-724-9068). North side at Jacksonville Landing; south side at Riverwalk. $2 one-way, $3 round-trip.

PARKING Metered parking is the norm throughout the city, so bring lots of quarters. Rates vary widely, and flat lots are infrequent. Most meters allow two to four hours of time for shopping.

MEDICAL EMERGENCIES For general emergencies, visit **Memorial Hospital Jacksonville** (main number 904-399-6111; emergency 904-399-6156; www.memorialhospitaljax.com), 3625 University Blvd S, Jacksonville. A medical destination within Jacksonville is the world-renowned Mayo Clinic Jacksonville (904-953-2000; www.mayoclinic.org/jacksonville), 4500 San Pablo Rd, Jacksonville.

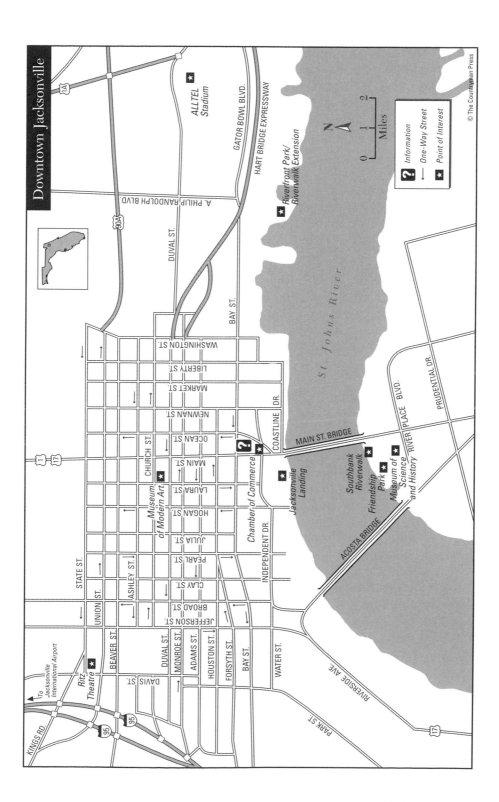

Downtown Jacksonville

ALLTEL Stadium

GATOR BOWL BLVD.

HART BRIDGE EXPRESSWAY

A. PHILIP RANDOLPH BLVD.

DUVAL ST.

BAY ST.

Riverfront Park/ Riverwalk Extension

St. Johns River

WASHINGTON ST.

LIBERTY ST.

MARKET ST.

NEWNAN ST.

OCEAN ST.

MAIN ST.

LAURA ST.

HOGAN ST.

JULIA ST.

PEARL ST.

COASTLINE DR.

Chamber of Commerce

INDEPENDENT DR.

Jacksonville Landing

MAIN ST. BRIDGE

Southbank Riverwalk

Friendship Park

Museum of Science and History

RIVER PLACE BLVD.

PRUDENTIAL DR.

ACOSTA BRIDGE

RIVERSIDE AVE.

PARK ST.

CHURCH ST.

Museum of Modern Art

STATE ST.

UNION ST.

ASHLEY ST.

CLAY ST.

BROAD ST.

JEFFERSON ST.

BEAVER ST.

DUVAL ST.

MONROE ST.

ADAMS ST.

HOUSTON ST.

FORSYTH ST.

BAY ST.

WATER ST.

DAVIS ST.

Ritz Theatre

To Jacksonville International Airport

KINGS RD.

N

Miles
0 1 2

? Information
→ One-Way Street
★ Point of Interest

© The Countryman Press

✳ To See

ART GALLERIES

Avondale

Set in the oak-shaded shopping district, **The Frame Shop Art Gallery** (904-389-6712), 3545 St. Johns Ave, showcases paintings of estuarine and beach scenes by local artists as well as palm tree pop art.

For discerning modern collectors, **R. Roberts Gallery** (904-388-1188 or 1-888-426-4302; www.rrobertsgallery.com), 3606 St. Johns Ave, offers lithographs and serigraphs by past masters and originals from today's internationally renowned fine artists, including paintings in the *Coyotes* series from Markus Pierson.

Neptune Beach

The temptation to indulge was overwhelming at **First Street Gallery** (904-241-6928), 216 First St. Intricate mosaics evoke ancient Crete; stained-glass windows offer a view into undersea worlds. Florida photography, turned wood, fine ceramics, fiber art, paintings of the beaches—you name it. You'll find a piece of art to call your own.

BREWERY TOUR Anheuser-Busch Budweiser Brewery Tour (904-751-8116; www.budweisertours.com), 111 Busch Dr, Jacksonville. This open-air tour overlooks the Brew Hall, where golden beers and amber ales are bottled and canned. Then sample the popular American beer. Great gift shop of logo items. Mon–Sat 9–4; free.

DINNER THEATER For nearly 40 years, the **Alhambra Dinner Theatre** (904-641-1212; www.alhambradinnertheatre.com), 12000 Beach Blvd, Jacksonville, has given Broadway-style performances like *Phantom of the Opera* coupled with a nice home-style dinner. Tue–Sun, with matinees on weekends, $39–46.

FERRY CROSSING In continuous operation since 1948, the **Mayport Ferry** (904-241-9969), Florida's only remaining public ferryboat, connects FL A1A from Mayport Village across to Heckscher Dr on Fort George Island; fee.

FOOTBALL Fall and winter, catch the **Jacksonville Jaguars** (904-633-2000; www.jaguars.com), 1 ALLTEL Stadium Pl, near the Hart Bridge, downtown.

HISTORIC SITES

Arlington

Fort Caroline National Memorial (904-641-7155; www.nps.gov/foca), 12713 Fort Caroline Rd. A replica of Fort Caroline, the first colony in Florida, sits along the St. Johns River inside this deeply wooded preserve, its size and shape based on the paintings of 1500s French settler and artist Jacques Le Moyne. Clamber up the battlements and peer over the sides. In 1565 the founder of St. Augustine, Pedro Menéndez, marched here with 500 troops to roust the French from Florida under the orders of King Phillip II. Taking the fort by surprise, they murdered 140 settlers, sparing only the women and children. Nearly 50 settlers, including Le Moyne, escaped by boat and returned to France. An interpretive center tells the story, and signs along the nature trails invoke the interaction between the French and Timucua. Open daily 9–4:45; free. A short drive to the end of Fort Caroline Rd takes you to the **Ribault Monument** on St. Johns Bluff, commemorating where the French first landed; it is a replica of the stone erected by Jean Ribault in 1562.

Timucuan Ecological & Historic Preserve (904-221-5568; www.nps .gov/timu), 13165 Mt. Pleasant Rd. A preserve of archeological and historic importance due to its massive Timucuan middens and a trail on which the Spanish trod en route to Fort

Sandra Friend

SLAVE CABIN RUINS AT KINGSLEY PLANTATION

Caroline, this deeply shaded park encompasses coastal scrub, freshwater wetlands, shady oak hammocks, and saltwater marshes, with several miles of biking and hiking trails. Open daily 9–4:45; free.

Fort George Island

Kingsley Plantation (904-251-3537; www.nps.gov/timu/indepth/kingsley/ kingsley_home.htm), 11676 Palmetto Ave. Established in 1791 by John McQueen, who sought his fortune under a policy of the Spanish government of Florida that invited Americans to homestead on land grants throughout eastern Florida, this Sea Island cotton plantation passed into the hands of Zephaniah Kingsley, a slave trader, in 1812. Zephaniah Kingsley lived here with his wife, Anna Madgigine Jai, a slave he had bought in Senegal and later freed, and their children. He strove to establish liberal policies for the freeing of slaves, and to ensure the rights and privileges of free blacks in Florida, but failed, and moved his family to Haiti in 1837. Tour the plantation home (a limited portion of it has been renovated) and the slave cabins; walk the waterfront along the St. George River. Open Mon–Sun 9–5; free.

AMERICAN RED CROSS VOLUNTEER LIFE SAVING CORPS BUILDING

Sandra Friend

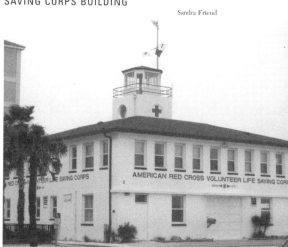

Jacksonville Beach

Learn about the history of the railways and beaches at **Pablo Historical Park** (904-246-0093), 425 Beach Blvd. Highlights on the free guided tour include the relocated Mayport railroad depot; Florida East Coast house #93, serving as a museum; and a Cummer and Sons locomotive from the cypress logging days, fresh off the old Mayport and Pablo Railway, which ended here at the beach in the late 1800s. Open Mon–Sat 10–3; donations appreciated. On the beach, the landmark **American Red Cross Volunteer Life Saving Corps Building** dates back to 1947. Established in 1912, the Corps provides volunteer lifeguards for the beaches, and historically provided rescue teams in lifesaving boats for ships in distress.

MUSEUMS

Avondale
Learn about the lifestyle and culture of the antebellum South at the **Museum of Southern History** (904-388-3574), 4304 Herschel St, covering politics, fashion, home life, and military memorabilia, as well as prehistoric Florida. Open Tue–Sat 10–5; fee.

Downtown Jacksonville
Museum of Science and History (MOSH) (904-396-7062; www.themosh .com), 1025 Museum Circle. This extensive museum will take you most of a day to explore. Permanent exhibits feature 12,000 years of local history and the marine animals of Northeast Florida; special exhibits and programs focus on topics like prehistoric beasts and the contents of the *Maple Leaf,* a sunken Civil War ship found in the St. Johns River. The Hixon Native Plant Courtyard showcases native plants that once grew on the banks of the river, and the Prehistoric Park leads you through the land of dinosaurs. Take a cosmic family camping trip under the stars with Bear Tales or listen to music in the starry night with Cosmic Concerts at the **Alexander Brest Planetarium** for an additional charge. Open Mon–Fri 10–5, Sat 10–6, Sun 1–6; $8 adults, $6.50 seniors, $6 ages 3–12.

The history of African Americans in Northeast Florida is depicted at the beautifully restored **Ritz Theatre and LaVilla Museum** (904-632-5555; www.ritz lavilla.org), 829 N Davis St, in the heart of the century-old LaVilla district. The 400-seat theater is home to exciting musicals and theatrical performances. The museum is open Tue–Fri 10–6, Sat 10–2, Sun 2–5; fee. Call the Ritz Theatre for a current schedule of performances.

Five Points

CUMMER ENGLISH GARDENS

Jacksonville CVB

With 40-plus years' experience in arts and gardens, the largest fine-arts museum in North Florida, the **Cummer Museum of Arts and Gardens** (904-356-6857; www.cummer.org), 829 Riverside Ave, displays its permanent collection from the Middle Ages to the present and is arguably one of the best fine-art museums in the state. As an art major I was in awe of the original works—from Glakens to Rubens—not often seen in Florida.

One of the more important pieces is Thomas Moran's oil painting *Ponce de Leon in Florida* (1878), which depicts the Spanish conquistador in the company of Native Floridians deep in the natural and mystical forests around the St. Johns River. The quaint 2.5-acre English and Italian Gardens overlook the St. Johns and are shaded by a 175-foot canopy from one of the oldest live oaks in the area. Other collections shown in the intimate galleries are 19th-century American landscapes, and Renaissance, baroque, rococo, and impressionist works. Open Tue and Thu 10–9; Wed, Fri, and Sat 10–5; Sun noon–5. $6 adults, $4 seniors, $1 children.

Museum of Modern Art (MOMA) (904-366-6911; www.jmoma.com), 333 N Laura St. Founded in 1924, the MOMA was the first institution in the city devoted to visual arts. It displays a fine selection of modern and contemporary works by locally and nationally acclaimed artists. A very special place is the Art Exploration loft, with lots of family interaction and education in the 16 interactive stations—and on Sunday it's free! All other days, a small fee is charged.

ZOOLOGICAL PARK You'll need to keep going back, because the **Jacksonville Zoological Gardens** (904-757-4463; www.jaxzoo.org), 8605 Zoo Pkwy, Jacksonville, continues to expand and bring in new exhibits each year. You'll enter the natural habitats of animals from around the world at the Main Safari Camp Lodge, with a hand-thatched roof created by 24 Zulu craftsmen from South Africa. You'll find a good showing of African wildlife from East Africa and the Rift Valley. In Wild Florida you'll discover the Florida panther, native bear, boar, eagles, and alligators in a wetlands environment. Kangaroos, wallabies, and koalas are in the Aussie exhibit, and the Range of the Jaguar exhibit showcases the neotropical rain forest with four jaguars, along with golden lion tamarins, tapirs, capybaras, giant river otters, anteaters, and reptilians, including the anaconda. The newest attraction is the Kid's Zone, 2.5 acres with life-size models of Florida's coastal animals, a splash zone, maze, climbing decks, and a forest play area. An animal care facility shows children how otters and squirrel monkeys are cared for. Daily 9–5; $11 adults, $9.50 seniors, $6.50 ages 3–12.

✳ To Do

BICYCLING The **Jacksonville-Baldwin Rail Trail** (www.coj.net) comprises 14.5 miles of an old CSX railway line through a dense canopy of forests, wetlands, and fields between Imeson Rd and CR 121. There are three separate paths: one for walking, jogging, and in-line skating; one for mountain bikers; and one for horseback riding. This historic route was the path taken by Union soldiers en route to and in retreat from the Battle of Olustee, as featured in the movie *Glory*.

MAKING FRIENDS AT THE JACKSONVILLE ZOOLOGICAL GARDENS

Sandra Friend

THE ATLANTIC COAST

Arlington

𝒮 A shady oasis in this urban area, **Tree Hill** (904-724-4646; www.treehill.org), 7152 Lone Star Rd, is a place for families to explore together, with more than 53 acres to roam on nature trails and boardwalks. Enjoy the butterfly garden; explore the **Florida Natural History Museum,** with its interactive exhibits on native wildlife, energy, and more; fee.

Jacksonville Beach

𝒮 **Adventure Landing** (904-246-4386; www.adventurelanding.com/jaxbeach), 1944 Beach Blvd. Get wet at **Shipwreck Island Water Park,** and then compete with the kids on go-carts, miniature golf, and laser tag. Fee.

𝒮 Eat, drink, and play at **Dave & Buster's** (904-296-1525; www.daveand busters.com), 7025 Salisbury Rd. Interactive games, simulators, arcades, and food and drink. Daily. After 10 PM on Fri and Sat, the facility is reserved for the grown-ups. Fee.

Mandarin

𝒮 You'll have a great time at the nicely landscaped **Mandarin Mill Family Golf** (904-262-7888), 10910 San Jose Blvd. Fee.

Southside

𝒮 Inside a cute castle that seems incongruous on this busy boulevard, the **Hands On Children's Museum** (904-642-2688), 8580 Beach Blvd, offers hands-on adventures for small children. They can make a deposit at the Mini Bank, be cashiers at the Winn-Dixie Little Grocery, or play with the puppets. Tiny tots have their own adventure room to explore, and everyone gets soapy in the Bubble Room. Fee.

SAILBOATS

Jacksonville CVB

GOLF With nearly 50 golf courses in the region, you'll find plenty of options. Search through them on the golfing section of the Visit Jacksonville web site (www.visitjacksonville.com/ visiting_jax/golf.asp), where you can dig through background information on the courses and book your tee times online.

HIKING Until I actively started searching for places to hike around Jacksonville, I had no idea there were so many opportunities. In addition to the listings in *Green Space*, you'll find nature trails—usually no more than a mile long—in many of Jacksonville's city parks (www.coj.net), among them **Ringhaver Park, Arlington Lions Club Park,** and **Westside Regional Park.** New to the city are preservation parks, where the land is left untouched except for minor visitor improvements like parking and trails. Of these, **Betz Tiger Point Preserve,** 12100 Pumpkin Hill Rd, and **Castaway Island Preserve,** 2885 San Pablo Rd S, are two of the newest to offer hiking trails. One of the most extensive and pleasant trail systems in the area is the 4.9 miles of interconnecting nature trails at the

Jacksonville CVB

A QUIET PADDLE

University of North Florida (904-620-2998), 4567 St. Johns Bluff Rd, South Jacksonville.

PADDLING **Black Creek Outfitters** (904-645-7003; www.blackcreekout fitters.com), 10051 Skinner Lake Dr, Jacksonville, is one of the most complete outfitters in Florida, with a full line of kayaking, surf, hiking, mountaineering, and climbing equipment. Call Keith Keller, director of outdoor activities, for the extensive list of guided tours around North Florida and beyond. Paddle on North Florida's scenic waterways with **Kayak Adventures** (1-888-333-2480), 413 Second St, Jacksonville Beach, in search of ospreys and pelicans.

✳ Green Space

BEACHES At **Kathryn Abbey Hanna Park** (904-249-4700), 500 Wonderwood Dr, Mayport, boardwalks lead through gnarled forests of sand live oak and over tall, windswept dunes topped with cabbage palms and sea oats to strands of white sand that attract sunbathers from all over the region. The park includes fishing ponds, separate hiking and biking trails, and two campgrounds—developed and primitive; fee. Wildly popular with the younger set, **Jacksonville Beach, Neptune Beach,** and **Atlantic Beach** all offer broad, sunny strands on which to nourish a tan; parking fee. North of the St. Johns River, beachgoers flock to **Huguenot Park,** a shifting sandbar at the mouth of the St. Johns River (see *Campgrounds*).

JACKSONVILLE'S BEACHES

Jacksonville CVB

PARKS Between Five Points and Avondale off St. Johns Ave, **Memorial Park** offers a broad open green space overlooking the St. Johns River, a gathering place for locals and a quiet place to read amid a neighborhood of stately 1920s homes.

Downtown Jacksonville

On a hot summer day, catch the mist off the world's first high-spraying fountains (more than 40 years old) at **Friendship Park & Fountain,** Southbank Riverwalk, on the St. Johns River. One of the oldest and largest live oak trees in Florida is at **Treaty Oak Park,** Prudential Dr at Main St. The tree spreads 160 feet across the branches.

Jacksonville CVB

FRIENDSHIP FOUNTAIN

Fort George Island

The site of numerous periods of human habitation and the highest hill on the southeastern Atlantic coast, **Fort George Island Cultural State Park** (904-251-2320; www.floridastateparks.org/fortgeorgeisland), 12157 Heckscher Dr, shows signs of the human touch—the former golf greens of the historic Ribault Club are being reclaimed by coastal forest. Opened in 1928, the Ribault Club attracted affluent guests with a yacht basin, lawn bowling courses, and nine-hole golf course. The island's human history dates back tens of thousands of years, however; explore it along the Saturiwa Trail driving tour; free. A new way to see the loop is on a cross-terrain Segway with Ecomotion Tours. The two-hour tour takes you 3 miles and visits the Kingsley Plantation at the north end of the island; reservations necessary (904-251-9477).

Jacksonville Beach

Oceanfront Park is a small access point (with parking) along First Street S, with beachfront access centered on a variety of sculptures that children love to play on, including a manatee and sea turtle. Interpretive information explains the creatures' roles in the local habitat.

PUMPKIN HILL CREEK PRESERVE

Sandra Friend

WILD PLACES Within city limits yet certifiably wild, **Pumpkin Hill Creek Preserve State Park** (904-696-5980; www.floridastateparks.org/pumpkinhill), 13802 Pumpkin Hill Rd, lies north of the St. Johns River off a maze of roads off Heckscher Dr (follow the signs). More than 4,000 acres are protected along the Nassau River, encompassing tall bluffs, scrub, and salt marshes. I've hiked out to the bluffs (where you'll find excellent birding) and along some of the multiuse trails, which are popular with the equestrian crowd. Free.

✳ Lodging

BED & BREAKFASTS

Avondale/Jacksonville 32204

The gorgeous 1912 Colonial-style
House on Cherry Street (904-384-1999; www.houseoncherry.com), 1844
Cherry St, is set directly on the St.
Johns River and is within easy walking
distance of Avondale Village. You'll
instantly relax once surrounded by the
elegant period antiques and Oriental
rugs, and in the nurturing hands of
friendly innkeepers Victoria and
Robert Freeman. There are many
reasons why people stay at B&Bs—for
the history, for the homemade food,
for the camaraderie (all found here),
or simply to know that someone cares
if you get up in the morning. Nursing
a bout of the flu while doing research,
I got progressively worse and can't
imagine what would have happened
to me if I had been in a large chain
hotel. Victoria not only nursed me
back to health with motherly care, but
also called to make sure I got home
okay. The inn is grandly elegant, but
not stuffy or fussy. You won't want to
miss evening conversations with these
intelligent innkeepers and their
worldly guests, sipping wine and sampling hors d'oeuvres on the spacious
screened-in back porch while dis-
cussing everything from politics to the
latest novel. Take a stroll on the large
lawn overlooking the St. Johns, where
you'll discover secret gardens and
hidden treasures, then rest on the
Crone's Bench and watch the dolphins play in the river. Breakfast is
equally elegant, with kayaker's quiche,
fresh fruit, and baked goods. The
small pecan grove and blueberry
patch produce just enough to make
fresh muffins for the occupants of the
four guest rooms. $85–115.

Jacksonville Beach 32250

🦐 Perched in the Bird Room of the
Fig Tree Inn (904-246-8855 or 1-877-217-9830; www.figtreeinn.com),
185 Fourth Ave S, I can see right
down the avenue. A willow bed frame
highlights this cozy nest, its walls and
surfaces accented with avian
tchotchkes—lamps, birdhouses,
prints, pillows, and a handmade quilt.
The room radiates Southern beach
charm, with its beadboard ceilings
and walls, and rustic doors and furnishings, yet it includes modern
amenities: small television with VHS,
coffeepot, phone, and wireless Internet. Out front, the scent of honey-
suckle greets you as you enter the
house through the arbor and gardens.
Built in 1915 as a summer beach cottage, it's now the proud possession of
Dawn and Kevin Eggleston, who renovated for eight years before they
opened the home to guests. On weekdays, guests enjoy a continental breakfast; on weekends, it's a sumptuous
feast whipped up by your innkeepers
and served on the screened porch.
The courses keep coming—fresh fruit
and yogurt, homemade pumpkin
bread, stuffed French toast, hash
browns, sausage—so come hungry!
After breakfast, grab your favorite

THE FIG TREE INN'S BIRD ROOM

Sandra Friend

novel and a beach chair and walk down to the end of the street to the beach; you can borrow bicycles and coolers, umbrellas and towels, too. Most guests can't help but return here every year for their beach vacation, so book early! There are six uniquely appointed rooms; two of them (the Coral and Palm) adjoin, perfect for families. $145–175.

A young, fresh B&B, the circa 1998 **Pelican Path B&B By the Sea** (904-249-1177 or 1-888-749-1177; www.pelicanpath.com), 11 N 19th Ave, is great for couples and single travelers. This is a place where you can pamper yourself. The gorgeous dining room overlooks the ocean, and all rooms have a bay window and king-sized bed; oceanfront rooms have an oversized hot tub. Rooms run $125–185, with Honeymoon and Anniversary as well as Senior Getaway packages available.

Riverside—Jacksonville 32204

In historic Riverside, just a short trip from downtown, is the **Inn at Oak Street** (904-379-5525; www.innatoak street.com), 2114 Oak St. Expect the unexpected at this not-so-typical B&B. The 1902 frame vernacular has a warm, comfortable environment accented with a rich use of color, exemplified in the Cabernet Room with rich wine-colored walls and queen sleigh bed. The nature-inspired Hemingway, with Audubon green walls, has a king grand mahogany sleigh bed and whirlpool spa tub. The spacious 1854 Room with gold walls and rich bed linens has a king-sized four-poster bed, an 8-foot-tall French armoire with amber glass doors, and a wine refrigerator. Business travelers will appreciate the wireless Internet and flat-screen TV with DVD/CD

player in their room. Children 12 and up welcome. $120–180.

HOTELS, MOTELS, AND RESORTS

Atlantic Beach 32233

Walk into the **Sea Turtle Inn** (904-249-7402; www.seaturtle.com), 1 Ocean Blvd, and you'll immediately feel the touch of class. Stay in an oceanfront room or suite to be left breathless at the perfection of an Atlantic sunrise. All rooms offer complimentary wireless Internet, refrigerator, coffeemaker, and evening turndown service. Rates start at $99 for coastal view. Aspiring novelists, note: Each room has a writing desk. Read John Grisham's *The Brethren,* written at one of these tidy desks, and discover your inspiration here, too.

Downtown Jacksonville 32202

From the classy **Hyatt Regency Jacksonville** (904-633-9095 or 1-866-613-9330; www.jacksonville.hyatt .com), 225 Coast Line Dr E, you can stroll the Riverwalk to the Landing, downtown's hot gathering spot. Rooms come in two flavors: Riverview or Cityview ($129–189). Suites are available on the Concierge Level, where visitors enjoy private breakfast in the Concord Club. The 19th floor has a rooftop fitness center, hot tub, and pool overlooking the river, and there are two restaurants and two bars in the massive complex.

Jacksonville Beach 32250

The Grande Dame of the beach is indisputably the **Casa Marina Hotel** (904-270-0025; www.casamarinahotel .com), 691 N First St. It opened on June 6, 1925, to great fanfare, the same day that Pablo Beach was rechristened Jacksonville Beach; the well-to-do flocked to this new Spanish Mediterranean hotel in droves. A parade of famous folks has stayed here through the years, from Al Capone to Harry S. Truman. And like many of Florida's historic hotels, it was commandeered for the war effort during World War II to house troops. Not until 1991 did it reopen as a hotel with the elegance of its former glory, with 24 individually decorated rooms and suites providing a taste of the regal past. A member of the Historic Hotels of America, it's a destination that no classic-hotel buff should miss. $89–289.

Neptune Beach 32266

All rooms face the ocean at the **Sea Horse Oceanfront Inn** (904-246-2175 or 1-800-881-2330; www.seahorse oceanfrontinn.com), 140 Atlantic Blvd, its exterior distinctively decorated with blue neon seahorses. Inside your room, savor the view, or better yet, head down to the famous Lemon Bar, an oceanside tiki bar that gets rolling well after dark. Standard rooms, $109–119, offer refrigerators and coffeemakers; suites and a penthouse are available.

CAMPING

Fort George Island 32226

Just across the St. George River from Little Talbot Island, perched at the mouth of the St. Johns, **Huguenot Memorial Park** (904-251-3335), 10980 Hecksher Dr, is one of the region's more popular remote beaches but is extra-special because it offers camping. Bounded by water on three sides, the size of the park expands and contracts with the tides, but the three campgrounds (inlet, river, and woods) remain the same—88 sites total. There are no hook-ups, but it's one heck of a bargain—$5 to 8 per night. Tents and RVs welcome.

✳ Where to Eat

DINING OUT

Atlantic Beach

"Delicious ambience" awaits at the intimate **Ocean 60** (904-247-0060; www.ocean60.com), 60 Ocean Blvd, where the experience starts in the Martini Room, with its infinite array of elegant delights and live music Wed–Sat. Move along to the main dining room to savor the day's specially crafted menu, which might offer pepper-seared Ahi tuna escabèché, drunken duck, or pan-seared ginger scallops with mango beurre blanc. Entrées are $12–30, but you won't want to stop there, not with oh-so-special salads and mouthwatering desserts to bookend your meal. You can drop a bundle with your date, but call it an education in "epicurean." Reservations strongly recommended.

Avondale

Biscotti's Expresso Café (904-387-2060), 3556 St. Johns Ave, is a foodie hot spot where the creative cuisine ($6 and up) matches the trendy coffee that comes in 20 different flavors. The "café bites" are exquisite, from grilled shrimp with roasted tomatillo salsa to crab and artichoke fondue. It's hard to pick a favorite, but at a minimum, come for coffee and their to-die-for chocolate desserts. The cozy tables inspire intimate conversations, especially over a glass of wine from their extensive wine list.

For relaxed dining, grab an early dinner at the **Brick Restaurant** (904-387-0606), 3585 St. Johns Ave, a local favorite where the bistro-inspired menu resonates well inside the restored 1926 Perkins Building. Entrées ($18 and up) include nori-crusted tuna (served with grilled bok choy and miso sauce) and New York strip with a truffle Shiitake demiglaze; for a real treat, try the Seafood Tower Salad, featuring lobster, shrimp, and guacamole.

Under the deep shade of a live oak tree, guests partake in *makdous* and the hubble-bubble of a hookah pipe at **The Casbah** (904-981-9966; www .thecasbahcafe.com), 3826 St. Johns Ave, where the ambience transports you to a secret hideaway deep within a Moroccan souk, complete with pillows on the floor and a belly dancer. Billing themselves as "Florida's Original Hookah Lounge," it's quite the draw for the late-night crowd. The food is pure Middle Eastern, and as my vegetarian friends and I did, order the *mazza* and share: Hummus, stuffed grape leaves, tabouleh, and baba ghanoush (with a side of *kibbe* for the carnivores) make an interesting meal (three *mazza* combo, $15).

Downtown Jacksonville

Known nationwide as one of the top steak house chains, **Morton's, The Steakhouse** (904-399-3933), 1510 Riverplace Blvd, doesn't disappoint in their Jacksonville location. Choose from nearly a dozen cuts and preparations of fine aged USDA beef from Chicago, or consider a whole baked Maine lobster. Save room for their legendary Hot Chocolate Cake topped with Häagen-Dazs vanilla ice cream, and expect a bill of at least $40 per person.

🍴 Sit and watch the river traffic at **River City Brewing Co** (904-398-2299; www.rivercitybrew.com), 835 Museum Cir, where the five-star meals are as much a draw as the location. In casual but elegant surroundings, the restaurant's menu relies heavily on fresh seafood, starting with

steamed tiger clams and calamari and moving on to jambalaya, tempura shrimp, and traditional gumbo, thick with oysters, shrimp, crab, crawfish, scallops, and andouille sausage. Local Mayport shrimp are featured as well, but landlubbers will appreciate the grilled New York strip and other beef and chicken choices. Salads and vegetables are à la carte, so dinner for two (before the wine) will run at least $75. It's well worth it.

Neptune Beach

Settle into a Mediterranean trattoria at **Mezza Luna** (904-249-5573), 110 First St, a place to relax over tempura shrimp (drizzled with sirachi aioli) or a goat cheese pizza with truffle sauce, and watch the world drift by. Entrées ($15–30) include "create your own pasta" from fresh ingredients. Save room for executive chef Tony Pels's handmade desserts!

Of course you'd expect seafood in Neptune Beach, and if you like it raw, **Tama's Fine Japanese Cuisine and Sushi** (904-241-0099), 106 First St, showcases the fine art of Hakarua Tamaki, who in 1981 was Jacksonville's first sushi chef and was classically trained to cut sushi in Tokyo. In addition to fine sushi, enjoy udon noodle soups, *gyoza*, tofu, *katsu*, and more, $5 and up.

San Jose

Since 1985, **Sorrento Italian Restaurant** (904-636-9196), 6943 St. Augustine Rd, has consistently delighted diners with fresh presentations of Neopolitan favorites such as sausage with peppers, veal rustica, and eggplant Parmesan. The trattoria atmosphere is perfect for an evening out with family.

San Marco

Creative cuisine is what you'll find at **bb's** (904-306-0100), 1019 Hendricks Ave, where sandwiches include crispy crabcake and grilled swordfish to complement their signature soup, a rich shrimp bisque. Savor the selections, starting at $7 (entrées $14–23) with a wine pairing from their extensive list.

🐾 Rated one of Jacksonville's best by its patrons, **Bistro Aix** (pronounced "X," like the city in France) (904-398-1949; www.bistrox.com), 1440 San Marco Blvd, melds French and Mediterranean influences for the best of both worlds. The 1940s brickwork and plush leather seats offer comfortable surroundings as you savor grilled tuna over whipped potatoes or a mushroom and fontina wood-fired pizza; entrées $10–32, with half portions of pasta available. At lunch, try the warm lamb "French dip" or salmon tartare, and don't miss the crispy homemade potato chips with warm blue cheese. It's a culinary experience you won't soon forget. Reservations aren't accepted, but you can call ahead for priority seating.

EATING OUT

Avondale

A retro diner with booths and counter service, the **Fox Restaurant** (904-387-2669), 3580 St. Johns Ave, should be your lunch stop for comfort food, from hand-patted hamburger patties to meat loaf and chicken potpie.

Atlantic Beach

🐾 Savor the aromas flowing from **Al's Pizza** (904-249-0002), 303 Atlantic Blvd, a local chain found all over the city. Settle into the snazzy bistro digs and order a to-die-for BLT pizza—I couldn't have believed how good it was until my husband and I polished one off. Al Mazur is the quintessential immigrant-makes-good success story, and he means a lot to the local community. The New York–style pies run $9–18, and the menu includes other Italian faves as well.

🐾 Since 1956, **Joseph's Italian** (904-270-1122; www.josephsitalian.com), 30 Ocean Blvd, home of the homemade crust, has fed a steady stream of satisfied customers. Homemade pasta is their forte—choose from six different kinds, and pick your own sauce and meats for a custom-tailored dinner, $7.25 and up. Bring Fido to the pet-friendly side patio to share your pizza pie, and leave a little room for the nightly gelato specials. Three locations, including Southside and North Jacksonville.

By day, the **Sun Dog** (904-241-8221; www.sundogjax.com), 207 Atlantic Blvd, is a funky neighborhood diner with sandwiches and burgers. By night, local bands transform the place into a pulsing dance floor with steak and seafood sides. Pick your mood, and arrive at an appropriate hour to enjoy this local favorite. Dinner entrées kick off with meat loaf (finished on the grill), $12 and up.

Downtown Jacksonville

The elegance of the marble and glass lobby of the Hyatt Regency (see *Hotels, Motels, and Resorts*) spills over to set the ambience of the **Trellises Restaurant,** which looks out across the lobby to the St. Johns River. The menu features fresh veggies and local fish. Their "famous grouper sandwich" stood up to its name, with fish so fresh it melts in your mouth; try it blackened for just a touch of spice. Breakfast, lunch, and dinner; sandwiches $7–8, entrées $12–20.

Five Points

Perched at *the* Five Points intersection, overlooking the blinker island, the **Derby House** (904-356-0227), 1068 Park St, is a hometown institution offering breakfast all day—my kind of place! I ordered mashed potato salad with my BLT for a heaping scoop of lunchtime delight. The offerings are diner standards with a little Greek twist (feta omelets, anyone?), $3 and up. Open daily 7–2.

Jacksonville Beach

Take in the view from the rooftop open-air bar at the **Beachside Seafood Market & Restaurant** (904-241-2702), 120 Third St S, or just stop by and grab a pound of fresh Mayport shrimp to steam back at the rental. Lunch is the busy time here, with their signature "shrimp burger" a perennial favorite.

Grab a quick bite at **Lubi's Hot Subs** (904-642-3800), 11633 Beach Blvd, home of "The Famous Lubi" ($5). Piled high on a steamed hero roll, it's like a Philly but has a Jacksonville twist—seasoned ground beef with mayo, mustard, American cheese, and a dash of hot pepper sauce. Wash it down with fresh-made cherry limeade!

Late night doesn't slow the crowd at the **Talk of the Town Bistro** (904-247-8757), 1504 Third St N, a bustling little restaurant with Asian and American specialties.

Mandarin

Savor a slice of Floridiana at a funky fish camp—**Clark's Fish Camp Seafood Restaurant** (904-268-3474; www.clarksfishcamp.com),

12903 Hood Landing Rd. With a menagerie of critters looking over your shoulder, you'll savor Southern favorites like fried green tomatoes and fried dill pickles, or choose an off-the-wall appetizer like antelope, smoked eel, or kangaroo (I just couldn't, but you might). Their "house special" oysters are the cream of the crop. Open daily for lunch and dinner, with an extensive menu ($7–19) —try the "Swamp Fest" if you can't make up your mind.

For comfort food, **Famous Amos** (904-268-6159), 10339 San Jose Blvd, can't be beat. It reminds me of the Howard Johnson's of the 1960s, but with a Southern twist. Think breaded pork chops, ham and pinto beans, gizzards . . . you get the picture. Each home-style entrée comes with your choice of three veggies or a slice of pie—you'll have a tough time deciding between chocolate cream pie or broccoli, right? Breakfast served 24 hours, including Southern fare like pecan waffles and fried tomatoes and grits. No matter what time of day, you'll walk out full for under $10.

Dinner with friends is always a fond memory, and I enjoyed one such dinner at **Santioni's** (904-262-5190), 11531 San Jose Blvd #6, after a charity fundraiser. The atmosphere is old-school Italian with traditional Neapolitan entrées, $8 and up.

Neptune Beach

Dine outdoors on picnic tables under a canopy or indoors in the cozy booths at the ever-popular **Sliders Oyster Bar** (904-246-0881), 218 First St, where folks gather for the super-fresh and inexpensive seafood (especially the oyster specials) and cheap beer. Try their Shrimp Dip, made with fresh Mayport shrimp, or a fish taco, with classic Southern sides like collard greens, pepperpot vegetables, and cheese grits; chase that hunger away for $5 and up.

San Jose
A landmark 1938 filling station has become a place where the whole neighborhood hangs out—and lucky me, I know the neighbors! Established in 1992, the **Metro Diner** (904-398-3701; www.metrodinerjax .com), 3302 Hendricks Ave, caters to eclectic and Southern palates with breakfasts like shrimp and grits, grilled three-cheese sandwich, and their specialty, the Breakfast Pie, packed with eggs, cheese, mushrooms, onion, bell peppers, red skin potatoes, and herbs. Enjoy lunch or brunch favorites like the Metro Pot Roast or chicken potpie. Most meals are under $10, and beverages run the gamut from fresh roasted coffee and lattes to Key West limeade. Open 7–2 daily.

San Marco
East of San Marco en route to the beach, **Beach Road Chicken Dinners** (904-398-7980), 4132 Atlantic Blvd, is one of those places that if the doctor didn't say fried chicken was such a no-no, we'd move in. It's been here forever, and it's just plain good Southern cooking—mashed potatoes and creamed peas, soft biscuits, and sweet tea to go with your done-just-right chicken.

Lunchtimes are busy at the **San Marco Deli** (904-399-1306), 1965 San Marco Blvd, where it's a pleasure to dine alfresco with the sound of the Three Lions fountain as a backdrop. The menu includes your typical run of deli delights, $4–6 for sandwiches, salads, and burgers.

Southside
Voted "Best in Jacksonville" for Indian cuisine eight years running, **India's Restaurant** (904-620-0777), 9802-8 Baymeadows Blvd, offers my kind of Tandoori—savory chicken *tikka masala* fresh from a North Indian–style clay oven. Lunch buffet.

COFFEE SHOPS & ICE CREAM PARLORS

Avondale
Lucky me, I walked in on the grand opening of **Perks! Coffeehouse** (904-388-6950; www.perksusa.com), 3651 St. Johns Ave, and plopped down on a plush couch to relax as my husband grabbed me a berry fruit tea smoothie blast. This little independent is a great gathering spot with lots of tables, chairs, sofas, and desserts to complement the artisan-roasted coffee, and cool stuff, including free Internet access.

Neptune Beach
Anchoring an intimate retail complex, **Shelby's Coffee Shop** (904-249-2422; www.beachtowncenter.com/shelby's/), 200 First St, is abuzz with patrons picking up lattes and ice cream en route to the live music offered in the courtyard on Fri and Sat evenings. They also serve panini, Reubens, and other creative salads and sandwiches like the Irie, with smoked turkey, Swiss, sprouts, Granny Smith apples, walnuts, and mayo on multigrain, $8. Open Sun–Thu seven AM–9 PM, Fri–Sat 7 AM–11 PM.

✳ Selective Shopping

Atlantic Beach
Patina (904-242-4990), 40 Ocean Blvd, showcases appealing home decor with upscale beach flair.

The scent of vintage paper envelopes you at **Tappin Book Mine** (904-246-1388 or 1-888-246-1399; www.tappin bookmine.com), 705 Atlantic Blvd, a libraryesque collection of used books where you can lose yourself for a few hours browsing hundreds of volumes, sheet music, and maps. The rarest items are under lock and key, but don't be afraid to ask.

Avondale

Reminiscent of the flower stalls in London's Covent Garden, **Anita's Garden Shop** (904-388-2060), 3637 St. Johns Ave, beckons you through its white gates flanked with blooms bursting from containers into a floral shop with garden extras.

Avondale Antique Mart (904-384-8787), 3651 Park St, isn't in the main shopping district but is worth the detour for antiques hounds who enjoy a browse through dealer booths.

A collector's destination, **Avondale Gift Boutique** (904-387-9557), 3650 St. Johns Ave, is distinguished by its fountain out front and elegant collectibles inside. Look for Lladro figurines, pottery, and glass art; don't miss the Christmas room.

Whimsy reigns at **Basket Case** (904-388-4106), 3575 St. Johns Ave, where you can pick up silly grown-up toys like wind-up cockroaches and desktop punching bags or more serious gifts like baskets of gourmet goodies, pet tchotchkes, and itty-bitty books.

Byrdies (904-384-0728), 3572-1 St. Johns Ave, has dealer booths with a little bit of everything, with an emphasis on glassware and linens.

The danger in reviewing shopping districts is the amount of money you can spend when you find the perfect store for gift shopping. **Cowford**

Traders (904-387-4557; www.cowford traders.com), 3563 St. Johns Ave, was just that kind of place. It's what you wished Woolworth's was like when you were little—a department store full of fun. Complementing a fabulous children's toy section are games and puzzles for adults, cards, and small knick-knacks. Outside along the sidewalk, you'll find a pet-friendly water trough.

Outfit your outdoor living space in finery at **Croatia Boutique** (904-389-6969), 3562 St. Johns Ave, with its imported ironware, tiles, and intricate metal work planters, tables, and chairs.

For upscale goodies for the little ones, head to **Khaki's** (904-384-2712), 3645 St. Johns Ave, with its fancy diaper bags, top-of-the-line strollers, and Lamaze toys.

Downtown Jacksonville

Locals just call it "The Landing," and it's *the* place to hang out downtown. **Jacksonville Landing** (904-353-1188; www.jacksonvillelanding.com), 2 Independent Dr, sits right along the river in the thick of things. Stop in first at the Convention & Visitors Bureau (904-791-4305) to get your bearings, and then pick up your trinkets to take home from **Destination Jacksonville** (904-598-5009), with its logo items and Florida foods. Collectors won't want to miss **Edgewater Treasures** (904-358-7007; www.edge watertreasures.com) for Swarovski, Pipka, and more. In all, there are 40 shops and 9 restaurants in the riverfront complex, with the late-night spot being **The Twisted Martini** (904-353-8464), with dining and live music Wed–Sun 4 PM–2 AM.

Five Points

It's just plain fun inside **Einstein's Kitsch Inn** (904-355-6620), 1051

Park St, where I bought a few wind-up sushi toys for friends and mused over a Jane Austen action figure with a writing desk (Jasper Fforde would be proud). Hula dolls, bobble-head Donalds, global warming mugs, Embarassmints—there's just no end to the great gifts you can stock up on.

Explore the nooks and crannies of **Fans & Stoves Antique Mall** (904-354-3768), 1059 Park St, and it may take you a while. These dealer booths are crammed to the hilt with cool stuff like paint-by-number kits, salt cellars, lobby cards, and Fiestaware. Someone walked past me with a huge L&N Railroad sign. There are literally thousands of items to sift through in this maze of a store.

Inertia Books & Records (www.my space.com/inertiajax), 820 Lomax St, reflects the "urban grunge" feel of the neighborhood, offering the Velvet Underground on vinyl next to punk and indie CDs and vegan activist epistles. It's a great little hangout thanks to Heartworks, a vegan bakery that

moved in to offer goodies like hummus and salad, fresh fruit tarts, vegan chocolate cookies, and Honest Tea.

Refined tastes seek **Lifestyles** (904-358-9898), 1029 Park St, where new age music drifts through the air while you look over the art glass, candles, lotions, potions, and spa treatments.

Midnight Sun (904-358-3869; www .themidnightsun.net), 1055 Park St, is the local center of imported exotica—fabrics, wind chimes, mobiles, gemstones, and other new age offerings, including yoga instruction.

In a little yellow house tucked under a magnolia tree, **Robin's Nest Antiques** (904-384-7144), 2000 Forbes St, offers "upscale retail" and crafts.

Jacksonville Beach

Since 1973, **Aqua East Surf Shop** (904-246-9809; www.aquaeast.com), 696 Atlantic Blvd, has been Surf Central for northeast Florida, with surf, wave, and skate gear.

A vision in white, **Ashes Boutique** (904-270-0220), 332 Second St S,

JACKSONVILLE LANDING

evokes heavenly thoughts as you browse their delicate children's and ladies' clothing. Artist Dana Roby's charcoal sketches are the perfect complement, and they can be transferred onto any clothing or tote. Bring your daughter for a cozy afternoon tea in their tearoom, open Mon–Sat.

At **Black Sheep Surf and Sport** (904-241-6612), 237 Fifth Ave S, stop in for kayak and Hobie cat rentals, beachwear, and surfboards; open daily.

Just a peek in the window caught my curiosity at **Cats MEOW Boutique** (904-242-2560), 328 Ninth Ave N, where you'll find fine contemporary clothing that's just purr-fect.

As befits its name, **Cottage by the Sea** (904-246-8411), 401 Third Street S, has rambling rooms with nautically themed glass: hand-painted folk art windows, stained glass, and art glass. It's not just about sea glass, however; wander from room to room and notice the richly embroidered pillows, handmade mermaids, and furnishings fit for a seaside retreat.

Direct from India, the luxurious dresses, handbags, and scarves at **Malabar Place** (904-339-0315), 204 Fourth Ave S, are set against the backdrop of a historic beach house. I couldn't resist a Rajasthani scarf, and the mother of pearl inlaid mirror tempted as well. Upscale home decor and clothing.

Seashells blanket lamps, treasure boxes, and chairs at **Not Just Chairs** (904-270-8665), 215 Fourth Ave S, a home-and-garden shop with vintage and new decor items. Original art hangs above classic French majolica garden plates; orchids fill a room of wicker with their bright colors. Fine soaps, gourmet foods, plants for the home—it's a great selection of items.

Sugarfoot Antiques (904-247-7607; www.sugarfootantiques.com), 228 Fourth Ave S, is a classic fine antiques store, specializing in European and Victorian furniture. But poke around a little and you'll find smaller treasures, as well—dolls, fine china, children's books from the 1940s, and a year-round Christmas room.

Mandarin

An eclectic two-story gallery, **Bamboo Global Art & Home Accessories** (904-292-0230), 9165 San Jose Blvd, features art and home decor items in natural fiber, wood, stone, and metal.

With more than 100 booths, **Sugar Bear Antique Mall** (904-886-0393), 3047 Julington Creek Rd, provides a place to search stacks of memorabilia, collectibles, and fun retro items.

Packed with antiques and collectibles in 30,000 square feet of dealer spaces, the **Tin City Antique Mall** (904-425-0000; www.tincityam.com), 11740 San Jose Blvd, will take most of the day to get through. From cigar dryers to fine furniture, they've got it all.

Neptune Beach

Boutique Unique (904-241-7109), 216A First St, features beach and casual wear, but what caught my eye were the brightly painted beach totes.

Art runs an eclectic range at **Hibernia Handmade** (904-249-7321; www.hiberniahandmade.com), 108 First St, where I expected Irish woolens but discovered sum-é fish platters and vessels, thick wood-block jigsaw puzzles, fine stemware, and metal art. Fine batik wall hangings from Ireland form the heart of the collection.

Riverside

Pier 17 Marine Inc. (1-800-332-1072), 4619 Roosevelt Blvd. Gifts wrapped in nautical charts? That's part of the charm of this massive nautical store, where you'll find everything from floating key chains to kayaks, outboard engines, canvas sails, and sailboats. Billed as the "South's Largest Outdoor Store," there's no doubting it'll keep you busy browsing for hours.

🐾 Pet lovers! Look for the pet boutique inside the **Primrose Antique Mall** (904-384-7671), 2730 Park St.

San Marco

🦆 I love the name! **Duck Duck Goose** (904-306-0606), 1972 San Marco Blvd, is a playful place with playful items for children (and the adults who love them), from children's books and clothing to a ride-upon (rocking horse–style) snail and butterfly.

ST. JOHNS PARK

In all of my travels around the world, I have *never* seen a bookstore with more books. **Chamblin Book Mine** (904-384-1685; www .chamblinbookmine.com), 4551 Roosevelt Blvd, boggled my mind. You can lose yourself all day in here, winding through a labyrinth of narrow passageways stacked floor to ceiling with books. No wonder they call it a mine—you could dig through it for years and never see it all. It's so comprehensive that the stacks are numbered like a library and authors broken out into their own sections. The staff claims there are more than a million books in stock, 95 percent used, and they've been accumulating inventory for 30 years. Bursting at the seams inside a former appliance store, this bookstore is one of the United States' top destinations for bibliophiles—even the obscure stuff is on the stacks. Serious

CHAMBLIN BOOK MINE   Sandra Friend

researchers will revel in the finds in the nonfiction section. For fiction, bring your life list! I found my whole library of books on Nepal echoed on their shelves, and some of my collection came straight from Kathmandu! Open Mon–Sat 10–6, trades welcome.

Gifts for the garden are the specialty at **Edward's** (904-396-7990), 2018 San Marco Blvd, where you'll find resin critters, garden flags, wind chimes, and collectibles like Lampe Berger.

Offering flirty, fun fashions, **5 Sisters Boutique** (904-399-1004; www .5sistersboutique.com), 1949-2 San Marco Blvd, has racks filled with clothes from trendy designers like Marisa K and Three Dot.

Local artists showcase their land-scapes and city scenes at **Gallery Framery** (904-398-6255), 2016 San Marco Blvd.

Enjoy a convivial evening of sampling fine wines at **The Grotto** (904-398-0726), 2012 San Marco Ave, where a wine bar complements the luxe wine shop.

From folk art angels with fine details (Jim Shore Designs) to Crabtree & Evelyn products, **III Lions** (904-396-9519), 1950 San Marco Blvd, provides a trendy selection of boutique items for you to browse, including pottery and handbags.

Something's cooking **In the Kitchen** (904-346-4222), 1950 San Marco Blvd, where you can sign up for a cooking class or fill your basket with gourmet goodies and cookware befitting a professional chef.

Fine glass and pottery take center stage at **Mimi's** (904-399-1218), 1984 San Marco Blvd, where I found a unique garlic-shaped bottle stopper amid the antique glass, table linens, and pewter.

Gourmet chocolates are prepared right before your eyes at the main offices of **Peterbrooke Chocolatier** (904-398-2489), 1458 San Marco Blvd. The chocolate production cen-ter has antique chocolate molds on display and offers rich chocolaty samples with the tour. Mon–Fri 10–5; tours at 10 only; fee. This well-known chocolate maker has locations in every shopping district, including just up the street at 2024 San Marco, where the cocoa aroma fills the store and you can pick up free samples or enjoy delights like chocolate-dipped potato chips and vanilla cream truffle eggs.

Upscale gifts abound at **Underwood Jewelers** (904-398-9741), 2044 San Marco Blvd, a San Marco institution since 1928. It's considered by some to be the *finest* fine jewelry store in Florida. In addition, think bridal registry—the most elegant china, crystal, and glass are showcased.

Southside

Headed out on a hike or a kayaking trip? Stop first at **Black Creek Out-fitters** (904-645-7003; www.black creekoutfitters.com), 10051 Skinner Lake Dr, an outfitter with the goods to get you on the trail and in the water. Open since 1984, it's the region's only substantial destination for outdoor gear.

U-PICK Rural Duval County is a hot spot for blueberry farming, thanks to the acidic soil; all those oak trees working overtime! In June, pick your own at the **Dowless Blueberry Farm** (904-772-1369), 7010 Ricker Rd, 2 miles South of 103rd St off I-295, and **Sellers Blueberry Farm** (904-781-7739), 10229 Old Plank Rd, off I-10.

✳ Entertainment

Atlantic Beach

On a Friday night, the "in" place to be is Atlantic Blvd, with parties on

ATLANTIC BEACH BOULEVARD

both sides of the street where Atlantic Beach and Neptune Beach meet at the shore. With a few dozen places to hang out until all hours, it's easy to find a nightspot to fit your mood, or try a pub crawl—there's one every few doors. Jazz lovers flock to **Ragtime** (904-241-7877), 207 Atlantic Blvd, a New Orleans–style establishment that goes on and on and on down the street. Featuring handcrafted beers, it's not *a* bar but a series of intimate spaces (each with its own bar) evoking the French Quarter, and it offers a full dinner menu and plenty of appetizers 'til late. Bouncers guard the doors at the **Lemon Bar,** the famous tiki bar at the Sea Horse Oceanfront Inn (see *Lodging*), and the place is wall-to-wall people late into the night. History buffs note: **Pete's Bar** (904-249-9158), 117 First St, was the first bar in Florida to reopen after Prohibition. You expect Mickey Spillane to step out of the shadows in this smoky noir setting with its dark booths and busy pool tables—"a serious bar for serious drinkers." For a more sedate experience, walk down to the next block; **200 First Street** (www.200first street.com) for "Music in the Courtyard" every Friday and Saturday evening, April through October, 7–10 PM. Local artists kick up the jams amid gleaming chrome at the Sun Dog (see *Eating Out*), and upstairs at **Caribee Key,** go for a taste of the Virgin Islands and some island rhythms at their tropical Cruzan Rum bar beneath bright Caribbean pastels; be sure to sample the avocado salsa and coconut shrimp!

Jacksonville Beach
Bring your beach chair or blanket and join the locals for **Moonlight Movies on the Beach,** offered at Jacksonville Beach all summer long, 9 PM on Friday evenings at the Sea Walk Pavilion; free.

San Marco
An art deco treasure, the **San Marco Theater** (904-396-4845), 1996 San Marco Blvd, designed by Roy A. Benjamin in 1938, is an elegant place to

take a date as the centerpiece of an evening out on the town. The theater shows both art films and cult classics, and in addition to popcorn, they serve up beer and wine. Call ahead for showtimes. Just down the street, the art deco Harold K. Smith Playhouse offers a slate of live theater September through June—and they're approaching their 90th season!

✳ Special Events

For an extraordinarily in-depth list of local festivals and special events, check the Visit Jacksonville web site (www.visitjacksonville.com). Here are some highlights:

May: The **Jacksonville Beer & Food Festival** at the Morocco Shrine Temple Auditorium features more than 130 exotic beers and food. The multicultural **World of Nations Celebration** in Metropolitan Park serves up exotic foods and fun. Take a self-guided **Historic Home Tour** through Riverside-Avondale. The **Kuumba Festival** celebrates African American heritage at Clanzel Brown Park, while high-flying dogs catch

Jacksonville CVB

KUUMBA FESTIVAL

Frisbees at the **Florida State Canine Frisbee Championships,** Bolles School. Join fellow bibliophiles at **Much Ado About Books** (904-630-1995; www.muchado aboutbooks.com), where big-name authors and Florida favorites rub elbows with their readers.

June–August: Seawalk Pavillion **jazz concerts** take place in Jacksonville Beach throughout the summer.

September: The **Riverside Arts Festival** arts and crafts show takes place at Riverside Park in Jacksonville.

October: The **Jacksonville Agricultural Fair** features livestock, a petting zoo, arts and crafts, midway rides, and live entertainment.

December: The **Holiday by the Sea Festival** takes place at the Seawalk Pavilion in Jacksonville Beach.

SAN MARCO THEATER

Sandra Friend

NASSAU COUNTY

AMELIA ISLAND, FERNANDINA BEACH, AND WEST NASSAU COUNTY

With its long, rich history, Amelia Island—the southernmost of the Sea Island chain and home of the colonial-era city of Fernandina Beach—has borne the rule of eight flags. In 1562, the French claimed this land, attempting to establish a colony along the St. Johns River to the south. The Spanish massacred most of the colonists in 1565 and divided the land into land grants. But because of its deepwater port at the mouth of the St. Marys River, Fernandina Beach always was up for grabs by anyone who wanted to challenge the authority of Spain.

By 1763, Fernandina Beach was a port of operations for the British, who had an uprising—the American Revolution—on their hands. When Britain passed control back to Spain, local patriots seized the deepwater port several times, hoisting three different flags (Patriots, Florida Green Cross, and Mexican Rebel) but never hanging onto control for more than a few years. In the wake of Thomas Jefferson's Embargo Act of 1807, all United States ports were closed to foreign shipping—but not Fernandina Beach. Its Spanish governor looked the other way as the port slid into the ribaldry echoed throughout lawless ports of the Caribbean, where smugglers met, pirates plotted, racketeers reconnoitered, and the seamy side of life stayed close to the surface. The city officially became part of the United States when Florida became a territory in 1821.

When the War Between the States broke out, Fort Clinch was considered a prime defender for the port of Fernandina Beach and the St. Marys River, the dividing line between Georgia and Florida. The Confederate flag rose above the fort, and Senator David Yulee came to town. He bankrolled Florida's first significant railroad system, the Florida Railroad, to move export goods from the deepwater port to the Cedar Keys, a shortcut for ships serving the ports of Mobile, New Orleans, and Havana. A few years after Florida rejoined the Union, naturalist John Muir arrived and walked the railroad route west as part of his "Thousand-Mile Walk to the Gulf." The railroad, too, shaped the destiny of this city; when Henry Flagler bypassed Yulee's stronghold, Fernandina Beach became a sleepy backwater in an otherwise robust new tourist industry along

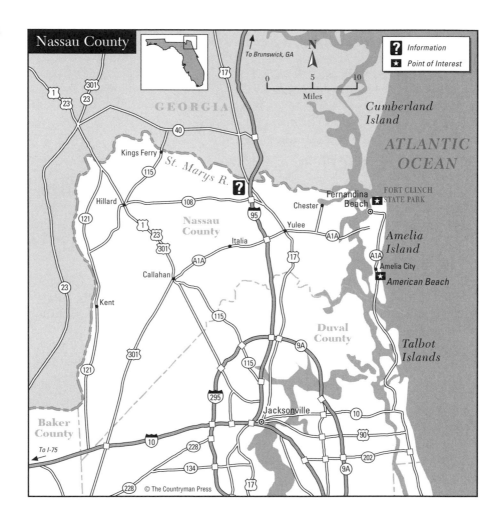

Florida's Atlantic Coast. A new industry came to the forefront—shrimping. Employing fishermen from Sicily, Portugal, Greece, and Germany, all of whom rowed boats while trawling their handmade nets, the shrimping industry grew quickly after 1900. The S. Salvador Company added refrigeration and better nets to motor-powered vessels, creating the first shrimp boats. Standard Marine (known locally as the Net House) started out making nets for the shrimp boats; now they also provide the nets used for Major League Baseball backstops.

As the city of Fernandina Beach grew, the population expanded farther south into the wilds along Amelia Island. Established in 1933 as a benefit for employees of the Afro-American Life Insurance Company, American Beach was Florida's first African American beach resort during segregation, boasting its own swinging nightclubs and hotels. If you've seen the John Sayles film *Sunshine State,* you know the rest of the story—half the residents sold out to developers, and now the historic beach is sandwiched between the Ritz-Carlton and Amelia

Island Plantation. Local character and beloved "Beach Lady," keeper of American Beach history, MaVynee Betsch, passed away in 2005. A 2,500-foot strip of public beach remains for all to enjoy, and historic preservation efforts continue to protect structures with cultural significance.

With the Intracoastal Waterway defining the western shore of Amelia Island and the Talbot Islands, Amelia Island's wild side is showcased in its vast acreage of natural preserves, from the Fort Clinch and St. Johns Aquatic Preserves offering protection to the seemingly unending stretches of estuarine marsh fringing the islands, to state parks like Fort Clinch, Big Talbot, Little Talbot, and Amelia Island. Inland, you'll find Simmons State Forest along the languid St. Marys River, and Cary State Forest, with its pitcher plant bogs amid the wet flatwoods. Western Nassau County remains a rural outpost, with farming and forestry its primary economy, its largest towns Hilliard and Callahan along US 301.

GUIDANCE Stop by the **1899 Florida Railroad Depot,** where you'll find the Amelia Island Welcome Center (1-800-2AMELIA), 102 Centre St, for on-the-spot travel planning assistance. Or plan your trip ahead of time on the **Amelia Island Tourist Development Council** web site at www.ameliaisland.org. For explorations in West Nassau County (Callahan and Hilliard), contact the **West Nassau County Chamber of Commerce** (904-879-1441), P.O. Box 98, Callahan 32011.

GETTING THERE *By air*: **Jacksonville International Airport** (see the Jacksonville chapter) is the nearest major airport, just 30 minutes south along I-95.

By car; **I-95** runs north-south through the region, connecting all major highways; **FL A1A** passes through all coastal communities, including Fernandina.

GETTING AROUND *By car*: From **I-95,** take **FL A1A** east to Amelia Island. A1A loops north through the Fernandina historic district, then turns east again to the beach. Head south on Fletcher Ave (FL A1A) through Fernandina Beach; the road turns west at Amelia City and connects with FL 105. The **Buccaneer Trail** (FL 105) continues past the roads leading to American Beach and then on to the Talbot Islands, turning to follow the St. Johns River, where you can take the Mayport Ferry to continue on A1A. **US 1** also connects Fernandina to Jacksonville. A1A continues west from Fernandina to **US 301,** which is the route from Folkston, Georgia, south through Hilliard and Callahan.

MEDICAL EMERGENCIES You'll find emergency services available at **Baptist Medical Center Nassau** (904-321-3500), 1250 South 18th St, Fernandina Beach.

✳ **To See**

ART GALLERIES Art galleries and studios showcase their works on

FORT CLINCH'S DEFENSES

Sandra Friend

Artrageous First Fridays (see *Special Events*). You'll enjoy such artists as **Sax/Designs on Gallery/Gifts** (904-277-4104), featuring American crafts, glass, wood, clay, and metal, and **Susan's Slightly Off Centre Gallery and Gifts** (904-277-1147), with unusual collections of ceramics, paintings, and glass, plus funky clothing. At the **Wall Art Gallery** (904-491-6303; www.wallartweb.com), 122 S Eighth St, formal gallery openings are followed by showings by world-renowned artists such as Hungarian-born bronze sculptor Armand Gilanyi and black-and-white photographer Kenneth Cain.

AVIATION TOURS The only way to see Fernandina Beach, Fort Clinch, and Cumberland Island all at once is from the air with **Island Aerial Tours** (904-321-0904), 1600 Airport Rd, Amelia Island. Bob and Chong Murphy take you on a magical journey over kayakers paddling the emerald green saltwater marsh-lands, wild horses running on the white sands, shrimp boats setting out to sea with dolphin escorts, and historic downtown Fernandina, including Fort Clinch. The small plane will hold two or three passengers. Call for customized tours and rates.

BOAT TOURS At **Amelia River Cruises & Charters** (904-261-9972), board the *Ryan-K* for fully narrated scenic tours exploring the backwaters of Amelia Island, discovering the area's rich history, or cruising around Cumberland Island to see horses galloping across the pristine white sands. North Amelia River or North and South Amelia Sunset $14 adults, $10 children. Two-hour Cumberland Island $20 adults, $16 children. The Amelia Island Lighthouse tour is only on Monday.

A private ferry departs from the docks in Fernandina for day or dinner trips to **Greyfield Inn Cumberland Island** (904-261-6408; www.greyfieldinn.com), Cumberland Island, Georgia (see *Lodging*).

Not your typical boat tour, the one at **St. Marys River Fish Camp & Campground** (904-845-4440 or 966-845-4443), 28506 Scotts Landing Rd, Hilliard, is along a quiet stretch of the river where you'll simply enjoy the ride, in a small bass boat, looking for alligators, deer, eagles, owls, and fish jumping in the rivers. Ahhhh!

CARRIAGE TOURS Old Towne Carriage Company (904-277-1555), Amelia Island. Take a 30- to 40-minute ride in a horse-drawn carriage through the Fernandina historic district while your narrator points out the history and culture of sites on the National Register of Historic Places in a 50-block area. $15 adults, $8 ages 3–12.

HISTORIC SITES With its 50-block historic district, **Fernandina Beach** is one giant historic site, a treasure trove for architecture and history buffs. More than 400 of the city's homes and shops pre-date the 1920s building boom. **Victorian mansions** are concentrated in the **Silk Stocking District,** and they come in all flavors—from Florida vernacular to Queen Anne. If you visit only one bar in Florida, make it the **Palace Saloon** (904-491-3332; www.thepalacesaloon.com), 117 Centre St, Florida's oldest. Opened in 1878, it boasts a 40-foot-long mahogany bar, handcrafted caryatids, and lush hand-painted murals—you can imagine pirates plotting (or are those Vanderbilts whispering?) in the dark corners.

Amelia Island Tourist Development Council

FORT CLINCH

Dating back to 1842, **Fort Clinch** (see *Green Space*) is one of the largest brick structures in Florida, and a must-see for architecture buffs. Designed as a Third System fortress, it utilizes some snazzy masonry tricks for roof support, including flying buttresses, vaulted archways, and hexagonal archway systems, with bricks facing downward in the ceilings in some of the tunnels. You'll even find a gothic pentagonal ceiling inside the bastion, echoing the fortresses of Europe. Built to defend the Fernandina port, Fort Clinch has a two-wall fortification: one masonry, one earthen. Batteries stand on the masonry walls. While construction started in 1842, it did not end until 1867. The fort was garrisoned during the Civil War and the Spanish-American War before the U.S. Government sold it in 1926. Thankfully, it was not torn down by the developer who bought it, and instead came into state ownership in 1935. Laborers from the Civilian Conservation Corps worked for six years on its renovation.

MUSEUM Stop by the old **Nassau County Jail** on Centre St, home to the **Amelia Island Museum of History** (904-261-7378; ww.ameliaislandmuseum ofhistory.org), 233 S Third St. Learn about why Amelia Island is the only location in America to have been ruled under eight flags, and enjoy the richly detailed quilt depicting historic sites around the city. Take a walking tour down Centre St, or a ghost tour beginning at St. Peters Cemetery. Open Mon–Fri 10–5, Sat 10–4.

✳ To Do

FISHING At **St. Marys River Fish Camp & Campground** (904-845-4440 or 966-845-4443; www.stmarysriverfishcamp.com), 28506 Scotts Landing Rd, Hilliard (see *Fish Camp*), you're so close the Georgia border you can cast your line across it. Take a ride down the black waters of the St. Marys in a small bass boat as it curves past white sandbars, cypress trees, and alligators, then under a train trestle. Fish or just enjoy the view. The river winds along a 130-mile path from the Okefenokee Swamp to the Atlantic. Given the connection to the ocean, tides play a role even this far up. Watch for shallow and narrow areas during low tide when sandy banks are displayed, especially in the narrower sections. Half day 2–4 miles, full day 12–20 miles.

HIKING Some of the don't-miss outdoor experiences in this region include the **Island Hiking Trail,** a 3.5-mile seaside loop at Little Talbot Island State Park;

the **Cary Nature Trail,** a short but satisfying stroll at Cary State Forest; and a walk on the back roads of Simmons State Forest, which lead to scenic views of the St. Marys River and past some of the rarest plants in Florida. My favorite short walk is **Blackrock Beach** at Big Talbot Island State park—it'll surprise you!

JET SKIING On Amelia Island, escape with a Jet Ski or parasail at **Adventure Amelia** (904-277-1161), located at Peter's Point, or **Island Water Sports** (904-261-1230).

PADDLING Rent a canoe or kayak from the folks at **St. Marys Canoe Country Outpost** (904-845-4440 or 966-845-4443; www.stmarysriverfishcamp.com), 28506 Scotts Landing Rd, Hilliard, and then explore the river on your own. Don't forget to pack a lunch: You'll want to stop for a relaxing break on the sandy banks.

Learn the correct way to kayak at **Kayak Amelia** (904-251-0016; www.kayak amelia.com), 13030 Heckscher Dr, in the saltwater marshes between Big and Little Talbot Islands. Jody Hetchka shows you safety first, and then carefully fits you with top-of-the-line paddles and kayaks. Head out into the saltwater marshes while your guide explains the history of area and local wildlife. You'll take a break and pull up on a pristine sandbar, where you can go for a refreshing swim. Special treats are warm chocolate chip cookies in summer and hot cider in winter. A single kayak runs $25 for a half day, $40 for a full day. A tandem kayak or canoe costs $40 or $55; a three-hour guided tour of the salt marsh ecosystem is $55.

SAILING Sail off the beaches of Fernandina with Charlie and Sandra Weaver on the **Windward's Child** (904-261-9125; www.windwardsailing.com), Fernandina Harbor Marina. Dolphins swim alongside the 34-foot Hunter sloop as you pass horses running on the beach on Cumberland Island. See Fort Clinch from the water, just as the Civil War blockade runners saw it. Move under the power of the wind with the quiet sounds of a warm sea breeze. Half-day, full-day, and sunset cruises.

SPA I'll always treasure that afternoon spent relaxing after a long day of hiking at the **Spa at Amelia Island** (904-432-2202 or 1-877-624-1854), where treatments include many varieties of massages, wraps, facials, and the vigorous Vichy shower.

TRAIL RIDING Jim Kelly holds the coveted Horseman of Distinction designation, so it's no wonder that his horses are in class-A shape and well trained to ride through the salt

KATHY WOLF TAKING NOTES WHILE ON A
KAYAK AMELIA ECOTOUR

Kathy Wolf

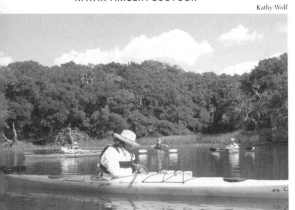

Amelia Island Tourist Development Council

AMELIA ISLAND IS ONE OF JUST A HAND-
FUL OF DESTINATIONS IN THE U.S. THAT
OFFERS HORSEBACK RIDING ON THE
BEACH.

marshes, white sand, and frothy surf of Amelia Island. At the **Kelly Sea-horse Ranch** (904-491-5166; www .kellyranchinc.com) you start out in a wooded area, and then ride along miles of open beach next to dolphins just offshore. One-hour rides $50, adults and ages 13 and up only. There's a 230-pound weight limit.

Country Day Stable (904-879-8383), Hilliard. Take a one-hour trail ride ($25) through 40 acres of north woods past the owners' re-creation of a medieval castle. The Horse Discovery ($10) lets small kids groom their horse, followed by a hand-led ride.

✳ Green Space

BEACHES **Fort Clinch State Park** (904-277-7274; www.floridastateparks.org/ fortclinch), 2601 Atlantic Ave, one of the oldest parks in the Florida State Park system, was acquired in 1935 when developers who planned to build along the peninsula couldn't pay their taxes; the state paid $10,000 with the "fort thrown in." Opened to the public in 1938, Fort Clinch State Park offers an array of sea-side activities. Besides hiking, biking, picnicking, and fishing, you can tour the historic fort, constructed in 1842, or enjoy the salt breezes through either of its two campgrounds on an overnight stay. Fee.

Talbot Island Geo-Park (904-251-2320; www.floridastateparks.org/bigtalbot island), 12157 Heckscher Dr. Divided into two adjoining state parks, Big Talbot Island and Little Talbot Island, these barrier islands provide an immersion into an undeveloped Florida shoreline, a rare and glorious experience. Short hiking trails lead out to the beaches, none more interesting than Blackrock Beach, where the lavalike "rocks" are made of naturally eroded peat and sand. The popular campground on Little Talbot Island sits in a bowl created by the dunes of the maritime forest; canoe rentals available. Fee.

GREENWAY A 300-acre strip that parallels Egans Creek, the **Egans Creek Greenway** (904-277-7350) is a grassy multiuse trail that leads through salt marsh and upland hammocks. It's a fabulous spot for wildlife watching—look for bobcats and deer in the uplands, and roseate spoonbills feeding on the salt flats. Access the

FORT CLINCH BEACH

Sandra Friend

BLACKROCK BEACH

Sandra Friend

greenway from trailheads at the Atlantic Recreation Center, 2500 Atlantic Ave; at Jasmine St; and at Citrona Dr. Open sunrise–sunset; free.

WILD PLACES & **Cary State Forest** (904-266-5021; www.fl-dof.com/state_forests/cary.html), US 301, Bryceville. Protecting pine flatwoods, cypress domes, and pitcher plant bogs, this state forest has an extensive network of trails open to equestrians. The 1.4-mile Cary Nature Trail is a great short jaunt for kids and people of limited mobility—well graded, good for a stroller, and wheelchair accessible with assistance. Families may wish to take advantage of the "primitive" campsites: tents only ($5 per night per tent), but with showers and restrooms provided. Fee.

More than 4,000 acres in the **Ralph E. Simmons State Forest** (904-845-3597; www.fl-dof.com/state_forests/ralph_e_simmons.html), off US 301, Hilliard, offer some of the most beautiful wildflowers in the state, and several nice campsites with a view of Georgia across the St. Marys River. The forest roads are used for hiking, biking, and trail riding; take a map along or you *will* get lost! Free.

✳ Lodging

BED & BREAKFASTS

Amelia Island 32034
The **Elizabeth Point Lodge** (904-277-4851; www.elizabethpointlodge.com), 98 S Fletcher Ave, just drew me in. Calling on my Maine roots, I

THE FLORIDA HOUSE INN

Amelia Island Tourist Development Council

suspect, the 1890s Nantucket shingle–style inn has a strong maritime theme. It's just steps from the ocean, and you can take in a breathtaking view from the porch or breakfast area. And even with 25 rooms, they are always booked. Rooms with breakfast $160–275.

🐾 ∞ Florida's oldest hotel, **Florida House Inn** (904-261-3300; www.floridahouseinn.com), 22 S Third St, dates back to 1857 and is located in the middle of the Fernandina historic district. With 25 rooms, it's more of a country inn than a B&B. Recently under new ownership, it has retained much of the original innkeeper's charm and staff, and still offers breakfast, lunch, and dinner in boarding-house style as well as an old English pub. Deluxe rooms feature vintage and decorator quilts, two-person

Jacuzzi, and working fireplace. Economy $99, standard $149–169, deluxe $179–219.

HOTELS, MOTELS, AND RESORTS

Amelia Island 32035

▼ Most visitors to **Greyfield Inn Cumberland Island** (904-261-6408; www.greyfieldinn.com), Cumberland Island, Georgia, depart from the docks in Fernandina, where the private ferry takes you across to a great escape from the hectic pace of the mainland. The remote island is teeming with wildlife, making it the perfect place to go for a nature walk or bicycle ride, paddle around in a kayak, or take a three-hour guided wilderness tour with a staff naturalist in the comfort of a Land Rover vehicle—all included in your overnight stay. Three fabulous gourmet meals are also included. Package rates start at $350 per night with a two-night minimum.

VACATION HOMES If you're bringing a large family on vacation, ask **Lodging Resources** (904-277-4851), 98 S Fletcher Ave, about **Katie's Light,** a three-bedroom, two-and-a-half-bath oceanfront home shaped like a lighthouse. This unique structure, with a 360-degree deck, also appeared in the movie *Pippi Longstocking.* Other beachfront properties are also available.

FISH CAMP

Hilliard 32046

✇ ⚅ Remember how life used to be? Down a dirt road in a quiet corner of the Ralph E. Simmons State Forest (see *Wild Places*), you come to **St. Marys River Fish Camp & Campground** (904-845-4440 or 966-845-4443), 28506 Scotts Landing Rd.

Steve Beck's family-oriented environment provides a great getaway place for safe, clean fun. You'll often see the kids up late at night playing basketball with him at the basketball court, just off the porch of the community store. Everyone hangs out here, and the sense is of community, caring, and Southern hospitality. Take to the water in fishing or pleasure boats to catch bream, catfish, or bass. Pull up on a sandy beach for a swim or picnic. Learn how to waterski. Search for the elusive goats on Goat Island. On weekends, watch a movie in the outdoor amphitheater, hike the many nature trails in the nearby state forest, or just relax and enjoy the beautiful solitude of the area—you'll run out of time before you run out of things to do. RV sites $25 daily, $120 weekly, $250 monthly. Primitive tent sites $10 daily.

✳ Where to Eat

DINING OUT

Amelia Island

Enjoy the charm of **Le Clos** (904-261-8100; www.leclos.com), 20 S Second St, while dining by candlelight in an intimate 1906 cottage. The creatively prepared French dishes by

CAMPSITE IN RALPH SIMMONS STATE FOREST

Sandra Friend

Cordon Bleu– and Escoffier-trained chef-owner Katherine Ewing are partnered with equally fine wines. Dinner nightly except Sun, $16–26.

EATING OUT

Amelia Island

Amelia Island Deli (904-261-9400), 5 S Second St. Light breakfast items, sandwiches, wraps, and platters ($4–6).

For a funky Florida adventure, visit **Palms Fish Camp** (904-251-3004), south of Amelia Island at Clapboard Creek. Art Jennette prepares authentic Florida Cracker–style seafood at fish camp prices. Go early (before 6:30) to take advantage of the buffet on Fri and Sat nights.

Callahan

Traveling up US 1, my son and I began to get hungry about dark. The **Florida Room Restaurant** (904-879-2006), 1335 S Kings Rd, looked like it might have a selection to satisfy both of us. I don't know what such a chef is doing so far out in the country, but I was grateful to have found this talented soul. The family-owned restaurant has a wholesome, comfortable atmosphere, with simple but charming decor carefully selected to enhance but not "stuffy up" the place. The self-taught chef is passionate about his cooking, and so we followed his dinner suggestions. My Orange Blossom Chicken would rival that of any chef in South Beach, and my son's Bucky Burger had to be the most enormous burger I have ever seen. Even with his bottomless stomach, he just couldn't finish it! This road stop is worth taking a country drive out from Jacksonville to visit.

Fernandina Beach

At the Florida House Inn, the Frisky Mermaid (www.friskymermaid.com)

For a jolly time, you'll always find your way to an Irish pub, and **O'Kanes** (904-261-1000), Centre St, is extra friendly. The Davis Turner Band has been playing here for over a decade, every night Wed–Sat. Dine on great Irish fare like steak and Guinness pie ($11), Shannon seafood au gratin ($17), and fish-and-chips ($11) in the pub or the dining room.

The Surf Restaurant (904-556-1059; www.thesurfonline.com), 3199 S Fletcher Ave, serves up lunch, dinner, and late-night snacks with live music on the huge outdoor sundeck. Salads, fried oyster or butterfly shrimp baskets, crab burgers, and Hawaiian chicken wraps ($9). Catch the Fri- and Sat-night all-you-can-eat buffets ($19 adults, $9 ages to 12).

Catch a big T-burger or portobello mushroom burger at **T-Ray's Burger Station** (904-261-6310), 202 S Eighth St, located inside the Exxon station at the corner of S Eighth and Ash streets.

Hilliard

Home-style Southern cooking and barbecue is on the menu at **Patricia Ann's** (904-845-2113), 551705 US 1. BBQ beef or pork plate ($7), liver and onions ($5), country-fried steak ($5); you won't go hungry with the Family Feast ($30), which includes regular slab whole chicken and large portions of both beef and pork served with three sides and garlic bread.

✳ Selective Shopping

Amelia Island

Whether you're fishing or dreaming about the coast, **Orvis Tidewater**

Outfitters (904-261-2202), 40 Amelia Village Cir, can feed your need. Stop in for fly rods, technical apparel, paintings by local artists, and gift items.

Fernandina Beach

Browse Centre St and many of its connecting streets, where you'll find great shopping like **Pineapple Patch** (904-321-2441), with Flap Happy and Fresh Produce kids' clothing. **Harbor Wear** (904-321-0061) has a great assortment of Life is Good women's quality sun and fun clothing. At the **Tilted Anchor** (904-261-7086) there's a nice selection of Brighton shoes and accessories along with interesting knickknacks like Cats Meow. The Irish-owned **Celtic Charm** (904-277-8009) takes me back to the motherland. **Amelia's Bloomin' Baskets** (904-277-2797) makes adorable gift baskets in a quaint island style. And the **Unusual Shop** (904-277-9664) really lives up to its name with artsy treasures. Expect the unexpected at **Terri Rauleson's Two Hearts** (904-321-1615), with whimsical gifts. Take the **Last Flight Out** (904-321-0510) and learn the history behind the name. The small shop offers a variety of gift and logo items and apparel.

🐾 Pets on leash are welcome at the **Bark Avenue Pet Boutique** (904-261-BARK; www.barkavenuepetboutique.com), 1008 Atlantic Ave, an upscale shop for pets carrying everything from doggy dresses and pet armoires to holistic pet food.

You'll think you're on the boardwalk at **Books Plus** (904-261-0303), 107 Centre St, where a wooden walkway winds among 3,800 square feet of shiny new tempting tomes in this one-of-a-kind independent bookstore. Owners Don and Margo Shaw started

the successful Amelia Island Book Festival and are respected contributors to national Book Sense picks.

Carrying all major brands of technical outdoor apparel, **Red Otter Outfitters** (904-206-4122), 1012 Atlantic Ave, is also your stop for biking and kayaking gear, Crocs, travel necessities, and guidebooks.

FARMER'S MARKETS AND U-PICK

Callahan

Hildebrand Farms (904-845-4254). Strawberries, tomatoes, melons, and cucumbers.

Fernandina Beach

You can't get shrimp any fresher than at the **Fernandina Seafood Market** (904-491-0765), 315 N Front St. Pay by the size and by the weight.

✳ Special Events

Year-round, first Fri of the month: The **Artrageous First Fridays** is an art walk with more than a dozen art studios and galleries open 6–9 PM in historic downtown Fernandina.

Year-round, first weekend of the month: See the blacksmith shop, jail, laundry, and kitchen come alive as park rangers reenact everyday life along with marching drills and artillery demonstrations at **Fort Clinch State Park** (see *Historic Sites*). Guided candlelight fort tours after sundown.

March: **Concours d'Elegance** (904-636-0027), Fernandina, is one of the nation's largest classic car shows, with more than 230 rare cars from private collections on display.

May: **Isle of Eight Flags Fernandina Shrimp Festival** (904-277-7274), in downtown historic Fernandina, is

THE FIRST WEEKEND OF EACH MONTH
SEES REENACTORS STEP FROM THE PAGES
OF AMERICAN HISTORY TO TRANSPORT
VISITORS BACK TO 1864.

closing in on a half-century of celebrating the shrimping industry with music, fine arts and crafts, antiques, pirates, and shrimp, shrimp, shrimp. Festivities include the Blessing of the Fleet (yes, shrimping is still a viable way of life here), the Shrimp Boat Parade, Family Fun Zone, fine arts and crafts show, a 5K run, food and vendor booths, and more. The festival kicks off with the solemn laying of a memorial wreath at the Shrimpers' Memorial, traditionally done by a member of the fleet.

June: Get your reservations well in advance for the **Amelia Island Chamber Music Festival** (www .islandchamber.org). World-renowned musicians perform chamber music at venues throughout the island in this fabulous annual event.

October: The **Amelia Island Book Festival** in Fernandina features book signings, readings, and workshops. Have "lunch with an author" or go on a "beachwalk with an author."

November–December: The Ritz-Carlton (1-800-241-3333) does it up big for **Christmas** as Santa and Mrs. Claus arrive in a horse-drawn carriage, giving the reindeer a rest before the big night. Enjoy a bonfire on the beach with hot chocolate and s'mores, campfire music, and storytelling. For the kids, there's an afternoon tea and storybook performances, and Santa will even tuck your little one in at night.

December: **Amelia Island Historic Christmas Tour of B&B Inns.** Not sure which B&B to stay at next time? Or just want to see the beautiful architecture decked out in holiday splendor? You'll want to make this favorite trek. The self-guided driving tour features 10 B&Bs filled with holiday music and light refreshments.

ST. AUGUSTINE, PONTE VEDRA, AND THE BEACHES

The breezy coastal city of St. Augustine invites the weary traveler to sit and stay a while, to soak in its Old World charm. Victorian houses sprout along narrow streets lined with palm trees. Coquina walls, made from seashell conglomerate quarried by the Spanish settlers, hide small gated gardens and patios. Each home, built with defense in mind, on orders of the king of Spain, has its main entrance off a courtyard brimming with greenery.

Many of the city's oldest buildings are of coquina quarried from Anastasia Island, including St. Augustine's defining landmark, the Castillo De San Marco, an enormous Spanish fortress that dates from 1695 and commands the seaward side of the nation's oldest city. Founded in 1565 by Spanish explorer Pedro Menéndez de Avilés, St. Augustine is the oldest continually occupied European settlement in the United States, a little slice of the Old Country on Florida's shores.

St. Augustine is a melting pot of cultures, a concentration of history in layers thicker than any other city in the United States. A thriving Greek community grew from Minorcan settlers who escaped the tribulations of a colony farther south at New Smyrna and sought refuge in the city. The oldest free black settlement in the United States—Fort Mose, established in 1738—sat just north of the Spanish settlement. Thirty years later, the dashing pirate Sir Francis Drake set the Spanish city aflame, blazing the way for British rule through 1784. Most of the Colonial homes you see today were built during the second Spanish Colonial Period, before Florida became a United States territory. St. Augustine is the only U.S. city with street patterns and architecture reflecting the Spanish Colonial ambience commonly seen in Caribbean and Latin American cities.

St. Augustine is also the birthplace of Florida tourism, thanks to Henry Flagler's grand hotels and railroad, built in the 1890s, which drew the first northern tourists to Florida "for their health." It is a city infused with history and art, timeless and yet chic. It's also my favorite city, in my humble opinion the most vibrant and charming destination Florida has to offer.

GUIDANCE **St. Augustine, Ponte Vedra & The Beaches Visitor & Convention Bureau** (www.getaway4florida.com) has a new web site where you can plan

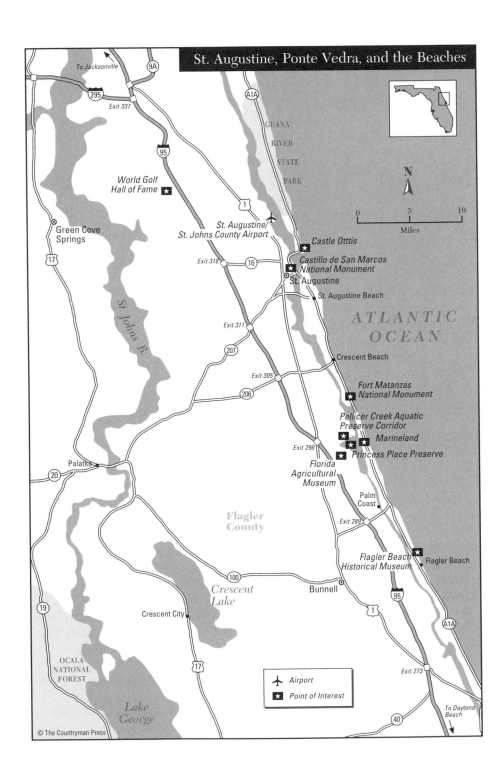

St. Augustine, Ponte Vedra, and the Beaches

To Jacksonville

GUANA
RIVER
STATE
PARK

N

0   5   10
Miles

Exit 337

World Golf
Hall of Fame

Green Cove
Springs

St. Augustine/
St. Johns County Airport

Castle Otttis

Castillo de San Marcos
National Monument

St. Augustine

St. Augustine Beach

ATLANTIC
OCEAN

Exit 318

Exit 311

Crescent Beach

Fort Matanzas
National Monument

Pellicer Creek Aquatic
Preserve Corridor

Marineland

Princess Place Preserve

Exit 305

Exit 298

Florida
Agricultural
Museum

Palatka

Palm
Coast

Flagler
County

Exit 289

Flagler Beach
Historical Museum

Flagler Beach

Crescent
Lake

Bunnell

Crescent City

OCALA
NATIONAL
FOREST

Lake
George

Exit 273

To Daytona
Beach

✈ Airport

★ Point of Interest

© The Countryman Press

your entire trip online, from reservations to ordering tickets. You also have the
option of stopping in at the prominent **St. Augustine Visitor's Center** on San
Marcos Ave near the city gates or the **Downtown Visitor Center** at the Government House Museum, King St. At the San Marco location, you can grab
brochures, on-the-spot reservations, and an introduction to the area via exhibits
and a video presentation. Right in front of the center, you'll discover the first of
a series of downtown maps that lead you through the historic district.

GETTING THERE *By air:* **Jacksonville International Airport** (See the Jacksonville chapter).

By car: Interstate 95 runs west of St. Augustine; exit at FL 16 and head east, or
follow US 1 south from Jacksonville, north from Bunnell. For the beach route,
follow A1A south from Jacksonville Beach to reach Ponte Vedra, Vilano Beach,
St. Augustine, Anastasia Island, St. Augustine Beach, Crescent Beach, and Summer Haven.

GETTING AROUND St. Augustine is a place to park and get out on foot: The
streets are narrow, with loads of pedestrian traffic. If you're planning to spend a
day or more and aren't staying in the city (free parking is a great perk that comes
with your room), ditch the car in one of the many flat-fee lots. A new parking
garage now looms behind the visitors center. There is free two-hour street parking along the waterfront and in residential neighborhoods, if you can find it;
there are some short-term metered spaces downtown along King St. Numerous
tour operators run trams through the city; see *To Do—Sightseeing Tours* for details.

PUBLIC RESTROOMS There are several sets of public restrooms along St.
George St, at the visitors center on San Marcos Ave, in the courtyard of the Flagler Museum, and at the marina.

MEDICAL EMERGENCIES **Flagler Hospital** (904-819-5155; flaglerhospital
.com), 400 Health Park Blvd, St. Augustine.

✳ To See

ARCHEOLOGICAL SITES The city of St. Augustine is one big archeological site,
so much so that any new construction requires a team of archeologists to assess
the site before building, since pottery shards, pieces of clay pipes, and the remains of 1800s yellow fever victims have routinely been discovered around town.
The **Tolomato Cemetery** on Cordova Street, circa 1777, was formerly a Tolomato Indian village.

At the **Fountain of Youth** (1-800-356-8222), 11 Magnolia Ave, amble around
the pleasant natural grounds at the site of the Timucuan village of Seloy, where
Ponce de León stepped ashore on April 3, 1513, to claim the land of *La Florida*
for Spain. In 1952 archeologists discovered the Christian burials of Timucua
here circa 1565, proving the site was the first Catholic mission in the New
World. A dripping rock spring is reverentially referred to as Ponce's Fountain of
Youth, and you're invited to take a sip—I did so back in the 1960s, and everyone

tells me I look 20 years younger than I am, so who knows? Judge for yourself; of course, you can take home bottled water from the spring for a small fee.

A little-known chapter in Florida history is that of **Fort Mose,** the first free black settlement in the southern United States. Founded in 1738 under the direction of the Spanish, this segregated community of emancipated slaves constructed a log fortress around their village along the salt marsh. In 1740 British invaders from Georgia overran the fortress; its inhabitants escaped to the Castillo de San Marcos in St. Augustine, where they joined a Spanish force to retake the strategic point. Visit the site at Fort Mose Historic State Park (904-461-2000; www.fortmose.org), at the end of Saratoga Blvd off US 1 north of St. Augustine.

ART GALLERIES St. Augustine is North Florida's cultural center, with more than 20 galleries showcasing local art. For ongoing arts events, check in with the **St. Augustine Art Association** (904-824-2310; www.staugustinearts.org), 22 Marine St, and the **Art Galleries of St. Augustine** (904-829-0065; www .staugustinegalleries.com), which holds Artwalks the first Fri of each month, 5–9 PM, showcasing the galleries in a moving festival. For those who aren't up for walking, the **St. Augustine Sightseeing Trains** (see *To Do—Sightseeing Tours*) offer free rides along the art route. **"Uptown Saturday Night"** is the gala monthly art walk through the San Marco Arts District, held on the last Saturday of each month. Pick up the **Art Galleries of Saint Augustine Guide** for the full scoop, and see *Selective Shopping* for additional galleries more strongly focused on retail sales.

Old St. Augustine

Stop and stare at the glorious depictions of aquatic life and waterfront scenes in the windows of the **Barry Barnett Collection** (1-800-535-8464; www.barry barnett.com), 1 King St, Ste 116. They'll tempt you!

At the **Brilliance in Color Fine Art Gallery** (904-810-0460), 25 King St, I found entrancing scenes of the Florida coastline glowing in giclee from Peter Pettegrew, and street scenes of Old St. Augustine from Arthur Fronckowiak. Representing local fine artists, the gallery showcases paintings, fine glass art, sculpture, and more.

Bold art will catch your eye at **The Crooked Palm Fine Art Gallery** (904-825-0010), 101 and 102 St. George St, such as the tropical fantasies in wavy frames by Steve Barton, Caribbean dreams by Dan Macklin, and strongly defined portraiture by Tim Rogerson.

My weakness is art glass, and **Eclectic Galleries** (904-825-4355), 1 King St, knew exactly how to press those buttons with aquatic life scenes in art glass that evoked the fluid motion of the sea. From milliflora paperweights to fine glass sculptures, this is a place an art glass aficionado will stare for hours.

The **P.A.S.T.A. Fine Art Gallery, Inc.** (904-824-0251), 214 Charlotte St, has more than 200 original pieces of art on display and changing monthly exhibits.

The oldest gallery in town is the **St. Augustine Art Association** (904-824-2310), 22 Marine St, dating back to 1924, with competitive shows and permanent exhibits.

Tripp Harrison Signature Gallery (904-824-3662 or 1-800-678-9550; www.tripp harrison.com), 22 Cathedral Place. In addition to historical paintings by this local artist with a distinctive and popular style, the gallery includes works by other sculptors and two-dimensional artists; I fell in love with the vivid blue hues of *Manatee Sunrise,* a giclee by Victor Kowal.

San Marco

The **St. Johns Cultural Council** (904-826-4116), 76B San Marco Ave, is a small gallery showing local artists in visual and performing arts.

Batik artist **W. B. Tutter** (904-823-9263), 76A San Marco Ave, offers an inviting gallery with marine-inspired pillows, fine framed batik art, cards, and sculptures.

San Sebastian

The neon sign outside the **Butterfield Garage Art Gallery** (904-825-4577; www.butterfieldgarage.com), 137 King St, will catch your attention—stop inside for a blast of "high-octane art" from this 12-artist co-op. It has large open spaces accommodating huge canvases, and you'll find many different media on display, like Estella J. Fransbergen's raku elephant ear leaves and Wendy Tatter's batik.

Energy Lab Art & Restoration Gallery (904-808-8455; www.energylab gallery.com), 137 King St, has an urban feel, a vibrant co-op where member artists display works in oil, clay, papier-mâché, and more; I felt drawn to the bold acrylics of Becki Hoffman and the haunting, muted scenes of St. Augustine by photographer Taylor Fansset.

The large, inviting spaces of the **Rachel Thompson Gallery** (904-825-0205; www.rachelthompsongallery.com), 139 King St, provide the perfect backdrop for Rachel's massive impressionist pastel still lifes, florals, and city scenes.

HISTORIC SITES

St. Augustine

No other U.S. city can boast the number of centuries spanned by historic sites found in downtown St. Augustine. Along Matanzas Bay, the imposing **Castillo de San Marcos,** completed in 1695 of coquina rock quarried from Anastasia Island, provided the city's coastal defense. Although the wooden town was burned several times by invaders, residents survived by taking refuge behind the fortress walls; the sedimentary rock absorbed cannonballs. Now a national park, the Castillo offers interpretive tours, a fabulous bookstore, and excellent views of the bay, 10–5 daily; fee. From the outer walls of the Castillo, a wood-and-stone rampart enclosed the city; visitors entered through the **City Gates,** which still stand at the entrance to St. George St.

THE OLDEST WOODEN SCHOOLHOUSE

St. Augustine CVB

❧ Built before 1763, the **Oldest Wooden Schoolhouse,** 14 St. George St, is indeed the oldest wooden school structure remaining in the United States. It's fun to take the kids through; fee.

❧ Along US 1, you'll see the **Old Jail** (see *To Do—Family Activities*), which looks like an 1890s hotel—Henry Flagler had it built in 1891 to move the undesirables away from his hotels to the edge of town, and it served its purpose until 1953. Flagler's Gilded Age also brought the stately Bridge of Lions on FL A1A, connecting St. Augustine with Anastasia Island. Residents have successfully fended off efforts to replace the bridge with a more modern structure, despite the traffic delays caused when the bridge opens to let ships through. If you're stuck on the bridge, grin and bear it—it's a small price for historic preservation of such a grand structure! Those woes won't last much longer, as a complementary span is being built in a similar style to offload some of the traffic.

Take a free guided boat ride out to **Fort Matanzas National Monument** (904-471-0116) on Rattlesnake Island, where you may be joined by dolphins or manatees. The military outpost has been here since 1565. The small but impressive fortress, built in 1740, protected Spanish St. Augustine from British encroachment. Nature walks and torchlight tours. Call for schedule.

❧ Dating back to 1874, the **St. Augustine Lighthouse & Museum** (see *Museums*) encompasses the entire light station complex. The light keeper's house is now a fun interactive museum with period items (including the original first-order Fresnel lens from the original tower, 1855–1871) and exhibits showcasing the history of light tending along the coast. From the top of the tower, you can see 35 miles on a clear day, fabulous for bird-watching from above.

Vilano Beach

As you drive along FL A1A north of Vilano Beach, you'll notice an Irish castle on the left. **Castle Otttis** (904-824-3274) was built in 1988 by Rusty Ickes as a landscape sculpture in "remembrance of Jesus Christ." The castle is an impression of one built more than a thousand years ago and was created under the guidance of the Catholic diocese to replicate the atmosphere of an Irish abbey. Amazingly, just two people, without outside aid, did all the masonry work. True to the castles of the period, the building is open to the environment. A privately owned structure, it is occasionally open for church services.

CASTLE OTTTIS

Kathy Wolf

HISTORIC HOMES With the discovery of coquina came solid buildings of stone. The **Gonzales-Alvarez House** (904-824-2872; www.oldcity.com/oldhouse), 271 Charlotte St, is the city's oldest house, its tabby floors laid in the early 1700s; during the British period in 1776, the house served as a tavern. Oldest House tours hosted by the St. Augustine Historical Society interpret the lives and times of its visitors and residents; fee. The nearby **Sequi-Kirby Smith House** (904-825-2333), 6 Artillery Lane, houses the St. Augustine Historical Society Research Library (open Tue–Fri 9–4:30) and was the family home of Confederate general Edmund Kirby-Smith; the house dates back to the Second Spanish Period. Built in 1798, the **Ximenez-Fatio House** (904-829-3575; www.ximenezfatiohouse.org), 20 Aviles St, is now open as a house museum with guided tours Tue–Sun 11–4. In the 1800s, it was an inn, so a walk through the home gives you a unique peek into the city's tourist past.

St. George and its cross streets are notable for homes dating back to the late 1700s—look for historical plaques with names and dates on each home. **The Peña-Peck House,** circa 1750, was the residence of the royal treasurer from Spain; it's managed as a house museum by a nonprofit, the Woman's Exchange (see *Selective Shopping*); fee.

✿ **Old Spanish Village** (904-823-9722), corner of Cordova and Bridge streets, provides an entire block's worth of historic homes to browse ($7 adults, $6 seniors, $5 students), nine houses dating from 1790 to 1910.

The **Colonial Spanish Quarter** (904-825-6830), 53 St. George St, is a living history museum set in 1740, showcasing a dozen historic homes and structures in a complex with traditional craftsmen—coopers, smiths, shoemakers, and more—in period dress tending to everyday life in the **Presidio de San Agustin,** a fascinating look into Florida's past. Open for self-guided tours 9–5:30 except Christmas; adults $6.50, children $4.

HISTORIC HOTELS When railroad magnate Henry Flagler built his destination hotels in the 1880s, he kicked off Florida tourism as we know it today. Stand at the corner of Cordova and King streets, and you can visually compare all three. Only one, the **Cordova,** remains a hotel, renovated in the 1990s into the elegant Casa Monica (see *Lodging*). The others are open to the public but serve different uses. The **Alcazar** is now city hall and the Lightner Museum (see *Museums*), where a café is tucked into the giant indoor swimming pool (the largest of its time in the 1880s), and visitors can wander through the original ballroom and baths. Flagler bequeathed his grand **Hotel Ponce de León** to become Flagler College (www.flagler.edu), a liberal arts college that started out as a women's school. Public access is limited, but you can join a walking tour (see *To Do—Walking Tours*) to immerse in the grandeur of Flagler's vision, as executed by interior decorator Louis Comfort Tiffany. The **Villa Zorayda,**

FLAGLER COLLEGE

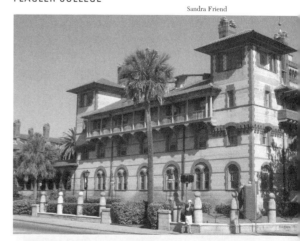

Sandra Friend

Sandra Friend

VILLA ZORAYDA

built in 1883 by Franklin Smith as a one-tenth-scale replica of the Alhambra in Spain, became a casino in 1922 and then an attraction, Zorayda Castle, in 1936. It is under restoration after sitting empty for years; check at the tourist office for details. Another quirky former hotel was **Castle Warden,** now better known as the Ripley's Believe It or Not Museum (see *To Do—Family Activities*). Built in 1887, it was purchased in 1941 and run as a hotel by Ocala hotelier Norton Baskin, who relocated to Crescent Beach; his wife, novelist Marjorie Kinnan Rawlings, soon followed.

HISTORIC CHURCHES When Father Francisco López de Mendoza Grajales offered the first Mass in St. Augustine, he did so at the **Mission Nombre de Dios** (904-824-2809), 27 Ocean Ave, more than four centuries ago. On the grounds of the ancient mission, a modern 208-foot stainless-steel cross marks the founding of St. Augustine in 1565; the statuette within the ivy-covered shrine of **Our Lady of La Leche** dates back to 1598 and was the first memorial to the Virgin Mary in the Americas. At St. George and Cathedral streets, the Cathedral Basilica, the first Catholic parish in the New World, was built in 1797 with stones from the ruins of the original mission. The **St. Photios Greek Orthodox National Shrine** (904-829-8205), 41 St. George St, is the only Greek Orthodox shrine in the United States. Henry Flagler and his wife are buried in a tomb within the **Memorial Presbyterian Church,** 32 Sevilla St, built in 1889 by Flagler.

MUSEUMS

Old St. Augustine
The **Government House Museum** (904-825-5033), corner of King and Cathedral streets, exhibits St. Augustine's finest collection of historical artifacts, with more than 300 colorful displays recounting life from Timucuan times through the founding of St. Augustine, the Seminole Wars, and the Flagler era. Open Tue–Sat 10–4; fee.

Otto C. Lightner, founding editor of *Hobbies* magazine, was a collector of

MISSION NOMBRE DE DIOS

Sandra Friend

collections. I remember the **Lightner Museum** (904-824-2874; www.lightner-muse um.org), 75 King St, which opened in 1948, when it showcased its treasures in a way a kid could understand—open a hotel room door, and you'd find a room full of postcards. Or a room full of buttons. Or a room full of teacups. Then City Hall moved into the Hotel Alcazar in 1971, saving the financially struggling museum but squeezing it into one segment of the hotel. Befitting its opulent setting, the museum shifted its emphasis to its upscale objets d'art—oil paintings, carvings, fine glasswork, and antique furnishings—although you can still find the button and matchbook collections tucked away in nooks, and one portion of the museum is devoted to the sciences, with minerals, archeological specimens, and an Egyptian mummy. As you stroll past the hotel's grand indoor swimming pool (the world's largest in 1888) and spa, you'll feel a part of the Gilded Age. Open 9–5 daily except Christmas; admission $8 adults, $2 ages 12–18, under 12 free with adult.

✍ **Florida Heritage Museum, Old Jail Complex** (see *To Do—Family Activities*), presents an excellent introduction to the region's long and storied past, from exhibits of Florida's First Peoples to the tale of Fort Mose (see *Archeological Sites*), the Spanish and British settlements, and the tale of Henry Flagler and his Model Land Company, the first snowbird real-estate scheme in Florida history. 10–5 daily; fee.

✍ Entered through an old Florida general store (complete with penny candies for the kids), the **Old Florida Museum** (904-824-8874 or 1-800-813-3208; www .oldfloridamuseum.com), 254-D San Marco Ave, captures the spirit of Florida's pioneer days. On your self-guided tour, learn how to use a mortar and pestle or pump a water pump; rope a "bull"; play with hoops, and write with a quill pen at the Pioneer School. Hands-on and perfect for families, it teaches Florida history by doing; fee.

The **Spanish Military Hospital** (904-827-0807), 3 Aviles St, provides a glimpse into 18th-century medical treatments at the Royal Hospital of Our Lady of Guadalupe on a narrated tour through this haunted building, with dioramas and artifacts like porcelain bedpans and scary-looking period medical instruments. Fee.

✍ **St. Augustine Lighthouse & Museum** (904-829-0745; www.staugustine lighthouse.com), 81 Lighthouse Ave, isn't just a working historic lighthouse but an entire light station complex. Built in 1871 and outfitted with a first-order Fresnel lens (still functional, but repaired in 1986 after damage from a vandal's bullets), the 165-foot lighthouse is the second permanent tower to stand along this coastline. Climb the steep spiral staircase (219 steps with landings) for a 30-mile view of the coast; look down and you can catch flocks of ibises in flight between their roosts at the St. Augustine Alligator Farm and their feeding grounds on the mudflats of Anastasia Island. The museum in the light keeper's house provides excellent interactive interpretive exhibits. Admission $6.50 adults, $5.50 seniors, $4 for ages 7–11.

St. Augustine
World Golf Hall of Fame (904-940-4000; www.wgv.com), 1 World Golf Place. I'll be the first to tell you that I don't play golf. But that doesn't mean that I'm

not intimately aware of the game. After having learned the game from none other than Humphrey Bogart, my dad spent 70 years on fairways and greens from Maine to Florida. And my mom, at 81, continues to play 9 to 18 holes a day. They would love the World Golf Village, so it was with their eyes that I approached this monument to legends and deeply rooted history. The museum will take you from the birth of the game in St. Andrews, Scotland, all the way through to today's champions. I was surprised to find that as a nongolfer I was very interested in the historical artifacts and in particular the Shell Hall, where a stunning crescent of acrylic pedestals honors Hall of Fame members. The second floor is set up much like 18 holes, with the front 9 covering the historical game, where you can walk across a replica of the famed St. Andrews Swilcan Burn Bridge, and the back 9 covering the modern game, where at one of the exhibits you'll see President Eisenhower's golf cart and at another discover the elements of golf course design. Test your swing at the virtual-reality exhibit. Open Mon–Sat 10–6, Sun noon–6. $12 adults, $7 ages 5–12.

WINERY At **San Sebastian Winery** (1-888-352-9463; www.sansebastianwinery .com), 157 King St, enjoy a tour of the processing plant in the arts district (the vineyards are off-site at a sister winery) with a complimentary wine tasting thereafter. A wine and jazz bar offers a laid-back place to chat with friends, or browse the Wine Shop for gourmet foods, kitchen items, and the signature wines of San Sebastian. Open daily.

ZOOLOGICAL PARK ✐ ᕫ I knew it as a kitschy place when I was a kid, with alligator wrestling and snake stunts, but the **St. Augustine Alligator Farm Zoological Park** (904-824-3337; www.alligatorfarm.com), FL A1A, is now a fully accredited zoological park that hasn't lost its funky charm. Dating back to 1893, it's one of Florida's oldest tourist draws, with pits filled with alligators. Marvel at the many reptilian species represented here, including albino alligators from Louisiana, endangered Nile crocodiles, caimans, and gharials that share their space with tiny muntjac deer. My favorite part of the park has always been the Alligator Swamp Nature Trail and Native Bird Rookery, where more than a dozen species of birds (including wood storks, green-backed herons, and least bitterns) build their nests in early March and raise their young in the trees, protected from predators like egg-stealing raccoons by the alligators cruising below. It's one of the few places I know where you can get close enough to photograph fledgling herons without disturbing them. There are other themed sections to the park, including the Great Down Under with Australian creatures and a section with animals of the rain forest;

PRESIDENT EISENHOWER'S GOLF CART AT THE WORLD GOLF HALL OF FAME

Kathy Wolf

daily shows now focus on interpretation of species behavior. Open daily 9–5, with admission $14.95 ages 12 and over, $8.95 ages 5–11, $7.48 wheelchair.

✴ To Do

BIRDING One of the best spots in the region for bird-watching is around the lagoons at **St. Augustine Alligator Farm** (see *To See—Zoological Park*), where the long-term presence of so many alligators assures the nesting colonies of egrets, herons, and wood storks that raccoons won't steal precious bird eggs. Along FL A1A in Crescent Beach, watch for nande conures, a variety of chartreuse parrot that has naturalized along the Intracoastal Waterway.

Sandra Friend

SOME OF THE RESIDENTS AT THE ST. AUGUSTINE ALLIGATOR FARM ZOOLOGICAL PARK

BOATING Rent or charter your own boat at the marina from **Bay Ray** (904-826-0010; www.bayrayrentals.com), 1 Dolphin Dr, which has miniature speedboats, pontoon boats, ocean kayaks, fishing charters, and a 33-foot sailing sloop. On **Sail Boat Adventures** (904-347-7183; www.villavoyager.com), Captain Paul Kulik provides an intimate sailing adventure for up to four people, $38 per person, tailored to your interests. The **Schooner *Freedom*** (904-810-1010), St. Augustine's one and only tall ship, takes guests out on relaxing three- and four-hour cruises on Matanzas Bay daily. This replica of a blockade runner is a 34-ton clipper, a family operation that lets guests take the wheel after passing through the Bridge of Lions—ride this, and you can be the one who holds up bridge traffic instead of waiting in it.

Sailing in to St. Augustine? You'll find plenty of slips at the **St. Augustine Municipal Marina** (904-825-1026); hail the harbormaster on VHF channel 16. Dockage (including use of showers and water) runs $4–5 per hour, $150 (minimum) weekly, $250 (minimum) monthly, electricity extra. Of course, it's a blast to pull in at the **Conch House Marina Resort** (see *Lodging*) and settle into a dining hut overlooking the water. Vessels from 20 to 120 feet can dock at this 194-slip marina; call ahead (1-800-940-6256) for availability and rates, which vary seasonally but start at $2 per foot per day.

ECOTOURS Go dolphin watching on the ***Victory III* Scenic Cruise** (1-800-542-8316; www.scenic-cruise.com), 4125 Coastal Hwy, St. Augustine, a narrated trip that departs from the St. Augustine Marina up to four times daily, or cruise with the *Lucky Ducky,* Blue Water Marina's (904-819-6741) dolphin trip twice daily from the marina.

FAMILY ACTIVITIES ✎ A fixture in St. Augustine, the **antique carousel** at Davenport Park on San Marcos Ave, still costs only a dollar for a ride. The **Old Jail** (904-829-3800; www.historictours.com), 167 San Marcos, with huge kid appeal, is just across the street. It's a historic building tour with a kitschy spin, where a loony prisoner leads you, the new guy, into lockup. Open daily 8:30–4:30; fee.

✎ Looking like an escapee from a Charles Addams cartoon, the original **Ripley's Believe It or Not Museum** (904-824-1606; www.staugustine-ripleys.com), 19 San Marco Ave, displays cartoonist Robert Ripley's weird stuff in a funhouse atmosphere; $12.95 adults, $8.95 seniors, $7.95 ages 5–12. At **Potter's Wax Museum** (1-800-584-4781; www.potterswax.com), 17 King St, the 160 wax stiffs don't move (mostly); in addition to the usual suspects (politicians and movie stars), there are lesser-known faces from history and art, including Voltaire, Sir Francis Drake, St. Augustine founder Menéndez, Rembrandt van Rijn, and Gainesborough. And what wax museum would be complete without a horror chamber, in this case direct from Vincent Price's House of Wax? Open 9–9; $9 adults, $8 seniors, $6 ages 6–12.

✎ Play miniature golf at **Anastasia Mini Golf,** 701 Anastasia Blvd, or try your hand at **Bay Front Golf,** the mini golf course between the marina and Bridge of Lions in the Old City.

FISHING Coastal Outdoor Kayaks (904-471-4144), 291 Cubbedge Rd, Crescent Beach, will rent you a boat, kayak (see *Paddling*), or canoe and all the gear and bait you'll need. Guides available.

A public pier along FL A1A provides access for saltwater anglers to try their stuff at St. Augustine Beach. For outfitting and access to the Intracoastal Waterway, visit **Devil's Elbow Fishing Resort** (904-471-0398; www.devilselbow fishingresort.com), 7507 FL A1A S. A local landmark, Devil's Elbow provides everything from bait to guide service and boat rentals, and has a handful of fish-camp-style vacation rentals on site.

GOLF St. Augustine's newest offering is the **Royal St. Augustine Golf & Country Club** (904-824-GOLF; www.royalstaugustine.com), 301 Royal St. Augustine Pkwy, with 18 holes carved out from pine forests and wetlands.

HIKING All regional and state parks offer nature and hiking trails, but you can't go wrong with a visit to any of the conservation areas (see *Wild Places*) managed by the St. Johns Water Management District. Backpackers will appreciate the primitive campsite overlooking the Matanzas River at **Moses Creek Conservation Area,** while day hikers who like to stretch their legs can revel in half a dozen different habitats (and benches with scenic views) on a 9-mile loop on the undeveloped southern portion of **Guana-Tolomato-Matanzas Reserve,** one of my favorite hikes in the state.

PADDLING With its dozens of uninhabited islands on which to stop and lunch or camp, the Matanzas River is a popular paddlers' getaway. You'll see manatees and dolphins cruising along this saline inland waterway, which runs between St.

Augustine and Summer Haven. Although there is no official "blueway" route, a navigational chart will help you chart your course among the many public lands that border the waterway. Most visitors put in at Faver-Dykes State Park or at the county park in Summer Haven. Canoe and kayak rentals and put-in are available at **Devil's Elbow Fishing Resort** (see *Fishing*).

Brad and Joyce Miller at **Coastal Outdoor Kayaks** (904-471-4144; www.coastal outdoorcenter.com), 291 Cubbedge Rd, Crescent Beach, have a great selection of kayaks, canoes, and ecotours available for everyone from the novice to the experienced paddler. Joyce can tell you all about Princess Place Preserve (see *To see— Historic Sites* in the Flagler County chapter) and how to get there—she used to be the caretaker! Take a two-hour birding tour, by kayak, of local salt marshes to get close to migrating wading birds as they feed on exposed oyster bars and sandbars. A naturalist will take you on a two-hour guided walking tour of Princess Place Preserve, Moses Creek Conservation Area, or Matanzas Inlet, pointing out local plant and wildlife. Or go on a four-hour combo walking/kayak tour, where you'll paddle to a small, remote island and lunch at Cresent Beach Cafe, followed by a walk around coastal marshes and upland pine while searching for wading birds and oysters. For about an hour and a half you can paddle at sunset on stable double kayaks through the saltwater marshes. If you have your Florida state fishing license, you'll want to try kayak fishing. All instruction, bait, and gear are included. Or rent kayaks or canoes and explore on your own. And hey, on Mother's Day, moms paddle free! Rental rates start at $12 per hour or $42 per day; tours start at $30.

GHOST TOURS The Ancient City has equally ancient ghosts—and a bevy of tour operators vying to introduce them to you. Standing atop the seawall, her scarf and 1790s attire fluttering in gusts of wind spawned by a distant hurricane, Amanda spun the tale of Jean Ribault's failed attack on St. Augustine and his armada's untimely demise. "For three days, the bay ran red with blood . . . the fishermen say to beware, when looking into the water after dark, of the faces of the slaughtered Huguenots . . ." Around her, the audience stood rapt with attention. Wrapping legend around history and serving it up as entertainment, St. Augustine's ghost tours do a bang-up job of spinning spooky stories that'll have your hair standing on end. Amanda's outfit, the granddaddy of ghost tours, is **A Ghostly Experience** (1-888-461-1009; www.ghosttoursofstaugustine.com), which was founded to provide visiting school groups with something to do after dark. Each walk is different, touching on a handful of the thousands of stories that permeate this city. Reservations are generally recommended for any of the ghost tours; other outfits include **Spirits of St. Augustine** (904-829-2396), 18 St. George; the **Haunted Pub Tour** (1-866-PUB-TOUR; www.ghostaugustine.com), 123 St. George; **Ancient City Tours** (1-800-597-7177; www.ancientcitytours.net), 3 Aviles St; **Pirate Ghost Tours** (904-501-7508), 27 San Marco Ave; and **Ghosts & Gravestones** (904-826-3663; www.ghostsandgravestones.com), 2 St. George St, which also offers rides on the "Trolley of the Doomed."

New to the St. Augustine scene, outfitter Zach McKenna runs **St. Augustine Eco Tours** (904-377-7245), leading guided trips that glide you past the Castillo de San Marcos. Call for rates and reservations.

PARASAILING Smile High Parasail Inc. (904-819-0980; www.smilehighpara sail.com), 111 Avenida Menendez #C, St. Augustine, offers crew-supported soars above the Matanzas River; up to three can fly together.

SCENIC DRIVES Few highways in the northern Florida peninsula match the beauty of FL A1A, the **Buccaneer Trail,** particularly in sections where the dunes remain preserved and free of development: between Ormond Beach and Flagler Beach, and north of St. Augustine through Guana River State Park. Designated a National Historic Scenic Byway, two-lane **A1A** provides a breezy seaside driving experience.

SIGHTSEEING TOURS Besides ghost tours and walking tours, St. Augustine offers some of the state's oldest narrated tours, including the **St. Augustine Sightseeing Trains** (1-800-226-6545; www.redtrains.com), 170 San Marco Ave, in operation since 1953 and offering complimentary pickup and drop-off at city motels as well as a truly educational tour of the city, with on/off privileges at all stops. Three-day ticket, $14 adults, $5 ages 6–12; package tours with historic and attraction admissions included run $20–70.

Old Town Trolley Tours (904-829-3800; www.trolleytours.com), running out of a depot at the Old Jail (see *Family Activities*), covers more than 100 points of interest with 20 stop-offs and reboarding privileges for three days on your ticket.

For a truly romantic tour, hop on board one of the **sightseeing carriages** along the bayfront near the Castillo de San Marcos, from **St. Augustine Transfer Company** (904-829-2391), $15 adults, $7 children 5–11. Or ride in style in a **1929 Model A** or **1955 Chrysler Imperial** on an Antique Car Tour; check with the Casa Monica Hotel (see *Lodging*) for details.

SPA Ponte Vedra Inn & Club (904-285-1111; www.pvspa.com), 200 Ponte Vedra Blvd, Ponte Vedra Beach. Come to this perfect haven for relaxation after a long day on the golf course or exploring neighboring St. Augustine. Wrap yourself in an elegant spa robe and sit with a light beverage while awaiting your treatment in the relaxation room or in the 2,000-square-foot Cascada Garden with oversized Jacuzzi and cascading waterfall. Then move on to your own private room for treatments like a reflexology massage ($80), a deep-cleaning facial or men's skin care treatment ($80), or a honeysuckle-algae scrub ($55).

WALKING TOURS In addition to leading ghost tours, costumed guides from **Tour St. Augustine** (904-825-0087), 6 Granada St, lead walking tours touching on many different themes, from architectural history to the Victorian era, as do the folks at **Old City Walks, Etc.** (904-797-9733). **Tours at Flagler College** (904-823-3378; www.flagler.edu), May–Aug, offer a look at the grandeur of Henry Flagler's flagship, the Hotel Ponce de León (now the college campus); fee. Or pick up a **Free Walking Tour Map** at the visitors center to take your own 32-stop self-guided tour of the Oldest City.

WHALE-WATCHING Each winter, right whales migrate from sites near Newfoundland to the shores of St. Johns County and their ancestral calving ground, where they give birth and raise their young. The right whale is the most endangered whale on earth, with only about 350 members of the species remaining. Working through a program coordinated by **Marineland** and the **Whitney Laboratory** (see *To See—Marine Park* in the Flagler

Sandra Friend

ST. AUGUSTINE SIGHTSEEING TRAINS

County chapter), volunteer whale-watchers take up positions along beaches in Crescent Beach, Summer Haven, and Marineland to record whale sightings. Each whale has a unique pattern of spots, making it easier to positively identify specific individuals.

WINDSURFING At Salt Run Inlet in Anastasia State Park (see *Green Space*), **Windsurfing St. Augustine** (904-460-9111; www.windsurfingstaugustine.com) rents windsurfers, sea kayaks, canoes, and catamarans, 10–6 daily. Sailing and windsurfing lessons offered by qualified instructors.

✳ Green Space

BEACHES Anastasia State Park (904-461-2033; www.floridastateparks.org/anastasia), 1340A FL A1A S, Anastasia Island. It's my favorite place to take a walk on the beach—an 8-mile unsullied round-trip to the tip of the island, right along Matanzas Pass, where you can sit and watch the sailboats come into the harbor at St. Augustine. Bird-watching is superb along the shoreline and the lagoons, and the campground in the coastal hammock can't be beat. Swimmers and surfers flock to these shores every summer, so it gets pretty busy on weekends. The park also includes the historic coquina quarries used by the Spanish to quarry blocks for the Castillo de San Marcos and other structures in the Ancient City, and windsurfing lessons and rentals are available at the lagoon. Fee.

PARKS

Anastasia Island
⚓ **Lighthouse Park** on Anastasia Island has a playground tucked under the windswept oaks and a boat ramp with access to the inlet.

Dupont Center
Faver-Dykes State Park (904-794-0997; www.floridastateparks.org/faver-dykes), 1000 Faver Dykes Rd. Nestled in oak hammocks along Pellicer Creek, this peaceful park offers camping, nature trails, and some of the best paddling along the coast. Bring your kayak or rent a canoe (reservations required) to enjoy

the Pellicer Creek Trail, gliding through mazes of needlerush as you paddle out to the Matanzas River. A new addition to the park, Mellon Island, is accessible only by boat and open to primitive camping. Fee.

Ponte Vedra Beach

Guana-Tolomato-Matanzas Reserve (904-825-5071; www.gtmnerr.org), 505 Guana River Rd. Most visitors come here for the beaches—they go on forever, it seems, paralleling FL A1A for several miles, with two large parking areas at either end. But I like the hidden treasure on the Intracoastal side of the park at the dam, the hiking and biking trail system that loops for 9 miles through a variety of habitats and provides fresh salt breezes as you walk under the oaks lining the Tolomato River. Fishing is superb in the Guana and Tolomato rivers, and a popular activity at the dam. Expect a beach parking fee during peak seasons and weekends. A new 21,000-square-foot Environmental Education Center opened recently to interpret this 60,000-acre reserve; stop in and see a 12-minute video, learn about the indigenous whales, stingrays, and fish; or stand on the back deck and watch flocks of birds coast over the grand estuary that surrounds the River of Palms. A gift shop offers scientific toys and books. Fee.

WILD PLACES The **St. Johns Water Management District** (386-329-4883; http://sjr.state.fl.us) is responsible for conservation areas that serve as buffers to the St. Johns River and its tributaries, and works with local land managers to administer the following preserves, which offer hiking, biking, paddling, and trail riding: **Moses Creek Conservation Area,** FL 206, Dupont Center, where you can backpack or ride your horse to a distant campsite with a sweeping view of the Matanzas River salt marshes; and **Stokes Landing Conservation Area,** Lakeshore Dr, which provides an outdoor classroom for local schools and beautiful panoramic views of the salt marshes along the Tolomato River for hikers.

Located just south of FL 206, the new **Matanzas State Forest** (386-446-6786; www.fl-dof.com) offers access from US 1 to nearly 5,000 acres along the Matanzas River. Outdoor recreation opportunities include wildlife and bird-watching along the network of walkable roads, and hunting in-season.

PELICANS ON ANASTASIA ISLAND

Sandra Friend

✳ Lodging
BED & BREAKFASTS

St. Augustine 32084
With 26 B&Bs at last count, St. Augustine provides a wide range of choices for the history-minded traveler. Check the **St. Augustine Historic Inns** web site at www.staugustineinns.com (immediate room availability at www.sahirooms.com) to find the best B&B to suit your needs. Here's a handful I personally explored:

Sandra Friend

MOSES CREEK

✎ & Delightfully classy and in the midst of the historic downtown, the **Agustin Inn** (904-823-9559; www .agustininn.com), 29 Cuna St, is a 1903 Victorian with 18 guest rooms, most with Jacuzzi and one (the Greensboro) with private entrance and wheelchair ramp. Your breakfast may include homemade Belgian waffles or house recipe quiche; dietary needs can be accommodated. Hurricane-prepared, the inn can run off a generator for up to three weeks. Rates start at $149 and increase dramatically on weekends; multiday packages are the best buy. Children over 12 are welcome.

✎ It's wonderful when travelers bring their experiences back to their own B&B, and you'll find that at **At Journey's End** (904-829-0076 or 1-888-806-2351; www.atjourneysend .com), 89 Cedar St, where the late-1800s Victorian is a backdrop for exotica—bedrooms themed after China, Egypt, and African safaris, as well as Key West and summer, with elegant beds and original art. The Key West suite is family-friendly and can handle a family of six; its own veranda

overlooks the garden. Rooms include cable TV and wireless Internet. A full breakfast is served every morning, with snacks and drinks available all day. $99–250.

Casa de La Paz (1-800-929-6269; www.casadelapaz.com), 22 Avenida Menendez. With a prime bayfront location, this Mediterranean Revival home has operated as an inn since the 1920s. Innkeepers Sherri and Marshall Crews now present seven romantic rooms ($169–299), several with sweeping views of the bay, romantic accoutrements, and wi-fi. It's the perfect place to cozy up with a loved one, and you'll love their gourmet two-course breakfasts with treats like banana-almond pancakes, raspberry-stuffed French toast, and eggs Benedict.

When I arrived at **Casa de Solana** (904-824-3555 or 1-888-796-0980; www.casadesolana.com), 21 Aviles St, the courtyard was abuzz with guests enjoying their breakfast. Built in the early 1800s, the historic main home is constructed of coquina stone and retains many of its original features, including handmade bricks. The adjacent de Palma house is now part of the complex. The decor reflects colonial St. Augustine with modern updates such as whirlpool tubs, cable TV, and wireless Internet. Gregarious guests will appreciate the evening social and desserts; those looking for a more intimate time will find it on the balconies and in the corners of the garden. Ten rooms, each uniquely decorated, $129–259.

& **Casa de Sueños** (1-800-824-0804; www.casadesuenos.com), 20 Cordova St. A chandelier sparkles over the whirlpool tub, funky black-and-white furnishings dress up the common areas, and each room uplifts the soul. This is the "House of Dreams," a 1920s Mediterranean Revival home along Cordova St, where guests can watch the world drift by from the vibrant sunporch or settle down for a read in the parlor. Each of the five rooms ($159–299) is a relaxing retreat, with comfy robes, fine literature, and a decanter of sherry on the dresser; two rooms boast a whirlpool. Enjoy a gourmet breakfast each morning.

Perfectly located—just a block off busy St. Georges on a quiet back street—**44 Spanish Street** (904-826-0650 or 1-800-521-0722; www.44 spanishstreet.com), 44 Spanish St, has rooms that are chic and bright, with luxurious linens, cable TV, irons, and hairdryers. The eight rooms come in several configurations with some connecting rooms and some with extra beds, making it great for girlfriend/sister getaways. My favorite is Rosewood, since it has its own private entrance from the street *and* a spare bed. $115–199.

∞ **The Kenwood Inn** (1-800-824-8151; www.thekenwoodinn.com), 38 Marine St, dates back to the 1860s, when it served as a boardinghouse. It has that wonderful feel of an old-time hotel, with narrow corridors, low ceilings, and mismatched floors. Each of the 14 spacious rooms ($95–185) has its own particular character; many are two-room suites. I enjoyed my stay in the Porcelain Room, with walls the color of Wedgwood china, where I could sway in a hammock on the balcony and listen to the carriages go by. The Bridal Suite ($175–250), which occupies the whole third floor, has a view of Matanzas Bay. All guests enjoy use of a private pool and secluded garden courtyard, where you can borrow a bicycle for a ride around town.

The Old Powder House Inn (1-800-447-4149; www.oldpowder house.com), 38 Cordova St. An 1899 Victorian with classic charm entices with its second-floor veranda, ideal for people-watching from the porch swing. From the frilly Queen Ann's Lace to the Garden, a three-bed girls' getaway, each of the nine elegant rooms offers a perfect 1900s ambience. $119–299.

Our House (904-824-9204; www .ourhousestaugustine.com), 7 Cincinnati Ave. Tucked in a residential neighborhood behind the San Marco Ave antiques district, Dave Brezing's two-story Victorian has a snazzy urban feel befitting its owner, a former *USA Today* editor. Bold monochrome walls set off the restored heart pine floor, art and literature accent each room, and a piano stands at the ready in the parlor. Two guest rooms, Greenhaven and Morningview, occupy the second floor; the first-floor Fern Garden guest room is nestled behind the parlor with a private entrance from a shady garden. Greenhaven features a romantic clawfoot tub, while wraparound windows suffuse Morningview with soft morning light. Each room ($149–220) has a large private bath and porch; Fern Garden has a two-person Jacuzzi. Guests also enjoy common sitting rooms and a secluded garden with fountain. Dave brings coffee to your room in the morning and cooks a great gourmet breakfast. Across the garden courtyard in a neighboring Victorian, he has two garden studios, Jasmine and Azalea. Each features queen-sized bed; sitting area; a kitchenette supplied with dishes, cutlery, coffee, and continental breakfast; large bath with whirlpool tub; private entrance; and porch. Azalea, with a convertible sofa, can accommodate up to four people. On-site parking and wireless Internet access are free. No pets; not suitable for children under age 12.

⚘ ♣ **The Painted Lady** (1-888-753-3290; www.staugustinepaintedlady .com), 47 San Marco Ave. You can't miss this Victorian decked out in purples and greens—it looks like a funky dollhouse. And indeed, it's one of the few B&Bs in town that welcomes children and pets. Will and Carri Donnan welcome the curious into three rooms ($79-plus) of their haunted home, where Miss Martha trysts with her lover and a ghost orange tabby leaves impressions on the daybed. It's all part of the ambience, since Carri is a fourth-generation spiritualist running a metaphysical shop downstairs where you can have your tarot read and aura photographed, or just browse through the crystals, dream catchers, incense, and racks of Eastern clothing.

⚘ ♣ **St. Francis Inn** (1-800-824-6062; www.stfrancisinn.com), 279 St. George St. With not a straight angle in the place, this is a three-story home with charm—how many B&Bs in the United States date back to 1791? Every room has its own unique shape, size, and furnishings befitting the character of Señor Gaspar Garcia; I'm drawn to the romantic Balcony Room, with its park view, sitting room, fireplace, and in-room whirlpool. A small swimming pool sits off the lush garden courtyard, and guests can enjoy the peace of St. Francis Park next door. Two chefs share the honor of creating gourmet breakfasts and delicious complimentary desserts each

evening. Rates run $129–269; at the high end, that's the rental of a family cottage across the street.

This is a first—a bed and *boat*. Docked at the municipal marina downtown, **SeaClusion** (www.bed -boat-st-augustine.com), slip 82, is an extension of Casa de Solana, offering guests an opportunity to sleep on the water in a well-appointed 38-foot trawler; guests can lounge on the deck or wander over to the B&B for amenities like a full breakfast and wireless Internet access. $249 and up.

Southern Wind (1-800-781-3338; www.southernwindinn.com), 18 Cordova St. My sister raved about her stay here, so I had to check it out. It's a beautiful 1916 Victorian home with one key feature—a wraparound veranda that's the perfect place to hang out and relax. Period furnishings and antiques add to the Gilded Age ambience of the inn's 10 rooms ($99–239, ranging from cozy nooks to spacious suites), and little touches like bottled water, bathrobes, and hair dryers make you feel pampered. Breakfast is served buffet style but always features one hot entrée like crabmeat omelets.

HOTELS, MOTELS, AND RESORTS
On Anastasia Island, just across the Bridge of Lions, you'll find numerous small nonchain motels with rates in the $30s. Poke around the northern fringe of St. Augustine for similar bargains. You'll also find excellent national chains along San Marco Ave and on St. Augustine Beach.

Anastasia Island 32080
⚘ **Anastasia Inn** (904-825-2879 or 1-888-226-6181; www.anastasiainn .com), 218 Anastasia Blvd. This pleasant, compact, newer offering has a small heated swimming pool and

Jacuzzi rooms, and a mini fridge, microwave, and coffeepot in every room; free continental breakfast. Rates start at $45 weekdays.

Was I delighted to find out the **Conch House** (904-829-8646; www .conch-house.com), 57 Comares Ave, wasn't just a restaurant but a hide-away for guests who can't get enough of that Key West atmosphere. The precious 13 units, recently renovated, offer crisp, tasteful decor, access by land or sea, and a variety of floor plans and sleeping arrangements. With some of the best eating and drinking in St. Augustine just steps from your door, *plus* a sparkling pool set amid lush tropical landscaping, why should you ever leave? Rates run $95–125 for standard rooms, $150–175 for suites, and $250–275 for two-bedroom efficiencies. Reserve your

CASA MONICA

St. Augustine CVB

spot well in advance; a three-day stay required for holiday weekends.

St. Augustine 32084

&. ∞ **Casa Monica** (1-800-648-1888; www.casamonica.com), 95 Cordova St. Stride into the Turkish-inspired lobby and take a step back into Henry Flagler's Gilded Age in this grand hotel, with its beaded Victorian lamps and painted beams, where the white-gloved staff usher you to your private abode. This is what Florida tourism meant in 1888, when the Casa Moni-ca (built by Flagler's partner, Franklin Smith) first opened its doors. After four months, Flagler bought the hotel and renamed it the Cordova. Restored to its original lavish glory several years ago by Richard Kessler, it now offers guests spacious rooms and opulent suites, $129–289, with modern appointments; it's a member of the Historic Hotels of America.

✐ ☙ **The Cozy Inn** (1-888-288-2204; www.thecozyinn.com), 202 San Marco Ave. Staying at this Superior Small Lodging during my last big hiking expedition, I appreciated being able to spread things out across a like-new two-story town house with a full kitchen, great for multiday stays ($130–200). Sparkling standard rooms with a Florida coastal atmosphere sport queen beds, $69–89. Pets welcome; a security deposit and cleaning fee applies.

I was upset to see some of my favorite waterfront motels disappear to rede-velopment until I *didn't* see new **St. Augustine Hilton** (904-829-2277; www.hilton.com), 32 Avenida Menen-dez, for the first time. Yep, that's right—I drove right past it, did a double-take, and came back around the block for another look. The facade fits in perfectly with the row of homes overlooking the bay, and that's a pleas-

CONCH HOUSE

ure to behold. You'll find the usual Hilton attention to detail within the 72 brand-new rooms ($169 and up) inside, but the best part is that you're within walking distance of all of Old St. Augustine.

✔ **St. George Inn** (904-827-5740 or 1-888-827-5740; www.stgeorge-inn .com), 4 St. George St #101. In the heart of the historic district, this hotel blends in seamlessly with the shops and restaurants of St. George St at the City Gates. Large, well-appointed rooms boast killer views of the down-town area; 22 units, with some very roomy suites ideal for families, $79–159. My favorite is Room 25, with a balcony that looks out on the Castillo and Matanzas Bay.

St. Augustine 32092
Adjacent to the World Golf Hall of Fame (see *To See—Museums*) is the **World Golf Village Renaissance Resort** (904-940-8000 or 1-800-WGV-GOLF; www.worldgolfrenais-sance.com), 500 S Legacy Trail. The resort borders the village's first cham-pionship course, at which hotel guests have full privileges, and offers guests preferred tee times to the Slammer

and the Squire. European accents, outdoor pool, professional golf simu-lators, 24-hour health club and sauna, billiards room, cigar room, and gift shop. Complimentary parking at a resort! Now, where do you see that anymore?

St. Augustine Beach 32080
Castillo Real (904-471-3505 or 1-866-941-7325; www.castilloreal.com), 530 FL A1A (Beach Blvd), is the new kid on the beach, a boutique hotel that's part of the Clarion chain. It feels nothing like its cousins, however, with its Moorish theme extending from the vaulted lobby with fountain to fine wood furniture and luxe linens in the guest rooms. Choose from stan-dard, Jacuzzi, or oceanfront rooms; rates start at $109.

The Mediterranean-themed **La Fies-ta Ocean Inn & Suites** (1-800-852-6390; www.lafiestainn.com), 810 FL A1A (Beach Blvd), has spacious rooms decorated in local artwork, tile entries, and great landscaping with a palm-lined pool. Oh, and the beach is just a stroll down the boardwalk over the dunes; rooms 216–219 have a beautiful sunrise view. $79–290, depending on season, size, and loca-tion; continental breakfast included.

🐾 I love a dog-friendly motel. **Vilano Beach Motel** (904-829-2651; www.vilanobeachmotel.com), 50 Vilano Rd, is light kitsch with pink flamingos and tropical decor—and a Hollywood location for the shooting of the WB series *Safe Harbor*. This clean 1950s motel is just off the beach and has cool tile floors in every room for your favorite pooch, plus a pool right outside your door. Each room has its own mural painted by a local artist, along with a small fridge and microwave. $85–125.

Ponte Vedra 32082

Rediscover the '20s at the **Ponte Vedra Inn & Club** (904-285-1111; www.pvresorts.com), 200 Ponte Vedra Blvd, where you'll experience all the grandeur of a famed winter resort for the wealthy and famous. Generations of guests continue to come back, and generations of staff continue to cater to their every need. The main inn was opened in 1938 and has retained much of its original grandeur. Choose from lagoon or ocean views in any of the 18 luxury rooms. The oceanside rooms are larger and feature two queen poster beds in a beautiful honey-blond finish. I wanted to have them ship one to my house. The European turndown service was new to me; the bed covers are removed, and two soft sheets surround your blanket for a much softer and more hygienic sleep. In the bathroom you'll find the television piped in so you won't miss the morning news; there's also a softly lit magnifying mirror. This resort is all about the little details, from intimate corner nooks to friendly personal service. Rooms start at $190 in the historic inn and $250 oceanfront.

Vilano Beach 32084

✒ Offering oceanview rooms and guest beach access, the friendly **Ocean Sands Beach Inn** (904-824-1112 or 1-800-609-0888; www.ocean sandsinn.com), 3465 Coastal Hwy, is a small motel scarcely more than a decade old with neat, clean motel rooms—your choice of king or twins. Each room has a mini fridge, coffeemaker, and hair dryer, and continental breakfast is served each morning in the breakfast room. It's a lovely little family-friendly place, and I especially like the pool just behind the motel, overlooking the North River, wonderful for cooling down after sunning on the beach. $99–139.

HOUSE RENTALS ✒ ♿ ❀ **The Beach Cottages** (1-888-963-8272; www.beach-cottages.com). Large families and friends traveling together often find house rentals an economical way to visit the beach. To enjoy the charm of 1890s Summer Haven, stay at **The Lodge,** a restored five-bedroom dogtrot cottage sandwiched between the Summer Haven River and the Atlantic Ocean, with breezy wraparound porches and gorgeous beadwork walls and ceilings, or **The Hut,** an adjacent funky little historic beach cottage with plank floors, lots of natural light, and a constant sea breeze. Specializing in family reunions, agent Win Kelly also represents another 13 beach cottages along the coast. Rentals range from $379 a night (three-night minimum) to $8,250 a month, depending on season, with weekly rentals preferred.

CAMPGROUNDS

North Beach 32084

✒ ❀ You'll find a shady campsite with a salt breeze at **North Beach Camp Resort** (904-824-1806; www.north beachcamp.com), 4125 Coastal FL A1A. Nestled on a barrier island between a remote stretch of A1A and the North River, it features beautifully landscaped sites ($40–42) shaded by mature trees. Tent campers enjoy sites ($38) within an easy walk of the river, so bring your fishing tackle! Facilities include a convenience store, playground, pool, Jacuzzi, and fishing pier; weekly rates available.

St. Augustine 32086

Indian Creek Campground (1-800-233-4324), 1555 FL 207. Tuck your camper into the shady forest, or choose a sunny pull-through space. RV spaces ($25) with gravel pads, each with picnic table; bathhouses scattered throughout the campground. Tent campers welcome but must check in before 6 PM.

St. Augustine Beach 32080

🏕 **Bryn Mawr Ocean Resort** (904-471-3353), 4850 FL A1A S. Just over the dunes from the Atlantic (with direct beach access), this campground has a mix of park models ($80–85), permanent residents, and RV spaces ($40 oceanfront, $47 beachfront), many with adjoining decks with picnic tables. Some sites are tucked in the maritime hammock, but most are out in the open along the ocean; the swimming pool is next to a nicely shaded playground area.

Ocean Grove Camp Resort (1-800-342-4007; www.oceangroveresort .com), 4225 FL A1A S. Set in a remnant maritime hammock with a grove of tall pines on Matanzas Bay, this campground with natural appeal has shady spaces (gravel and grass pads, $45), rustic one-room log cabins with air-conditioning ($60, sleeps four), and tent spaces ($38) with beautiful views across the salt marsh. Dock with boat launch, fish-cleaning station; a camp store has marine items.

✳ Where to Eat

DINING OUT

Anastasia Island

🍴 It's not just dinner—it's an experience. A little taste of St. Croix along Salt Run, the **Conch House Restaurant** (904-829-8646; www.conch -house.com), 57 Comares Ave, has been pleasing customers since 1946. Dress is strictly casual, and the atmos-

phere is, too. You might catch a reggae band in the courtyard. Dine upstairs and watch the pink moonrise over the dunes, or dangle your feet in one of the palm-thatched chickees over the water. You can even sit next to live alligators and watch them watch you. And if that isn't enough to start, it's the food and the attentive wait staff that rate the "Dining Out" category. Start with banana pepper calamari or their famous baked stuffed clams, $9. For the main course ($19–27), try the fresh homemade lobster ravioli, or shrimp Anastasia; order up Minorcan pork back ribs with Mrs. Ponce's famous barbecue sauce. Light appetites will appreciate the Nutty Fish Salad, which to me was a delight—grouper rolled in crushed macadamia nuts, flash fried, garnished with edible orchids, and surrounded by fruit and a coconut dipping sauce. Its artful presentation was mirrored in every dish I saw around the room. The portions are huge—even the salad came supersized. Consider sharing your meal with your companion; I almost didn't have room to share the mile-high Key lime pie. The drink menu is as extensive as any Caribbean bar, and I'm sorry I had to pass on it. Next time, I'll let someone else be the designated driver (or stay next door; see *Lodging*) so I can try the Goombay Smash!

North Beach

At **The Reef** (904-824-8008; www .thereefstaugustine.com), 4100 Coastal Hwy, soak in the ambience of the dunes while looking out over the Atlantic and savoring dilled shrimp salad, made with the local catch, or crab Florentine, with thick chunks of blue crab. The extensive menu includes regional favorites like shrimp and grits, Florida rock lobster, and jambalaya, $10–25. Open for lunch and dinner daily, but Sunday brunch is their forte—for $28, the extensive spread includes crab legs and eggs Benedict made to order, and you'll enjoy jazz or classical guitar in accompaniment to the strum of the waves outside.

🍴 **Cortesses Bistro and Flamingo Bar** (904-825-6775), 172 San Marco Ave. Classy presentation and wonderful textures in a perfect bistro setting —dining at this newcomer to the northern end of town is a delight. Step into the traditional courtyard with its booths and tables shaded by garden finery, and you won't want to leave. Indoors and out, intimate dining spaces set the tone for fine creations from executive chef Roger Millecan, including herb-crusted New Zealand lamb, Chicken Cortesse (chicken breast stuffed with prosciutto and provolone, sautéed in white wine), and Atlantic salmon grilled with a peppercorn mélange. An extensive wine list complements your meal. Don't pass up the appetizers, either: I savored the blue crab and corn cakes ($7) presented with a drizzle of lemon

CONCH HOUSE SALAD

Sandra Friend

garlic aioli, and the daily special (grouper) was tender with a spicy edge. Entrées $15–24; Sunday live jazz brunch 1–5, $9–14, or catch live music most nights in the popular Flamingo Bar.

Le Pavillion (904-824-6202), 45 San Marco Ave. In a grand old home in the antiques district, this elegant French restaurant is one of St. Augustine's top dining experiences. For lunch, enjoy the special oyster platter and salad ($11), or crêpes stuffed with seafood, beef, spinach, or chicken ($10); dinner entrées include filet mignon, half roast duckling, fresh trout sautée almandine, and their famous rack of lamb for one ($17–27).

Tucked into an 1879 Victorian home under the trees along the avenue, it's as inconspicuous as it is delicious. For more than 20 years, the **Raintree Restaurant and Steakhouse** (904-824-7211; www.raintreerestaurant .com), 102 San Marco Ave, has delighted diners with its award-winning entrées and extensive wine list. Choose from lamb shank osso buco, grilled portobello napoleon, beef Wellington, and more: $14–26. Don't miss the dessert bar, where the chef creates bananas Foster and crêpes tableside. Open for dinner; reservations suggested.

Old St. Augustine
95 Cordova (904-810-6810; www .95cordova.com), 95 Cordova St. Settle back into that comfortable chair and savor St. Augustine's most upscale dining experience, presented by chef Renee Nyfeler and the staff of the Casa Monica (see *Hotels, Motels, and Resorts*). Take a trip back in time to the 1880s, when Henry Flagler's railroad brought the crème de la crème of New England society to this very

place; although evening attire isn't required, you'll want to be dressy for this occasion. The menu is a changing palette of entrées ($18–29) of the caliber of sesame-seared sea scallops and fusion herb-crusted redfish and polenta. Winner of the Wine Spectator "Award of Excellence"; reservations recommended. One insider tip: **The Market at 95 Cordova,** the café along King St, serves gourmet food in a more casual atmosphere, with a bakery and fudge shop to tempt passersby.

St. Augustine

🍴 **Creekside Dinery** (904-829-6113; www.creeksidedinery.com), 160 Nix Boatyard Rd. Set off the mainstream of US 1, this gabled replica Cracker house looks like someone's home—until you step inside. The vast open rooms and wraparound porches along Oyster Creek blur the line between indoors and outdoors. Imagine toasting marshmallows tableside as the crickets buzz at twilight under the magnolia trees: You can do that at Creekside on an open tabby grill pit. The focus of the menu is seafood, with fresh grouper, plank-cooked salmon, and other specialties presented on fish platters. Ask for the piquant and spicy house dressing on your salad, and if the squash casserole is available as the night's vegetable, don't miss it! The fried entrées are a little heavy on the breading, but the grilled fish will leave you with a smile—I recommend the Crock a' Shrimp for shrimp lovers. Entrées, $8–17.

Vilano Beach

🍴 A rockin' 1920s fish camp gone upscale, **Cap's On The Water** (904-824-8794; www.capsonthewater.com), Myrtle St, is hidden back in a neighborhood along the Intracoastal Water-

way. Boaters can find it easily enough; you'll have to follow the signs. With the doors thrown wide open and the whole place shaded by giant live oak trees, it blurs the line between indoors and outdoors—with a killer view of the Tolomato River estuary thrown in for good measure. Try some Vanilla Grouper, a nut-encrusted fresh catch with a sweet vanilla rum sauce, a Stilton Salad, or classic St. Augustine Fried Shrimp, dipped in egg wash and rolled in cracker meal. Entrées, $8–14. Stopping here for a late lunch, I nibbled on Shrimp Vilano, a fiery little concoction melding fresh local shrimp with a garlic-chile sauce, set on a bed of crispy spinach with Asiago crumbles. Just writing about it makes me want a snack. Despite how well it's hidden, this is a busy, busy place on weekends —come at an off-hour if you don't want a long wait. Oh, and the restaurant faces west across the water, making it a perfect place to savor a sunset.

Fiddler's Green Oceanside Bar & Grill (904-824-8897; www.thefiddlersgreen.com), 2750 Anahma Dr (FL A1A). The view says it all—right on the beach nestled into the dunes. And the lineage doesn't hurt, either, as this restaurant is cousin to the ever-popular Saltwater Cowboys and Creekside Dinery. The menu includes a little something for everyone, but their forte is seafood, with local favorites like Shrimp Aviles (pan-seared fresh shrimp with garlic, shallots, mushrooms, sun-dried tomatoes, and tasso ham in a light bourbon cream sauce over penne) and Blackened Fish Matanzas (fresh catch dredged in hot Cajun peppers, pan seared and served with drawn butter). Entrées $10 and up; full bar.

THE VIEW FROM CAP'S ON THE WATER

EATING OUT

Anastasia Island

Gypsy Cab Company (904-461-8843; www.gypsycab.com), 828 Anastasia Blvd. Decked out in Caribbean pastels on the outside and with a jazzy New York bistro feel on the inside, the award-winning Gypsy Cab Company dishes out "urban Italian" treats like vegetable *formaggia* (one of the weekday lunch specials served 11–3) with just-crunchy vegetables in a strong garlic and cheese sauce ladled over ziti and topped with fresh bread crumbs. Of the soup selections, the wild mushroom bisque delivers with a velvety texture and just the right amount of mushrooms; sandwiches $7–8, salads $8, dinner entrées $12–17. Top off your meal with tiramisu, or go for the chocoholics' favorite, their rich and creamy chocolate mousse.

🍴 They say fried shrimp was invented in St. Augustine, and **O'Steen's Restaurant** (904-829-6974), 205 Anastasia Blvd, has been the local hot spot for fried shrimp and pileau (pronounced *per-loo*)—a classic regional dish of seasoned rice, shrimp, and Minorcan sausage—since 1965. The lines get long here, so sign up at the window and browse next door in the antiques shop while you listen for your name on the loudspeaker. Open Tue–Sat for lunch and dinner ($6–20); cash only.

Crescent Beach

South Beach Grille (904-471-8700; www.southbeachgrill.net), 45 Cubbedge Rd. It's a surreal scene: 1940s music spills across the dunes as you sip a margarita and watch the waves crashing on the beach. With a full complement of beach drinks, from the Goombay Smash to Blue Island Ice Tea, the South Beach Grill is *the* hot spot in Crescent Beach. Choose the open-air back porch for best effect and enjoy steamed shrimp with datil-pepper corn bread, or the thick seafood jambalya. Entrées run $10–17, but you can opt for wraps or burgers for a lighter meal. My suggestion: Stop by for a drink and a bowl of their outstanding roasted corn and blue crab corn chowder, a crunchy, buttery concoction that will have you ordering seconds.

Old St. Augustine

🍴 **A1A Ale House** (904-829-2977), 1 King St. With its upstairs dining area (overlooking Matanzas Bay) jazzed up with fish tanks and snazzy nautical decor, this is a place for funky fusion seafood like a delicious blue crab BLT, a snapper burger (made with fresh-ground snapper topped with mango ketchup), and shrimp and grits. Lunch and dinner (entrées $13 and up); open daily.

Acapulco's (904-804-9933), 12 Avenida Menendez, offers Mexican dishes like *carne asada, pollo colorado,* and *mole poblano* in the shadow of the Castillo de San Marcos, with a stellar view of Matanzas Bay from their upper floor; serving lunch and dinner ($10–18) in a comfortable atmosphere.

Decorated with murals depicting the founding and settlement of St. Augustine, **Athena Restaurant** (904-823-9076; www.athenacafe.com), 14 Cathedral Place, provides a unique setting for classic Greek dishes like *pastitsio, moussaka,* and *saganaki* (entrées $14 and up), but the big deal here are the desserts (baklava, napoleons, and more) that beckon from the front bakery case. Open for breakfast, lunch, and dinner.

🦐 A delightful unpretentious bistro that would be my local hangout if I lived here, the **Aviles Market Café** (904-829-6033), 11C Aviles St, offers up breakfast faves like French toast (made with fresh French bread), biscuits and gravy, and three-egg omelets. Impressionistic paintings of local estuaries and other intriguing art draw your attention to the walls, and folks chat across the room like they've known each other forever. Grab a hearty breakfast for less than $5, or come in for lunch specials like pressed turkey and avocado sandwiches, and chicken Caesar salad. Part of the café is indeed a market, selling fresh veggies and fruit.

🦐 **Barnacle Bill's** (904-824-3663; www.barnaclebillsonline.com), 14 Castillo Dr. My favorite stop in town boasts hearty seafood selections, fabulous chowder, and the don't-miss Datil Do-It Shrimp, a spicy delight sea-

soned with local datil peppers. Lunch and dinner, $11–20, plus market-price fresh catches. Additional location on FL A1A at St. Augustine Beach.

A great spot for people watching, the **Bunnery Bakery & Café** (904-829-6166), 121 St. George Ave, opens early to offer breakfasts ($3 and up) like Southern Eggs—laid atop fluffy biscuits with homestyle sausage gravy and grits. Yum.

If you love omelets, don't miss **Mary's Harbor View Café** (904-825-0193), 16A Avenida Menendez, where 11 choices await along with an extensive breakfast and lunch menu. It's a small but bustling bargain breakfast bistro, opening at 7 AM.

O. C. White's (904-824-0808), 118 Avenida Menendez. Jazz floats across the walled courtyard on a stiff breeze from Matanzas Bay. Classy but casual, this unique dining venue—the General Worth House, circa 1791—overlooks the bay at the marina, offering a large outdoor patio with live music nightly. Lunch and dinner offerings focus on seafood, like shrimp and scallop scampi, crabby grouper, and seafood gumbo over rice ($7–23).

Catering to the British palate, the **Prince of Wales Restaurant** (904-810-5725), corner Spanish and Cuna St, is the place for mushy peas and Yorkshire pudding as sides with your entrée, and sticky toffee and treacle as a treat. Have a classic bangers and mash, "curry of the day" with an authentic Kingfisher beer, or a ploughman's lunch, $8–14. This is the first place in Florida I've discovered hard cider on draft!

Art and a bagel—it's an early morning wake-up. **Schmagel's Bagels & Deli** (904-824-4444), 69 Hypolita St, is in the heart of the shopping district. Choose from 10 different types of freshly baked bagels topped with everything from lox to hummus (my fave: green olive cream cheese). Deli sandwiches and panini for lunch, all selections under $6. The deli connects to the **Mullet Beach Gallery** through a courtyard (see *Selective Shopping*).

Since 1976, the **Spanish Bakery** (904-471-3046; www.thespanish bakery.com), 42½ St. George Ave, has served up tempting treats from the historic Salcedo Kitchen. Stop in for empanadas, cinnamon cookies, and rolls and munch down on your goodies under the shade of an old cedar tree. Open daily at 9:30 AM.

Orangedale

Watch for seaplanes as they land and take off by **Outback Crab Shack** (904-522-0500), 8155 CR 13 N at Six Mile Marina on the St. Johns River (take FL 16 west—it's worth the drive). You'll get your money's worth,

as they dish out enormous platters of fried scallops ($14), alligator ($12), and catfish ($15). Lobster, crawfish, blue crab, and clams are steamed to perfection. They'll even blacken or stir-fry your meal. Get your daily requirement of veggies with the steamed Low Country tender potatoes, onions, corn, broccoli, mushrooms, and sausage for $5. Open daily for lunch and dinner.

St. Augustine

Since 1967, **Johnnies** (904-824-0308), 138 San Marco Ave, has served up their signature cheesesteaks to diehard fans, including variants on the classic Philly—the "Pittsburgh," with shoestring potatoes and grilled onions; the "Pizza Steak," with provolone, mushrooms, pepperoni, and marinara; and the "Blue Bacon Steak," with cheese, bacon, grilled onions, and blue cheese dressing. Enough already, I'm getting hungry. Subs and more subs, half or full, $5.55 and up. Open Mon–Sat 10–3.

The **Kings Head British Pub** (904-823-9787), 6460 US 1 N, looks like it dropped out of an Elizabethan painting: an ivy-covered cottage with bright red British phone booth (à la Dr. Who) outside; inside, real Brit food from bangers and mash to Scotch eggs, ploughman's platter, various meat pies, and fish-and-chips, $7–13. Lunch and dinner, closed Mon.

🍴 A delightful restaurant with many vegetarian choices, **The Manatee Cafe** (904-826-0210; www.manatee cafe.com), 525 FL 16, Westgate Plaza, offers breakfast goodies ($5–10) like burritos, fruit-topped pancakes, and omelets, and main dishes ranging from tofu Reuben and chili to Cajun chicken. Herbal teas, carrot juice, and other "good for you" foods, too! Serv-

PRINCE OF WALES RESTAURANT

Sandra Friend

ing breakfast and lunch 8–8 (except Sun, 8–3); a portion of all sales goes to manatee preservation funds.

You'll say "I'm all right" at the **Murray Bros Caddyshack** in World Golf Village. Tee up with nachos with chili ($10) or chicken wings ($7), tour the greens with the Wedge Salad ($8), and check out the back nine with the Caddyshack Classic—a 12-ounce USDA strip steak ($21). The 19th Hole has domestic and imported beers.

St. Augustine Beach

Right on the beachfront, **Beachcomber Restaurant** (904-471-3744), A St, is a local favorite with classic American fare—burgers, sandwiches, salads—for lunch, $4–7. Local seafood figures in with their spicy homemade Minorcan clam chowder, fried gator tail, shrimp dip, and fried shrimp and scallops, $7–15. Open for breakfast, too, except Tue.

Cafe Eleven (904-460-9311), 501 FL A1A (Beach Blvd), is a snazzy combination of bistro and performance space, with live music on weekends. Breakfasts include funky treats like a feta, spinach, and cheese croissant and praline French toast, but I gravitate to the enormous fresh salads —pear 'n' berry, bruschetta, tomato mozzarella—and big sandwiches; $4–6. The pastry case will tempt you, too. Open 6:30 AM–midnight.

Saltwater Cowboys (904-471-2332; www.saltwatercowboys.com), 299 Dondanville Rd. Good luck finding a parking space at this wildly popular fish camp on the Matanzas River; your best bet is arriving for lunch or a very early dinner. It's all about fish, of course—fried, broiled, baked, blackened, and steamed, but they've got killer Florida barbecue as well. Try a

Florida Cracker specialty like frog legs or cooter, or the hot and spicy jambalaya. Entrées $7–19, plus market-price fresh catches.

Breakfasts come hearty at the **Sea Oats Café** (904-471-7350), 1073 FL A1A, tucked away in the Publix plaza. For less than $10 you can fill up on their pancakes (bacon, cheddar-filled, chocolate chip, banana, blueberry) or try out the homemade cheddar grits (I loved 'em) with a shrimp, cheese, and tomato omelet. This was the only non-hotel breakfast spot open along the beachfront on a Sun morning, and I'm glad I found them.

Sunset Grille (904-471-5555; www.sunsetgrilleA1A.com), 421 FL A1A (Beach Blvd). Enjoy huge seafood pasta platters (shrimp and scallops Rockefeller, $15), the "world's best" coconut-crusted shrimp ($15), and the smoothest margaritas along the beach in this casual, award-winning local favorite. Lunch and dinner, $7–20, with nightly specials—AYCE crab legs on Mon!

Vilano Beach

Next to the Vilano Beach Motel (see *Lodging*), **TwoCan Terry's** (904-819-9101) serves up beach fare like oyster "po'boy" and crabcakes along with deli sandwiches and subs, seafood and steak platters, burgers and assorted nibbles— including fried plantains and fried baby spinach. My pick: baked burritos, just the way I like 'em, smothered in cheese and enchilada sauce. Open for lunch and dinner, $4–15.

COFFEE SHOPS & ICE CREAM PARLORS

Old St. Augustine

A Michigan chain, **Kilwins** (904-826

0008), 140 St. George Ave, tempts you inside with display cases filled with chocolate goodies; they sell ice cream as well. Sip a chai or grab some ice cream at **St. Augustine Gourmet** (904-823-1991), 20 Castillo, a pleasant place to take a break while walking the Ancient City. The funky **St. Augustine Coffee Company** (904-824-0036), 8 Granada, opens early to offer espresso, bagels, salads, and desserts. But the granddaddy of sweet stuff in the Old City is **Whetstone Chocolates** (www.whetstone chocolates.com) on St. George Ave, a local fixture since 1967. Their chocolate factory is moving into the San Sebastian district (at the corner of King St. and US 1) and will reopen for tours in 2007.

St. Augustine

Jasmine's Coffeehouse (904-826-0865; www.jasminescoffee.com), 149 San Marco Ave, is an Internet café and free wi-fi hot spot serving breakfast (egg sandwiches, bagels, lox, and organic granola) all day along with its upscale coffees and iced drinks. Their lunch options include freshly made salads and different deli sandwiches, such as a smoked ham, apple, and Brie melt for $6. Open Mon–Fri 8–4:30, Sat 8–3.

✳ Selective Shopping

Anastasia Island

Known well to locals as the place to browse while you're waiting for your seat at O'Steen's, **Anastasia Antique Center** (904-824-7126), 201 Anastasia Blvd, offers dozens of dealer booths within a broad, open space. You'll find Blue Mountain pottery, ruby and Vaseline glass, guitars and books.

Anastasia Books (904-824-0648), 13 Anastasia Blvd. Nice selection of Floridiana (new and used) as well as plenty of children's books and textbooks for homeschoolers. Large used-book section, including the area's largest selection of science fiction and fantasy.

In an urban chic old storefront, **The Final Groove** (904-824-6520), 115 Anastasia Blvd, screams retro with its '60s and '70s clothing, hats, and furniture. I found the perfect purse here to complement a Victorian outing.

Filled with my kind of fun, flamboyant art, **Simple Gestures Art & Gifts** (904-827-9997), corner of White St and Anastasia Blvd, gets the nod not just because of their copious supply of funky stuff by local artists—including Roadside America kitsch, Story People, art sets for kids, mosaics, and garden art—but also because they unearthed part of a local mystery in their front yard, the rails to the old streetcar line that ran from downtown to the beach nearly a century ago. How cool is that? Ask for their "free phantasmagorical gift wrap" for the treasures you're bound to pick up.

Near the corner of A1A and Alternate A1A, explore a Florida roadside classic —**Tom's Souvenirs & Sea Shells,** a roadside stand filled with all that said "Florida vacation" in my childhood, from seashells to corals and sponges, nautical decor, Florida candies, gator heads, and kitschy Florida gifts.

Ponte Vedra

Pineapple Post Gift Shop (1-877-757-7678; www.pineapplepostgifts .com), 2403 South Third St, offers great gifts and home accessories with southern hospitality; complimentary gift wrap.

St. Augustine

With more than 100 stores to choose from, you could spend most of a week browsing the shops of historic St. Augustine. There are three major shopping districts: **Old St. Augustine** tends toward touristy with a touch of art, especially along St. George St, which is lined with shops from end to end and has everything a tourist could want and more, from T-shirts and tchotchkes to postcards and paintings. **San Marco Ave** is the antiques district to the north of the City Gates, and **San Sebastian** is the up-and-coming arts district along King St near the San Sebastian Winery. I've listed highlights for each area.

Old St. Augustine
Around the World Marketplace (904-824-6223), 21 Orange St. The burble of fountains makes browsing a pleasant experience as you poke through colorful imports—Tavalera porcelain, onyx chess sets, masks, statues, mirrors, and wall art.

Mermaid sketches and tropical scenes caught my attention at **Art & Ornaments** (904-824-8613; www.myornaments.org), 5 Spanish St, Ste B, a fine place for engraved wooden Christmas ornaments.

Bouvier Maps & Prints (904-825-0920; www.bouviermaps.com), 11-D Aviles St. If you're looking for a map to go with St. Augustine's history, this is the place to visit. Dealing in original antique maps and prints, this shop is as rare a find as its incredible inventory. Closed Tue and Wed.

Dreamstreet Too (904-829-5220; www.dreamstreettoo.com), 64 Hypolita St, a place for the soul to soar, is a new age shop replete with angels and fairies, music, and books; I love the uplifting sayings on the walls.

Frantiques (904-823-1818), 6 Cordova St. Tourist trains stop here for a look at the "love tree," an intertwined growth of cabbage palm and live oak. Step inside for vintage clothing, furniture, glassware, and books, or grab a fresh fruit smoothie at the Love Tree Juice Bar in the back of the building.

Grover's Gallery (904-824-5738), 14B St. George St. Big pieces, low prices: That's the philosophy of artist Grover Rice, who has spent more than 30 years carving wood into art such as life-sized sea turtles and pelicans, tikis made from palm trunks, and model villages.

For historic tomes, stop in at **La Libreria** on St. George St, the official bookstore of the Colonial Spanish Quarter (see *To See—Historic Homes*).

It's one of the most interesting locations I've ever seen for an antiques store, so I suggest you go out of your way to the **Lightner Antique Mall** (904-824-9948), 25 Granada St, located *inside* the original swimming pool of the historic Alcazar Hotel, now the Lightner Museum (see *To See—Museums*). Go around the back of the museum to enter.

All things nautical—that's the theme at **Mariner's Manor** (904-808-7014), 107 St. George St, where you'll find paintings of ships, books on sailing, and nautically themed home decor.

Think gifts with attitude at **Materialistic** (904-824-1611), 125 St. George St, where even the T-shirts are smarmy. Pick up a punching rabbi, a dashboard hula dancer, or a Brahman lunch box.

At **Metalartz** (904-824-6322; www.metalartz.net), 58 Hypolita St, mobiles and glass balls dangle from the ceiling, and lizards and dragonflies cling to a tree that rises from the floor. With art glass, paintings, metal sculptures, and much more, this kaleidoscope of artistry represents 15 local artists and their very creative expressions.

The **Mullet Beach Gallery** (904-829-6831; www.mulletbeach.com), 51 Cordova St #B, features local artists in watercolors, acrylics, pottery, and more. Patrick Madden's bright acrylics jump off the walls, and Brenda Phillips creates oils on canvas with colors that'll jazz up any space. Don't miss Evie Auerbach's functional and fun fish platters!

For your fix of Jimmy Buffett T-shirts and related paraphernalia, stop in at **Palm Bay Republic** (904-829-2291; www.palmbayrepublic.com), 162 St. George St, a colorful shop fronting the Heritage Walk mini-mall.

Browse through global imports at **The Rising Moon** (904-829-0070), 58 Spanish St, a tasteful gift shop in a historic home.

ST. GEORGE STREET

Sandra Friend

St. Augustine Art Glass (904-824-4916), 54 St. George St, isn't just about glass—check out the raku art sculptures and playful metal sculptures in the tranquil garden behind the building.

Second Read Books (904-829-0334), 51 Cordova St, keeps a brisk business going with used books for sale or trade just a block from Flagler College. Look for a good local section, fine literature, and a broad young-adult selection.

The Woman's Exchange (904-829-5064), 143 St. George St, is a volunteer organization dating back to 1892 that manages tours through the historic Peck Piña House (circa 1700) in order to run a consignment outlet for top-quality home crafters. Their motto is "Creative need is as important as the financial need," and their creativity runs the gamut from watercolor notecards and cookbooks to clothespin dolls, hand-smocked dresses, hand-crafted soaps, and hand-painted glass.

San Marco Ave
A huge selection of beads and necklaces waits at **The Bead Chick** (904-829-8829), 72 San Marco Ave. Sit and create your own strands of beauty.

A historic two-story home now beckons as **Eden** (904-829-2122), 82 San Marco Ave, with "temptations for the home." Inside, look for beaded dresses and jackets, chic lamps, gifts, and large pieces of antique furniture.

I spent quite of bit of time browsing **Jena's Antiques & Art** (904-806-4274), 56 San Marco Ave, turning up treasures like classic wooden toys, Tiffany glass, a dry sink, vintage mirrors, and hand-painted fruit.

Mineral lovers note: **The Jewel Box Goddess Shop** (904-827-1030; www

SAN MARCO AVENUE ANTIQUES

.jewelboxgoddess.com), 208 San Marco Ave, offers a fine selection of crystals in matrix (including one of my favorites, sky-blue celestite) and creative lapidary designs by the store's owner, Gloria Danvers. It's also the home of psychic James Bullock, who does readings Fri–Sun.

St. Augustine Antique Emporium (904-829-0544), 62 San Marco Ave, features 22 dealer booths in a refreshingly open setting, making it easy to keep track of the rest of your group as you browse through the art glass, jewelry, postcards, salt cellars, stained glass, and other ephemera.

Featuring fine artists and craftsmen of the First Coast, **San Marco Gallery & Gifts** (904-826-4434), 78B San Marco Ave, showcases original paintings and sculpture, jewelry, and greeting cards with original photos.

Fine glassware, lamps, furnishings, and home decor are the tip of the iceberg at a **Step Back in Time** (904-810-5829), 60 San Marco Ave.

Gleaming diving helmets set the tone at **Treasures by Marc Anthony** (904-823-0008), 74 San Marco Ave, where a pirate greets you as you walk in to explore classic nautical decor such as glass diver balls, ship's wheels, and, of course, treasure chests.

At **Uptown Antiques** (904-824-9156), 63 and 67 San Marco Ave, look through the mini-mall of dealer booths and you'll unearth treasures like historic postcards of St. Augustine, movie memorabilia, posters, and books.

Wolf's Head Books (904-824-9357 or 1-800-521-5061; www.wolfshead books.com), 67 San Marco, Ste B. I walked in here to look around and walked out with a rare book in my favorite field of study, Florida natural history. This is a true antiquarian bookseller. You will find books here you can't even find on the Internet, especially in the Florida section, with great prices and a superb selection. Open daily.

San Sebastian

The heart of the arts district is **Rembrandtz** (904-829-0065), 131 King St, the gallery that started it all back in 1995. Lovingly tended by Lynne Doten and Kimberly Hunt and representing more than 75 artists, this funky shop carries art glass, fabric arts, paintings, photography, pottery, and more; my eyes were drawn to Ray Brilli's colorful scenes of St. Augustine.

St. Augustine Beach

🖉 Out at the beach, you'll find all the usual surf, swimming suit, and T-shirt shops you've come to expect from every beachfront town. Drive FL A1A to explore, and you'll find gems like **Sunburst Trading Company** (904-461-7255), 491 FL A1A (Beach Blvd), the shell shop for the region, with a selection of shell crafts, burbling Mexican fountains, Latin imports, and, of course, shells. Bring the kids:

The incredible selection starts at 20¢, and there are fossils and coral to choose from, too. An additional location is at 146 St. George St in the Old City.

FARMER'S MARKET Farmer's and Art Market. Now here's a twist—a farmer's market that's evolved into a weekly art gathering, where you can peruse the works of local sculptors and painters while picking up the perfect peck of potatoes. Every Wed 7:30–noon at the St. Augustine Beach pier.

✳ Entertainment

St. Augustine
Between Memorial Day and Labor Day, families gather at Plaza de la Constitucion for free weekly **Concerts in the Plaza,** Thu evening 7–9, with jazz, blues, folk, and country artists keeping the crowd swinging. Catch live music 5–8 and 9–close nightly at the **Tropical Trade Winds Lounge** (904-829-9336; www.trade windslounge.com), 124 Charlotte St, where the house band Matanzas plays Jimmy Buffett and a jammin' collection of their own home-grown St. Augustine–style tunes, or settle back with a beer on the rooftop of the **Old Mill House** on St. George St for breezy acoustic music. For a real immersion into history, stop in at the **Taberna del Gallo,** one of St. Augustine's original watering holes, at the Colonial Spanish Quarter (see *To See—Historic Homes*) to raise a tankyard to the Bilge Rats as they draw you back to 1734 with their repertoire of seafaring tunes. Open Thu–Sat 2–9:30, Sun noon–7.

The play's the thing at the **Limelight Theatre** (1-866-682-6400; www .limelight-theatre.org), 11 Old Mission Ave, with year-round performances ($10–24) that include professional productions like *I Hate Hamlet* and *The Diary of Anne Frank.* Florida's official state play, **The Cross and Sword,** depicts the settlement of St. Augustine, with performances Thu–Sat at 8:30 PM at the St. Augustine Amphitheater on Anastasia Island (904-471-1965). Special plays are offered during Lent and Christmas.

Catch the **Comedy Club at the Gypsy Bar & Grill** (adjacent to the Gypsy Cab Company; see *Eating Out*) for live national acts Thu–Sat; tickets $10.50.

✳ Special Events

Visit www.getaway4florida.com for a full roster of annual events.

February: **Menéndez Birthday Festival,** St. Augustine. A weekend's worth of parades, music, and heritage celebrations commemorating the founder of St. Augustine, with events throughout the Old City.

April: Having been brought up on Maine potatoes—and being an Irish lass—I had to inquire about Hastings's "Potato Capital of the World" Annual **Potato and Cabbage Festival.** So it was back to the basics with mouthwatering potato stew and cabbage soup, and some new treats like potato cupcakes and potato fudge (we call them *needhams* in Maine). The tiny town of Hastings really knows their spuds—ayuh!

May: **Gamble Rogers Folk Festival** (904-794-0222; www.gamblefest.com), St. Augustine Amphitheatre, first weekend. One of Florida's top folk music weekends, with dozens of performers honoring one of the strongest voices in Florida folk music, and vendors and craftspersons with Florida art. Weekend pass $45, ages 13 and up; daily performances $15–25, children free with paying adult (except Sat, $10).

May: **Florida's First Coast Nature Festival,** mid-month, St. Augustine Amphitheatre. I've been a regular at this event since it started a few years back, a nature-based festival offering workshops and seminars on birding, native wildlife, and enjoying the outdoors.

June: **Drake's Raid,** St. Augustine, first weekend. I love the plug for this one: "the largest 16th-century reenactment in the United States." As if

there could be another? Only the most studious of history lovers know that swashbuckling pirate Sir Francis Drake came ashore and set fire to St. Augustine in 1586, sacking the city.

September: **St. Augustine Birthday Festival.** Founded on September 8, 1565, this city has plenty to party about, with reenactments and live entertainment. Join the countdown to the half-millennium!

October: **Colonial Folk Arts and Crafts Festival,** St. Augustine, Spanish Quarter. Browse 17th-century arts and crafts—everything from weaving to blacksmithing—in one of the most interesting living history festivals in Florida.

FLAGLER COUNTY

PALM COAST, BUNNELL, FLAGLER BEACH, BEVERLY BEACH

I t's one of the first Florida places etched in my memory, the wind whipping through our 1955 Ford as Dad drove with the windows open down A1A, the Atlantic Ocean spreading off to the horizon. I remember a day spent at Marineland, a soft plastic toy as a souvenir, and holding my nose at the smell of the sulfur springs at Washington Oaks. South of St. Augustine, north of Daytona Beach, Flagler County has been a quiet place—until recently. Now condos rise from the dunes south of Marineland and at the edge of the junglelike forests of Hammock, and Palm Coast continues to spread. Yet there are still many corners of the county where you can recapture the wild that has always been, along its placid creeks and salt flats, beneath the towering oaks, and beside tidal pools on the shore.

THE FLAGLER PIER

Visit Florida

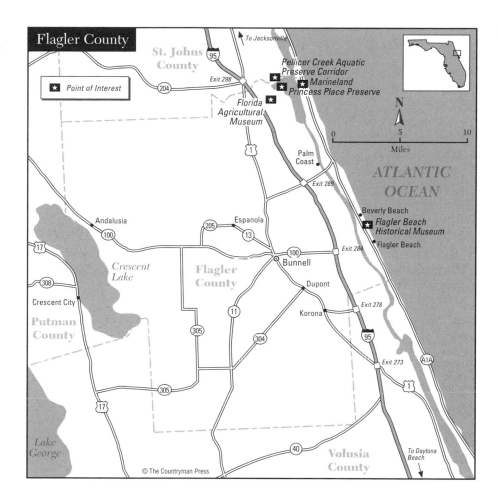

Flagler County

St. Johns County

★ Point of Interest

To Jacksonville

Pellicer Creek Aquatic Preserve Corridor
Marineland
Princess Place Preserve

Florida Agricultural Museum

N

ATLANTIC OCEAN

Miles
0   5   10

Palm Coast

Exit 298

Exit 289

Andalusia

Espanola

Beverly Beach
Flagler Beach Historical Museum
Flagler Beach

Exit 284

Crescent Lake

Flagler County

Bunnell

Dupont

Crescent City

Putman County

Korona

Exit 278

Exit 273

A1A

Exit 273

Lake George

Volusia County

To Daytona Beach

© The Countryman Press

Spanish land grants shaped this region, where plantations were carved out along the coast in the early 1800s. One such, Bulowville, boasted the largest sugar mill in Florida; it can now be seen at Bulow Plantation Ruins State Park. Carved out of neighboring St. Johns and Volusia, Flagler County was established in 1917 with Bunnell as the county seat.

GUIDANCE **Flagler County Tourism Development Council** (1-800-788-0613; www.visitflagler.org), 1200 E Moody Boulevard #1, Bunnell 32110, and **Flagler County Parks & Recreation** (386-437-7490; www.flaglerparks.com).

City of Beverly Beach Town Office (386-439-6888), 2770 N Oceanshore Blvd, Beverly Beach 32136; for Flagler Beach, contact the **City of Flagler Beach** (386-517-2000; www.flaglerbeach.org), P.O. Box 70, Flagler Beach 31236, or **Flagler Beach Chamber of Commerce** (904-439-0995 or 1-800-298-0995).

GETTING THERE *By air:* From the north, fly into Jacksonville International Airport (see the Jacksonville chapter), or from the south, fly into Daytona Beach International Airport (386-248-8069; www.flydaytonafirst.com).

By car: Interstate 95 provides access to the highways that lead to Flagler's back roads. Exit at Dupont Center, US 1, Palm Coast, and Flagler Beach.

GETTING AROUND A car is necessary to make your way around the county. FL A1A and US 1 are the major north–south routes, with FL 100 connecting Flagler Beach and Bunnell.

MEDICAL EMERGENCIES **Florida Hospital—Flagle**r (386-586-2000), 60 Memorial Medical Pkwy, Palm Coast.

✳ To See

ARCHEOLOGICAL SITES Located in a maritime hammock, the **Mala Compra Plantation Archaeological Dig** can be found at Bings Landing Park (386-437-7490; www.flaglerparks.com/bings/preserve.htm), 5880 N Oceanshore Blvd (FL A1A), Palm Coast. The former home of Brigadier General Joseph Martin Hernandez stretched over 724 acres; in the early 1800s he grew sea island cotton, corn, and oranges. Purchased in 1816 for the then-tidy sum of $1,500, the plantation was burned to the ground in 1836 by Seminoles during the Second Seminole Indian War. Artifacts from the dig are on display at the Flagler Beach Historical Museum (see *Museums*). General Hernandez was Florida's first delegate to the U.S. Congress, and also its first Hispanic member. The 8-acre park is a great place for picnics or fishing (from the pier). On weekends you can rent kayaks for a gentle paddle on the Intracoastal. Bings Landing Park is located on the west side of A1A, approximately 2 miles north of the Hammock Dunes Bridge.

ART GALLERIES

Flagler Beach
You'll find designer clothing along with a variety of works by local artisans at **Down By the Sea Boutique & Art Gallery** (386-439-2255), 208 S Third St. Open Mon–Sat 10–4.

Hammock
Tucked beneath the live oak canopy, the **Baliker Gallery** (386-446-0069; www .paulbaliker.com), 5928 N Oceanshore Blvd (FL A1A), beckons you to stop with its larger-than-life driftwood sculptures. Step inside to surround yourself with vivid acrylics of Florida forests and estuaries, and delicate bronze statuettes. The creative spirit of Paul Baliker and Cynthia Spiriti hums through this open space, where the figures of sailfish, sea turtles, and sprites emerge out of the natural curves of driftwood. Gallery open Sat–Sun 10–5; garden open daily 10–5.

Palm Coast
For elegant works of art by local and national artists, visit **Arte de Palm** (386-597-5277; www.artedepalm.com), 101 Palm Harbor Pkwy #114 at Piazza in the

European Village Resort (see *Lodging*). Among the artists, Jacksonville native Henry Von Genk III stands out with his evocative Old Florida landscapes. Open Tue–Sat 11–6.

HISTORIC SITES

Bunnell
The **Bunnell State Bank Building** (circa 1917), 101–107 N Bay St, was the only bank in Flagler County from 1917 to 1932. Today the two-story mason vernacular is known Citizens Bank of Bunnell.

Built in 1915, the **Old Dixie Highway** was built using convict labor. A narrow, 9-foot-wide segment of the original road can be driven through the towns of Hastings, Espanola, and Bunnell between Flagler and St. Johns counties.

Flagler Beach
At **Bulow Plantation Ruins Historic State Park** (see *Green Space—Parks*), take a walking tour through the oldest and most extensive colonial-period sugar works remaining in Florida.

Old Kings Road. Paralleling US 1 and I-95 you'll find segments of the Old Kings Rd, Florida's first highway. Before the American Revolution, Colonel James Grant, governor of British Florida, sought to connect plantations along the East Coast by following an old Indian trail, and he put his lieutenant governor, John Moultrie, in charge. He eventually achieved the objective: connecting St. Augustine to Andrew Turnbull's New Smyrna plantation. By 1774, the shell-surfaced road had pine logs for crossing the swampy sections and numerous bridges, and it was used by settlers and military patrols.

Palm Coast
Princess Place Preserve (386-437-7490, ext 240), Princess Place Rd, off Kings Rd in north Flagler County. It will take a few turns and a long drive down a dirt road to reach this unique historical treasure. It's magical! The oldest homestead in Flagler County, the beautiful 1886 home looks out over Pellicer Creek and the Matanzas River. Or go by kayak (see *To Do—Paddling*) and pull up on shore to have lunch on the veranda or by Florida's first in-ground artesian pool (no swimming in the pool is allowed, however). Open Wed–Sun 7–6; free.

MARINE PARK ✍ **Marineland** (904-460-1275 or 1-888-279-9194; www.marine land.net), 9600 Ocean Shore Blvd, just south of Summer Haven on FL A1A, is the world's oldest marine park, opened in 1938. But it's not your grandpa's Marineland anymore—the iconic old three-story-tall Marine Studios tank gave up the ghost, and along with it went the original buildings and most of the aquatic life. When I stopped in, I was pointed up an oceanfront sidewalk past the rubble of the old buildings to the new, state-of-the-art Dolphin Conservation Center, built atop the old Whitney Park. Here, Nellie (who celebrated her 53nd birthday recently) still reigns as the doyen of the dolphins, and the focus is on dolphin interaction. Guests can sign up to swim and otherwise interact with the dolphins, reinforcing behaviors such as playing ball and jumping. Encounters, which must be booked well in advance, range from $65 to $275, depending on the length of the interaction. If you just walk in, like I did, you can watch those folks having fun for a $5 fee ($2.50 child). Future plans include an artificial reef for snorkeling and a restaurant on the 60-acre preserve. Open daily 8:30–4:30.

MARINELAND

Sandra Friend

At the adjacent **Whitney Laboratories** (904-461-4000; www.whitney.ufl .edu), managed by the University of Florida, scientists and students delve into the secrets of the deep to apply to biomedical and biotechnical research. "Marine invertebrates are great models for human beings," said Maureen Welch as she showed me recent studies that used sea slugs to model the neurological problems of Alzheimer's patients. In addition to its permanent exhibits at Marineland, the lab holds an open house each spring. Groups can arrange private tours. A free lecture series provides informative background on marine topics, Jan–May, on the second Thu of each month.

MUSEUMS

Bunnell
Holden House Museum (386-437-0600), 204 East Moody Blvd, was built in 1918 by Mr. and Mrs. Tom Holden, who lived there until 1970. The rooms are decked with authentic furniture of the times, and the gables are inset with pieces of apothecary bottles, antique colored glass, and old pieces of dishes. Open Wed 10–1.

Flagler Beach
Trace the history of the city to the early 1900s at the **Flagler Beach Historical Museum** (386-517-2025), 207 S Central Ave. Fossils, Indian tools, newpaper clippings, and old photographs are on display Tue–Fri 10–4 and the second Sat of the month noon–3.

Palm Coast
Florida Agricultural Museum (386-446-7630; www.flaglerlibrary.org/history/ agrimuseum/agri1.htm), 1850 Princess Place Rd, brings the First Coast's heritage alive in a 300-acre living history educational park. Learn about the first farmers—the Timucua—in a Native American village, the European influence and Spanish colonial agriculture through rare breeds of Cracker cattle and horses, and an 1890s rural town with a sawmill and turpentine operation. The museum is still under development; call for special events and programs.

BICYCLING A paved bicycle path stretches more than 12 miles south from Marineland toward Flagler Beach, paralleling scenic FL A1A.

BIRDING One of my favorite spots for bird-watching is **Boardman Pond,** just north of the Volusia County line. Park your car along Walter Boardman Rd and watch from the bank, or wander down the Bulow Creek Trail (see *Green Space—Parks*) to a blue-blazed trail leading to the Audubon observation deck.

Next to the **Flagler Beach Library** off South Flagler Ave, there is a beautiful walkway leading into the marshlands toward the Inland Waterway.

ECOTOURS For an exploration of the estuary, take a tour on **Discovery Cruises** (386-931-0356; www.discoveryrivercruises.com), 139 Avalon Ave, Flagler Beach, departing either from the Dockside Marina or Gamble Rogers State Park, depending on the time and day. Narrated eco-historic cruises let you glimpse dolphins, manatees, and birds along the waterways; choose a two-hour Flagler River Cruise or one- to one-and-a-half-hour Tomoka "Jungle" Cruise. Adults $15 and 20; seniors, military $18; children $10. Open Tue–Sun.

FAMILY ACTIVITIES ✍ Take the kids bowling at **Coquina Lanes** (386-445-4004), 11 Old Kings Rd N, Palm Coast, where all 24 lanes have bumpers available. Open daily 9:30 AM–2 AM; $2.25–3.50 per person.

FISHING A popular spot with saltwater anglers, the **Flagler Beach Pier** is a great place to get a line wet or just to get a great view of the beach. Grab your supplies at **Roy's Bait House,** 105 N Second St, before hitting the pier. For a meander through the shallows on a flats skiff with an expert captain, contact **Palm Coast Fishing** (386-437-2545; www.palmcoastfishing.com).

HIKING ✍ My first Florida hiking was along the trails at **Washington Oaks Gardens State Park** (see *Green Space—Botanical Garden*) as a youngster— they're short and fun to explore, especially with your kids. Another don't- miss short and free spot for families is the boardwalk at **Haw Creek Conservation Area** (see *Gren Space—Wild Places*) outside Bunnell, where alligator sightings are assured. But my favorite here is the **Bulow Creek Trail** at Bulow Plantation Ruins Historic State Park (see *Green Space— Parks*), which leads you into truly primeval hammocks of ancient oaks and pines. Pretty much all of the public lands in the county have somewhere to hike. To learn more, read *50 Hikes in North Florida*.

BULOW CREEK

Sandra Friend

PADDLING Tropical Kayaks (386-445-0506; www.tropicalkayaks.com), at the Palm Coast Golf Resort Marina, Palm Coast. Take a two-hour guided ecotour ($35) past historical treasures or rent a surfing kayak and explore the local beach and inlets for manatees, dolphins, and jumping mullet. A two-hour rental, $15; four hours, $25; double kayaks for 24 hours, $35. Bicycle rentals available at $5 per hour or $20 per day. Please call 386-446-6370 for bike rentals.

Paddlers with their own craft can put in at **Princess Place Preserve** or the Guana-Tolomato-Matanzas Reserve (see *Green Space—Parks* for both) access at Marineland and paddle for miles through the estuaries, enjoying dozens of uninhabited islands on which to stop and lunch or camp.

The folks at **Coastal Outdoor Kayaks,** in Crescent Beach, will take you on guided tours to Princess Place Preserve (see *To Do—Paddling* in the St. Augustine, Ponte Vedra, and the Beaches chapter).

SCENIC DRIVES Few highways in the northern Florida peninsula match the beauty of FL A1A, the **Buccaneer Trail,** particularly in sections where the dunes remain preserved and free of development between Ormond and Flagler beaches. Designated a National Historic Scenic Byway, two-lane A1A provides a breezy seaside driving experience.

WHALE-WATCHING The calving ground of the right whale can be seen from both Marineland and neighboring Summer Haven and Crescent Beach in St. Johns County; check with Marineland to become an official whale-watcher during the winter calving season.

COQUINA BEACH AT WASHINGTON OAKS

Sandra Friend

BEACHES Sunbathers enjoy the strand just south of **Marineland,** where a large county parking lot and boardwalk provide access, as well as the strips of shell-dotted sand along Matanzas Inlet. Parking areas and dune boardwalks flank the highway after you cross the inlet. Just a few miles south, the **Coquina Beach** at **Washington Oaks Gardens State Park** (see *Green Space—Botanical Garden*) is one of Florida's true geological treasures, a natural sculpture created by the sea digging into an outcropping of the shell-laden Anastasia limestone of the Atlantic Coastal Ridge. You can't swim here, but it's worth a visit to take a walk on the beach and marvel at the incredible rock formations and tidal pools sculpted from coquina. Fee.

At Beverly Beach, your best place to soak up the sun is **Varn Park** on FL A1A, a county park with beach access, changing rooms, and outdoor showers. There isn't much beach left at Flagler Beach below the seawall promenade, so continue south to **Gamble Rogers Memorial State Recreation Area** (386-517-2086; www.floridastateparks.org/gamblerogers), 3100 S FL A1A, Flagler Beach. With soft sands tinted orange by coquina shells and an expansive 144-acre beachfront, this is a park for relaxing and catching some rays. Thirty-four campsites (no shade) directly overlook the Atlantic Ocean, with 30-amp and water hook-ups, hot showers, and a dump station. The park is also home to the annual Gamble Rogers Folk Festival. Fee.

BOTANICAL GARDEN **Washington Oaks Gardens State Park** (386-446-6780; www.floridastateparks.org/washingtonoaks), 6400 N Oceanshore Blvd. On the site of the first Spanish land grant in the region, these formal gardens were lovingly cultivated between 1936 and 1964 by Owen D. Young, chairman of the board of General Electric, and his wife. Meandering pathways lined with azaleas and camellias make a maze through a hammock of ancient live oaks, past benches set in scenic spots for quiet contemplation. On the wilder side of the park, walk the short Mala Compra Trail to explore mangroves and needlerush along the Matanzas River en route to a popular picnic area; hike the 1.7-mile Bella Vista Trail to see coastal scrub, maritime hammock, and dense hardwood forests. Fee.

ROSE GARDEN AT WASHINGTON OAKS

Sandra Friend

PARKS At **Bulow Plantation Ruins Historic State Park** (386-517-2084; www.floridastateparks.org/bulow plantation), CR 2001 south of FL 100, it's not just about the historic

BULOW PLANTATION RUINS

Sandra Friend

sugar plantation ruins. Bring a kayak or rent a canoe and launch into the needlerush-lined waterways of Bulow Creek, or walk the Bulow Creek Trail beneath a canopy of ancient live oaks through a forest floor dense with coontie, a primitive plant that was once common in North Florida's hammocks.

Protecting sensitive lands along the Matanzas River, **Guana-Tolomato-Matanzas Reserve** (904-825-5071; http://nerrs.noaa.gov/gtm) is home to the northernmost stands of mangrove on the Atlantic coast as well as rich oyster beds that can wreak havoc with your boat if you don't heed the tides. Straddling both sides of the waterway and including pristine islands such as Mellon Island, a palm hammock reached by kayak offshore from Summer Haven, this southern segment reserve offers endless waterways for kayakers to explore. The primary public access point for the preserve is the new, county-managed **River to Sea Preserve** (www.flaglerparks.com/riversea/preserve.htm) straddling both sides of the road at Marineland. Nature trails and other facilities are under construction on the west side of A1A; on the east side, a parking area provided access to the coquina-studded shores of the Atlantic Ocean.

Princess Place Preserve (386-437-7490; www.flaglerparks.com/princess _place1.htm), off US 1, includes the historic Cherokee Lodge and Florida's first in-ground swimming pool (see *To See—Historic Sites*); camp in the deeply shaded campground and walk the network of short trails that take you to freshwater and saltwater marsh views and around a sulfur spring, or launch your kayak into

CHEROKEE LODGE POOL

Sandra Friend

Pellicer Creek or the Matanzas River (the preserve is at their confluence) and paddle away! Open Wed–Sun 7–6; free.

WILD PLACES The St. Johns Water Management District (386-329-4883; sjr.state.fl.us) is responsible for conservation areas that serve as buffers to the St. Johns River and its tributaries, and works with local land managers to administer the following preserves that offer hiking, biking, paddling, and trail riding: **Graham Swamp Conservation Area,** along Old Kings Rd south of Palm Coast, protects a fresh-

HAW CREEK IRISES

water floodplain that creates a barrier against saltwater intrusion from the Atlantic Ocean; a mile-long hiking trail lets you explore the swamp. **Haw Creek Conservation Area,** CR 2007, near Bunnell, has a fabulous boardwalk along a pristine creek; you will see many alligators here. **Pellicer Creek Conservation Area,** off US 1 near I-95, protects almost 4,000 acres of wetlands between Faver-Dykes State Park and Princess Place Preserve.

✳ Lodging

HOTELS, MOTELS, AND RESORTS

Bunnell 32110

Clean rooms can be found at **Country Hearth Inn** (386-437-3737; www.countryhearth.com), 2251 Old Dixie Hwy, where you will also find their "InnCredible" breakfast and sparkling outdoor pool. Rates for queen and king beds start at $59.

Flagler Beach 32136

Reasonably priced accommodations can be found at the **Beach Front Motel** (386-439-0089 or 1-888-221-4722; www.beachfrontmotel.com), 1544 S Oceanshore Blvd: $54–79 per night, $295–425 per week, $895–1,500 month, depending on the season. Also check out the **Lazy Hours Motel on the Beach** (386-439-3300), 1316 S A1A, located within a short walk to the fishing pier ($55–80).

&. ⌺ Romance is in the air at **Island Cottage Villas by the Sea** (386-439-0092 x2 or 1-87-ROMANCE-2; www.islandcottagevillas.com), 2316 S Oceanshore Blvd. Toni and Mark Treworgy radiate warmth and simplicity in this quaint "island" hideaway. The immaculate rooms and suites are just across from their own private beach, while the heated pool is the centerpiece surrounded by lush gardens and enchanted surprises. This is a surfside destination—a fine-dining restaurant on the property offers romantic ambience, eclectic wines, and gourmet cuisine on Sat eves, and the "Tropical Breeze Spa" pampers you in an intimate garden setting. Toni, an accomplished writer and vocalist, is also a very talented watercolorist and has many of her lithographs and originals on display for sale. $149–319; a two-night minimum is required.

Ten one- and two-bedroom suites ($99–129) are within easy walking distance to local restaurants and the beach at the **Plaza Caribe Hotel** (386-439-3020; www.plazacaribehotel.com), 301 S Central Ave.

🐾 Bring your favorite pet to the **Whale Watch Motel** (386-439-2545 or 1-877-635-5535; www.whalewatchmotel.com), 2448 S Oceanshore Blvd. The quaint family-run motel features only 10 rooms nestled in four separate buildings. Choose from rooms and efficiencies to full cottages. No phone in the room, but do you really need one? If yes, there is one available for use on the property. $69–89 per night; $400–600 per week.

Treat yourself to luxury at the beachfront **White Orchid Inn & Spa**

(386-439-4944 or 1-800-423-1477; www.whiteorchidinn.com), 1104 S Oceanshore Blvd. In the "Room with It All" you can enjoy a king-sized canopy bed, crisp white linens, a Jacuzzi big enough for two, and a poolside veranda. The "Courtyard and Lilac Green" room features a beautiful glass-block shower and covered lanai. You'll enjoy beautifully landscaped grounds, a swimming pool, and a heated mineral pool. The onsite holistic spa features a variety of massages, wraps, facials, and hand and feet care. $159–269.

Palm Coast 32137

There something for everyone at the all-suite **European Village Resort** condo hotel (386-597-5200 or 1-888-675-3000; www.evresort.com), 101 Palm Harbour Pkwy, where you can enjoy a full array of luxury amenities like in-room 42-inch plasma TV and Tempurpedic bed. Play golf and tennis, swim in the heated pool, or stroll through the European Piazza, browsing unique shops where three gargantuan video screens show everything from sporting events to movies. Suites start at $139 for a Standard 1 bedroom condo overlooking the Piazza. Premiere suites have Roman tubs. Add $20 resort fee per suite. Special discounts for AARP members and Florida residents.

CAMPGROUNDS

Beverly Beach 32136

You can't get any closer to the beach than at the **Beverly Beach Campground and RV Resort** (386-439-3111 or 1-800-255-2706; www.beverlybeachcamptown.com), 2816 Oceanshore Blvd. With your RV parked facing the Atlantic Ocean, you'll greet each day with a stunning sunrise. Oceanfront sites are $65–85, ocean view $50–$70, tent sites $35.

Bunnell 32136

Set in piney woods along Hog Pond, **Thunder Gulch Campground** (386-437-3135 or 1-800-714-8388; www.thundergulchcampground.com), 127 Lantana Ave, is a peaceful place to settle in with your rig. Full hook-up with 30-amp electric, $30–32; primitive campsites $26.

Flagler Beach 32136

🐾 You'll love fishing in the ocean or the Intracoastal while at **Flagler By the Sea Campground** (386-439-2124; www.floridacamping.com), 2982 N Oceanshore Blvd, where there's always something to do outside. Leashed pets okay. RVs only; full hook-ups with 30-amp electric. Oceanfront sites are $40–50.

✳ Where to Eat

DINING OUT

Flagler Beach

Pier Restaurant (904-439-3891), 215 FL A1A. If watching the pounding surf is high on your to-do list, stop in for a late lunch or early dinner with a spectacular view. Enjoy the delightful shrimp salad or a slice of their homemade Key lime pie. Open daily starting with breakfast at 7. Most entrées under $10.

EATING OUT

Beverly Beach

Next to Beverly Beach Campground and RV Resort (see *Campgrounds*), bright lemon yellow and turquoise beckon you to come into the beachfront **Shark House Seafood Restaurant,** where the seafood is fresh, and Elvis is in the building. Get your teeth into "Jaws" with Shark Bites ($6), or try a hot cup of conch chowder ($3) or tasty platter of coconut shrimp ($13). Open Mon–Thu for dinner 4–10, Fri–Sun for lunch and dinner 11:30–10.

Bunnell

For the best BBQ around, head inland to **Woody's Bar BQ** (386-439-5010), 99 Flagler Regional Plaza. The Family Value Meal is your best bet, with a portion of chicken thighs and legs, ribs and sliced pork, and beef or turkey with four large sides ($23 for two; $33 for four). Open daily for lunch and dinner.

Flagler Beach

Grab a cup of coffee, a pastry, or a scoop of ice cream and say hi to Carol and Tony at **Cafe CARA** (386-439-3131), 420 S Central Ave. They serve up mostly sandwiches, and nothing costs more than $10. Open Mon–Sat 11–6, closed Sun.

❧ Sea shanties and windjammer ships decorate the walls of **Fisherman's Net** (386-439-1818), 500 S FL A1A, where you get fresh seafood and fabulous service at a great price; reduced-price dinners 4–6. Known for the best Chilean sea bass; entrées range from $8–25. A simple but nice wine list. Open Tue–Sun 11–9, Fri–Sat 11–10. Closed Mon.

Gail and Carol always have great hamburgers and beer-battered shrimp at **High Tides at Snack Jacks** (386-439-3344), 2805 S FL A1A, where you can relax on the screened porch and look out over the ocean. Valet parking available. Open daily for lunch and dinner, 11–10. Entrées $4–19.

Manny's Pizza House (386-439-6345), 1848 S FL A1A, packs them in all day long! For breakfast expect a bit of a wait as patrons line up for Manny's Waffle Favorite, complete with two eggs, waffle, bacon, sausage, or ham ($6). The Surfer's Special is two eggs with two pancakes or two slices of French toast ($5). For lunch or dinner (entrées $8–28), make sure to try their house specialty, Greek salad. Open daily 7 AM–10 PM.

There's always a line at **Martin's Restaurant & Lounge** (386-439-5830), 2000 S Oceanshore Blvd, as chef-owner Kevin Martin serves generous portions priced between $10–22. Open daily for lunch and dinner, 11:30–9.

Hammock

Be nice to Steeler fans at **Mad Dog's in the Hammock** (386-447-5731; www.maddogfan.com), 5949 N Oceanshore Blvd, where die-hard Pittsburgher Tim Dougherty spends his winters after he's done attending every Steeler game of the season, as he's done since 1972. The can't-miss-it building is done up in black and gold and features baskets with Angus burgers, clams, gator tail, and the like ($8–10), as well as full seafood and steak dinners ($16–24).

SEA BREEZE SWEET SHOP

Sandra Friend

After a swim at the beach, nothing's better than soft serve from the **Sea Breeze Sweet Shop**, 5861 FL A1A. Besides the cones, shakes, and sundaes, they can whet your whistle with burgers, nachos, dogs, and subs.

Palm Coast

At **High Jackers Restaurant** (386-586-6078; www.highjackers.com), 202 Airport Rd, they've got one of my favorites on the daily menu— Wisconsin Beer Cheese Soup! Entrées are strictly steak and seafood, done up as kabobs and fried fish platters in the HoJo tradition. Located at the Flagler County Airport, they're a spinoff of High Tides at Flagler Beach. Give 'em a whirl!

✳ Selective Shopping

Palm Coast

A stop for the Red Hat Ladies, **Ms. Cynthia Black's Studio** (386-446-4662), 5861 N Oceanshore Blvd, has those necessary purple and red boas, Hollywood glam attire, and African items. Located directly across from Bings Landing (see *To See—Archeological Sites*) in the Hammock. Open daily 11–7, closing at 6 during daylight savings.

Stroll through cobblestone walkways, lush gardens, and cool fountains of **Piazza del Fontana** at the center of the European Village Resort (386-597-5200 or 1-888-675-3000; www.evresort.com), 101 Palm Harbour Pkwy (see *Lodging*). Step in to favorites such as, **Oh! Naty Children's Boutique** (386-597-5242), where you'll find the latest designer fashions, such as Lily Pulitzer and Madonna's line, and **Arte de Palm Fine Art Gallery** (386-597-5277; www.artedepalm.com) for original

painting, sculpture, and jewelry (see also *To See—Art Galleries*). Don't miss **Shakespeare's English Tea Shop** (386-446-6323) for a spot of tea and English scones.

FARMER'S MARKETS, SEAFOOD STANDS, AND U-PICK An old-fashioned market is set in the center of Flagler Beach with fresh-baked goods, fruits, vegetables, and nuts; Fri 7–2 at the corner of FL 100 and FL A1A. For more information, call the Flagler Beach Chamber of Commerce (904-439-0995 or 1-800-298-0995).

✳ Special Events

March: **Art in the Park** (386-871-8895; www.flaglercountyartleague.com), Palm Coast Community Center, third weekend. Some of the region's finest artists are showcased at this juried exhibit and festival that includes artists' booths, storytelling, children's activities, and more.

April: **Earth Day Celebration** at Washington Oaks State Park (see *Green Space—Botanical Garden*), third weekend. This long-standing outdoor celebration of Earth Day features reenactors with living history demonstrations of pioneer Florida, live entertainment by Florida folk musicians, hands-on activities for the kids, and local arts and crafts.

October: **Creek Side Festival** (386-437-0106; www.flaglerchamber.org/creeksidefestival) at Princess Place Preserve (see *Green Space—Parks*), third weekend. This family-oriented outdoor extravaganza features Florida bluegrass and blues musicians boogying down along scenic Pellicer Creek. See artists in action, take kayak or walking tours of the preserve, visit the food booths, or check out the antique tractor displays.

THE ST. JOHNS RIVER

The St. Johns River is one of only 14 rivers designated an American Heritage River. This top fishing spot covers 70 square miles of rivers and lakes, with several towns settled along its banks. In 1513 Ponce de León is said to have discovered the Fountain of Youth at De Leon Springs. Around 1570 the resident Timucua Indians were beginning to lose their foothold on their land; by the 1700s the area was populated with early pioneers and traders. With the timber and turpentine industries well established, the steamboats of the late 1800s brought the wealthy down from the north to vacation near the mineral-rich springs.

Putnam County spans both sides of the river south of Flagler County, while Clay County hugs the western shore south of Jacksonville. These rural retreats have a long and storied history, from Palatka's role in the Civil War to Green Cove Springs—a destination for wealthy northerners who wanted to "take the waters" for their health. On Lake Santa Fe, **Melrose** was established along the Bellamy Road in 1887, and you won't find a better place to study early Florida architecture: There are nearly 80 buildings in town on the National Register of Historic Places. At the north end of Lake Santa Fe, **Keystone Heights** shows off its 1920s charm.

GUIDANCE Nearest to Jacksonville, the **Clay County Tourism Division** (904-394-7401; www.claycountytourism.com), 1764 Kingsley Ave, Orange Park 32073, can help you with your travel planning. In Palatka, stop by the **Putnam County Chamber of Commerce** (386-328-1503; www.putnamcountychamber.org), 1100 Reid St, Palatka 32178, or in Crescent City (386-698-1657) at City Hall.

GETTING THERE *By air:* **Jacksonville International Airport** (see the Jacksonville chapter) or **Gainesville Regional Airport** (see the Alachua and the Historic Lake District chapter) are the nearest major airports.

By bus: **Greyhound** (1-800-231-2222).

By car: From Jacksonville, take **US 17** about 50 miles south. From the St. Augustine area, take **CR 16** from I-95 to Green Cove Springs. **FL 207** connects St. Augustine and Palatka.

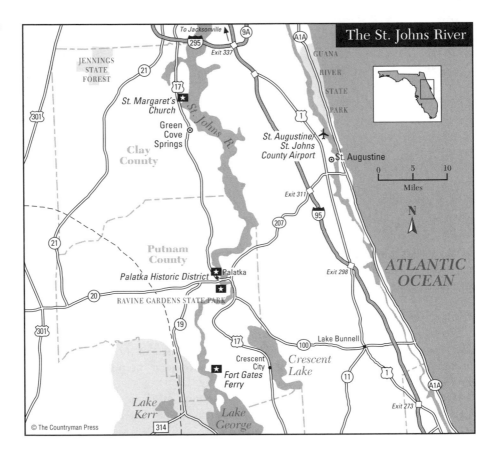

To Jacksonville · 9A · 295 · Exit 337 · GUANA · A1A · The St. Johns River
JENNINGS STATE FOREST · 21 · 17 · RIVER · STATE
301 · St. Margaret's Church · PARK
Green Cove Springs · St. Johns R. · 1 · St. Augustine/ St. Johns County Airport · St. Augustine
Clay County · 0 5 10 Miles
N
Exit 311 · 95
21 · 207
Putnam County · ATLANTIC OCEAN
Palatka Historic District · Palatka · Exit 298
20 · RAVINE GARDENS STATE PARK
301 · 19
17 · 100 · Lake Bunnell
Crescent City · Crescent Lake · 11 · 1 · A1A
Fort Gates Ferry · Exit 273
Lake Kerr · Lake George
© The Countryman Press · 314

By sea: From Jacksonville, follow the St. Johns River south and dock in Orange Park or Green Cove Springs; continue another 10 miles south to Palatka.

GETTING AROUND US 17 runs from Orange Park south along the St. Johns River past Green Cove Springs into Palatka and continues south through Crescent City, passing Welaka. **CR 16** runs east–west from Green Cove Springs past Penney Farms and Camp Blanding in Starke to the Bradford county line. Take **CR 21** from Orange Park south to reach Middleburg and Keystone Heights. **FL 100** connects Palatka with Keystone Heights and Flagler Beach.

MEDICAL EMERGENCIES Orange Park Medical Center (904-276-8500; www.opmedical.com), 2001 Kingsley Ave, Orange Park. **Putnam Community Medical Center** (386-328-5711), FL 20 W, Palatka.

✳ To See

AGRICULTURAL TOURS Visit fern fields, potato and cabbage farms, and an agricultural museum on the **Putnam County Agricultural Extension Agritours**

(386-329-0318). Working with Jacksonville's sister city of Masan, Korea, **JaxMa Orchids** (904-284-4442), US 17 south of SR 16, sells and distributes imported *Phalaenopsis* orchids. Their acres of greenhouses are open for public viewing Mon–Sat 8–5; free.

AQUACULTURAL TOURS Learn about warm-water fish production and native Florida fish conservation at **Welaka National Fish Hatchery and Aquarium** (386-467-2374), CR 309, Welaka. Open daily 7–4; guided group tours. Free.

ART GALLERIES Florida School of the Arts Galleries (386-328-1571), 5001 St. Johns Ave, Palatka. Serving as a public library until the 1980s, the Larimer Arts Center (386-328-8998), 216 Reid St, Palatka, is now the home of the Arts Council of Greater Palatka and the council's monthly exhibits. The gallery is open Thu and Fri 1–5, Sat 10–2. **Melrose Bay Gallery** (352-375-3866), 103 FL 26, Melrose, represents fine regional artists in a variety of media. Open Fri–Sun.

HISTORIC SITES

Crescent City
Charles & Emily Cheatham House, 102 Main St. Emphasizing horizontal planes and wide eaves, this Prairie-style home showcases the American architectural style of Frank Lloyd Wright. Henry G. Hubbard, who was the first to bring the camphor tree and Japanese persimmon to Florida, built the **Hubbard House**, 600 N Park St. Now a private residence, the circa-1879 dwelling is surrounded by elaborate botanical gardens.

Green Cove Springs
Green Cove Spring and Swimming Pool, a popular tourist spot in the late 1800s, is thought to be Florida's first therapeutic mineral springs. A decorative railing surrounds the clean and clear spring, about 20 feet in diameter, set amid tall oaks and palm trees. You can look down about 31 feet, where it tapers to a

FOLKLORE While traveling through the small community of Bardin off FL 100, peer into the piney woods and look closely; you might just catch a glimpse of the Bardin Booger. Local legend has it that a giant, shaggy-haired creature, much like the elusive Sasquatch, was first sighted in the mid-1980s. Said to smell much like rotting cabbage and stand 13 feet tall, the apelike creature has been touted as northeast Florida's Bigfoot. The Bardin Booger was immortalized in the late Billy Crain's "Bardin Booger" song, which is still played at many festivals and events along with the occasional appearance of the Booger itself. The curious and disbelievers can view a scrapbook filled with news clippings and illustrations at Bud's Store, the Bardin community gathering spot. You'll also find Jody Delzell's 1995 book *The Enigmatic Bardin Booger* at Andrea's Book Store in Palatka.

narrow entrance into the cavern. This section is out of sight, but it opens to 25 feet wide and descends another 150 feet before flowing toward the St. Johns River. The spring keeps the neighboring 50-by-100-foot swimming pool at a constant 72 degrees year-round, then overflows down a stream about 300 feet to the St. Johns. You'll note the sulfurous odor, but the water is safe for swimming and at one time was bottled as drinking water. The spring is open year-round; swimming in the pool is allowed only during summer months.

Hibernia

Bubba Midden is located on the east bank of Black Creek, 2 miles north of its confluence with the St. Johns River in the vicinity of Hibernia.

A long drive down a narrow dirt road is richly rewarded when you reach the quaint **St. Margaret's Episcopal Church** (904-284-3030; www.stmargarets .org), Old Church Rd. George Fleming emigrated from Ireland and established Hibernia (Latin for "Ireland") Plantation on the 1,000 acres now known as Fleming Island. The church, a gift for his wife, Margaret Seton Fleming, was completed in 1878. With only 50 seats, the Gothic-style sanctuary requires three services on Sun. The annual Tour and Tea (see *Special Events*) re-creates the Civil War era with guided tours of the plantation grounds; high tea is served.

Interlachen

The quaint 1892 **Interlachen Town Hall** (386-684-3811), 311 Atlantic Ave, on the National Register of Historic Places, was the social center in the early 1900s, holding such town hall activities as dances, ladies' society meetings, and voting—events it hosts to this day.

Keystone Heights

Keystone Beach (see *To Do—Swimming*) dates back to 1928, with its historic bathhouse and dance hall perched on Lake Keystone.

Melrose

Boasting one of the highest concentrations of historic sites in Florida, with 79 classic homes and businesses, **Melrose** is a town where history is part of everyday life. Many buildings are more than a century old but remain well kept and occupied as residences; see *To Do—Walking Tours* for how to explore local history.

Middleburg

Middleburg Methodist Church Cemetery and the 1847 Middleburg United Methodist Church are next to the Middleburg Historical Museum (see *Museums*).

Orange Park

Since 1921, the **Loyal Order of Moose at Moosehaven** (904-278-1210) has been a part of the Orange Park community. The fraternal organization dedicated to bettering the lives of children and the elderly, along with helping their communities, donated many sites and buildings, which are now the town hall, fire station, and library, to the town of Orange Park. The retirement community resides on 63 acres along the St. Johns River and has its own chapel, library, and a state-of-the-art assisted-living health care center.

See the register from the **Parkview Resort Hotel** (circa 1890) and rare photographs from the late 20th century at the Orange Park Town Hall (904-264-9565), 2042 Park Ave, Mon–Fri 8–5.

Palatka

The 1854 **Bronson-Mulholland House** (386-329-0140), 100 Madison St, has seen its share of history. The former residence of Judge Isaac Bronson, the home also served as a school for freed slave children and a Red Cross center in both world wars. The beautifully restored antebellum plantation home is open Tue, Thu, and Sun 2–5.

Built by the Atlantic Coast Line in 1908, the **Historic Union Station** (see *Railroadiana*) showcases the architectural style of H. H. Richardson with its random window openings and hexagonal dormered bays.

The Georgian-style **Tilghman House** (386-325-8750), 324 River St, built around 1887, now operates as an active arts center. Note the half-gabled veranda supported by Greek Doric columns and the Palladian window in the gable dormer. Open Mon–Fri 9–5.

Penney Farms

The **J. C. Penney Memorial Church** (904-529-9078), as well as buildings in the surrounding area, was built in 1927 as a community for retired ministers.

Welaka

Mount Royal Indian Temple Mound, CR 309, is believed to be the largest shell mound in the state. The 100-foot-high site of the Timucua Indian ceremonial ground dates back to A.D. 1200–1600.

MURALS Pick up a map at the Chamber Visitor Center at 1100 Reid St and stroll through the **"Mural City of Northeast Florida"** seeking out the **25 Palatka Murals** (386-328-6500) scattered throughout the downtown historic district. These building-sized, breathtaking murals beautifully depict the history, landscape, and culture of Palatka. You'll find a cattle drive, Ravine Gardens (see *Green Space—Botanical Garden*), and the sailboats of the annual Mug Race (see *Special Events*). Look for the tiny gray church mouse in the Billy Graham mural (it's on the church porch).

A PALATKA MURAL

Kathy Wolf

MUSEUMS

Crescent City

The Crescent City Women's Club takes on a labor of love filling the **Little Blue House Heritage Museum and Art Center** (386-698-4711 or 386-698-1991), 602 N Summit St, with pieces of the past. The former home, dating back to 1871, showcases the history and art of South Putnam. Open Tue–Sat 2:30–5.

Green Cove Springs

& Local history is well documented at the **Clay County Historical Museum** (904-284-9644 or 904-284-5243), 915 Walnut St. And with the addition of the Railroad Museum you'll enjoy the collection of photographs, fine china and silverware, timetables, bells and whistles, step boxes, and baggage tags once part of the Clay Street Hill Railroad. Look for Phantom Train ACL 76. Open Sun 2–5.

Keystone Heights

On 170,000 acres of sand pine and scrub oak in the heart of the Florida wilderness, **Camp Blanding** was home to 800,000 World War II soldiers from 1940 to 1945. Nine infantry divisions prepared for conflict in ankle-deep sand on arguably one of the toughest training grounds anywhere. The **Camp Blanding Museum and Memorial Park** (904-682-3196), Starke, is dedicated to these soldiers but also honors all who served in Korea, Vietnam, and Desert Storm. The newest addition is the Black Soldiers Memorial Park, dedicated in 1998. Life at Camp Blanding during the 1940s is depicted in the museum through colorful displays of weaponry, photos, memorabilia, and even a life-sized bunkhouse. In the Memorial Park, monuments honor the original nine army infantry divisions and the 508th Parachute Infantry Regiment; several World War II aircraft and vehicles are on display. Actors Demi Moore and Viggo Mortensen worked long hours in the harsh environment during the filming of *GI Jane,* and real military drill instructors put 16 civilians through basic training for TV's *Boot Camp.* The current site, now reduced to about 73,000 acres, continues to train members of the U.S. National Guard, Active Army, and Army Reserves from all over the United States. The museum gift shop has a fine selection of books, pins, and patches. Open noon–4 daily.

CAMP BLANDING MUSEUM

Kathy Wolf

Middleburg

Black Heritage Museum (call Maude Jackson at 904-282-4168, Mamie Oliver at 904-282-5223, or Sarah Weeks at 904-282-5205 for tours), Longmire Ave at Hunter-Douglas Park, is a sensitive and thought-provoking view of black culture during the late 1800s displayed in a one-room schoolhouse.

Photographs and displays of the early turpentine, timber, and phosphate industries depict one of the oldest continuous communities in Florida at the **Middleburg Historical Museum** (904-282-5924), 3912 Section St. Open Sun 2–4.

Palatka

Originally part of Fort Shannon during the Indian Wars (1832–1845), the

Kathy Wolf

UNION STATION, PALATKA

Putnam Historic Museum (386-325-9825), 100 Madison St, is the oldest dwelling in the Palatka area. Open Tue, Thu, and Sun 2–5.

RAILROADIANA All aboard at the **Historic Union Station** (386-329-5538) and **David Browning Railroad Museum** (386-328-1539) at the corner of 11th and Reid streets, Palatka. The Union Depot is open daily with railroad memorabilia, historical documents, and photographs of the Palatka area. But you'll want to plan your trip when all the members run their trains at the Browning Museum—on the first Sun and third Sat of the month. Look for the 31-foot HO-scale model train, one of the longest in the world, chugging along the tracks for the enjoyment of young and old. The museum is open daily.

✳ To Do

BICYCLING Whether you ride city streets or rough and rural, several great off-road touring and mountain bike paths can be found throughout the county. The Northeast Regional Planning Council (904-363-6350) produces **Bikeways of Northeast Florida,** Clay and Putnam counties, which can be picked up at the Clay County Tourism Division (904-264-2651; www.claychamber.org), 1764 Kingsley Ave, Orange Park. There is a nice **paved bicycle path along US 17** from Doctors Lake south about 7 miles; or you can veer off onto Pine Ave for views of the St. Johns River. For off-roaders, head to the rolling sandhills of **Gold Head Branch State Park** (see *Green Space—Parks*), then down FL 21 to CR 352 for a leisurely lakeside ride. For a challenge, start at the Maintenance Building on Putnam County Blvd in East Palatka and head west on FL 207A, traveling 17.8 miles through riverfront farmlands and neighborhoods reflecting rural Florida. The trail ends at Federal Point Rd.

RAVINE GARDENS

Sandra Friend

BIRDING Hundreds of osprey nests top the trees and beacon markers along the St. Johns River. Great blue herons and snowy egrets are a common sight along the banks, especially around the fish camps. The roadside observation tower at the **Beecher**

Unit of the Welaka National Fish Hatchery and Aquarium (see *To See—Aquacultural Tours*) provides excellent viewing, in winter and spring, of sandhill cranes, southern bald eagles, and a variety of egrets and herons. The **Welaka State Forest** (see *Green Space—Wild Places*) Mud Trail is a good place to see woodpeckers, Osceola turkeys, and owls. Thousands of azaleas bloom in spring, making **Ravine Gardens State Park** (see *Green Space—Botanical Garden*) a great place to view cedar waxwings, cardinals, hummingbirds, and a variety of butterflies. View limpkins, gallinules, anhingas, and white ibises at **Kenwood and Rodman Recreation Areas** off US 19 (see *Forests, National* in *What's Where*).

BOATING Dock Holiday Boat Rentals (904-215-5363; www.dockholiday boatrentals.com), 3108 US 17 S, Orange Park, provides weekend-long rentals for fishing boats, $175–300; pontoon boats, $175–300; and houseboats, starting at $750. **Venture Up** (904-291-5991), 2216 S Mimosa, Middleburg, rents canoes or paddleboats for $25 per day; kayaks $20 a day.

River Adventures (1-866-OUR-BOAT; www.riveradventuresinc.com), Crystal Cove Marina, Palatka. Motor down the St. Johns River while living on board a 60-foot luxury houseboat. Stretch out on the sundeck, then slip down the water slide for quick refreshment. These large houseboats accommodate up to 20 people and can be rented daily starting at $575, which includes a captain. Or they'll show you how to pilot the boat yourself, then let you take it for a week ($2,400–3,000). Groups of five or fewer can take advantage of the well-equipped fishing boats ($65 a day).

DRIVING TOURS Fans of Lynyrd Skynyrd will want to find **Brickyard Road** in Green Cove Springs, where Ronnie Van Zant lived before his untimely death. Unfortunately, other fans kept stealing the sign, so the county erected a concrete pillar with the street name painted on it.

For the shortest route from US 17 to US 19, take the **Fort Gates Ferry** (386-467-2411), CR 309, Welaka. The oldest operating ferry in Florida, this tiny two-car barge has transported auto passengers back and forth across the St. Johns River continuously since 1856. Access to the ferry dock is a mile off CR 309 on the east at Gateway Fishing Camp (see *Lodging*) and 17 miles through the Ocala National Forest from the west. Caution should be observed in the wet season, as both are dirt roads. If arriving from the west, honk your horn to alert the ferry captain. Autos $9, motorcycles $5. Open 7–5:30. Closed Tue.

Pick up *A Driving Tour of Putnam County* to explore the scenic byways in the area; the brochure does a great job of linking together sites of cultural and historical interest.

ECOTOURS Learn more about the environment and local waterways with **Whole Earth Outfitters of Florida** (904-471-8782; www.wholeearthoutfitters.com). Canoe, kayak, and camping tours take small groups through lakes, rivers, and coastline inlets to discover natural and historic Florida. Launch from the family homestead in Georgetown and paddle the St. Johns River, Lake George, and

Salt Springs Run in search of bald eagles and alligators. Push off from a sandy beach in St. Augustine (see the St. Augustine, Ponte Vedra, and the Beaches chapter) into a sheltered waterway for a different view of the St. Augustine Lighthouse, Castillo de San Marcos, and Bridge of Lions. Half- and full-day trips $45–85. Overnight trips available.

FISHING The well-known places to fish here are **Lake George,** the **Rodman Pool,** and of course the **St. Johns River,** but don't pass up the deep waters of **Crescent Lake.** Often neglected by anglers, this 12-mile body of water quickly drops from the 3-foot shoreline flats to depths reaching 14 feet. You may want a depth finder to locate the 12- and 13-pound bass lurking under the tea-stained water, or catch them as they move to the shallows to feed in such places as Shell Bluff and Sling Shot Creek. When fishing Crescent Lake, stop by **Landing Lake Crescent Resort** (386-698-2485; www.lakecrescent.com), 100 Grove Ave, Crescent City (see *Lodging*), for all your bait, tackle, and marine needs. Fifteen-foot fiberglass fishing boats are available for half-day ($35) or full-day ($65) rentals. Pontoon boats run $75 for a half day, $130 for a full day. Off CR 309 several marinas and fish camps (see *Lodging—Fish Camps*) lead down to the St. Johns River; bait and tackle is plentiful, and you can rent boats, guides, or lodging.

GOLF In Green Cove Springs, try **Cattail Creek Golf Club** (904-284-3502). Orange Park has **Eagle Harbor Golf Club** (904-269-9300) and **Golf Club at Fleming Island** (904-269-1440); in Middleburg you'll find **Ravines Golf Resort** (904-282-1111) in a lovely setting between Black Creek and Black Creek Ravines Preserve.

GREYHOUND RACING **Jacksonville Kennel Club** (904-680-3647), 20455 Park Ave, Orange Park. **Orange Park Greyhound Track** (904-646-0001), Orange Park.

SCENIC DRIVES Paralleling the St. Johns River, FL 13 and CR 13 are designated the **William Bartram Scenic Highway,** passing through farmland and river bottom between Hastings and Jacksonville.

SWIMMING Revive yourself in a chemical-free community pool: The constant 72-degree water of the **Green Cove Spring** (see *To See—Historic Sites*) feeds directly into the pool and then out to the St. Johns River, ensuring clean, mineral-rich water at all times. The pool is open only during summer months. Step back in time at **Keystone Beach** (352-473-7847), 565 S Lawrence Blvd, Keystone Heights. Established in 1924, it's a place where you can splash around on a sandy beach outside the historic bathhouse on Lake Geneva.

WALKING TOURS The **Clay County Historical Society** (904-284-3615) provides guided tours through two historic districts on the National Register of Historic Places. You'll find 85 structures in the **Green Cove Springs Historic District,** mostly around Walnut St and bounded by Bay St, the CSX railroad tracks, Center St, Orange Ave, St. Elcom St, and the St. Johns River. There are a dozen buildings in the **Middleburg Historical District** along Main and Wharf streets.

The Historic Melrose 125 Years: A Celebration Tour brochure outlines a walking tour of the 79 historic sites in town, from businesses to private homes, churches, and cemeteries. I found the brochure while visiting the Micanopy Historical Society Museum, but you may want to write to Historic Melrose, P.O. Box 704, Melrose 32666, for a copy. Or just explore on your own: Amble down the narrow back streets (many unpaved) along the Lake Santa Fe chain of lakes on foot or by car to see genteel homes set in lush landscaping under ancient live oaks.

The "Golden Age" is beautifully represented in **Crescent City**, whose streets are lined with ornately decorated Victorian architecture under a generous canopy of live oaks. A brochure, detailing the location of 20 of these historical homes (see *To See—Historic Sites* for two examples), churches, and commercial buildings, is available from Crescent City (904-698-2525), 115 N Summit St.

Seek out the many murals (see *To See—Murals*) and extensive Victorian architecture in historic **downtown Palatka.** Pick up *Palatka and Putnam County Through the Ages,* a detailed walking and driving tour brochure, at the Putnam County Chamber of Commerce (see *Guidance*).

✳ Green Space

BEACH The sandy beach and crystal-clear water at **Keystone Beach** (352-473-4807), Keystone Heights, make this a great place for swimming, snorkeling, and catching some rays.

BOTANICAL GARDEN You'll want to take in the burst of color Jan–Apr at **Ravine Gardens State Park** (386-329-3721; www.floridastateparks.org/ravinegardens), 1600 Twigg St, Palatka, when thousands of azaleas burst into full bloom. Drive 1.8 miles

SUSPENSION BRIDGE IN RAVINE GARDENS
Sandra Friend

through canopies of live oaks surrounded by thick blankets of tropical and subtropical flora. Stroll through the 182-acre park, stopping at the observation terraces 100 feet above the ravine, or just sit and watch hummingbirds and butterflies in the formal gardens. There's a great place to picnic near the amphitheater. Open daily 8 AM–sunset; fee.

PARKS One of Florida's newest state parks, **Dunns Creek** (386-329-3721; www.floridastateparks.org/dunnscreek), 320 Sisco Rd, Pomona Park, protects sandhills and scrub along a sharp bend in the St. Johns River. Stop for a picnic, or follow the 1.5-mile nature trail to Blue Pond.

Mike Roess Gold Head Branch State Park (352-473-4701; www.floridastateparks.org/goldhead), 6239 FL 21, Keystone Heights, centers on an incredible ravine dripping with ferns, from which the sand-bottomed Gold Head Branch is born. Nature trails let you climb down into the deep ravine and follow the stream's course to Little Lake Johnson, where you can grab a canoe and paddle across the expanse. Three miles of the Florida Trail (see *What's Where*) pass through the park, with a primitive campsite along the way; developed camping and cabins from the Civilian Conservation Corps era are also available.

FOREST AT DUNNS CREEK
Sandra Friend

SPRINGS The spring and pool are the focal point of this pretty little park on the edge of the St. Johns River, but the view from the spring at **Spring Park** (904-529-2200), Green Cove Springs, looks out over the St. Johns River, making this a great place for picnics. Gentle breezes blow through the shady canopy of tall and graceful live oaks covering the children's play area. A truly wild place, **Mud Spring** in Welaka State Forest (see *Wild Places*) shimmers like an underwater garden, an aquatic pool teeming with life.

WILD PLACES Bayard Point Conservation Area (904-529-2380), FL 16, Green Cove Springs. Access this 10,000-acre preserve from the John P. Hall Sr. Nature Preserve entrance off FL 16 near the St. Johns River Bridge to follow the trails through pine flatwoods and scrub out to a beautiful campsite on the banks of the St. Johns River. It's a popular place for trail riding and fishing, and it's used for environmental education classes for the local school district. Free.

Black Creek Ravines Conservation Area (904-269-6378), Green Rd north of CR 218, Middleburg. If you've always wanted to see pitcher plants in bloom, stop here and walk the trails out to the vast bogs beneath the high-tension lines. The reason for

MUD SPRING
Sandra Friend

Kathy Wolf

BLACK CREEK

this preserve, however, is the rugged terrain—bluffs up to 90 feet above sea level, deeply cut with ravines that channel rainwater down to Black Creek. Primitive camping, biking, and horseback riding are permitted; bring your camera for the showy parade of spring wildflowers! Free.

Dunns Creek Conservation Area (386-529-2380), off FL 100 S of San Mateo, has a splendid array of bog wildflowers along its trails in spring; there's one primitive campsite.

Etoniah Creek State Forest (386-329-2552), FL 100 N, Florahome, protects one of Florida's most beautiful ravines at Etoniah Creek, where hikers can look down a 40-foot bluff to see tapegrass waving in the current of the stream at the bottom; visit in springtime, when the azaleas and dogwoods put on a show. The Florida Trail (see *What's Where*) runs through the state forest, with designated campsites and a screened-room camping shelter at Iron Bridge. Free.

Jennings State Forest (904-291-5530; www.fl-dof.com/state_forests/jennings .html), 1337 Long Horn Rd, Middleburg. Popular with equestrians for its dozens of miles of riding trails, this high-and-dry forest amid the sandhills outside Jacksonville also offers several hiking trails; try out the Fire & Water Nature Trail for an interpretive introduction to the habitats found here, including seepage slopes with pitcher plants. The North Fork Black Creek Trail offers primitive camping within a stone's throw of the waterway. Free.

Murphy Creek Conservation Area (386-329-4883), CR 309-B, is a two-part preserve with a loop trail through floodplain forest off Buffalo Bluff Rd, near Welaka, and a loop trail on Murphy Island, leading to rare high bluffs above the St. Johns River, accessible only by boat; camping permitted. Free.

Rice Creek Conservation Area (386-329-4404) is a very special preserve off FL 100 N, 3 miles west of Palatka. From the new trailhead, follow the main road back to the T intersection and turn right to find the Florida Trail (see *What's Where*). A 2-mile blue-blazed loop follows impoundments built in the 1700s by British settlers who scraped an indigo and rice plantation from the floodplain forest; dozens of bridges carry you across blackwater waterways between ancient cypresses. Free.

Welaka State Forest (386-467-2388; www.fl-dof.com/state_forests/welaka .html), CR 309 south of Welaka, is one of the best places in the area for an overnight campout. Grab your backpack and walk 4 miles along the Johns Landing Trail to one of two spectacular primitive campsites right on the St. Johns River. Or take the kids on an easy stroll through the floodplain forest on the nature trail at the fire tower, or along the short Mud Spring Trail to see Mud Spring, a crystal-clear garden of aquatic plants. Fee.

✳ Lodging
BED & BREAKFASTS

Green Cove Springs 32043
Take in the cool river breeze of the St. Johns while sitting on the veranda of an 1887 inn on the National Register of Historic Places. Just across from the Green Cove Mineral Spring (see *To See—Historic Sites*) is the **River Park Inn Bed & Breakfast** (904-284-2994; www.riverparkinn.com), 103 S Magnolia Ave. During its heyday in the late 1800s and early 1900s, the spring was a mecca for wealthy tourists. This three-story frame vernacular home is just one of the "cottages" built to accommodate the well-heeled crowd. Five guest rooms, all with private bath, feature vintage decor. The Master Suite has a two-person Jacuzzi and sitting room. A part of the historic district, the inn is within easy walking of the fishing pier, antiques shopping, dining, and movies. Rooms with breakfast $75–200.

Palatka 32177
Talking with Doug de Leeuw about the love and enthusiasm he and his wife, Jill, have for the 1878 **Azalea House Bed & Breakfast** (386-325-4547; www.theazaleahouse.com), 220 Madison St, I couldn't help but feel that I'd come home. Surrounded by more than 100 pieces of needlework, you'll want to create some of your own. And you can! Jill not only stocks needlework supplies, but she also offers a Stitcher's Retreat complete with culinary delights and a special commemorative sampler kit. Jill, an accomplished pastry chef, also prepares a delicious full breakfast served in the formal dining room. Wander throughout the Victorian home and relax in the formal parlor and library-style living room, or step outside to the open verandas that stretch around the home overlooking the tropical swimming pool, gardens, and fishpond. When you're ready to retire, curl up in an iron sleigh bed overlooking a magnolia tree in the Magnolia Room or (my favorite) the large Garden Room, with mission-style furnishings and "Button Bunny" needlework, recalling the rabbits in Richard Adams's *Watership Down.* This former home of Benjamin Alexander Putnam's grandson Benjamin Alexander Calhoun, and former vice president John C. Calhoun, has six rooms with 14-foot ceilings, four of which have private bath. Open all year; $70–135.

HOTELS, MOTELS, AND RESORTS
Orange Park 32073
While it bills itself as a bed & breakfast, the **Club Continental and River Suites** (904-264-6070 or 1-800-877-6070; www.clubcontinental .com), 2143 Astor St, is so much more. Still owned by heirs of the Palmolive Soap Company, the 27-acre estate retains the atmosphere of a private club.

Walk amid the splendor of the carefully manicured gardens and fountains set in intimate courtyards. Towering 200-year-old live oaks bend to frame the three swimming pools. The seven rooms in the main Mediterranean-style mansion reflect Old World elegance, while 15 river suites, some with Jacuzzi and four-poster king-sized bed, all have a private riverfront balcony. Rooms with continental breakfast $80–175.

CAMPGROUNDS

Lake Kingsley 32091

On the sandy shores of spring-fed **Lake Kingsley at Camp Blanding** (see *To See—Museums*) you can pitch your tent under shade trees. The primitive campground has latrines, showers, and a designated swimming area. The RV-only campground is separate from the primitive and has full-hook-up facilities with a children's playground. Contact the Morale, Welfare, and Recreation office (904-682-3104) for sites. The MWR also rents canoes, inner tubes, camping gear, and bicycles.

🐟 Fish, swim, or just lounge around at **Kingsley Beach RV Park Campground and Resort** (904-533-2006), 6003 Kingsley Lake Drive, off FL 16. There's a lot to do at this family-oriented 30-acre park. Scuba lessons, banana boat rides, paddleboats, and Jet Skis are just some of the water amenities on this clear blue lake. If you don't want to cook, the restaurant serves all three meals. Bait-and-tackle shop, game room, and live outdoor entertainment. RV sites $25–40 a day, $125–300 a week. Don't own an RV? The resort also rents one- to three-bedroom furnished cabins for $50–145 a day and $175–650 a week.

Orange Park 32003

An angler's getaway since 1963, **Whitey's Fish Camp** (904-269-4198; www.whiteysfishcamp.com), 2032 CR 220, has 44 sites ($28) with full hook-ups, a restaurant (see *Eating Out*), boat and canoe rentals, and, of course, fishing.

FISH CAMPS

Crescent City 32112

Landing Lake Crescent Resort (386-698-2485; www.lakecrescent .com), 100 Grove Ave, sits on the west side of the largely undeveloped Crescent Lake (see *To Do—Fishing*). It's here you'll find black crappie, bream, black and striped bass, and catfish. Fish from the pier or rent a boat and explore the lake's hidden depths. The camp features efficiency rooms with cable TV and full kitchen (one has a fireplace), suites, RV sites, covered marina slips, swimming pool, recreation room, a pub/deli, and bait-and-tackle store. Rooms $58–120, RV sites $19–23, marina slips $5–10.

Crescent City 32139

Quiet and rustic, the **Gateway Fishing Camp** (386-467-2411), 229 Fort Gate Ferry Rd, is located in the heart of bass fishing country, between Little Lake George and Lake George. Stay in the air-conditioned cottages, complete with stove, where you can fry up your catch of the day. Fish off the private boat ramp or take to the river in a rental boat. Cottages $35–50 daily, $210–300 weekly. Rental boats $35 a day. You can also pitch your tent for $10.

Satsuma 32189

The vintage **Stegbone's** (386-467-2464; www.stegbones.com), 144 Norton Fish Camp Rd, will take you back to the way life used to be: RVs, Jet Skis, and cell phones are not allowed at this vintage 1946 fish camp. Choose from one of five classic Florida cabins, the upscale three-bedroom Riverfront Getaway cottage, or a single-wide trailer ($70–185).

Welaka 32193

At the other end of comfort is the **Floridian Sports Club** (386-467-2181; www.floridiansportsclub.com), 114 Floridian Club Rd, with in-room Jacuzzi, wet bar, and screened porches overlooking the river; $159 and up.

✳ Where to Eat

DINING OUT

Melrose

✿ **Blue Water Bay** (352-475-1928), 319 FL 26. With a formal dining room in shades of oceanic blue, this classy restaurant pulls in patrons all the way from Gainesville with entrées ($13– 40) like lemon-steamed snow crab legs, Cajun étouffée, and their famous seafood platters. French night is Tue; buffets on Fri and Sat at 5. Their sushi and desserts are some of the best I've ever sampled.

Orange Park

Looking for a romantic evening? You'll find it at the restaurant at **Club Continental** (904-264-6070 or 1-800-877-6070; www.clubcontinental.com), 2143 Astor St. Tall ceilings, white tablecloths, candles, and an incredible view of the St. Johns River are just part of the Old World elegance in the main house, where an extensive gourmet menu is complemented by fine wines and rare cognacs. This members-only restaurant allows you entrance only if you stay over in the main house or river

suites (see *Lodging*). Open Tue–Fri for dinner, Sun brunch.

EATING OUT

Crescent City

What a treat to find **3 Bananas** (386-698-2861), 11 South Lake St. This tropical paradise, just off the lake, offers up a large chicken Caesar salad ($7), Caribbean jerk chicken ($6), lightly fried Crescent catfish ($9), and a half-pound paradise burger ($5). Sit on the outside deck and look for the sunken pirate ship while drinking Rum Runners and piña coladas for only $3. Live island music on weekends. Open every day except Tue.

East Palatka

The fresh and friendly **Musselwhite's Seafood & Grill** (386-326-9111), 125 US 17 S, serves up such dishes as Florida alligator tail with a tangy twist ($4); tangerine tuna marinated with citrus, soy, ginger, and honey ($16); and New York strip cut and grilled to your liking ($11–15). Save room for dessert: Key lime pie and chocolate peanut butter pie are only $3.

Keystone Heights

Johnny's Bar-B-Q Restaurant (352-473-4445), 7411 FL 21. Eat in, walk up, or drive through at this busy local icon, where families gather for great barbecue and burgers. The waitresses know everyone by name, and service is in a snap, even during the lunch rush. Historic photos and memorabilia from Keystone Heights line the walls. Daily lunch specials ($5) and dinner plates ($6–8) pack in the crowds; salads (with your choice of barbecue meat) appeal to the lighter palate.

Sabo's Italian-American Restaurant (352-473-2233), 7448 FL 21.

The portions are huge, the blue cheese dressing homemade, and the prices can't be beat: $7–10 for baked-to-order entrées with salad and tasty garlic rolls. My friends raved about the traditional Italian favorites; you won't be disappointed. Lunch and dinner; closed Mon.

Middleburg

Inside the cozy **Country Cabin Bar-B-Que** (904-282-6700), 2216 S Mimosa Ave, Gail and Smokey Boston prepare some of the best barbecued delights around in their oakwood smoker. The "Feast for Two" ($19) includes a hefty portion of barbecued ribs, pork, beef, or turkey, along with coleslaw and garlic toast.

Orange Park

Whitey's Fish Camp (904-269-4198), 2032 CR 220. Catfish is the specialty at this recently renovated restaurant with Florida flair. All-you-can-eat catfish ($13) is only for those with a big appetite. Petite eaters can order a basket with slaw, fries, and hush puppies ($6). If you're not into catfish, then there's just about any other type of fish you can think of—and you can choose grilled, blackened, broiled, fried, or pecan- crusted. Seafood platters ($14) include shrimp, oysters, scallops, and grouper. A really healthy appetite commands the Deluxe Dinner ($19), which seems to cover just about everything on the menu, including frog legs and 'gator tail. Fear not, landlubbers: You can get a 16-ounce rib eye ($19) or marinated chicken breast ($10). The outdoor terrace has live music on the weekends.

✳ Selective Shopping

Green Cove Springs

The **historic district** in Green Cove Springs is an excellent place for antiquing.

Hibernia

Fleming Island ("the Island," as the locals refer to it) is located on US 17 in Hibernia and is the community's center for restaurants and modern shops.

Melrose

Ann Lowry Antiques (352-475-2924), 1658 SE Fifth Ave, housed in a historic church under a canopy of ancient live oaks, showcases classy home decor items and furnishings. Ann shares the building with **East Coast Antiques** (352-475-5771), which offers an eclectic selection of furniture, books, home ephemera, and a bargain basement with more books and board games.

In the Hilton-Brinson House, an 1886 landmark, the new **Bellamy Road Fine Arts, Literature, and Film** (352-475-3435; www.bellamyroad arts.com), 5910 Hampton St, offers a nod to the region's history and combines the interests of its owners to offer an antiquarian bookstore and art gallery featuring artists that capture the soul of Florida, as well as film screenings. Hours are limited; call ahead.

Middleburg

Country Charm Mercantile (904-282-4512), 4544 Alligator Blvd. Hand-crafted quilts bulge from the shelves; wind chimes dangle from the ceiling. This five-room home is jam-packed with gift items and home decor, from Heritage Village miniatures to Yankee Candles, gourmet foods, and Beanie Babies. Closed Sun.

Palatka

Andrea's Book Store (386-325-2141; www.andreasbookstore.com), 308 S

US 19, has a great selection of local folklore (see the Folklore sidebar) along with national best-sellers. The web site provides excellent reviews of selected favorites.

FARM STANDS Stop by **County Line Produce,** near the Putnam–St. Johns line as you travel along FL 207. Get buzzing and head to the self-serve **1947 Honey Stand** (386-749-3562), 303 E FL 100, San Mateo, where you'll find pure, raw Florida honey. Choose from orange blossom, gallberry, or wildflower in 1-, 2-, and 5-pound jars.

✷ Entertainment

Thrasher Horne Center for Performing Arts (904-276-6815; www.thcenter.org), 283 College Dr, Orange Park. This state-of-the-art 84,666-square-foot theater is fully equipped with a multiuse theater and two art galleries. Its first event is scheduled for fall 2004. Expect performances of professional theater, dance, and music, along with visual arts exhibits.

✷ Special Events

January: The **Putnam County African-American Cultural Arts Festival** (386-325-9901), downtown Palatka, always on Martin Luther King Day, is a celebration of African American history, arts, and culture.

March: Downtown Palatka hosts the annual **Florida Azalea Festival** (386-326-4001), always the second weekend.

You'll find traditional agricultural exhibits, entertainment, and midway rides at the **Putnam County Fair** (386-329-0318), Putnam County Fairgrounds, East Palatka.

April: Best place to skin a catfish is at the **Catfish Festival** (386-698-1666), Crescent City. The championship catfish-skinning contest is one of many events, including the catfish run, a parade (led by King Catfish), a bluegrass concert, an antiques show, and an arts and crafts fair.

On the St. Johns River you can watch the rowing regatta of the **Gainesville Crew Classic and Masters** (352-378-6837).

May: ♿ Not to be missed is the annual **St. Margaret's Tour and Tea** (904-284-3030; www.st.margarets.org), Old Church Rd, Hibernia. The one-hour tour of Margaret's chapel (see *To See—Historic Sites*) and the Fleming family plantation is followed by high tea. Civil War reenactments, Virginia reel dancing, period costumes, and Southern hospitality are just some of what's on offer. A limited number of golf carts are available for the handicapped or those unable to walk the area. $9 for ages 12 and up, $6 seniors.

One of this area's major events, the 42-nautical-mile **Mug Race** (904-264-4094) sets sail from the Palatka riverfront and races to Jacksonville along the St. Johns River.

You'll find not only hot steaming blue crabs at the annual **Blue Crab Festival** (386-325-4406; www.bluecrabfestival.com), downtown Palatka, but also such delights as soft-shell crabs, shrimp, and alligator. Four days of entertainment, rides, and arts and crafts. Always on Memorial Day weekend.

June: Wake up early and head to the **Bostwick Blueberry Festival** (386-329-2658) for the blueberry pancake breakfast, where you can pick up blueberry-related foods, arts, and crafts.

August: **Soul Food Festival and Parade of Pride,** Vera F. Hall Park, Green Cove Springs.

October: Get your caboose to the **Palatka Railfest** (386-649-6137), Union Station, corner of 11th and Reid, where you can learn about model and full-scale trains or enhance your HO, S, and N collection at the many railroad exhibits.

November: The **Bronson-Mulholland House** (see *To See—Historic Sites*) is centerpiece to the Fall Antique Fair (386-329-0140), where local and out-of-town vendors display and sell several fine antique and estate pieces.

Relive the **Battle of Horse Landing** (386-328-1281), Rodeheaver Boys Ranch on the St. Johns River, with living history demonstrations including a Civil War reenactment and military ball.

December: Take a tour through Crescent City, where many of the grand and glorious homes are decorated in holiday splendor (386-649-4534).

On the **Clay County Historical Society Holiday Tour of Homes & Sites,** walk through Green Cove Springs' authentic Victorian homes decorated for the holidays; $10.

EVENTS AT CLAY COUNTY FAIRGROUNDS Throughout the year there are several events at the Clay County Fairgrounds (904-529-3617), 2497 CR 16 W, Green Cove Springs. In Jan equestrians gather for the $25,000 **Hunter Jumper Grand Prix.** In Feb, celebrate Celtic heritage with the **NFL Scottish Highlands Games** (904-264-2635). The **Clay County Agricultural Fair** (904-281-1615; www.claycountyfair.org) is in Apr. By Nov, get ready for 24 hours of bluegrass and gospel music at **Sheila's Bluegrass Festival** (904-923-5222), while later in the month canines jump for joy at the **Paws and Pals Agility Dog Show.**

Original Florida 2

ALACHUA AND THE HISTORIC LAKE
DISTRICT

THE LOWER SUWANNEE

THE BIG BEND

THE UPPER SUWANNEE

Visit Florida

ALACHUA AND THE HISTORIC LAKE DISTRICT
ALACHUA, BRADFORD, AND UNION COUNTIES

I n 1765, botanist William Bartram described a visit to the village of Cuscowilla, on the edge of a vast prairie, where he met with the great chief Cowkeeper. Cowkeeper's descendants, the Seminoles, were pushed south off their ancestral lands by settlers eager to claim the rich prairies, oak hammocks, and pine flatwoods as their own. After Florida became a U.S. territory in 1821, Congress authorized the construction of the Bellamy Road, a wagon route from St. Augustine to Tallahassee, leading settlers to this region. But it was not until the establishment of the University of Florida in 1853 that **Gainesville,** now the largest and most vibrant city in the region, became a major population center. All three counties maintain their rural roots, where farming and ranching surround small historic communities.

Gainesville started out as Hogtown, an 1824 settlement of 14 inhabitants on a creek that snaked its way into the vast prairie south of town. Named for General Edmund Gaines, commander of U.S. Army troops in Florida during the Second Seminole War, Gainesville won out over Lake City for the location of the newly formed University of Florida, becoming the county seat in 1854. Civil War skirmishes in downtown streets added a touch of excitement in the 1860s, but it wasn't enough to dissuade a steady stream of settlers. Gainesville incorporated as a city in 1869.

Historic but hip describes the towns north along US 441, mingling old and new, with historic structures reinvented into cafés, art galleries, and theaters. Settlers coming down the Bellamy Road moved into **High Springs** on the Santa Fe River as early as the 1830s; Florida's phosphate boom accelerated the town's growth in the 1870s, and it retains that turn-of-the-century feel. The Bellamy Road also brought settlers to the pastoral town of **Alachua,** founded in 1905. Blink, and you'll miss the turnoff from US 441 to Alachua's Main St, just a mile south of I-75. But it's worth the stop. Although only a few blocks long, downtown Alachua is crammed with unique shops and restaurants.

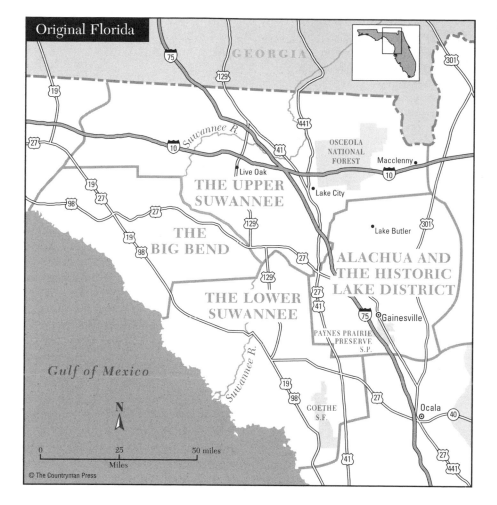

Original Florida

GEORGIA

OSCEOLA
NATIONAL
FOREST

Macclenny

Live Oak

Lake City

THE UPPER
SUWANNEE

THE
BIG BEND

Lake Butler

ALACHUA AND
THE HISTORIC
LAKE DISTRICT

THE LOWER
SUWANNEE

Gainesville

PAYNES PRAIRIE
PRESERVE
S.P.

Gulf of Mexico

N

GOETHE
S.F.

Ocala

0   25   50 miles

Miles

© The Countryman Press

In Bradford County, the county seat of **Starke** lives in infamy as the home of the Florida State Prison and its electric chair, but downtown Call St shows the genteel side of this historic city. South of Starke on US 301 is **Waldo,** founded in 1858 as a railroad town. In the 1960s Waldo became infamous for its speed traps along US 301, so much so that a former officer wrote a book about it. *Waldo* remains a synonym for *speed trap* in Florida, so watch that gas pedal when you drive through!

The railroads also ran through **Hawthorne,** established in 1880 as a junction for trains from Gainesville to Ocala and Waldo. The Lake District continues in a sweep southward past Newnans Lake and the historic village of **Rochelle** down to Lake Lochloosa and Orange Lake, where Pulitzer Prize–winning author Marjorie Kinnan Rawlings put the fishing village of **Cross Creek** on the map. Nearby **Evinston,** established in 1882 on the Marion County border, was a major citrus center until the deep freezes of the 1890s killed the groves. And

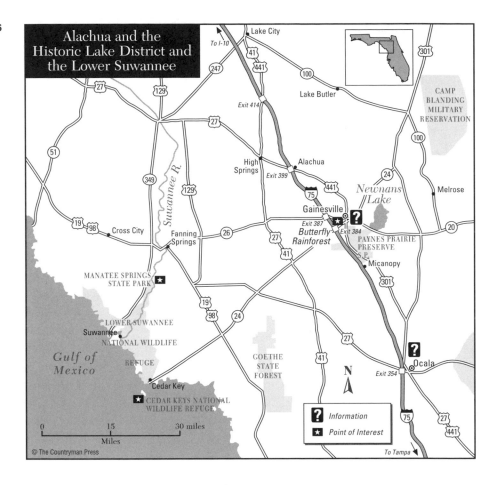

Alachua and the
Historic Lake District and
the Lower Suwannee

Micanopy, founded in 1821 near Paynes Prairie, is one of Florida's top destinations for antiques shopping, its downtown a snapshot of the late 1800s.

In western Alachua County, history buffs will appreciate tiny **Archer** for its railroad museum and Civil War history. Florida's phosphate boom built the town of **Newberry** in 1870, where workers dug deep pits to extract the black nuggets used for fertilizer. In more recent times, paleontologists have had a field day in Newberry's phosphate pits, pulling out fossilized crocodiles, turtles, and other creatures whose bones are on display at the Florida Natural History Museum in Gainesville.

GUIDANCE Stop in at the **Gainesville/Alachua County Visitors & Convention Bureau** (352-374-5231; www.visitgainesville.net), 30 E University Ave, Gainesville 32801. For points east of Gainesville, visit the **North Florida Regional Chamber of Commerce** (904-964-5278; www.northfloridachamber .com), 202 S Walnut St, Starke 32091.

GETTING THERE *By air:* Continental, Delta (ComAir), and USAir provide daily commuter service to the **Gainesville Regional Airport** (352-373-0249; www .gra-gnv.com), located east of town off FL 20.

By bus: **Greyhound** (352-376-5252), 516 SW Fourth Ave, Gainesville.

By car: I-75 runs through the heart of Alachua County, paralleled by US 441; US 301 passes by the lakes of Bradford and Union counties. FL 20, 24, and 26 radiate out of Gainesville to reach points east and west in Alachua County, and US 41 provides an often-canopied scenic rural route between High Springs, Williston, and Archer.

By train: **Amtrak** (352-468-1408) stops in Waldo, west of Gainesville.

GETTING AROUND *By bicycle:* Gainesville is one of Florida's most bicycle-friendly cities, with rail-trails, dedicated urban bike paths, and bike lanes connecting the city core and the University of Florida with the suburbs.

By bus: Given the University of Florida's large student population, local bus service via **Regional Transit System** (352-334-2600) is frequent and comprehensive; call 352-334-2614 for a schedule.

By taxi: **A1 Yellow Cab** (352-374-9696).

PARKING Although there are some free parking spaces in downtown Gainesville (two-hour limit), it's mostly metered parking (50¢ an hour, two-hour limit in most places). One parking garage serves the downtown district. At the University of Florida, if you can't find metered parking along the edge of campus, it's essential to pick up a visitors pass (free) at one of the staffed parking permit kiosks off University Blvd or SW 13th St. Park only in permit areas that match the color of your pass—even in metered areas—or you'll face a parking ticket, payable immediately at the main parking office on North-South Rd. In Alachua, High Springs, and Starke, you'll have no problem finding free street parking within easy walking distance of shops and restaurants.

PUBLIC RESTROOMS You'll find public restrooms in High Springs in a replica train depot housing the chamber of commerce at the south end of the antiques district.

MEDICAL EMERGENCIES In Gainesville, **Shands HealthCare** (352-265-0111; www.shands.org), 1600 SW Archer Rd, is one of the nation's top medical facilities; you also have the option of **North Florida Regional Medical Center** (352-333-4000; www.nfrmc.com), 6500 W Newberry Rd.

✳ To See

ARCHEOLOGICAL SITES Thanks to the archeologists of the University of Florida, Gainesville, many significant sites have been identified throughout Alachua County. Some, like the **Law School Burial Mound,** are open to public inspection. Located on the University of Florida campus near Lake Alice, this burial mound dates back to A.D. 1000. It contains the remains of the ancestors of the

Potano culture, also known as the Alachua Tradition peoples. The **Moon Lake Villages** were a series of Alachua Tradition villages on the site now occupied by Buchholz High School in Gainesville. Accessed by the trails in **Gum Root Swamp Conservation Area** (see *Wild Places*), villages along **Newnans Lake** were occupied as early as 3000 B.C., and more recently by the Seminoles, who called the lake *Pithlachocco*: "the place where boats are made." More than 100 aboriginal canoes were unearthed from the lake in 2000, the largest such find in Florida. Most remain buried in the mud. Another Paleo-Indian site has been identified near the boardwalk along US 441 in the middle of **Paynes Prairie**. At **San Felasco Hammock Preserve State Park** (see *Green Space—Wild Places*), one of the first Spanish missions in North America was established in 1608 and occupied until 1706. Its exact location is not marked, but you can walk through the woods around the mission along the Old Spanish Way trail, where Alachua County's original seat, **Spring Grove,** has also vanished under the thick cover of hardwood forest.

ART GALLERIES ✍ ♿ **Samuel P. Harn Museum of Art** (352-392-9826; www.harn.ufl.edu), SW 34th St and Hull Rd, Gainesville, showcases thematic exhibits of fine arts from their extensive collections as well as rotating traveling exhibits. The tall, open rotunda provides access to the main galleries. In the Richardson Gallery, you might encounter an exhibit of fine turn-of-the-20th-century American oils, but you'll always find the museum's masterpiece on display—Monet's *Champ d'Avoine.* Take a seat and enjoy some quiet time studying this impressionistic masterpiece. Looking for more to aid your art appreciation? Stop in the Bishop Study Center to peruse their library of fine-art books, or examine the computers for exhibits from virtual galleries. In addition to books, jewelry, and fine-art reproductions, the Museum Shop carries artsy games and toys for kids, and the artistic works of several local artisans. Tue–Fri 11–5, Sat 10–5, Sun 1–5. Closed on state holidays. Donation.

Santa Fe Gallery (352-395-5621), 3000 NW 83rd St, Building P, Room 201, Gainesville. The first community college approved for loans of high-security exhibits from the National Gallery of Art and the Smithsonian Institution, the Santa Fe Community College displays rotating exhibits of contemporary art in their gallery. Mon–Fri 10–3, Tue 6–8. Free.

Thomas Center Galleries (352-334-5064), 302 NE Sixth Ave, Gainesville. Serving the community as the Hotel Thomas from 1928 to 1968, this is now a cultural center housing a small history museum, an art gallery with rotating exhibits, and the city's Department of Cultural Affairs. Roam the galleries and enjoy the beautiful surrounding gardens. Free.

THOMAS CENTER GALLERIES
Gainesville/Alachua CVB

Gainesville, include the University Gallery in Fine Arts Building B, with contemporary national and regional art displays (Tue–Sat); the Focus Gallery in Fine Arts Building C (Mon–Fri), featuring student art and emerging artists; and the Grinter Gallery in Grinter Hall, with its international art displays (Mon–Fri). Free.

HISTORIC SITES

Archer

In 1865 David Levy Yulee, U.S. senator and head of the Florida Railroad, stashed the personal effects of Confederate president Jefferson Davis at his Cottonwood Plantation while Davis attempted to flee to Florida after the surrender of the Confederacy. Yulee's servants led Union soldiers to the prize, and Yulee was jailed for treason. **A plaque near the old Archer Depot** (see *Museums*) tells the story; the plantation house burned in 1939.

Cross Creek

At the **Marjorie Kinnan Rawlings Historic State Park** (352-466-9273; www .floridastateparks.org/marjoriekinnanrawlings), CR 325, house tours take you through the living and working space of this Pulitzer-winning novelist beloved by regional historians for her accurate depictions of rural North Florida. Set in what remains of her original orange grove from the 1940s, this dogtrot Cracker home offers some quirks specific to its northern resident, including the "liquor cabinet" with firewater on top and firewood on the bottom, as well as her use of inverted mixing bowls as decorative fixtures for lights. Cary Grant, Spencer Tracy, and many other legends stayed in Marjorie's guest room. Costumed guides explain what life was like in Cross Creek when Marjorie sat on the front porch and typed the drafts of her novels, including *The Yearling*. Fee.

Gainesville

Several historic districts surround the city core of downtown Gainesville, where the original **Courthouse Clock** (circa 1885) resides in a new housing at the corner of University and First St in front of the new courthouse. B&Bs (see *Lodging*) stake a claim in the historic **Southeast Residential District,** Gainesville's earliest suburb, settled in the 1880s. Wander through these streets for some fine examples of Victorian and Cracker architecture. In the lushly canopied **Northeast Historic District**, covering a few blocks around the Thomas Center, 12 historic homes show off their Victorian charm beneath the live oaks and magnolias. Start your tour at the **Thomas Center** (see *Art Galleries*). Built in 1906, this restored Mediterranean Revival hotel began as the home of Major William Reuben Thomas, the man instrumental in attracting the University of Florida to Gainesville. Founded in 1853, the **University of Florida** boasts its own historic center. In 1989 the **Pleasant Street District** was placed on the National Register of Historic Places, the first predominantly African American community in Florida to gain that designation. Comprising a 20-block area to the northwest of downtown, it contains 35 points of historical interest, including the St. Augustine Day School, 405 NW Fourth Ave, an 1892 mission for African Americans, and the Dunbar Hotel, 732 NW Fourth St, a favorite of jazz musicians and the only Gainesville lodgings available to African American travelers from the 1930s through the 1950s.

High Springs

High Springs itself is a historic downtown; many of its buildings date back to the late 1800s. A remnant of the original wagon road that brought settlers to this region, the **Old Bellamy Road** can be accessed from US 41 north of High Springs: Follow the Bellamy Road east to the interpretive trailhead. Just south on US 41 is the **De Soto Trail** monument, commemorating the route of explorer Hernando de Soto and his men as they traversed the Florida peninsula in 1539.

Kanapaha

Established in 1855, the **Historic Haile Homestead** (352-336-9096; www .hailehomestead.org), 8500 SW Archer Rd, provides a glimpse into the life of Florida's territorial settlers on a 40-acre remnant of the original 1,500-acre Sea Island cotton plantation. Open Sun for tours noon–4; adults $7, under 12 free.

Micanopy

More than 35 historic sites crowd Micanopy's small downtown, best enjoyed as a self-guided walking tour (see *To Do—Walking Tours*). Some don't-miss stops include the **Old Presbyterian Church,** built 1870; the 1890 **Thrasher Warehouse,** housing the Micanopy Historical Society Museum (see *Museums*); the 1880 **Calvin Merry House,** the oldest home on the east side of the street; the **Victorian Gothic Revival Powell House,** from 1866; the 1895 **Brick School House;** the 1875 **Simonton-Herlong House** (see *Lodging*); and the **Stewart-Merry House,** built around the 1855 log cabin where Dr. James Stewart practiced medicine. None of the homes are open for public inspection, although many of the historic business buildings now house the town's shops.

Newberry

For a ramble through a preserved homestead, visit **Dudley Farm Historic Site State Park** (see *Green Space—Farms*), where rangers in period costume take you through a day in the life of a turn-of-the-20th-century Florida farmer. The museum at the visitors center interprets the several generations of family who lived here, and how farming changed over the years; the tour will open your eyes to how difficult life was for Florida's early settlers.

OLD PRESBYTERIAN CHURCH, MICANOPY
Sandra Friend

Starke

The historic **Bradford County Courthouse** anchors the west end of Call St to US 301; the **Gene Matthews Museum** marks the east end of the historic district. A restored theater shows first-run movies. As renovation of the historic district continues, expect to see more of the storefronts fill in.

MUSEUMS

Archer

Housed in the former railroad depot, the **Archer Historical Society Museum** (352-495-9422), Magnolia and Main streets, displays local history and railroad memorabilia, including a lab-model Edison phonograph, an original telephone and telegraph from the depot, and the curator's antique camera collection. Open Sat 3–6, Sep–June. Donation.

Gainesville/Alachua CVB

CANNED GOODS AT THE DUDLEY FARM

Gainesville

Alachua County Historic Trust and Matheson Museum (352-378-2280; www.mathesonmuseum.org), 513 E University Ave. In addition to its interpretation of Alachua County's history, the museum houses a historical library and archives, with an extensive collection of Florida history books and documents. Closed Mon. Free. The trust also administers the historic **Matheson House,** the second-oldest residence in Gainesville, and the **Tison Tool Museum,** both open by appointment only. Fee.

✄ ♿ **Florida Museum of Natural History** (352-846-2000; www.flmnh .ufl.edu), SW 34th St and Hull Rd. Interactive and engaging, the Florida Museum of Natural History continues to evolve with new picture-perfect 3-D dioramas and hands-on activities. Kids and adults love the walk-through Florida cave, which now funnels you into the permanent exhibit called Northwest Florida's Waterways and Wildlife, showcasing everything from karst topography and carnivorous plants to indigenous peoples and the creatures of the salt marsh. In the South Florida People and Environments gallery, shrink down to the size of a killifish to explore the world beneath the mangroves, and walk into the home of a Calusa chieftain. Dinosaurs never walked Florida's soil, but we've had saber-toothed tigers, mastodons, and shoveltuskers; learn more about them in the newly refurbished Florida Fossils exhibit. New to the museum is the Butterfly Rainforest, a separate (fee-based) exhibit that

DOWNTOWN STARKE

Sandra Friend

will surround you with these winged wonders (see the Butterflies sidebar). Don't miss the Collectors Shop, a must for picking up educational toys and books for the kids. Mon–Sat 10–4:30, Sun 1–4:30. Donation.

The **Institute of Black Culture** (352-392-0895), 1510 W University Ave, exhibits African, African American, and Caribbean art on the University of Florida campus. Mon–Fri 8 AM–9 PM; free.

Hawthorne

Hawthorne Historical Museum (352-481-4491), 7225 SE 221st St, is housed in a restored 1907 church; artifacts, exhibits, and primitive arts illustrate the long history of this rural village.

Sandra Friend

MICANOPY HISTORICAL SOCIETY MUSEUM

Micanopy

Micanopy Historical Society Museum (352-466-3200; www.afn.org/~micanopy), corner of Cholokka and Bay streets. Housed in the Thrasher Warehouse (circa 1890)—the "Home Depot of its day," says volunteer Paul Oliver, built along the railroad tracks—this small but comprehensive museum gives an overview of life in and around Micanopy, from the ancient Timucua and William Bartram's visit to Cuscowilla in 1774, through the town's settlement as a trading post in 1821, and on into this century, with special exhibits of historical railroad items, relics from the Thrasher Store (now Tyson Trading Company), and period pieces from the Simon H. Benjamin Collection. There's also a small gift shop and bookstore with historical tomes on the region. Open 1–4 daily. Donation.

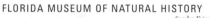

FLORIDA MUSEUM OF NATURAL HISTORY

Sandra Friend

Starke

Boat Drain School Museum, 581 N Temple Ave. In 1893 this one-room pine board schoolhouse served the needs of Bradford County's small population; today it's a small museum dedicated to the history of Bradford High School. **The Gene Matthews Bradford County Historical Museum** (904-964-4606), 201 E Call St, showcases Bradford County's history, with a special emphasis on turpentine, logging, and railroads. Open Tue–Sun 1–5; free.

RAILROADIANA At Magnolia and Main in Archer, the Archer Historical Society Museum (see *Museums*) occupies the **old railroad depot;** across the street at the Maddox Machine Works, a gleaming **Seaboard Air Line steam engine, circa 1910,** is on display. Visit the Micanopy Historical Society Museum (see *Museums*) for historical information and relics from the **Gainesville, Rocky Point & Micanopy Railroad,** circa 1895. After it became the Tampa & Jackson Railroad, locals called the T&J the "Tug & Jerk." It stopped at Thrasher's Warehouse, which now houses the museum.

High Springs grew up around Henry Plant's Seaboard Air Line; the man credited with putting Tampa on the map selected High Springs as his distribution center. On Railroad St (south of Main), look for the **original passenger depot,** a historic site now housing the Station Bakery & Café (see *Eating Out*). To the west of the station, vast rail yards, roundhouses, and engine shops kept busy with mighty steam engines; the only reminder of their passing is a bright red **Seaboard Coast Line caboose** tucked behind city hall.

Railroads shaped the towns of Starke, Waldo, and Hawthorne as well. You'll find a **working railroad depot at East Brownlee Street** (FL 16) in Starke at the railroad crossing just west of US 301, and a **retired caboose** sitting on a siding southwest of the junction of US 301 and FL 20 in Waldo.

ZOOLOGICAL PARK ✪ **Santa Fe Community College Teaching Zoo** (352-395-5604; www.inst.sfcc.edu/~zoo), 3000 NW 43rd St, Gainesville. For more than 20 years, this unique, hands-on zoo has taught generations of animal technicians (once known as zookeepers) how to create exhibits and handle animals. Guests travel with a guide through the deeply forested complex, learning about bald eagles, muntjac, otters, and more while watching students at work, learning how to care for their charges. Open weekends 9–2, with tours held every 10 to 15 minutes. Weekday tours by reservation only; closed holidays and semester breaks. Free.

✳ To Do

ALLIGATOR SPOTTING In 2002 artists created alligator sculptures that were placed throughout Gainesville, then auctioned off as a fund-raiser for the arts. To track down the remaining whimsical pieces, ask around for the *Gator Trails* brochure, or look it up online on the *Gainesville Sun* web site (www.gainesvillesun.com). To spot hundreds of live alligators, visit **Alachua Sink** in Paynes Prairie Preserve State Park (see *Green Space— Wild Places*) or visit the University of Florida campus, where a network of nature trails surrounds **Lake Alice.**

WALDO'S RETIRED CABOOSE

Sandra Friend

Sandra Friend

LAKE ALICE

Visitors get up close and personal with the university's real-life namesakes—but don't ramble down the pathways after dark! The daytime sightings of 10-foot alligators sunning themselves along the trail are thrill enough. Parking areas on Museum Rd are restricted to student use until 3:30 PM.

BAT-WATCHING On the University of Florida campus at Lake Alice, the **Bat House** in the Student Agricultural Gardens on Museum Rd contains a colony of more than 20,000 brown bats. Visit at dusk to see the incredible display of bats pouring out of the house and into the skies. At the **Lubee Center** (352-485-1250; www.lubee.org/center.aspx) north of Gainesville, researchers care for endangered fruit bats under the auspices of the Lubee Foundation, formed by rum magnate Louis Bacardi. Group tours are offered by reservation only.

BICYCLING Gainesville is a city for serious bicycling; many residents use bikes as their sole means of transportation. For a map of the urban bikeway network, contact the **Gainesville Bicycle/Pedestrian Program** (352-334-5074), 306 NE Sixth Ave, Gainesville. **The Gainesville-Hawthorne State Trail** (see *Green Space—Greenways*) starts at Bouleware Springs Park in southeast Gainesville and runs to downtown Hawthorne, providing riders with a 34-mile round-trip. **San Felasco Hammock Preserve State Park** (see *Green Space—Wild Places*) has more than 12 miles of shady, rugged mountain biking routes. Check on bike rentals at **Spin Cycle** (352-373-3355), 424 W University Ave in Gainesville, and **Santa Fe Bicycle Outfitters** (352-454-BIKE), 10 N Main St, High Springs.

BIRDING At **Paynes Prairie Preserve State Park** (see *Green Space—Wild Places*) birders head for open ground—look for overlooks from **Bolen's Bluff** and the **La Chua Trail,** and along US 441. You'll see more waders these days since the prairie's been flooded for several years. Encounter dozens of trilling species around the water gardens at **Kanapaha Botanical Gardens** (see the Botanical Gardens sidebar). Any spot with a marsh is a major haven for birds; check the *Green Space* section for ideas.

DIVING Northwestern Alachua County lies along the spring belt, offering open-water and cave diving at **Poe Springs** as well as underwater adventures in adjacent Gilchrist County at **Ginnie Springs** and **Blue Spring** (see *Green Space—Springs*). At High Springs check in at **Extreme Exposure Adventure Center** (1-800-574-6341; www.extreme-exposure.com), 15 S Main, for rental

BUTTERFLIES The **Florida Museum of Natural History** (see *To See—Museums*) now sports **Butterfly Rainforest**, a permanent conservatory where butterflies float like autumn leaves across a backdrop of tropical forest under glass. The conservatory is part of the **McGuire Center for Lepidoptera and Biodiversity**, hosting the world's second-largest collection of mounted specimens amid 39,000 square feet of research labs. What will catch your eye from the museum floor and draw you into this new space is the Wall of Wings, with thou-

Sandra Friend

BUTTERFLY RAINFOREST

sands of colorful and unique specimens; outdoors, enjoy the **Florida Wildflowers & Butterflies Garden**. Open Mon–Sat 10–5, Sun 1–5; closed Thanksgiving and Christmas. Adults $8.50, Florida residents $7.50, students/seniors $6.50, ages 3–12 $4.50.

GREATHOUSE BUTTERFLY FARM

Sandra Friend

In Earlton, near Melrose, visit native Florida butterflies at the **Greathouse Butterfly Farm** (1-866-475-2088; www.great housebutterflyfarm.com), 20329 SR 26 E, where tours of this working butterfly farm lead you through gardens and greenhouses and into the Butterfly Barn, a magical experience. Tours offered daily at 10 AM; fee. Deluxe tours (for smaller groups) are available by appointment: adults $8, children/seniors $6.

equipment, instruction, and pointers on the area's best dives. **Water World** (352-37-SCUBA), 720 NW 13th St, a full-service dive shop, rents snorkeling and scuba gear, holds dive training, and offers information on more than 50 dive sites within an easy drive of Gainesville.

ECOTOURS Author and river rat Lars Anderson runs regular **guided kayaking trips** out of his Adventure Outpost in High Springs (see *Paddling*).

GOLF **Ironwood Golf Course** (352-334-3120), 2100 NE 39th Ave, is a city-owned public course with PGA pro Bill Iwinski on staff; 18 holes, par 72, on an Audubon-approved natural course established in 1962. West of I-75 on FL 26, the **West End Golf Course** (352-332-2721) features the world's largest and longest night-lighted course (18 holes, par 60), along with a driving range.

HIKING Home to the state office of the **Florida Trail Association** (1-877-HIKE-FLA; www.floridatrail.org), 5415 SW 13th St—where you can stop in and pick up hiking information and hiking-related gifts—Gainesville is ringed with dozens of excellent opportunities for hikers, including more than 20 miles of trails at **Paynes Prairie Preserve State Park** and another 12 miles of trails at **San Felasco Hammock Preserve State Park** (see *Green Space—Wild Places*). Or opt for an easier stroll at one of the nature centers or wilderness areas. Check out *50 Hikes in North Florida* for details on the best hiking in the region.

POE SPRINGS

PADDLING Two outfitters in High Springs can get you in the water and down the Santa Fe or the nearby Ichetucknee in Columbia County. At **Santa Fe Canoe Outpost** (386-454-2050; www.santaferiver.com), US 441 at the Santa Fe Bridge, rent a canoe (shuttle included) or take a guided trip (including overnights!) on the Santa Fe or Ichetucknee rivers. In addition to their "menu" of guided trips and a selection of canoes and kayaks for sale or rent, the **Adventure Outpost** (386-454-0611), 815 NW US 441, High Springs, has technical clothing, camping equipment, and a nice selection of regional guidebooks. Owners Lars and Patsy keep the shop well stocked: You'll even find pottery and other gift items from local artists. Kick back and thumb through a book, or relax at the picnic tables outside under the trees.

PRAIRIE OVERLOOK **Paynes Prairie Overlook,** I-75 rest area southbound. Notice the DANGEROUS SNAKES warning signs around the rest area, intimidating visitors from getting too close to the edge of Paynes Prairie, North Florida's largest prairie. Reflecting this theme, the Florida Department of Transportation built a snake-shaped walkway out to an observation deck overlooking the prairie. To northbound travelers, the walkway and deck look like an enormous snake, complete with a ribbon of concrete creating a forked tongue.

SCENIC DRIVES The **Old Florida Heritage Highway** (www.scenicus441.com), a newly designated Florida Scenic Highway, circles the Gainesville area, using US 441, CR 346, CR 325, and CR 2082 to create a beautiful drive around Paynes Prairie and along canopied roads. Along **CR 234,** from FL 26 south through Rochelle to Micanopy along the east side of Newnans Lake, you'll cruise past historic homes under a canopy of ancient live oaks.

WALKING TOURS

Gainesville
Check with the Thomas Center (see *To See—Art Galleries*), the Gainesville CVB (see *Guidance*), or the Matheson Center (see *To See—Museums*) for brochures outlining walking tours of historic Gainesville, such as the **Pleasant Street Historic Walking Tour** and **Historic Gainesville: A Walking Tour,** which covers the Northeast Historic District around the Matheson Center.

Micanopy
Stop in at the Micanopy Historical Society Museum (see *To See—Museums*) to purchase an inexpensive **walking tour booklet** that details the history and location of 38 significant sites in the historic district.

✳ Green Space

FARMS ✐ Bring a bag of carrots for admission to the **Mill Creek Farm Retirement Home for Horses** (386-462-1001; www.millcreekfarm.org), CR 235A in Alachua, open Sat 11–3. In the 1840s farmstead at **Morningside Nature Center** (see *Nature Centers*) kids learn what life in Old Florida was really like during living history demonstrations on weekends. Let them visit with the barnyard

BOTANICAL GARDEN 🖉 ♿ 🐾 With more than 14 distinct garden areas spread across 62 acres bordering Lake Kanapaha, **Kanapaha Botanical Gardens** (352-372-4981; www.kanapaha.org), 4700 SW 58th Dr, provides a peaceful retreat on the western edge of Gainesville. Come in spring to revel in the aromas of azalea and camellia in bloom; come anytime to walk more than a mile of pathways between the burbling water gardens, the palm hammock, and the woodland gardens, where you can pause and sit on a bench next to a reflective pool, or watch an artist at work painting one of the many lovely garden scenes. Plant identifications add to your understanding of native plants and popular botanicals. Children will appreciate the new children's garden, as well as the many places to duck beneath bowers of plants. Art glass aficionados should note the collection assembled in the gift shop; you'll always find fine art on display in the Summer House, and plants available from the on-site nursery. Managed by the North Florida Botanical Society, this is one of Florida's little-known beauty spots. Dogs on leash permitted. Closed Thu; fee.

KANAPAHA GAZEBO

animals and join in on a cane-grinding session. At **Dudley Farm Historic Site State Park** (352-472-1142; www.floridastateparks.org/dudleyfarm/), 18730 W Newberry Rd, visitors amble through a working 19th-century Florida farm, where park rangers in period costume present ongoing living history demonstrations of sugarcane harvesting and daily farm chores. Farm open Wed–Sun 9–4, grounds 8–5. Guided tours available. Fee.

GREENWAYS The paved **Gainesville-Hawthorne State Trail** (352-336-2135) runs along a 17-mile section of the old railroad line between the two towns, with termini at Bouleware Springs Park in southwest Gainesville and in downtown Hawthorne, and additional parking areas at all major road crossings. Enjoy biking, hiking, or horseback riding along the adjoining grassy strip. Passing through Hampton on US 301, the new **Palatka–Lake Butler State Trail,** when completed, will connect these towns on a ride through rural Putnam and Bradford counties.

NATURE CENTERS ✍ **Bivens Arm** (352-334-2056), 3650 S Main St, Gainesville. Stroll the interpretive paths under shady live oaks along the edge of this marshy extension of Paynes Prairie, a great spot for bird-watching. Daily 9–5; free.

✍ **Morningside Nature Center** (352-334-2170; www.natureoperations.org), 3540 East University Ave. Preserving 278 acres of forest on the eastern edge of Gainesville, the Morningside Nature Center provides a living history farm, interpretive exhibits, and a network of hiking trails through longleaf pine flatwoods and sandhills. Free except during special events. *good birding*

PARKS As befits a large town with a lot of greenery, Gainesville has an extraordinary number of small parks with picnicking, playgrounds, and other fun family activities. One of the more unusual parks in the area is the **Devil's Millhopper Geological State Park** (352-955-2008; www.floridastateparks.org/devilsmillhopper), 4732 Millhopper Rd, where you can walk down 232 steps to the bottom of a 120-foot sinkhole lush with vegetation. At **Bivens Arm Nature Park** (352-334-2056), 3650 S Main St, nature trails and boardwalks circle a willow marsh.

Dogs are welcome to roam off-leash at 🐾 **Squirrel Ridge Park,** 1603 SW Williston Rd, a city park with an open fenced area for dogs to play. For a theme park for your dog, visit 🐾 **Dog Wood Park** (352-335-1919; www.dogwoodpark.com), 5505 SW Archer Rd, where Fido can romp and play across a 15-acre preserve, a true doggy delight with swimming ponds, a walking trail, and doggy playground equipment. Open to nonmembers Sun only; $8.25 for first dog, $2.50 for additional pooches (accompanying human free).

A FEW OF THE 232 STEPS AT DEVIL'S MILL-HOPPER PARK

Sandra Friend

SPRINGS On CR 340 outside High Springs, there are three major parks centered on the region's largest springs. **Blue Springs** (386-454-1369) forms the centerpiece of a county park with picnicking, nature trails, and camping, but most visitors dive and snorkel in the springs. Open 9–7 daily. $10 adults, $3 children 5–12; no pets. Just over the line in neighboring Gilchrist County, **Poe Springs Park** (386-454-1992) is a 197-acre county park with rolling hills and steep bluffs along the Santa Fe River. At nearby **Ginnie Springs** (386-454-7188; www.ginniespringsoutdoors.com), overnight campers can swim in the springs until midnight; it's a mecca for cave divers. Tube and canoe rentals available; open 8–sunset. (See also *Green Space—Springs* in The Lower Suwannnee chapter.)

WATERFALLS Visit **Devil's Millhopper** (see *Parks*) during the rainy season, and you'll see cascades dropping more than 100 feet down the walls of this steep sinkhole, creating an atmosphere much like a tropical rain forest for Florida's southernmost natural waterfall.

WILD PLACES Nowhere else in North Florida can compare to **Paynes Prairie Preserve State Park** (352-466-3397), 100 Savannah Blvd, a 22,000-acre wet prairie defining the southern edge of Gainesville. Herds of bison and wild horses roam the vast open spaces, while alligators collect en masse in La Chua Sink at the north end of the prairie. With more than 20 miles of hiking, biking, and equestrian trails and a beautifully shaded campground, it's one of the best places in the region for wildlife-watching. Open 8–sunset daily; fee.

Enjoy 12 miles of rugged trails through the hills of **San Felasco Hammock Preserve State Park** (386-462-7905) on Millhopper Rd, a lush preserve with Appalachian-like landscapes formed by Florida's limestone karst. Open 9–5 daily; fee.

Conservation areas are some of the wilder spots around the region's lakes, where hikers, bikers, and equestrians can roam miles of old forest roads and developed trails through floodplain forests. Visit **Gum Root Swamp Conservation Area** on FL 26 for a glimpse of Newnans Lake; the **Newnans Lake Conservation Area** (with three tracts: Hatchet Creek, North, and South) off CR 234 and FL 26; and the **Lochloosa Conservation Area,** where you can hike out to an observation platform on Lake Lochloosa from a trailhead adjoining the fire station in Cross Creek. All are managed by the St. Johns Water Management District (386-329-4483; http://sjr.state.fl.us).

✳ Lodging

BED & BREAKFASTS

Gainesville 32601
🐾 ♿ **The Laurel Oak Inn** (352-373-4535; www.laureloakinn.com), 221 SE Seventh St. After two years of renovating this roomy 1885 Queen Anne in Gainesville's historic residential district, Monta and Peggy Burt can be proud of the results—they won the city's top beautification award in 2003. The Laurel Oak Inn is a place to

unwind. Sit on the spacious porches and watch the owls from the comfort of your rocking chair, or enjoy the pampering afforded by the soft robes, fragrant lotions, and candles that accompany your in-room hydro-jet massage tub. It's a hit with honeymoon couples, and business travelers appreciate the DSL Internet access in every room ($90–170). You won't go away hungry, as a steady parade of artfully presented gourmet treats appears on your breakfast plate. A ground-floor room accommodates wheelchairs with an appropriately sized wheel-in shower.

The Magnolia Plantation Inn (1-800-201-2379; www.magnoliabnb .com), 309 SE Seventh St. In 1991 Joe and Cindy Montalto opened the Baird House, an 1885 Victorian, as the first B&B in Gainesville. In addition to the five lavish rooms in the main house, each with private bath ($99–150), their plantation now encompasses six lovingly restored cottages ($185–270) connected by lush, shaded gardens developed by Joe, a landscape architect. Full breakfast served in the Baird House, and wireless Internet is available to all guests.

○○ **Sweetwater Branch Inn** (1-800-595-7760; www.sweetwaterinn .com), 625 E University Ave. Cornelia Holbrook's complex of four historic buildings just outside downtown provides a selection of tastefully themed rooms and the private Honeymoon Cottage, popular with newlyweds who take their vows at McKenzie Hall, the Victorian-style banquet room on site. Sit on the broad, breezy veranda to enjoy complimentary wine and hors d'oeuvres each evening, or stroll the lush gardens and listen to the burble of the fountains. $90–140.

🐾 **Hampton Lake B&B** (1-800-480-4522; www.hamptonlakebb.com), US 301. On Lake Hampton, this massive winged A-frame with a native stone fireplace and pecky cypress walls is the dream home of Freeman and Paula Register; the antique gas pumps were handed down from Grandpa, who was the local Gulf Oil distributor in the 1930s. This is a retreat for those who love the outdoors, with fishing tackle and a pedal boat waiting at the pier, walking trails winding through 18 acres of pines, a porch swing and rockers overlooking the lake, and a hot tub for relaxing after play. Outdoorsy decor accentuates the spacious Wade Room, big enough for an entire family. Four rooms of varying sizes, $80–140. Fisherman's packages available; dinner prepared for an additional fee with notice.

High Springs 32643

○○ Enjoy spacious accommodations in a romantic setting at the **Grady House** (386-454-2206; www.gradyhouse.com), 420 NW First Ave, a charming two-story mansion from 1917 with intimate formal gardens in the backyard. The aroma of home-cooked muffins wafts through the dining room; settle down by the fireplace and read a book. Five rooms, $90–140; or Skeet's Cottage with two bedrooms sleeping four, $190–210 (two-night minimum).

At the **Rustic Inn** (386-454-1223; www.rusticinn.net), 3105 S Main St, Tom and Wendy Solomon offer relaxation in six modern rooms ($79–149) with nature themes, from the Everglades to sea mammals; settle into a rocking chair on the porch or take a lap around the pool on this 7-acre mini ranch. A continental breakfast basket is left at your room each evening so you can set your own pace in the morning.

Micanopy 32667

⊚ **Herlong Mansion** (1-800-HER-LONG; www.herlong.com), 402 NE Cholokka Blvd. When guests come to this neoclassical 1875 mansion, they take to the verandas, where comfortable chairs overlook the expansive lawns. Of the four suites, five rooms, and two private outbuildings, sisters and girlfriends traveling together will especially appreciate Pink's Room, with its two antique cast-iron beds and a daybed; brothers will like the masculine Brothers' Room, with a double bed and a daybed. The mansion features private baths, classy antiques, and original push-button electric switches throughout. For a touch of history, settle back in the Music Room and watch *The Yearling* or any of several other movies filmed in the region. Full breakfasts on weekends; continental breakfasts weekdays; no special orders. No children, no pets, no smoking on premises. $79–249.

HOTELS, MOTELS, AND RESORTS

Gainesville 32601

& **Cabot Lodge** (352-375-2400; www.cabotlodgegainesville.com), 3726 SW 40th Blvd. It's always happy hour at the Cabot Lodge, where guests get cozy in the massive great room, sharing cocktails, snacks, and stories as the sun sets. The large, comfortable rooms ($76–120) ensure a good night's rest, with all the usual amenities.

& **University of Florida Hilton** (352-371-3600; www.ufhilton.com), 1714 SW 34th Place. Top-notch chain hotel with T-1 lines to every room ($169 and up), fitness center, heated

pool and spa; visit Albert's Restaurant for fine dining, American-style, including a Sun brunch with complimentary mimosas. Shuttle provided to airport.

High Springs 32643

🐾 **Cadillac Motel** (386-454-1701), 405 NW Santa Fe Blvd. Built by Dynamite Jones in 1950, this modest family motel has clean, spacious rooms, each with cable TV and coffeemaker; $38–45.

🐾 **High Springs Country Inn** (386-454-1565; www.highsprings.com/cinns/), 520 NW Santa Fe Blvd. This 1960s family-run offering has cute landscaping outside its period rooms ($38 for one bed, $53 for two), which vary in size from small to suite; each is sparkling clean, with small tiled bathroom, fridge, microwave, and cable TV.

CABINS

Cross Creek 32640

Secret River Lodge (352-466-3999), 14531 S CR 325. Tucked behind the Yearling Restaurant (see *Dining Out*), this eclectic collection of restored fish camp cabins on Cross Creek provides a quiet venue for relaxing in a sleepy little town. Each cabin is named for one of Marjorie Kinnan Rawlings's books and varies in amentities from a simple bed and bath ($89) to a two-bedroom cabin with full kitchen ($129).

CAMPGROUNDS

High Springs 32643

⚲ **High Springs Campground** (386-454-1688; www.highspringscampground.com), 24004 NW Old Bellamy Rd, provides camping in a family-oriented atmosphere, with playground, swimming pool, tent sites ($16), and full hook-ups ($22).

River Rise Resort (386-454-7562; www.riverriseresort.com), 252 SE Riverview Circle. With horseback riding, camping, canoeing, swimming, and nearby hiking trails, it's a centrally located mecca for outdoor recreation along the Santa Fe River.

Starke 32091

🐾 **KOA** (904-964-8484; www.starke koa.com), 1475 US 301. Large campground, partially shaded, with exceptional amenities like free wireless Internet and wide, 70-foot pull-through spaces ($30–38). Heated swimming pool, playground, cabins ($42); no tents.

✳ Where to Eat

DINING OUT

Cross Creek

🍴 The **Yearling Restaurant** (352-466-3999), CR 325. A regional favorite since 1952, the Yearling reopened in 2002 under new ownership with the same devotion to quality Cracker fare. Although the outside looks like an old shack along Cross Creek, the main dining area features dark, rich wood and windows on the creek. If you're lucky enough to end up in the overflow section, it's an antiques shop replete with a fishing skiff, booths from the original restaurant, and shelves lined with classic books like the sci-fi thriller *Thuvia, Maid of Mars* by Edgar Rice Burroughs. This is a funky place celebrating the legacy of their neighbor Marjorie Kinnan Rawlings, where you're as likely to rub elbows with the poet laureate of Tennessee as you are with local fishermen. Cheese and crackers kick off each meal, which you can supplement with an appetizer like the large portion of freshly battered fried mush-

rooms. Outstanding "Cross Creek Traditions" ($12–28) include crawdads, alligator, frog legs, venison, soft-shell crab, catfish, and pan-fried quail, as well as a variety of steaks and combination platters. Coated in a light breading, the fresh venison medallions are surprisingly tender and juicy; the stuffed flounder contains a mass of succulent buttery crabmeat. Lighter fare is available between noon and 5 PM on weekends, including a unique "Creek Boy" sandwich served up with your choice of fried shrimp, oyster, or alligator with coleslaw and Jack cheese. For dessert, try the sour orange pie, a tiger-striped creation with the taste of a chocolate orange truffle. Live music Fri and Sat.

Gainesville

Amelia's (352-373-1919; www.afn .org/~links/unionst/amelia), 235 S Main St, Ste 107. Gainesville's top pick for fine Italian cuisine, Amelia's Italian bistro entices you off the street with the aromas of fresh sauces bubbling in the kitchen; entrées $10–15. Open for lunch Thu and Fri, dinner Tue–Sun. Closed Mon.

Dragonfly Sushi & Sake Company (352-371-3359; www.dragonflysushi .com), 201 SE Second Ave, Union Street Station. Purple walls and velvety black and red chairs accentuate the op-art feel of sushi served up by Gainesville's only certified sushi chef. Lunch and dinner sushi served à la carte ($5–10).

Emiliano's Café (352-375-7381), 7 SE First Ave. With a daily selection of Spanish tapas, Cuban and Caribbean sandwiches, and Cuban entrées in a setting with a special Spanish-Caribbean flair, Emiliano's provides Gainesville's best choice for fine Latin cuisine. Lunch ($7–9) served Tue–

Sat; dinner ($12–20) every day but Mon; Sun brunch.

🍴 Winner of numerous awards, **Mildred's Big City Food Café and Wine Bar** (352-371-1711; www .mildredsbigcityfood.com), 3445 W University Ave, is a hot spot for those who love wine, good food, and desserts to die for. Setting a mood with gleaming chrome, dark wood, and snappy 1940s jazz, the New Deal Café (open 11–5, Mon–Sat) provides quick-stop diners with creative quiches, pasta du jour, salads, and sandwiches such as grilled ham and Brie, fried eggplant and prosciutto, and the delicious hummus, which comes loaded with layers of roasted peppers and a black olive tapenade on fresh focaccia (lunch $7–11). Don't walk out without a slice of cake ($5, huge portion). I couldn't resist the chocolate mocha ganache, but it was a tough choice stacked up against a raspberry whipped cream torte, a French silk torte, and the decadent Chocolate Fudge Corruption.

Panache Bistro (352-372-8446), 113 N Main St. Part of The Wine & Cheese Gallery (see *Selective Shopping*), this upscale lunch spot (11–2:15) serves up unusual daily specials, such as the sweet potato quesadilla, a hot blue cheese and green apple sandwich, or the cheeseboard with three cheeses, French loaf, and fruit du jour; lunch offerings $6 and up. For atmosphere, sit out in the shaded patio garden to sip your choice (4 to 10 options daily) from the wine bar. My lunch companions gave the Florida Sunshine Cake "delightful" and "scrumptious" ratings for the orange-rich flavor, delicate frosting, and white chocolate garnishes.

Paramount Grill (352-378-3398), 12 SW First Ave. In this sophisticated downtown, European-style bistro, chef-owner Clif Nelson draws on nearly 20 years of local experience to create provocative fusion food. I enjoyed my chilled cucumber, yogurt, and almond soup du jour and artfully presented salad with four types of farm-fresh berries and baby asparagus over baby greens. Entrées include such creative gems as spicy Thai-style prawns with Asian vegetables, linguine, fresh basil, and coriander; seared garam masala–spiced tuna steak served over green onion hummus with tomato cucumber chutney, grilled papadam, and vindaloo vinaigrette; and pan-roasted prime Angus fillet served over garlic mashed potatoes with Shiitake mushroom sherry wine sauce, poached asparagus, puff pastry, and white truffle oil. Entrées, $15–24 with salads à la carte. Lunch weekdays 11–2, dinner daily; Sun brunch 10–4. Reservations suggested.

EATING OUT

Alachua

🍴 **Conestogas Restaurant** (386-462-1294; www.alachua.com/conestogas), 14920 Main St. Loyal customers just keep filling up the dining room at Conestogas, where they're celebrating more than 15 years in the business. In this unpretentious, Western-themed restaurant, you'll nibble on peanuts while waiting for one of the tender house sirloin steaks ($10–17), marinated in the family's secret marinade recipe. Burgers are the other big thing—fresh handmade burgers ($5–7) cooked the way you want them. The Main Street Monster Burger ($18) challenges *Guinness Book of World Records* appetites with

48 ounces of beef on an extremely oversized bun. Open for lunch and dinner; closed Sun.

Gainesville

Bistro 1245 (352-378-2001; www .bistro1245.com), 706 W University Ave. This tiny speck of a café near the busiest corner in Gainesville serves fabulous lunches in a classy atmosphere. I was impressed by my choice: portobello mushroom with apple jam, smoked Gouda, and red pepper aioli on fresh bread. Sounds odd, but it works! Sandwiches run $6–10, dinner entrées $8–16; wine tastings and live jazz on Fri 5–8; Sun brunch 11–4.

❦ **Book Lovers Café** (1-888-374-0090), 505 NW 13th St. Tucked inside busy Books Inc., the Book Lovers Café serves creative vegetarian and vegan salads and entrées ($6 and up), going well beyond tofu burgers and sprouts. Check the artsy menu board for the day's offerings, which may include gourmet salads such as Thai cucumber, with crunchy fresh cucumbers in rice vinegar, and red beans in walnut sauce, a tasty combination of textures in olive oil. If you can't make up your mind, try the 3 Salad Sampler. Savor a cup of authentic Indian chai, or enjoy freshly squeezed lemonade. Seating is scattered throughout the bookstore, but if you sit near the kitchen, you'll smile at the young chefs singing along to mellow music behind the counter as they prepare your meal. Themed dinners showcase macrobiotic and ethnic foods.

❦ **Burrito Brothers Taco Company** (352-378-5948; www.burritobros .com), 16 NW 13th St. A Swedish chef serves up Mexican take-out, and the burritos are out of this world. The new digs feature a garden patio dining room. It's a popular student stop just off campus with vegetarian and vegan choices; don't miss the excellent fresh guacamole. $3–6; order from the web site—they ship!

❦ **Chop Stix Cafe** (352-367-0003), 3500 SW 13th St. Vietnamese noodle bowls, Thai and Chinese entrées, a sushi bar, and a wide variety of vegetarian choices, all presented in a soothing Asian atmosphere with giant carp and a sweeping view of the alligators cruising Bivens Arm. Fabulous food, fabulous prices—$5–9 covers everything from giant noodle bowls to combination platters. Closed Sun.

Copper Monkey Restaurant & Pub (352-374-4984; www.thecopper monkey.com), 1700 W University Ave, is a popular local hangout with fabulous burgers $6 and up, plus healthier options like salads and veggie sandwiches.

David's Real Pit BBQ (352-373-2002; www.davidsbbq.com), 5121 NW 39th Ave. Cheap, fast, and good: It's not supposed to be possible, but this award-winning barbecue place pulls it off. Plates of barbecued ribs, chicken, beef, turkey, and pork run $9–11, hearty sandwiches $4–5, and you can choose your sauce from the "wall of fire." They even do omelets and pancakes for breakfast, $2–6. The surroundings are nothing fancy, but the food is sublime.

Harvest Thyme Café (352-384-9497), 2 W University Ave. It's somewhere to kick back and read the morning paper while sipping coffee, tea, or chai. Enjoy shakes and smoothies, fresh fruit, sandwiches, soups, salads, and wraps, $6 and up; my fave is 32 South Main, stuffed full of homemade hummus. Open 8–4; the menu is posted on a colorful chalkboard over the kitchen.

I stopped at **The Swamp** (352-377-9267; www.swamprestaurant.com), 1642 W University Ave, between sessions this spring and enjoyed a great lunch with friends in this renovated 1915 professor's home right across from campus. We ordered ahi tuna wontons, Bermuda salad, and my Parmesan-crusted grouper, and everyone went away happy. With a sports bar atmosphere, it's a raucous place, but the meals are great; $8–11.

The Top (352-337-1188), 40 N Main St. Think pop art and paint by number: This place is a step back into the 1970s, with chairs like my 1976 high school cafeteria. But it's a hip young crowd that hangs here, with food to match: I loved the spinach salad with roasted peppers, onions, pecans, goat cheese, and a mango vinaigrette, and the speedy service made it possible to get back to my conference in record time. Lunch $5–7; dinner entrées ($8–13) like pecan-crusted tofu and ginger orange stir-fry show off the chef's creativity.

🍴 **Wise's Drug Store** (352-372-4371), 239 W University Ave. Since 1938, Wise's has had an old-fashioned soda fountain in their drugstore—and they charge less than $1 for a scoop of ice cream! They'll make sundaes,

FLOYD'S DINER

Sandra Friend

shakes, banana splits, and flavored sodas, too. Lunch sandwiches, burgers, and dogs for under $5. Open 8:30–4.

High Springs

Floyd's Diner (386-454-5775; www.floydsdiner.com), 615 Santa Fe Blvd. Gleaming chrome, glass block, classic hot rods, and a neon pink flamingo welcome you to a great diner experience along US 41, where you'll step back into the 1950s and sink your teeth into huge burgers, overflowing salads, and pan-sautéed pastas. There's a dizzying array of menu choices ($5 and up), from a BLT to filet mignon, so I can only say: Explore! And save room for an old-fashioned shake or malted milk. Lunch and dinner 11:30–9 daily.

In the old railroad depot, the **Station Bakery & Café** (386-454-4943), 20 NW Railroad Ave, offers great sandwiches on fresh-baked bread ($2–4), including the classic "fluffernutter," as well as salads, ice cream, and fresh-baked goods. Open for lunch daily.

Micanopy

For flatbread and antipasto, it's worth the drive to **Blue Highway** (352-466-0062), 204 NE US 441, a bistro evoking a French country kitchen with its bold colors and bright local artwork. Their handcrafted pizzas come with creative but sensible combination toppings like Rustica, Greek, and BBQ Chicken, but I love their Blue Highway Salad, crunchy with toasted pecans and feta, the best. Open Tue–Sun for lunch and dinner; $6–12.

Aunt Sherry's chicken salad is the draw for me and my lunch buddies at **Coffee N Cream** (352-466-1101), 201 Cholokka Blvd, where you can sit out on the shaded porch and enjoy the sunshine or plop back into a couch with your coffee cup. Other menu favorites ($5 and up) include the Micanopy Salad and Frito pie. The café is an ice cream parlor and a breakfast/lunch stop that sees me more often than my mother does; open daily.

Old Florida Café (352-466-3663), 203 NE Cholokka Blvd. A funky antiques-shop-cum-lunch-spot under the shade of giant live oaks, the Old Florida Café provides tasty home-made soup, black beans and rice, and chili as well as a gamut of "generous sandwiches," hot Cubans and Reubens, and fabulous thick BLTs ($4 and up). Browse the shelves while waiting for your order, or stake out a place on the front porch and watch the world wander past. Don't miss out on their desserts, especially the piquant McIntosh wild orange pie. Open 11–4; closed Mon.

Pearl Country Store (352-466-4025), US 441 and CR 234. On the outside, it looks like your basic convenience store. Step inside, and you'll be treated to down-home breakfast sandwiches, hotcakes, French toast, and omelets served 6–11 AM, followed by a parade of barbecue ($5 and up): sandwiches, dinner platters, and barbecue-by-the-pound, as well as daily dinner specials. It's all tucked away in David Carr's eclectic country store, where local baked goods, organic veggies, and books on natural Florida share the floor with more traditional convenience store fare. Barbecue served Sun–Thu 11–7, Fri and Sat 11–8.

Starke

Granny's Best (904-964-4678), 200 E Call St, mingles an ice cream parlor with a sandwich shop, offering sweet tea and lemonade, soups and salads, hamburgers and sandwiches, and tasty desserts; daily lunch specials, $2–6.

✳ Selective Shopping

Alachua

Little Hearts Desire (386-462-7706), 14925 Main St. A sweet little shop with local country crafts and ceramics accenting an array of consignment antiques. Closed Sun.

Inside a lovely little pink cottage, **Pink Porch Books** (386-462-9552; www.pinkporchbooks.com), 14720 Main St, boasts more than 7,000 "previously loved books" that'll take you hours to browse. Stop in and sit a spell!

Evinston

Wood & Swink (352-591-1334), 18320 SE CR 225. Built in 1884 of heart pine, this general store and local post office is one of the few remaining historic post offices in the United States, complete with original decorative (and still functional!) postboxes. It's a welcoming place with a jumble of antiques, crafts, groceries, fresh produce, books on local culture and history, and gift items. Stop by and say hello!

Gainesville

Artisans' Guild Gallery at Greenery Square (352-378-1383; www.gainesvilleartisansguild.com), 5402 NW Eighth Ave. It's the place in Gainesville for local art, from colorful textiles to turned wood, art glass, and pottery, in an artists' co-op representing more than local 50 artisans. Open 9–6, Sun noon–5.

Brasington's Adventure Outfitters (1-888-438-4502; www.brasingtons.com), 2331 NW 13th St. If you're headed out to the trail or to one of the pristine nearby rivers, stop in and get outfitted at Brasington's, one of only a handful of outdoor adventure outfitters in Florida where you can pick up backpacking gear. With paddling equipment, camping supplies, technical clothing, and a wide variety of travel and outdoor adventure guides, you'll find everything you need for outdoor recreation in North Florida.

Goerings Book Store (352-378-0363; www.goerings.com), 3433 W University Ave. Truly a bookstore in touch with its town, this well-established independent bookseller offers an interesting intellectual mix of books, from modern fiction and nonfiction to poetry, with an emphasis on Florida authors. Gainesville bestsellers are placed prominently in the front of the store. Grab a coffee and browse Gainesville's most comprehensive newsstand, especially deep in political and spiritual enlightenment magazines. The children's section provides breadth and depth, and features little non-book goodies like science toys and stuffed animals. Several bookcases are devoted to books on

Florida, including an antiquarian section. If you're looking for an offbeat literary or artistic gift, perhaps a calendar by Edward Gorey or a set of magnetic poetry, you'll find it here. A smaller location is on the UF campus at Bageland, 1717 NW First Ave.

Gypsy Palace (352-379-1116), 4000 Newberry Rd. Its gaily painted front will catch your eye as you drive down Newberry Rd, with only a hint of the exotic experience to come. Step into the shop for a true sensory experience, where a cloud of incense accents the Asian music as you browse through Rajasthani pillow covers, carvings of gods and goddesses, and clothing imported from India, Turkey, Morocco, China, and Japan.

Harold's Frames & Gallery (352-375-0260; www.haroldsframes.com), 101 SE Second Place. Showcases stunning images of natural Florida by local photographers, including some of my favorites by John Moran.

Hyde & Zekes (352-376-1687), 1620 W University Ave. A fixture since my college days, Hyde & Zekes helps university students gain a little pocket cash while spreading a wealth of out-of-print music across Gainesville and beyond. If you're looking for small bands and independent labels, this is the place—and yes, they still sell vinyl!

Paddiwhack (386-454-3751; www.paddiwhack.com), 3842 Newberry Rd 1G, next to Talbot's. "Art for Life" is the theme of this most eclectic of art shops, where creativity molds colorful, playful, vibrant pieces ranging from mirrors and wall hangings to large pieces of furniture, each signed by one of the many artists represented.

WOOD & SWINK

Sandra Friend

Still Life in G (352-372-5155), 201 SE Second Ave, Ste 114. Step into this classy art gallery on the Hippodrome Square, featuring both local and national artists, for an eyeful of fine art. Frequent special events including weekly wine-and-cheese do's.

Thornebrook Village (352-378-4949), 2441-6D NW 43rd St. A trendy and popular collection of galleries and boutiques at the north end of Gainesville; my favorite shop in the complex is the **Thornebrook Gallery** (www.thornebrookgallery .com), showcasing the work of fine Florida artists.

Wild Iris Books (352-375-7477; www.wildirisbooks.com), 802 W University Ave. It's loud, it's proud, and it's feminist. The merchandise at Wild Iris runs the gamut from raunchy greeting cards and comics to tomes on Zen Buddhism, Wicca, and artistic inspiration. The back room houses used books, while culturally sensitive children's books rate their own special corner, and the main section contains a special emphasis on strong female voices in fiction and nonfiction.

The Wine & Cheese Gallery (352-372-8446; www.wineandcheese gallery.com), 133 N Main St. More than 4,000 types of wine line the floor-to-ceiling shelves at this 30-year-old fixture in downtown Gainesville, a necessary stop for the discriminating gourmand. In addition to the perfect wine, you'll find imported chocolates, microbrew beers, and a wide array of gourmet food items. Lunch served in their Panache Bistro (see *Dining Out*).

High Springs
In a 1905 home, **Heartstrings** (386-454-4081), 215 N Main St, has a coun-try feel, with room after room of primitives, painted windows, glass and china, and a smattering of gift items.

High Springs Emporium (386-454-8657), 660 NW Santa Fe Blvd. In its new location north of downtown, detached from the rest of the retail district, this shop has a heavy focus on beautiful Asian- and African-import home decor items: sculptures and carvings, jewelry, wall hangings, and trinkets. But the real reason to stop here is to check out their collection of rocks and minerals, with everything from new age quartz points to assemblages of crystals that will impress the most serious mineral collector—as will the owner, who knows her stuff about geology.

High Springs Gallery (386-454-1808; www.highspringsgallery.com), 115 N Main St. Representing works from more than 700 artists (with 30 percent local content), this gallery soars with art with a natural feel, from the playful painted metal flowers and creatures of Sarasota artist Brian Meys to the large amount of art glass on display.

Take the kids to **His & Her Hobby Shop** (386-454-5365), 65 NW First Ave, for a real treat—a huge eight-car slot car track where they can race each other. Their stock also includes model aircraft and model trains, including HO and N track and cars.

Joann's Antiques, Gifts, and Collectibles (386-454-7505), 70 N Main St, intersperses McCoy pottery, classic glass, and Barbie dolls with large items like 1890s cash registers and huge measuring scales.

Main Street Antique Mall (386-454-2700), 10 S Main St, is chock-full of small items like saltcellars, antique glassware, and kitchen items.

Wisteria Cottage (386-454-8447), 225 N Main St. A true period piece, this tin-roofed Cracker home with bead-board walls and ceilings has numerous spacious rooms filled with country crafts and collectibles, a kitchen filled with gourmet foods, and an Americana room.

Micanopy

One of the top antiquing towns in Florida, downtown Micanopy dates back to the 1820s. Enough shops crowd Cholokka Blvd (Micanopy's "Main Street") to allow you to spend the entire day shopping. Some of my favorites include:

O'Brisky Books Inc. (352-466-3910), 112 NE Cholokka Blvd. Bursting with books, O'Brisky deals mostly in used nonfiction and features an excellent Florida section in the front of the store. Bring your want list—I've been surprised at the gems I've discovered in the stacks, and manager Gary Nippes runs a free search service for those tough-to-find items.

The Micanopy Country Store (352-466-05100), 202 Cholokka Blvd. Open daily. Focus on antique glassware, dishes, and bottles, including those elusive milk bottles.

House of Hirsch Too (352-466-3744), 209 Cholokka Blvd. High-end antique furnishings, modern quilts, and home decor items.

The Garage at Micanopy, Inc. (352-288-8485), 212 Cholokka Blvd. Fun ephemera fills the booths in this 1920s garage, from figurines and postcards to toys and glassware at reasonable prices.

I've picked up many a gift at the **Shady Oak Gallery & Art Glass Studio** (352-466-3476; www.shady oak.com), 201 Cholokka Blvd, where in addition to selling the whimsical creations of local artists, they teach hands-on art glass courses at very reasonable prices. Check their web site for full details.

The Shop (352-466-4031), 210 Cholokka Blvd. Every nook and cranny brims with botanical gifts in this garden-themed shop, where you'll also find crafts, antique glassware and furnishings, and quilts. Closed Tue.

Treasured Collection by Macy (352-466-8000), 190 Cholokka Blvd. Macy's salute to Victoriana includes flower-topped women's hats, original art and prints, and a secret garden behind the store.

Smiley's Antique Mall (352-466-0707; www.smileysantiques.com), CR 234 and I-75 (Micanopy exit). With more than 200 booths, this mini mall of antiques will keep you browsing for hours. Open daily 9–6.

Starke

When I was a kid, US 301 was Main Street for tourists headed down to Central Florida, and the shops and attractions along the way were geared to wide-eyed northerners. Signs proclaimed RARE 16 FOOT ALBINO ALLIGATOR!, SEE THE WALKING CATFISH!, and FREE ORANGE JUICE! Most of those old-time tourist traps (and I say that with affection) are now gone, but the stretch of US 301 north from Starke to Lawtey hosts a few hangers-on. At **Textile Town** (904-964-4250), housed in an old Stuckey's, you can nab chenille bedspreads, towels by the pound, and T-shirts at three for $10. With its giant tepee out front, the **Silver Lining American Indian Trading Post** (904-964-5448) has Native American crafts, moccasins, antiques, and turquoise jewelry. And a former Horne's restaurant hosts **Florida Souvenir Land,** with pecans and candies, T-shirts and towels, and all sorts of ticky-tacky ephemera that the kids will love.

Scarlett's Custom Framing and Gallery (904-964-9353), 139 E Call St, deals in antique advertising and sheet music, as well as a fine selection of quilts. Open Thu–Sat.

Packed full of antique bargains, **Sister's Antiques & Gifts** (904-368-0846), 301 E Call St, opens after school each weekday and on Sat.

Waldo
Waldo Antique Village (352-468-3111), US 301. Adjoining the flea market, this big barn full of antiques has been around for more than 20 years—the large farm implements outside are just a sample of the primitives and country items you'll find here. Open daily.

Waldo Farmer's and Flea Market (352-468-2255), US 301. The reason to stop in Waldo: a sprawling complex of more than 800 vendors across 40 acres on both sides of the highway, showcasing the best produce that North Florida has to offer. Sat and Sun 7–4.

FARMER'S MARKETS, PRODUCE STANDS, AND U-PICK One thing the Gainesville area is known for is blueberries. I have friends who make their annual pilgrimages every May to pick their own at farms totaling more than 700 acres of these tasty natural treats. Much of this area is rural, so you'll often see farmers selling fruits and vegetables in-season at temporary stands and off the backs of their trucks.

Earlton
Growing their blueberries the organic way, **Berry Bay Farm** (352-468-2205), 20256 NE 114th Ave (CR 1469), is open for U-pick and pre-picked blueberries from mid-May through mid-June; call for directions.

Gainesville
Alachua County Farmer's Market (352-371-8236), 5920 NW 13th St, corner of US 441 and FL 121. Fresh produce from local farmers, Sat 8:30–1.

Downtown Farmer's Market (352-334-7175). Fruits and plants, vegetables and fruits—bountiful local produce stacked up at the corner of SE First St and University Ave. Wed 4–6:30 PM.

Union Street Farmer's Market (352-462-3192), downtown at the Hippodrome. Local produce, baked goods, candles, plants, and live acoustic music. Wed 4–7:30 PM.

Hawthorne
Brown's Farm (352-475-2015), FL 26 east of US 301. A permanent roadside stand selling straight from the farm; stop in for fresh honey, veggies, and fruits, including strawberries, peaches, and onions in-season.

WALDO ANTIQUE VILLAGE

Sandra Friend

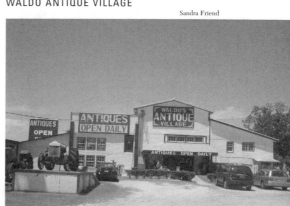

High Springs

High Springs Farmer's Market, next to the railroad tracks, downtown, has local vendors with seasonal fresh produce. Thu 4–7 PM.

Starke

In addition to the **Starke State Farmers' Market,** 2222 North Temple Hwy (US 301), and **Wainwright's Pecans, Produce, and Seafood** (904-964-5811), 302 N Temple Hwy, the bountiful produce of Bradford County (well known for its excellent strawberries) fills fruit and vegetable stands all along US 301 from Starke north to Lawtey. Some are permanent locations, like **Kings Kountry Produce** (904-964-2552), 18079 US 301 N, open daily, and **Norman's Roadside Market** (904-964-9152), US 301; others are transient stands that show up during the growing season.

✳ Entertainment

Gainesville

Check with the **Gainesville Cultural Affairs Office** (352-333-ARTS; www.gvlculturalaffairs.com) for their latest slate of **free public concerts** down-town on Fri night, presented year-round. Since this is a university town, the place to see and be seen is downtown, of course, on the patio bars and cafés surrounding Sun Center and the **Hippodrome State Theater** (352-373-5968), 25 SE Second Pl, where vibrant live productions take the stage. For those into student-driven nightlife, nightclubs line Main and University.

Dance aficionados enjoy the **Gainesville Ballet Theatre** (352-372-9898; www.gainesvilleballettheatre.org), 1501 NW 16th Ave, a 30-year-old nonprofit regional ballet company. **Dance Alive!** (352-371-2986; www.dancealive.org), 1325 NW Second St, presents modern works and classic ballet as the State Touring Company of Florida. After 20 years, the **Gainesville Chamber Orchestra** (352-336-5448), performing at a variety of venues around the city, continues to delight its fans. One of those venues, the **Philips Center for the Performing Arts** (352-392-2787), 315 Hull Rd, can be counted on for a wide variety of shows.

High Springs

The Priest Theater (386-454-SHOW), 15 NW First St, is Florida's oldest movie theater, built in 1926 as a minstrel and vaudeville venue. Movies are shown here on vintage X-16 projectors from the 1940s, on Mon, Fri, and Sat evenings for $2 and up.

✳ Special Events

February: ♦ **Hoggtown Medieval Faire** (352-334-ARTS), at the Alachua County Fairgrounds, 39th Ave, Gainesville. The largest and longest-running (21 years in 2007) Renaissance Faire in Florida, the

THE HIPPODROME STATE THEATER

Sandra Friend

Hoggtown Medieval Faire spans two weekends each February with active participation by the Society for Creative Anachronism, a playful bunch that usually keep their events off-limits to the public. At Hoggtown more than a third of the crowd dresses in medieval drag; it's a place to get in touch with your inner knight (or princess), where wandering minstrels strum on mandolins; fairies, dwarves, and witches roam the streets; and the vendors take "Lady Visa and Master Card." Kids will have a blast with street theater, magic shows, medieval carnival games, and manually powered amusement rides you won't see anywhere else, like the Barrel of Bedlam and the Hippogriff. Vendors include an alchemist with real charms, tarot readers and other mediums, and artisans crafting in fiber, wood, and wax. Even the food court is a little different: You'll see knights fresh off the battlefield toasting each other with cobalt bottles of frothing cherry ale. Daily events include jousting, live chess battles, and the court processional through the streets of Hoggtown. Fee.

March: **Spring Garden Festival, Kanapaha Botanical Gardens** (see the Botanical Gardens sidebar), Gainesville. A weekend's worth of gardening tips, landscaping tricks, and environmental awareness set in the beauty of this region's largest garden.

April: ✿ **Farm & Forest Festival, Morningside Nature Center** (see *Green Space—Nature Centers*), Gainesville, features cane grinding and other pioneer crafts, displays of fire engines, and hands-on activities for the kids.

May: **High Springs Pioneer Days** (386-454-3120; www.highsprings .com). Annual celebration of local history, arts and crafts, held the first weekend of the month.

Commemorate a noble vegetable at the **Windsor Zucchini Festival,** second weekend, Windsor.

June: **Yulee Day,** Archer, second Sat. Celebrating the birthday of David Levy Yulee, Florida's first U.S. senator and founder of the Florida Railroad, the town that was his home hosts exhibits, crafts, and vendors at the historic railroad depot.

October: Drift into the **Florida Butterfly Festival,** Florida Museum of Natural History (see *To See—Museums*), second weekend, for live native butterfly exhibits, a photography contest, lectures, field trips, and on-site vendors.

November: **Alachua County Fair** (352-372-1537; www.alachuacounty fair.org), first week, at the fairgrounds on 39th Ave, Gainesville. A traditional county fair attracting farmers from around the region, showing off their cattle, chickens, vegetables, and more in friendly competition. Top country music acts and exhibitions from vendors; fee.

Micanopy Fall Harvest Festival (352-466-7026; www.afn.org/~mica fest), Micanopy. Since 1973, this celebration of harvesttime brings together artisans, craftspeople, and musicians with more than 200 display booths throughout town.

THE LOWER SUWANNEE

PURE WATER WILDERNESS: DIXIE, GILCHRIST, AND LEVY COUNTIES

I f you've come to Florida for peace and quiet, you'll find it "way down upon the Suwannee River" in the Pure Water Wilderness, a region known best for its rivers, springs, and estuaries, part of the laid-back western shore of Florida known as the "Nature Coast." Settlers trickled into the region in the 1850s when state senator David Levy Yulee (son of Moses Levy, founder of Levy County) ran his Florida Railroad from Fernandina Beach to **Cedar Key,** providing the first shipping link across Florida. In 1867 naturalist John Muir followed the path of the Florida Railroad on his 1,000-mile walk to the Gulf of Mexico. Arriving at the Cedar Keys, he fell ill with malaria and spent several months living in the village, which had a booming pencil industry. The fine southern red cedars and white cedars growing on scattered islands throughout the Gulf made the perfect housing for pencil leads. The original settlement on Atsena Otie Key included several houses and the Eberhard Faber Pencil Mill. After the island was devastated by a tidal surge in 1896, business shifted to Depot Key, today's downtown Cedar Key.

Cedar Key sits between the mouth of the Withlacoochee River, on which the towns of **Yankeetown** and **Inglis** sprang up, and the mouth of the Suwannee River, home to the fishing village of **Suwannee.** The railroad line (now the Nature Coast State Trail, a rail-trail) connected Fanning Springs, where Fort Fannin was built along the river in 1838 as part of a chain of forts during the Seminole Wars, with the turpentine and lumber towns of **Old Town** and **Cross City.** On the southern shore of the Steinhatchee River, the fishing village of **Jena** grew up around the abundant mullet and crab, with packing houses shipping out seafood to distant ports.

CEDAR KEY

Sandra Friend

Dixie County boasts the lowest per-capita population in the state, and Gilchrist County has only a single traffic light, at the crossroads in the county seat of **Trenton.** Sleepy riverside hamlets and end-of-the-road fishing villages provide a natural charm found only in rural Florida.

GUIDANCE **Pure Water Wilderness** (352-486-5470; www.purewaterwilderness .com), P.O. Box 779, Cedar Key 32625, is the primary contact for the region, which comprises six distinct chambers of commerce.

GETTING THERE *By air:* Gainesville (see the Alachua and the Historic Lake District chapter) provides the only "nearby" commuter access, an hour or more from most points on the Nature Coast.

By bus: **Greyhound** stops along US 19 in Cross City and Chiefland.

By car: Alt US 27, US 129, US 27, and US 19 are the major north–south routes through this trio of rural counties. To reach them from I-75, use US 27 from Ocala or High Springs, or FL 24 or FL 26 west out of Gainesville.

MEDICAL EMERGENCIES Serious emergencies should be deferred to **Seven Rivers Community Hospital** (352-795-6560), 6201 N Suncoast Blvd in Crystal River (10 miles south of Levy County on US 19) or to Gainesville (see the Alachua and the Historic Lake District chapter), 40 miles east; call 911. For lesser problems, contact the **Cedar Key Health Clinic** (352-543-5132) or the **Nature Coast Regional Hospital** (352-528-2801), US 41, Williston.

Important: In these rural counties, cell phone coverage is sporadic to nonexistent, depending on your carrier.

✳ To See

ARCHEOLOGICAL SITES At the end of CR 347 in the **Shell Mound Unit** of Lower Suwannee NWR (see *Green Space—Wild Places*), a short trail takes you to the most significant archeological feature in this region, a 28-foot-tall shell midden created between 2500 B.C. and A.D. 1000 by the ancestors of the Timucua who once inhabited this coastline. Just off CR 351 at Old Railroad Grade in Dixie County, the **Garden Patch Archeological Site** at Horseshoe Beach has several burial and ceremonial mounds and two large middens.

ESTUARINE CREEK NEAR SHELL MOUND
Sandra Friend

HISTORIC SITES **Atsena Otie Key,** abandoned by most of its settlers after an 1896 hurricane-driven storm surge, is now part of the Cedar Key NWR (see *Green Space—Wild Places*), only accessible by boat (see *Ecotours* and *Paddling* under *To Do*). Buried under cover of maritime hammock along the short hiking trail from the dock are reminders that this was the original town of Cedar Key. Bricks scattered around a deep hole are all that's left of the Eberhard Faber Pencil Mill. The deep hole contained the machinery of the mill, driven by water flowing through a sluice. Workers sawed cedars into the small slats required for making pencils. In an ironic twist of nature, a grand cedar now crowns the spot. The trail ends at the town's cemetery, set on a bluff overlooking the salt marshes. The marble tombstones date back to 1882, some fallen, some as clean as the day they were erected. A wrought-iron fence cordons off one tiny corner, a private family plot under the windswept oaks. **Seahorse Key,** part of the island chain, has a small cemetery with Union soldiers who died while occupying the **Seahorse Key Lighthouse,** which can be visited on open-house days during the fall seafood festival (see *Special Events*).

In Fanning Springs work is under way to reconstruct **Fort Fannin** on its original site just north of US 19. Back in 1838, U.S. Army troops built and manned a small wooden fortress at the river crossing, Palmetto, as part of a string of defenses during the Second Seminole War. Renamed Fort Fannin in honor of Colonel Alexander Fannin, the name became corrupted over time to Fanning. As the war raged on and Fannin attempted to round up Seminoles for deportation to the West, the garrison grew from a dozen men to nearly 200 in 1843. Yellow fever ravaged the troops. Abandoned in 1849, the remains of the fort vanished back into the forest.

MUSEUMS

Cedar Key

Cedar Key Historical Society Museum (352-543-5549), 609 Second St. Exhibits and artifacts trace the history of this coastal town from its founding through Civil War occupation, the rise and fall of the pencil industry, and current advances in aquaculture; an excellent resource for researchers and amateur historians in understanding Florida's Gulf Coast. Open Mon–Sat and holidays 11–4, Sun 1–4; donation.

Cedar Key Museum Historic State Park (352-543-5340; www.floridastate parks.org/cedarkeymuseum). Follow the signs out through the residential area to this large compound established in 1962 as the first museum to capture Cedar Key's long history as presented by St. Clair Whitman, a colorful local man who started his own personal museum of artifacts and seashells. Whitman's house is under restoration on the property; a small trail leads along the edge of the estuary. Closed Mon and Tue; fee.

Levyville

& Amid the farms and fields of Levy County, quilting is one of the favored pastimes. At the **Levy County Quilt Museum** (352-493-2801), 11050 NW 10th Ave, quilters come together to perfect their craft. The modern log structure contains plenty of space for active quilting while displaying prizewinning quilts (and other related handicrafts) around the rooms.

RAILROADIANA Although the railroad no longer carries cypress logs through Bell, the **historic train depot** (circa 1905) along US 129 now houses the town hall. On US 19 in Cross City, the old **railway freight station** sits along the rail-trail near Barber Ave; you'll find the **Chiefland railway depot** undergoing restoration at the southern terminus of the Nature Coast Trail (see *Green Space —Greenways*). At Cedar Key the **depot** marking the historic western terminus of the Florida Railroad is still on Railroad St, but the trestle leading to the coast has been obliterated by condos. South on US 19, watch for "3 Spot," a **steam engine circa 1915** in a small wayside park just north of the blinker at Gulf Hammock. One of the few pieces of original rolling stock displayed in Florida, it pulled logging cars to the Patterson-McInnes sawmill.

WINERY ♿ **Dakotah Winery & Vineyards** (352-493-9309; www.dakotah winery.com), 14365 NW US 19, Chiefland. Established in 1985, this premier Florida winery features wines and other products produced from cultivated muscadine grapes. It's a unique place with a touch of the romantic: Antique windmills stand tall over the vineyard, and visitors relax under an arbor overlooking the vines and a duck pond. Inside the tasting room, owner Rob Rittgers buzzes around, answering questions and pouring wine for each new group of guests. Art fills the spacious room, from hand-painted wine bottles with Florida scenes to woodcraft, paintings, quilts, and sketches by local artists. Mon–Sat 10–5, Sun noon–5.

✳ To Do

BICYCLING On the **Nature Coast Trail** (see *Green Space—Greenways*), enjoy a 32-mile paved bike path connecting the communities of the Lower Suwannee. Mountain bikers frequent the trail system at **Manatee Springs State Park** (see *Green Space—Springs*).

BIRDING You'll always see pelicans at the **Cedar Key dock,** but don't miss the Pelican Man, who tosses fish to a crowd of pelicans every evening. At **Cedar Key NWR** (see *Green Space —Wild Places*), each island has colonial bird rookeries and beautiful beaches; beware of the high snake population in forested areas. Seahorse Key is off-limits to all visitors Mar–June due to its fragile pelican rookery. **Lower Suwannee NWR** (see *Green Space—Wild Places*) offers great birding opportunities along the trails at the Shell Island Unit, where you'll see Louisiana

GULF HAMMOCK
Sandra Friend

herons, willets, and other wading birds in shallow saline ponds near Dennis Creek, and belted kingfishers along the hammocks. In spring follow the Road to Nowhere (see the sidebar of the same name) through the **Jena Unit of Big Bend WMA,** and take the side roads (if wet, only navigable by four-wheel drive or on foot) west to the Gulf hammocks to see seaside sparrows, clouds of migratory birds (from robins to vireos and warblers), and nesting pairs of black rails. At any time, you'll see wading birds roadside in the salt marshes.

BOATING For a map of **boat ramps along the Suwannee River,** contact the Suwannee River Water Management District (386-362-1001); one of the easiest to access is off US 19-98 at the Gilchrist-Dixie county line. Recreational boaters enjoy playing on a segment of the **Cross Florida Barge Canal** accessed at Inglis, off US 19. In **Cedar Key** parking gets tight around the public marina (downtown) on weekend mornings. **Island Hopper Tours** (352-543-5904; www .cedarkeyislandhopper.com), City Marina, rents boats and provides guided tours and drop-offs (see *Ecotours*) on the Gulf of Mexico. At **Suwannee** several marinas provide access to the Suwannee River and the Gulf of Mexico.

DIVING Scuba divers have several unique venues to try out their skills. At **Devil's Den** near Williston (see *Lodging*), a shimmering pool of 72-degree ice-blue water fills an ancient cave. As you descend stone steps to access the open water underground, a chandelier of ivy dangles down through the sinkhole, with rays of sunlight filtering through the opening. It's a surreal and beautiful scene. Divers delight in discovering prehistoric fossils on the limestone bottom. Dive fee $27, additional $10 for night dives, gear rental $62 (includes dive fee). Cave certification not required. Full dive shop and instruction on site. At nearby **Blue Grotto** (352-528-5770; www.divebluegrotto.com), 3852 NE 172nd Court, cave-certified divers can descend up to 100 feet into the Floridan Aquifer, dropping down into a cave system from the bottom of a sinkhole; dive shop with rentals on site. The many **springs of the Suwannee River** are open to open-water diving, but only cave-certified divers should venture *into* the crevices from which the waters pour. Wreck diving is a popular pastime, as divers can visit sunken steamboats such as the *City of Hawkinsville,* the very last of the Suwannee River steamboats, sunk just south of Fanning Springs in 1922. It's a designated underwater archeological preserve. For support, check with **Suwannee River Scuba** (352-463-7111), 17950 NW 90th Court, for guided trips, cold air, rentals, and instruction.

ECOTOURS **Island Hopper Tours** (see *Boating*). Catch a ride out to the outer islands of the Cedar Keys with

ENTERING THE DEVIL'S DEN

Sandra Friend

the Island Hopper, offering island drop-offs (perfect for exploring Atsena Otie or Seahorse Key), one-hour scenic cruises, and sunset cruises. $12 adults, $6 children under 12.

🐾 **Lady Pirate Boat Tours** (352-543-5141), Slip 16, City Marina. Take the 22-foot pontoon on any of several tour options—bird-watching, sand dollar collecting, sunset trips, or island drop-offs. $12 adults, $6 children.

Nature Coast Expeditions (352-543-6463) runs photographers' field trips along the Suwannee River and the Cedar Keys; enjoy an afternoon with a professional guide for $75 for up to three people.

Visit Florida

FRESHWATER FISHING

Paddle with Brack Barker at **Wild Florida Adventures** (1-877-WILD-WAV; www.wild-florida.com), where you'll explore the estuaries at a leisurely pace; destinations include Cedar Key, Steinhatchee, Waccassa, and Suwannee, and half-day tours ($50) include a gourmet picnic.

FISHING For recommended **fishing guides and charters in Cedar Key,** check with the Cedar Key Chamber of Commerce (see *Guidance*). Bait and tackle are available at **Fishbonz** (352-543-9222) in Cedar Key. In Suwannee the full-service **Suwannee Marina** (352-542-9159), 219 Canal St, has a boat ramp, charters, dry dock, gasoline, bait and tackle, and mechanics on site. At Inglis, **Lake Rousseau** is a hot spot for bass anglers; check in at the fish camps (see *Lodging—Fish Camps*) along CR 40 for guides.

HIKING Hiking in the region is limited to short day hikes leading out to scenic points along the Suwannee River and the Gulf estuaries, mainly in the **Lower Suwannee National Wildlife Refuge** (see *Green Space—Wild Places*) and state parks; I especially enjoy the nature trails at Manatee Springs State Park (see *Green Space—Springs*). At **Andrews Wildlife Management Area** (see *Green Space—Wild Places*), trails lead past state and national grand champion trees.

HOUSEBOATING

Visit Florida

HOUSEBOATING **Miller's Suwannee Houseboats** (352-542-7349 or 1-800-458-BOAT; www.suwanneehouseboats.com), CR 349, Suwannee, rents houseboats for cruises up the 70-mile meander of the Suwannee River from Suwannee to Fanning Springs—head

out for an overnight, a few days, or a week. You have all the amenities of home, minus the yard, as you drift past shorelines crowded with red maple and sweetgum, and sight a manatee or two. Rates vary by season and number of days, starting at $400 for two days and going up to $1,300 for a week; special deals for active military personnel on leave.

HUNTING Off US 19 in Fanning Springs, **Andrews Wildlife Management Area** (386-758-0531) is a popular fall hunting ground for deer and wild hogs.

PADDLING Freshwater paddlers have numerous **launch points into the Suwannee River;** contact the Suwannee River Water Management District (386-362-1001) for a map. There are **canoe liveries** at Manatee Springs State Park, Fanning Springs State Park, and Hart Springs Park (see *Green Space— Springs*), and rentals are available at some of the riverside campgrounds, such as Big Oaks River Resort (see *Lodging—Campgrounds*).

Outfitters with rentals for exploration of the Cedar Keys include **Fishbonz** (352-543-9922) and **Nature Coast Expeditions** (352-543-6463). From Cedar Key, you can launch into numerous wilderness waterways; see *Green Space—Wild Places* for details. With or without a guide, there are hundreds of miles of saltwater passageways to explore. The southern terminus of Florida's longest and most rugged sea kayaking route, the 91-mile **Historic Big Bend Saltwater Paddling Trail,** is the town of Suwannee. From there, you follow the coastline north along the Big Bend Aquatic Preserve, with stops at Shired Island, Horseshoe Beach, and Sink Creek before reaching Steinhatchee to begin rounding the Big Bend (see The Big Bend chapter). This is a vast wilderness area, so don't set out unless you have appropriate maps and navigational aids, camping gear, and an adequate supply of fresh water and food. Obtain information about the trail from the Office of Greenways and Trails (850-488-3701), 325 John Knox Rd, Bldg 500, Tallahassee 32303. For a gentler immersion in this part of the Gulf estuary, head down the Road to Nowhere (see the sidebar of the same name) and put your kayak in at the **Cow Creek Bridge,** where a maze of estuarine waterways cuts through the plain of black needlerush out to the Gulf. Similarly, you can launch into the creeks off the **Dixie Mainline Trail** (see *Scenic Drives*), but be sure you find somewhere to park that isn't blocking the road. On a day trip into the estuary, consider carrying a GPS, and make sure you mark a waypoint at your car so you can find it again.

MANATEE SPRINGS STATE PARK

Sandra Friend

THE ROAD TO NOWHERE Imagine, if you will, a lengthy paved road in the wildest and most inaccessible portion of a generally wild and inaccessible part of Florida, ending abruptly in the salt marshes of the Big Bend Aquatic Preserve: the **Road to Nowhere.** This highway didn't access a single home or a fishing pier: It was a clandestine airstrip. During the 1970s and 1980s, smugglers landed planes as big as a DC-9 on this highway to drop off loads of marijuana destined for points north. After the operation was shut down by law enforcement, a legacy remains—a ribbon of pavement with unparalleled views of the salt marshes, now used by anglers and paddlers, bikers and birders. One warning: If you drive down the Road to Nowhere, there are two short unpaved sections. Don't go too fast on the second one, or you'll miss the end of the road and end up in the salt marsh! The Road to Nowhere runs through the Jena WMA (see *Green Space—Wild Places*) and is most easily accessed from CR 358 from the Steinhatchee Bridge (see The Big Bend chapter).

THE VIEW FROM THE ROAD TO NOWHERE

Sandra Friend

SCALLOPING Charters run from **Gulfstream Marina** (352-498-8088; www.gulf-streammotelmarina.com), CR 358 in Jena, where they'll be happy to set you up with a captain who knows the prime scalloping grounds. See The Big Bend chapter for more details on this unique take on fishing in the Gulf of Mexico.

SCENIC DRIVES Showcasing the remote southern fringe of Dixie County in Lower Suwannee Wildlife Refuge, the **Dixie Mainline Trail** is a one-of-a-kind scenic drive, a 9-mile one-lane hard-packed limestone road through the wilds of

Sandra Friend

ALONG THE DIXIE MAINLINE TRAIL

the cypress-and-gum floodplain of the California Swamp, with one short stop at Salt Creek for a walk out on a boardwalk. Don't expect to drive more than 20 mph, and watch for oncoming traffic. There are pull-offs every mile to allow vehicles to pass. Check with the refuge before utilizing the drive to ensure it's not flooded.

SKYDIVING At **Skydive Williston** (352-528-2994; www.skydivewilliston .com), US 41 just south of Williston, you can tandem jump with profession-al, USPA-certified instructors as you learn to skydive.

SWIMMING For refreshing plunges into cool, fresh water, try the swimming area at **Fanning Springs State Park** and the open springs at **Hart Springs** and **Blue Spring** (see *Green Space—Springs*). At **Cedar Key City Park,** a small waterfront park adjacent to the City Marina provides the village's only public beach on the Gulf of Mexico; several motels have their own private beaches, but the best ones are found on the outer islands, accessed only by boat. Shallow Gulf waters invite at **Shired Island** and **Horseshoe Beach.**

TRAIL RIDING **Goethe State Forest** (see *Green Space—Wild Places*) is a favorite, with more than 100 miles of equestrian trails. Look for trailheads at Black Prong, Apex, and Tidewater along CR 336. Equestrians can also parallel the paved **Nature Coast Trail** (see *Green Space—Greenways*).

WALKING TOURS Stop in at the Cedar Key Historical Society Museum (see *To See—Museums*) for the **official walking tour of Cedar Key,** which leads you past sites in the old town and explains the history of the outlying islands.

✳ Green Space

GREENWAYS From its start in Dixie County at Cross City, the 32-mile **Nature Coast Trail** (352-493-6072) forks in Fanning Springs. One prong heads east to Trenton, ending at the historic train depot; the other heads south to end at the Chiefland railroad depot. Equestrians may use the grassy strip parallel to the paved biking trail.

FANNING SPRINGS STATE PARK

Sandra Friend

SPRINGS There's a big reason they call this the Pure Water Wilderness. Fresh water abounds! Large public springs accessible by road include **Poe Springs Park** (386-454-1992), a 197-acre county park with rolling hills and steep bluffs along the Santa Fe River, and **Ginnie Springs** (386-454-7188; www.ginnie springsoutdoors.com), a 200-acre park that's a mecca for cave divers. Open eight AM–sunset; canoe and tube rentals available. **Hart Springs** at Hart Springs Park (352-463-3444), 4240 SW 86th Ave, is a Gilchrist County park with swimming, hiking, and camping; the crystalline spring pours out 62 million gallons each day. **Fanning Springs** at Fanning Springs State Park (352-463-3420), US 19-27, has a well-developed swimming area and canoe rentals. **Manatee Springs** at Manatee Springs State Park (352-493-6072), NW 115th St, outside Chiefland, has swimming, boating, fishing, hiking and biking trails, and a large campground. At the end of CR 339A off Alt US 27 between Bronson and Chiefland, **Blue Spring** at Devil's Hammock Park creates a natural 72-degree pool as it feeds the Waccasassa River. Spend an afternoon picnicking under the shady oaks at this Levy County park. Fee for all but Blue Spring; contact the Suwannee River Water Management District for a map of spring locations in the Suwannee River for additional diving and swimming choices.

WILD PLACES Encompassing more than 40,000 acres, the **Lower Suwannee National Wildlife Refuge** (352-493-0238), 16450 NW 31st Place, protects the floodplain of the Suwannee River as it reaches the Gulf of Mexico. Most of it is inaccessible except by boat, although there are short hiking trails at Shell Mound and the park headquarters. In Fanning Springs, **Andrews Wildlife Management Area** (386-758-0531) off US 27 is notable for the number of national and state champion trees in its dark riverside forests, reached by dirt roads and short hiking trails.

HART SPRINGS PARK

Sandra Friend

Near Blue Spring, **Devil's Hammock WMA** off Alt US 27 is crisscrossed with old logging roads usable for hiking, biking, and horseback riding; be mindful of hunting season for your own safety.

Extending through most of southern Levy County, **Goethe State Forest** (352-447-2202), 8250 SE CR 336, has three large tracts for recreation and a new visitors center, plus a showcase cypress tree at Big Cypress.

At **Cedar Key Scrub State Reserve** (386-758-0531) off FL 24, hikers meander through a coastal scrub, rare in this wetland region.

Hunters make more use of **Jena WMA,** a massive preserve along the Road to Nowhere (see the sidebar of the same name), where rugged side roads reach pristine beaches along the grassy shores of the Gulf estuary.

Boaters and paddlers have an extensive watery wilderness to explore. In addition to the backwaters of the Lower Suwannee NWR and the 90-mile **Big Bend Aquatic Preserve** to the north of Suwannee (see *To Do—Paddling*), they can visit the islands making up **Cedar Key National Wildlife Refuge** (352-493-0238), off Cedar Key. And at Waccasassa Bay State Preserve (352-493-0238), 31,000 acres between Cedar Key and Yankeetown, boaters have the place all to themselves—it's a wet wilderness suitable for paddling and fishing, with primitive campsites available to paddlers.

✳ Lodging

BED & BREAKFASTS

Cedar Key 32625
Cedar Key Bed & Breakfast (352-543-9000 or 1-877-543-5051; www
.cedarkeybandb.com), corner of Third and F streets, P.O. Box 701. Innkeepers Bill and Alice Philips take you back to Cedar Key's heyday as an exporter of fine cedar for buildings and pencils. Built in 1880, this home was used as a boardinghouse by the daughter of one of Florida's first senators, David Levy Yulee. Within an easy walk of shopping and the docks, it's an ideal place to unwind under the paddle fans with a good book. Five romantic rooms and a Honeymoon Cottage, each decked out with period antiques, $105–210.

Island Hotel (352-543-5111 or 1-800-432-4640; www.islandhotel-cedar key.com), Second and B streets. Don't look for right angles in this historic tabby-and-oak hotel, built just before the Civil War—it's the place in town to sleep with history. Each room ($80–135) has a private bath; full breakfast in the restaurant downstairs is included with your stay.

Inglis 34449
Pine Lodge Country Lodge (352-447-7463; www.pinelodgefla.com), 649 CR 40 W. Enjoy lazy days and quiet nights amid romantic Victorian decor ($89–129) in Old Crackertown. A beautiful sunset is just steps away on the antique porch rockers, and a hearty country breakfast awaits you in the morning. Elvis fans will appreciate being immersed in part of the set of *Follow That Dream*, which was filmed along this highway out to the Gulf.

Morriston 32688
The Bayer's Lair Bed, Barn, and Breakfast (352-486-4314; www
.thebayerslair.com), 11751 SE 16th Ln. Hitch up that horse trailer and head for the hills near Goethe State Forest (see *Green Space—Wild Places*), where more than 100 miles of equestrian trails await. The Bayers offer a

ISLAND HOTEL

Sandra Friend

pleasant room, suite, and studio ($30–70), each with private bath, coffeemaker, microwave, toaster oven, and compact fridge. Guests pay an extra $10 a night for stall space and turnout for each horse. No horse? No problem! You'll still enjoy this off-the-beaten path retreat.

Williston 32696

The Ivy House (352-528-5410), 108 NW Main St. Built by the founder of Williston, the Ivy House once served as a hospital. You wouldn't guess that today by the broad parlor filled with Victorian furnishings, nor by the three bedrooms (Blue Willow, Rose, and Wisteria, $95), each bed piled with pillows, each room with private bath. With breakfasts prepared by the kitchen staff of the adjoining fine-dining Ivy House restaurant (see *Dining Out*), you'll be in the lap of luxury.

HOTELS, MOTELS, AND RESORTS

Bronson 32621

❅ A haven for horse lovers, **Black Prong Equestrian Center** (352-486-1234; www.blackprong.com), 450 SE CR 337, is surrounded by Goethe State Forest (see *Green Space—Wild Places*). In addition to being a playing and training ground for your favorite steed, it's also a secluded getaway with modern, well-appointed one- and two-bedroom apartments ($88–110), all manner of campsites ($15–30), and stalls for your horses ($32–40).

Cedar Key 32625

❀ ♿ ❅ Although it's one of the older lodges on Dock Street, **Dockside Motel** (1-800-541-5432; www .dockside-cedarkey.com), 491 Dock St, delivers with large well-kept suites overlooking either the marina or the Gulf ($60–85). Open up those mas-

sive picture windows and let the sea breeze pour through. Ten units; small pets accepted.

❅ **Faraway Inn Motel & Cottages** (352-543-5330; www.farawayinn.com), Third and G streets. Harking back to vacation memories, the rooms and cottages ($60–115) at the Faraway Inn sweep you back into the great age of Florida tourism—the funky beach cottage of the 1940s. Small pets accepted.

❀ ❅ **The Gulf Side Motel** (1-888-543-5308; www.thegulfsidemotel .com), 552 First St. Located at the very end of FL 24, this 1950s-era motel sits right on the Gulf, enabling visitors to kick back and relax on the fishing pier, porch swing, or Adirondack chairs overlooking the water. Neat and recently redecorated after extensive renovations, all rooms are nonsmoking. Choose from efficiencies

THE IVY HOUSE

Sandra Friend

or standard rooms ($80–109) and be sure to check out Room 8, with its great Gulf view. Nine units; small pets accepted.

❦ **Harbour Master Suites** (352-543-9146; www.cedarkeyharbourmaster .com), 390 Dock St. Settling in for an extended stay? Here's luxury for you —a choice of six suites with apartment-style amenities, available by the night, week, or month. Rates start at $80. Each suite features tastefully furnished rooms with large windows; two provide full kitchen.

❦ **Sawgrass Motel** (352-543-5007), P.O. Box 658. Perched above the classy Sawgrass Gallery (see *Selective Shopping*) on Dock St, this duo of immaculate rooms ($75) overlooking the marina presents a quandary—to choose the darker nautical theme, or the bright and airy space? Both include a microwave, coffeemaker, refrigerator, and TV; no phone.

Seahorse Landing (1-877-514-5096; www.seahorselanding.com), 4050 G St, provides a fabulous view of sunset over the Gulf from newer large condo units (1,024 square feet, sleeping four or six) equipped with washer and dryer, dishwasher, microwave, full dishes and linens, television and VCR; DSL available in some units. $150–170.

🐾 **Sunset Isle Motel & RV Park** (1-800-810-1103; www.cedarkeyrv.com), FL 24. Along the estuary, this pleasant family motel has rooms with refrigerator, microwave, and coffeemaker ($45) as well as cottages ($85) and RV spaces ($16); tent campers welcome.

Chiefland 32626
🐾 **Best Western Suwannee Valley Inn** (352-493-0663), 1125 N Young

Blvd, has the feel of a small family motel, with a coin laundry and soda machines in the breezeway and a pleasant pool out front. Central to everything, they have 60 large rooms, many with desk and dataport, some with microwave and refrigerator; $70 and up.

Cross City 32628
Carriage Inn (352-498-3910), US 19-27-98. At this family motel, the wrought-iron railings remind me of the French Quarter. Enjoy well-kept, reasonably sized 1960s-style rooms ($39–45), with a swimming pool, shuffleboard court, and adjacent restaurant; across the road from the Nature Coast Trail.

Fanning Springs 32693
Cadillac Motel Inn & Suites (352-463-2188), 7490 N US 19, has real curb appeal: a tropical oasis, from the sparkling swimming pool to the flowering bushes in front of the rooms. This well-kept, family-run motel dates back to the 1950s, with large rooms and original small tiled baths in retro colors. Furnishings are bright and tropical, and each room has a microwave and mini fridge. Twenty-nine units, including family-sized multibed suites; $45 and up. Walk to Fanning Springs State Park and the Nature Coast Trail.

Suwannee 32692
Suwannee Shores Motor Lodge (352-542-7560), 525 Canal St. At this pleasant family-owned motel, enjoy being able to walk down the boardwalk to the river's edge and cast in a line, or put in your boat at the ramp. Older, spacious rooms (some kitchenettes) with a nautical atmosphere; $65 and up.

COTTAGES

Cedar Key 32625

🐾 My friends love to stay at **Mermaid's Landing** (1-877-543-5949; www.mermaidslanding.com), 12717 FL 24, an easy stroll from town and a great place to launch a kayak. Set in a funky beach atmosphere, each cottage ($65 and up) comes with an equipped kitchen. Kayak rental on site.

🐾 At **Pirates Cove** (352-543-5141; www.piratescovecottages.com), FL 24, each cottage ($69–95) comes fully equipped with dishes and linens; free use of bicycles for exploring Cedar Key, or fishing equipment to settle back on the shore and cast a line.

CAMPGROUNDS

Bell 32619

🍃 **Hart Springs Park** (see *Green Space*) on SW CR 344 west of Trenton offers both primitive tent and hook-up sites, dump station, grills, picnic tables, and hot showers. $11–13; weekly and monthly rates available. No pets.

Branford 32008

🍃 🐾 **Ellie Ray's River Landing Campground** (386-935-9518; www.ellieraysriverlanding.com), 3349 NW 110th St. A high canopy of oaks shades this expansive campground along the Santa Fe River, a great place for river rats to hang out. You've got swimming in a horseshoe-shaped spring on the river, canoeing and kayaking down to the Suwannee, boating, fishing, plenty of springs nearby for divers, canoe and paddle-boat rentals, and an on-site lounge. $19–25; weekly and monthly rates available. Leashed pets only.

THE LOWER SUWANNEE

Cedar Key 32625

Shell Mound County Park (352-543-6153), CR 326, on the edge of Lower Suwannee NWR, provides basic tent and camper sites cooled by breezes off the salt marsh. Ideal for hikers, paddlers, and anglers who like to get an early start; boat ramp, picnic tables, and privies.

Inglis 34449

Big Oaks River Resort and Campground (352-447-5333; www.bigoaksriverresort.com), 14035 W River Rd. An extremely appealing spot on the Withlacoochee River, with full-hook-up sites ($25), cabins with cable TV ($55 and up), and the main house (from $125). Enjoy the swimming pool, and make use of the campground store, which rents canoes and kayaks, johnboats and pontoon boats, and tubes (including shuttle service).

Old Town 32680

🐾 **Suwannee River Campground** (1-888-884-CAMP), FL 349. With campsites tucked in the deep shade of the river forest, this is one beautiful hideaway set above the river. Choose from tent sites ($18), pull-through sites with full hook-ups ($22), or camping cabins (no bathrooms, $30).

SHIRED ISLAND

Sandra Friend

Swimming pool, boat ramp, and fishing dock.

Suwannee River Hideaway Campground (352-542-7800; www.river hideaway.com), CR 346-A. You're greeted by a cute replica of an old general store at check-in at this new campground along the Suwannee, with pretty full-hook-up spaces ($22–24) under the pines and oaks. Tenters ($12) get the primo access to the river; a boardwalk leads from the bathhouse area down to the river.

🐾 The only area campground with a significant amount of river frontage, the **Yellow Jacket Campground** (352-542-8365; www.yellowjacket campground.com), FL 349, blends well into its natural surroundings. Over more than two years, the new owners renovated this former fish camp into a place of beauty. A rope swing with a grand view of the Suwannee River hangs off an ancient live oak tree next to shady riverside campsites; guests enjoy a beautiful swimming pool and spa area. $22 tents, $32 riverbank RV sites, $110 for their extremely pleasant cottages.

Shired Island

It's the epitome of rustic—a flush toilet (not in the best of shape) your only amenity. But if you really want to get away from it all, pitch your tent or bring your trailer to **Shired Island County Park** (352-498-1240), the most remote campground on the Nature Coast, at the end of CR 357 right on the Gulf. Launch your sea kayak from the beach, and enjoy a sunset that's all yours. Self-serve $9; nearby boat ramp.

Yankeetown 34498

🐾 **B's Marina and Campground** (352-447-5888; www.bmarinacamp

ground.net), 6621 Riverside Dr. Campsites ($20) along the pine-and-palm-lined Withlacoochee River, with paved pads and picnic tables. Bring your boat and take advantage of the dock, or come by boat and arrange overnight dockage. It's a great place to launch a kayak and head out to the Gulf, with rentals available.

DIVE RESORT

Williston 32696

Devil's Den (352-528-3344; www .devilsden.com), 5390 NE 180th Ave. Surrounding its world-renowned dive venue (see *To Do—Diving*), Devil's Den provides a full-service dive resort with 30 RV sites ($22), 20 tent sites ($7–11), and 3 kitchenette cabins ($75–80, sleeping four) perched on the rim of a large sinkhole. Campers enjoy use of bathhouses and a heated pool on site. In addition to the must-dive grotto, enjoy swimming, snorkeling, and scuba in spring-fed Ray's Fish Pond, ranging up to 22 feet deep, and picnicking in the covered pavilions or open tables under the forest canopy. No pets permitted.

FISH CAMPS

Inglis 34449

Big Bass Village Campground (1-877-GO-FISH2; www.bigbassvillage .com), 10530 SE 201st St, on Lake Rousseau, is the place to go if you're after trophy-sized largemouth bass on this snag-filled lake. In addition to primitive ($12) and full-hook-up sites ($15), they have rustic cabin rentals ($35–50, includes cable TV, fully equipped kitchens), a bait-and-tackle shop, and boat rentals.

✳ Where to Eat

DINING OUT

Cedar Key
The Island Room Restaurant at Cedar Cove (352-543-6520; www .islandroom.com), 10 Second St. The island's dressiest restaurant serves up proprietor-chef Peter Stefani's specialties, like grouper Savannah (pecan crusted, served with a sherry beurre blanc) and New Zealand rack of lamb; entrées $13–25. Reservations suggested.

Williston
The Ivy House (352-528-5410), 108 NW Main St. Featuring recipes handed down for more than 50 years through the Hale family, The Ivy House presents gourmet Southern cooking in a 1912 Victorian home; five differently themed rooms provide unique backdrops to the main attraction, the food. From Southern-fried grouper ($10) to a Big South sampler of a Delmonico steak, grouper, and shrimp ($19), you'll find something to fit every appetite, served up with roasted vegetables, corn bread, yeast rolls, and their trademark baked potato with cheese. Leave some room for a homemade dessert, like their classic milk cake. Open for lunch and dinner; closed Sun. A gift shop occupies one room near the entrance, with an array of feminine gift items.

EATING OUT

Bell
Captain Hugh's (352-463-7670), US 129. If you're in the mood for mounds of food, stop by Captain Hugh's, where buffets will keep you sated. Breakfasts under $4, lunches $3 and up, and dinners $9–14, including local favorites like catfish, clams,

grouper, quail, shrimp, and snow crab.

Cedar Key
The Captain's Table (352-543-5441), 222 Dock St. Savor the sunset while partaking in the fabulous mullet dip at the Captain's Table, a great choice for seafood on the Gulf and one of my usual stops, where dinner for two runs under $25. Save some room for the excellent Key lime pie! Closed Tue.

🏮 **Pat's Red Luck** (352-543-6840), 490 Dock St. Consistently excellent for both lunch and dinner ($6–17). The oysters here are always fresh and lightly breaded, making my top lunch pick the New Orleans Peacemaker, a Cajun rendition of the po'boy sandwich.

♿ **Seabreeze on the Dock** (352-543-5738), 520 Dock St. One of the few eateries in Cedar Key that a wheelchair can reach, the Sea Breeze offers good fresh Gulf seafood with a great view. Try their creamy oyster stew as a starter, and move on to entrées ($10–24) showcasing local favorites—grouper strips, mullet, roast clams, blue crab claws, and stone crab. For something completely different, try the hearts of palm salad as a side—served with peaches, dates, and pineapples, and topped with peanut butter ice cream dressing. Yum!

Chiefland
Bar-B-Q Bill's (352-493-4444), US 19 and FL 320. This place is always packed, and it took but one meal to understand why: fine barbecue that even impressed my friends from Texas. Served with traditional fixings, barbecue comes as sandwiches ($2 and up) and plates ($6 and up), with optional salad bar. Daily lunch

specials served 11–3; open lunch and dinner.

Bells Family Restaurant (352-493-4492), 116 N Main St. The buffet is the centerpiece of this longtime hometown favorite, where even at lunch you can grab piles of fresh peel-'n'-eat shrimp and stacks of fried fish. Every day means a slightly different feature on the buffet, from frog legs and 'gator tail to quail and catfish ($8–14), with daily specials. There's an extensive menu, too, with items like country-fried steak and grouper Reubens. Country breakfasts served 7–11 ($1.49–7); breakfast buffets Sat and Sun ($5).

Cross City

Cypress Inn Restaurant (352-498-7211), US 27 and CR 351-A. Since 1928, they've been serving up heaping helpings of Southern cooking in this beautiful pecky cypress building; sit down and make yourself at home. Prime rib special ($10), seafood dinners ($7–9, including fresh mullet and grouper), and everything comes with your choice of home-style sides like fresh acre peas, baby limas, fried okra, and corn nuggets. Open 5–9:30; cash or ATM debit cards only.

Fanning Springs

Always packed for dinner, the **Lighthouse Restaurant** (352-463-2644), US 19 across from the state park, serves fresh Gulf seafood and thick steaks that folks come for from miles around. Try the Swamp Thing ($17), with 'gator tail bites, catfish strips, and golden-fried deviled crab, or the Dinghy ($9) for small appetites, with flounder, shrimp, crab, and oysters. Entrées $8–28; open 11–11 daily.

Sandra Friend

THE TRENTON COCA-COLA BOTTLING PLANT

Suwannee

Salt Creek Restaurant (352-542-7072), CR 349, is a spacious restaurant with seating overlooking the Gulf estuary. It's worth the drive to the end of the road for their succulent seafood, including fresh oysters, mullet, bay scallops, and their steamer pots (six choices of seafood, $9 and up) cooked with veggies and red potatoes. Entrées run $11–19, including a Fisherman's Platter with blue crab. Open Wed–Sun 11–10.

Trenton

Inside the spacious Suwannee Valley Quilt Shop (see *Selective Shopping*), the **Cypress Swamp Café** offers delightful daily specials like crab salad on croissant: $5 including tea or coffee. You'll be tempted by slices of pie —like cashew, sawdust, and tin roof— displayed prominently in a bakery case on the edge of this gardenlike space inside the historic Coca-Cola bottling plant. Open Tue–Sat 10–5.

Williston

🦐 **Driftwood Grill** (352-528-5074), 515 E Noble Ave. Enjoy a heaping helping of comfort food in this comfy down-home cafe, where a plateful of pancakes with your choice of toppings (blueberry, chocolate chip, or peaches and cream) will run you less than $3; lunches $2–7, Southern-style dinners $6–13.

Hale's General Store (352-528-5219), 8 NW Main. It's a gift shop (check out the quilts) and an old-fashioned ice cream parlor open 10–3, serving deli sandwiches and salads as well as steamed seafood. Closed Sun.

✳ Selective Shopping

Cedar Key

From gift and home decor items to one-of-a-kind pieces of art, you'll find a great selection in artsy Cedar Key. The shopping district encompasses Second St, its cross streets, and Dock St along the Gulf. A handful of places you shouldn't miss:

The Cedar Keyhole (352-543-5801), 457 Second St. Representing more than 20 local artists and a handful of consignments, this gallery tempts with art in virtually every medium. Fused art glass captures the motion of ocean waves, and Cindy's gourd handbags add a touch of humor. Despite ceramic slugs and hand-painted dresses, the art reflects island themes. Ongoing gallery events, including nationally juried exhibits, occupy the second floor.

Curmudgeonalia (352-543-6789), corner of Second and D streets. Every little town needs an independent bookstore, and none so much as Cedar Key, being an enclave of artists and writers. Curmudgeonalia fills the

niche, with an excellent selection of tomes on Florida and by Florida authors, and a children's section that caters to inquisitive outdoorsy kids.

Dilly Dally Galley (352-543-9146), 390 Dock St. Dark woods accent the nautical theme in this seaside shop, with wooden signs, wood carvings, and antique ephemera tucked away in the back rooms. The front desk also serves as the check-in for the Harbour Master Suites (see *Lodging*).

Haven Isle (352-543-6806), 582 Second St. Dating back to 1884, this little white gingerbread cottage houses the usual gift items found in small tourist towns, but with a twist—the owner is a well-respected stained-glass artist, and the back of the shop serves as his studio. Look high up on the walls for original art in glass, wood, and metal by local artists.

Island Arts (352-543-6677), C St. Just around the corner from Second St, this vibrant artists' co-op features playful art with a maritime theme. Follow the purple fish inside for a parade of pop art, clever cards, and other island treasures.

The Natural Experience (352-543-9933), 334 Second St. A working wood and clay studio occupies one

HALE'S GENERAL STORE

Sandra Friend

corner of this classy gallery, where Don Duden works the lathe, creating hand-turned wood vessels. In addition to Don's fine work, several other artists are represented, including noted author and photographer Jeff Ripple and his stunning "One With Nature" collection of original outdoor photography. Pottery and art glass, enameling and impressionistic Florida landscapes round out the collection.

Sawgrass Gallery (352-543-5007), 451 Dock St. Featuring artists from around America, the Sawgrass Gallery displays an eclectic mix of glass, metal, ceramic, and fabric art. My eyes immediately locked on the "sublimely weird sculptures" of Julie Borodin, a parade of one-of-a-kind pillows, and the free-form pottery of Connie Mickle, flowing shapes expressed in earth tones. From fused glass to foam-core 3-D collages, the artistry sings.

The Suwannee Triangle Gallery (352-543-5744; www.suwannee triangle.com), 491 Dock St. Take a pinch of Connie Nelson, with her island watercolors of houses, waterbirds, and Florida's colorful flora, and add a dash of Kevin Hipe, with his offbeat mosaics and photography that captures the spirit of the Cedar Keys, and you've been drawn into the Suwannee Triangle. In addition to the prolific output of these two excellent local artists, the gallery features fine jewelry, prints of collages, and Brian Andrews's distinctive "story people."

Chiefland
Every weekend Chiefland has flea markets as bookends—**Shaw's,** a small enterprise, at the south end of town near SW Fourth Ave, and the **Chiefland Farmers Flea Market** (352-493-2022), Sat and Sun 8–4.

Comb through the stalls for country bargains!

Magnolia Mist Unique Gifts & Antiques (352-493-7877), 711 N Main, stands out along US 19 in downtown Chiefland with a good selection of antiques and gift items.

Old Town
Intrigued by the stacks of driftwood outside **Catch the Drift** (352-542-7770), 410 US 19 S, I stopped to take a look and was glad I did. C. Emery Mills's decade-old gallery is all about nature as art, with 10 local artists creating sculptures from wood, shells, and coral.

Suwannee
You'll find **Souvenirs & Things,** CR 349, with original stained-glass art, carved wooden fish sculptures, and other nautical gifts along Salt Creek adjoining the Salt Creek Restaurant (see *Eating Out*).

Trenton
Suwannee Valley Quilt Shop (352-463-3842), 517 N Main St. It's not just a quilt shop; it's a piece of history. Grab lunch at the Cypress Swamp Café (see *Eating Out*) or browse the selection of stained-glass supplies. But if fabric's your thing, you'll find plenty of options here!

Williston
Cedar Chest Antiques (352-528-0039), 48 E Noble Ave. Modern home decor items like carved hope chests share space with beaded Victorian lamps, Vaseline glass, and collectible dolls in a virtual showroom of antique furniture. Open Wed–Sat.

Cindy's Cottage (352-528-2200), 533 NE First St, is a cute corner shop in a historic home. I practically had to drag my husband out of here, he was so fascinated with the old books and ephemera, and walked away with a vintage drawing board.

Dixies Antiques (352-528-2338), 131 E Noble Ave. It's a mini mall overflowing with antiques and collectibles, with a heavy emphasis on kitchenware and dishes—look for your missing Fenton glass, Fiestaware, and enamelware here. But you'll also find country crafts, western home decor, rustic wooden furniture, and ironworking by a local blacksmith in among the stacks of paperbacks, Hardy Boys mysteries, and soda pop bottles—a little something for everyone. Closed Sun. The produce stand in the parking lot carries seasonal fresh fruit and vegetables.

Williston Peanut Factory Outlet (352-528-2388), 1309 US 41. Small outlet with offerings of peanut goodies made on site, from roasted peanuts to peanut butter and peanut brittle; open during production hours.

Yankeetown
Riverside Antiques & Gallery (352-447-2717), 3B 63rd St. An antiques mall and art gallery featuring local artists, with primitive art, nautical-themed items, and garden art in the historic Yankeetown Garage.

U-PICK R&S Produce (352-528-0100). Fresh fruit and vegetables out of a permanent, canopied fruit stand just west of US 41 on FL 121, south of Williston.

✳ Entertainment

Catch live music at **Frog's Landing** (352-543-9243), 490 Dock St, Cedar Key, on weekends.

✳ Special Events

February: **Suwannee Valley Bluegrass Festival** (1-800-576-2398), Trenton. Enjoy live bluegrass from Florida performers.

March: **Suwannee River Fair** (352-486-5131) is the combined county fair for the three-county region, with livestock and vegetable judging, rides and crafts, and more. Suwannee River fairgrounds.

April: **Cedar Key Sidewalk Arts and Crafts Festival** (352-543-5600; www.cedarkey.org). Enjoy the works of local artists, with a taste of seafood for good measure.

May: **Red Belly Day** (352-463-3310; www.dixiecounty.org), Fanning Springs State Park. One of the most amusing Memorial Day weekend celebrations in Florida, centered on the town's favorite member of the bream family (which makes for a great fish fry), with families participating in sack races, melon chunking, and the ever-popular belly-flop contest.

September: **Down Home Days** (352-463-3467), Trenton. More than 180 artists, craftspeople, and food vendors, with music for a "down-home" time.

October: **Cedar Key Seafood Festival** (352-543-5600; www.cedarkey. org), third weekend. Thousands converge on this tiny village for samplings of local seafood and a large arts and crafts show, as well as special tours of the Cedar Key lighthouse.

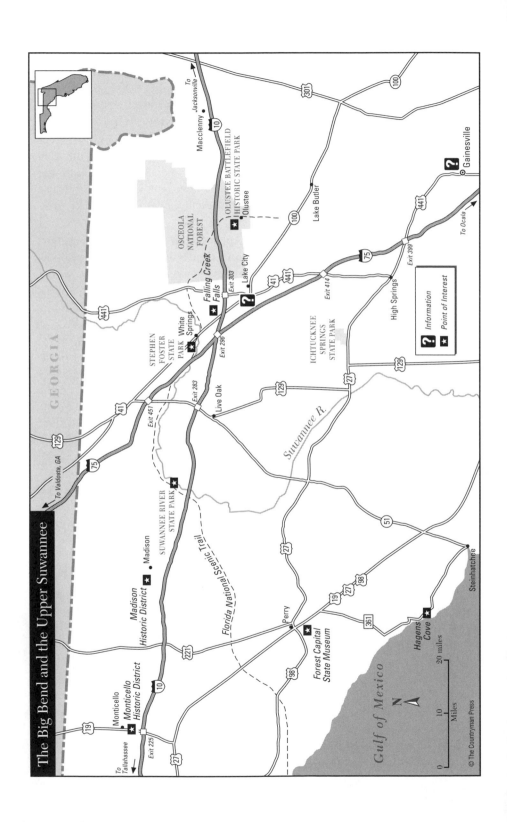

The Big Bend and the Upper Suwannee

THE BIG BEND
TAYLOR AND LAFAYETTE COUNTIES

Encompassing the sweep of Florida's coastline where the peninsula meets the Panhandle, the Big Bend is a wild and wondrous place. Once the domain of the Timucua Indians, the region saw Spanish explorers in 1529, when Pánfilo de Narváez came looking for gold and marked Deadman's Bay on the map; he was soon followed by Hernando de Soto and his men. Building two small missions near the Fenholloway River, the Spanish attempted to convert the Timucua, but diseases ran rampant, decimating the tribes. By the 1700s, the Seminoles, descendants of Maskókî peoples, moved south to take their place. In 1818 General Andrew Jackson brought U.S. forces against the Seminoles at the Econfina River and marched his troops south across the Steinhatchee River at the falls. During the Seminole Wars of the 1800s, the area was a hotbed of military activity, with Fort Frank Brook erected near the mouth of the Steinhatchee, and four more forts built along the Econfina and Fenholloway rivers. General Zachary Taylor led more troops into the region in 1838, attempting to force the Seminoles to reservations in the West. Taylor County bears his name.

Along the Gulf Coast, you'll find **Steinhatchee** near the mouth of the eponymous River, founded by pioneers looking for cedar to feed the pencil factories in the Cedar Keys (see The Lower Suwannee chapter). In the 1940s Greek sponge divers moved into the area to work the vast sponge beds in the Gulf of Mexico, and the fishermen followed. Although the sponge divers are long gone, you

CANOEING ON THE STEINHATCHEE RIVER
Steinhatchee Landing

can see reminders of Greek culture in the offerings on local menus. Up the coast, **Adams Beach** and **Keaton Beach** are quaint fishing villages along the vast estuary of the Big Bend. **Perry,** the seat of Taylor County, grew up around farming in the 1860s, but the economy shifted to lumber and turpentine after Reconstruction, when timber companies removed vast tracts of virgin pines and cypress, and processed the harvest in two enormous timber mills. The Forest Capital Museum (see *To See—Museums*) tells the story of Florida's timber industry, centered at Perry.

Lightly populated and agrarian, both Taylor and Lafayette counties provide quiet getaways for folks looking to get well off the beaten path.

GUIDANCE Contact the **Lafayette County Chamber of Commerce** (386-294-2510), P.O. Box 416, Mayo 32066, and the **Perry/Taylor Chamber of Commerce** (1-800-257-8881; www.taylorflorida.com), P.O. Box 892, Perry 32348.

GETTING THERE *By car*: US 19-27 runs through the heart of Taylor County, but you'll want to take CR 361 and FL 51 to explore its Gulf Coast communities. FL 51 and US 27 meet at Mayo, the center of Lafayette County, passing through all of its major towns. Steinhatchee is a three-hour drive north from Orlando.

MEDICAL EMERGENCIES The nearest medical center is in adjoining Suwannee County at Live Oak (see The Upper Suwannee chapter). Call 911 for emergencies.

✳ To See

GHOST TOWNS In 1870 **New Troy,** near Troy Springs, boasted busy steamboat docks and steady commerce. It was the seat of Lafayette County, but after an arsonist torched the courthouse in 1892, county residents voted to move the courthouse to Mayo; New Troy was abandoned soon after.

HISTORIC SITES Steinhatchee Spring, a historic spa and the birthplace of the Steinhatchee River, is off FL 51 north of US 27. Visit downtown **Perry** for a look at the historic district, centered on the Taylor County Courthouse; the Lafayette County Courthouse in Mayo dates back to 1908. At **Steinhatchee Falls** (see *Green Space—Waterfalls*), examine the rock above the falls closely; when the water is low, you can see ruts left behind by heavy wagon wheels from territorial settlers crossing in the 1820s.

LAFAYETTE COUNTY COURTHOUSE
Lafayette County CVB

MUSEUMS Forest Capital Museum State Park (850-584-3227; www .floridastateparks.org/forestcapital), 204 Forest Park Dr, Perry. In Florida's

heart of forestry, this lively museum focuses on the importance of Florida's timber, particularly its pine forests. In addition to a diorama on the historic turpentine and naval stores industries, there are life-sized replica habitats and a talking
tree to teach the kids about the life cycle of Florida's trees. A wooden map of
Florida showcases the variety of native trees in the state (314 types), with each
county made out of a different type of wood. Outside the museum, walk beneath
the stately longleaf pines through a reconstructed Cracker homestead. Open
9–5; closed Tue and Wed.

✳ To Do

BICYCLING Perfect for beginners, the **Allen Mill Pond** bike trail runs 4.2 miles
between Allen Mill Pond and Lafayette Blue Springs along the Suwannee River.
For information, contact the Suwannee Bicycle Association (386-397-2347),
White Springs.

BIRDING **Cooks Hammock,** hidden in a maze of forest roads off FL 51 at the
Lafayette Hunt Club, has a colony of white and glossy ibises; hang out at
Hagens Cove (see *Green Space—Beaches*) to watch flocks of shorebirds,
including black skimmers.

BOATING In Steinhatchee you can rent boats and pontoons at many marinas,
including Gulfstream Motel (see *Lodging*), **Sea Hag** (352-498-3008; www
.seahag.com), **Ideal Marina and Motel** (see *Lodging*), **Paces Cabins** (352-
498-0061), and **Woods Marina and Campground** (352-498-3948). Marinas
provide dockage and storage (including dry dock) at varying rates. A public boat
ramp is located at the end of CR 358 on the north side of the river; turn right at
the end of the bridge.

DIVING From diving and snorkeling offshore on the **reefs of the Big Bend** and
around its **submarine springs** to diving in the crystalline waters of the **Suwannee River,** this area offers many options for divers. Check in at the dive shop at
Ideal Marina and Motel for offshore opportunities and outfitting, and at River
Rendezvous for freshwater diving (see *Lodging* for both). Important note: Many
open-water divers have died in this region while attempting cave diving. Do not
enter an underwater cave or spring unless you are a certified cave diver. Most
springs must be accessed by boat, and a DIVER DOWN flag is necessary while diving.

FISHING With more than 60 miles of wilderness coastline, the Big Bend has
always attracted a steady clientele of saltwater anglers in search of grouper,
cobia, and trout. Toward that end, you'll find plenty of **fishing guides,** especially
around Steinhatchee. Ask around at the marinas (see *Boating*) regarding specific
captains' specialties, and expect a day's worth of guided fishing (which includes
your license) to cost $350–700, depending on what you're after. At Keaton
Beach, a fishing pier provides access to the Gulf.

Inland, anglers head for **Koon Lake,** a 110-acre fish management area west of
Mayo on US 27, where largemouth bass and bluegill provide spring sport. If

ORIGINAL FLORIDA

you're fishing along the banks of the Suwannee River, target sunfish around the snags and channel catfish in the deep holes.

HIKING The **Florida Trail** (www.floridatrail.org; see *What's Where*) traverses two particularly scenic areas in this region—Goose Pasture and the Aucilla River Sinks (see *Wild Places*). Don't miss **Steinhatchee Falls** (see *Green Space— Waterfalls*), with its 6-mile round-trip trail along the Steinhatchee River. Two short hiking trails in the **Tide Swamp Unit of Big Bend WMA** lead through coastal pine flatwoods along the tidal marshes near Hagens Cove; **Dallus Creek** is the most scenic.

HUNTING Deer hunting is big sport between Thanksgiving and Christmas in the thousands of acres of natural lands making up the **Big Bend Wildlife Management Area,** which stretches south into Dixie County. Check the Florida Fish and Wildlife Conservation Commission web site, www.floridaconservation.org, for hunt locations and dates.

MUD BOGGIN' Ever wonder what folks do with those monster pickup trucks? Stop by **North Florida Mud Boggin',** US 27 between Branford and Mayo, on the second and fourth Sat each month at 6 PM to watch the gears grind and the mud fly.

PADDLING For a tiny taste of white-water thrills, head to Steinhatchee with your kayak to leap the **Steinhatchee Falls** (see *Green Space—Waterfalls*). The 8-mile trip from the falls to Steinhatchee along this obsidian-colored waterway winds through dark river hammocks and forested residential areas before meeting the tidal basin, offering several Class I rapids. Rent kayaks from Steinhatchee Outpost (see *Campgrounds*); take-out is at Fiddler's Restaurant (see *Dining Out*). Of course, the Suwannee River is the region's prime canoeing venue, outlining the eastern border of Lafayette County. Put in at **Troy Springs State Park** (see *Green Space—Springs*) or the CR 51 bridge crossing north of Mayo to follow the central section of the **Suwannee River Wilderness Trail** (see The Upper Suwannee chapter).

Estuary dominates the central and most remote portion of a rough but scenic 91-mile saltwater paddle attempted by a handful of people every year: the **Historic Big Bend Saltwater Paddling Trail** (see The Lower Suwannee chapter). Paddlers on this segment can find services at Steinhatchee, Keaton Beach, and Econfina, where sea kayakers put in at **Econfina River State Park** (see *Green Space—Wild Places*) for direct access to the Gulf of Mexico. On US 98 you'll find picnic tables and a boat

FROM THE TRAIL ALONG DALLUS CREEK
Sandra Friend

ramp on the Econfina River, a junglelike paddling route that heads south 6 miles to the state park. A little farther west, paddlers can also put in at the Aucilla River and head upstream along the **Wacissa River Canoe Trail** into Jefferson County; the Aucilla quickly peters out as it disappears through its famed sinks.

SCENIC DRIVES Contact the Perry/Taylor County Chamber of Commerce (see *Guidance*) for a brochure on **The Loop** in Taylor County, a nearly 100-mile circuit taking you through the scenic fishing villages along the Gulf Coast and through the heart of the "Forest Capital of Florida." A truly wild and scenic drive, the **Road to Nowhere** (see The Lower Suwannee chapter) in Jena is best accessed from Steinhatchee.

✳ Green Space

BEACHES The Big Bend isn't noted for its beaches—it's an estuary. But you will find a **soft white strand at Hodges Park** in Keaton Beach at the end of CR 361, along a grassy strip with restrooms and a covered picnic pavilion. Between Steinhatchee and Keaton Beach on CR 361 in the Tide Swamp Unit of Big Bend WMA, **Hagens Cove** is a prime destination for scalloping, especially for families with small children. Don't expect a beautiful white-sand beach here. It's an accessible piece of shoreline along an infinite stretch of mudflats, a beautiful place to sit and watch the sunset.

PARKS In downtown Mayo, ancient live oaks shade **Mayo Town Park,** which has a playground, picnic area, and historic Cracker home. Just off US 27 near Cindy's Motel (see *Lodging*).

SPRINGS Contact the Suwannee River Water Management District (386-362-1001) for a map of spring locations on the Suwannee River for diving and swimming. In this region you can visit tiny **Conviction Springs** at River Rendezvous (see *Lodging*), but you shouldn't miss **Troy Springs State Park** (386-935-4835), 674 NE Troy Springs Rd off US 27 near Midway, where the water is nearly 75 feet deep and contains the remains of the *Madison,* a steamboat scuttled in 1861 when her owner left to fight for the Confederacy in Virginia. Adjoining **Ruth Springs** is a third-magnitude spring open for swimming and diving; **Lafayette Blue Springs** (386-294-1617) along CR 350A has primitive camping, nature trails, picnic pavilions, and a boat ramp.

TROY SPRINGS

Sandra Friend

SCALLOPING Dropping off the back of a 32-foot Ocean Cat, I plunge into the warm waters of the Gulf of Mexico, mesh bag in hand. It's my first time snorkeling in many years, and the fins on my feet feel unfamiliar, the scene surreal, dreamlike. I glide noiselessly through hues of green above a waving pasture of turtle grass, where silvery pinfish glimmer against the shifting textures and a jellyfish pumps briskly against the seafloor. I spot my goal ahead, a patch of rocks and bright white sand with tall strands of Christmas tree grass rising to the surface. There, at the base of the waving grass—bay scallops! It takes a few swift kicks of the flippers to make the dive and then surface with the clacking shellfish in hand, the beginning of a seafood dinner gathered under my own power.

For many years the estuar-

SCALLOPING

Sandra Friend

WATERFALLS Steinhatchee Falls rates as Florida's broadest and most interesting waterfall. This limestone shelf along the Steinhatchee River served as a crossing point for wagons as settlers pushed their way south along the Gulf Coast, and the wagon ruts are still visible in the limestone on both sides of the river. A riverside park has interpretive information, picnic tables, and a boat launch; a hiking trail starts just outside the gate. The trailhead and falls are off CR 51, 2 miles west of US 19-27.

WILD PLACES During hunting season, you'll see plenty of pickups pulling into **Hickory Mound WMA** near Perry, and the **Big Bend WMA** surrounding Steinhatchee. Off-season, Hickory Mound's extensive dike trails are great for birding and alligator watching; the Jena Unit of Big Bend WMA provides fabulous birding (accessed best from Steinhatchee, it's actually in adjoining Dixie County). The **Tide Swamp Unit of Big Bend WMA** is the home of Hagens Cove, the region's swimming and scalloping beach. Off CR 355, the **Mallory Swamp WMA** provides access to nearly 30,000 acres of remote wilderness south of Mayo. Off US

ies of the Big Bend have been the only place where enough scallops naturally breed to be harvested; their estuarine nurseries in other parts of the state had been overcollected and poisoned by runoff. Although more counties along the Gulf Coast have had their waters reopened for an annual scalloping season, Steinhatchee remains the destination of choice for serious shellfish harvesters. Your success is in direct proportion to the weather: Too much rain, and the scallop

Steinhatchee Landing

SHUCKING A SCALLOP

population suffers. The season runs Jul 1–Sep 10, and you must abide by state-mandated limits of 2 gallons of whole scallops per person per day. If you snorkel from your own boat, you must have a saltwater fishing license and display a DIVER DOWN flag. Many local marinas arrange charters; **Big Bend Charters** (352-498-3703; www.bigbendcharters.com) specializes in scalloping trips. No fishing license is required when you scallop with a charter, nor if you head for **Hagens Cove** (see *Green Space—Beaches*), where you can wade into the Gulf and collect to your heart's content.

98 east of the Aucilla River bridge, the **Aucilla River Sinks** and **Goose Pasture** provide access to one of the strangest rivers in Florida—after rushing across rapids, it vanishes beneath the limestone bedrock and pops up time and again in "windows" in the aquifer, deep sinkholes with water in motion. Use the **Florida Trail** (see *What's Where*) to explore this unique area. At the end of CR 14, **Econfina River State Park** (850-584-3026; www.floridastateparks.org/econfina-river) gives paddlers a put-in to the vast Gulf estuary.

STEINHATCHEE FALLS

Sandra Friend

✳ Lodging

BED & BREAKFASTS

Mayo 32066

ₕ **Le Chateau de Lafayette** (386-294-2332; www.lechateaumayo.com), Bloxham and Fletcher streets. Step back in time in these tastefully appointed romantic suites in the former county courthouse (1883–1907), restored to its historic splendor and lovingly cared for by Donna Land. Six rooms in French Provincial style, $65–80, include continental breakfast; full breakfast available. Fine dining Tue–Sat evenings in The Golden Pear (see *Dining Out*).

HOTELS, MOTELS, AND RESORTS

Keaton Beach 32348

Keaton Beach Marina Motel & Cottages (850-578-2897), 20650 Keaton Beach Dr. Sandy Beach (honest!) runs this family motel with spacious rooms; the unit I checked out had a glassed-in porch overlooking the channel. It's an older building, with uneven floors, but that just adds to its charm. $59 for motel rooms, $89 for cottages (which require a two-night stay).

Mayo 32066

🐾 **Cindy's Motel** (386-294-1242), 487 W Main St (US 27). A blast from my past: a spotless 1950s motel (period furnishings, even!) harking back to family road trips in the days before interstate highways, where every room has air-conditioning, cable TV, and ample space for Mom, Dad, and the kids. The property is shaded by grand live oaks and sits just across from the city park and behind the Mayo Café. $45–50.

Perry 32348

Chaparral Inn (850-584-2441), 2519 S Byron Butler Pkwy. From the pre-interstate days when Perry was a bustling junction of major U.S. highways, the Chaparral has aged gracefully. Each modest room ($38–45) includes cable TV, phone, and air-conditioning; enjoy the pool or sit in a porch swing on the well-manicured grounds.

ℐ ₕ The **Hampton Inn** (850-223-3000), 2399 S Byron Butler Pkwy, comes with a guarantee of top-notch customer service: It's ranked fifth in the nation for its chain. In addition to an expanded continental breakfast, look for cookies and chocolate-dipped strawberries in the dining area every afternoon; families crowd the swimming pool on weekends. Rates start at $90; reservations recommended, especially during football season, when they catch the spillover of fans from Tallahassee.

Steinhatchee 32359

ℐ ₕ 🐾 **Gulfstream Motel and Marina** (352-498-8088; www.gulfstream motelmarina.com), CR 358, is actually in Jena (Dixie County) but part of the Steinhatchee community. With 20 newly refurbished units in the middle of the action, it's perfect for folks headed out on fishing or scalloping trips. Large, well-maintained units ($60 and up) feature kitchenettes, television, and plenty of beds for the kids; there's even a unit with bunk beds, and family-friendly cabins. Connecting rooms make it possible to bring the extended family. You'll find the Crabhouse Café and the Sportsmen Den tiki bar on the premises, as well as charters, boat rentals, live-aboard marina slips, marina store, and fish-cleaning stations. Guests receive docking and launching privileges with their room.

❧ ♿ 🐾 **Ideal Marina and Motel**
(352-498-3877; www.steinhatchee
.com/ideal), 114 Riverside Dr. Jody
and Scott Peters run this pretty little
place right on the river, with walk-
out-the-door access to your boat at
the marina. Each sparkling room has
pine board walls and tile floors, cable
TV, and nice-sized bathroom; most
have a small refrigerator, and guests
share a patio and grill area. Boat slips
are included in the room price, $59–
79. A full-service marina, they offer
boat rentals, guide service, fishing
licenses, bait and tackle, marine supplies, and a dive shop. The Peterses
also own the small **Fisherman's Rest**
(see *Campgrounds*) across the street.

Pelican Pointe Inn (352-498-7427;
www.pelicanpointeinn.com), 1306 SE
Riverside Drive. With condos converted to motel rooms in 2002, Pelican Pointe offers a riverfront view and
dockage in front of your room, adjacent to Fiddler's Restaurant (see *Dining Out*). Amenities vary, but all of
the spacious rooms have cable TV and
screened balcony; $99–175.

🐾 **Steinhatchee River Inn** (352-
498-4049; www.steinhatcheeriverinn
.com), Riverside Dr, has 17 large and
tidy units on a hillside above the river,
offering a variety of room configurations (most are two-room suites) for
$60 and up, with wireless Internet
access. The swimming pool overlooks
the river.

🌹 At **The Sunset Place** (352-498-
0860; www.thesunsetplace.com), 115
First St SW, every condo has a full
kitchen and sweeping view of the
Gulf estuary along the Steinhatchee
River; watch the sunset from your
balcony or at the pool. $85–120, with
surcharge for scalloping season.

Perry 32348
🐾 **Perry KOA** (850-838-3221; www
.perry-koa.com), 3641 US 19 S, provides a mix of shady and sunny pull-
through sites with full hook-ups or tent
sites ($20–29) and new Kamping
Kabins and Kottages with bath ($45–
85). Amenities include a swimming
pool and hot tub, and wireless Internet.

Steinhatchee 32359
🌹 **Fisherman's Rest** (352-498-3877),
115 Riverside Dr. Across from and
owned by the Ideal Marina and Motel
(see *Hotels, Motels, and Resorts*),
this relaxing campground offers high,
dry campsites shaded by live oaks,
with full-hook-up (including cable)
pull-through sites ($20) and a tent
camping area with bathhouse ($8).
Easy walk to restaurants and the
marina.

THE IDEAL MARINA

Sandra Friend

🦆 🛶 ♿ 🐾 ⊙ **Stein-hatchee Landing Resort** (352-498-3513; www.steinhatch eelanding.com), FL 51. It's a magical place, with the feel of a turn-of-the-20th-century village on the shores of the Steinhatchee River, where ancient live oaks shade Old Florida and Victorian gingerbread

THE HONEYMOON COTTAGE

Steinhatchee Landing

homes that melt into the landscape. When owner Dean Fowler came to Steinhatchee from Georgia in the 1970s to fish, he saw a need for a place where the whole family could come and relax while the family angler was out on a fishing trip. At Steinhatchee Landing, the 31 tasteful, old-fashioned homes come with modern interiors: a step from Florida Cracker into a page out of *House Beautiful,* with hardwood and tiled floors, high ceilings, gleaming modern kitchens, and inviting overstuffed beds. Most of the homes are owned privately and leased for rental through the 35-acre resort, where guests are free to roam and enjoy the riverside pool, health center, petting farm, children's playground, and miles of walking trails; canoes and kayaks, guided pontoon tours, and bicycles are available for a nominal fee. In addition to a conference center accommodating 60 guests, the newly christened

🦆 **Steinhatchee Outpost** (1-800-589-1541), US 19 and FL 51, offers open and shaded sites ($8–22) for tents and RVs, adjacent to the Steinhatchee River, as well as a private pond for paddling, canoe and kayak rentals for trips on the river, and quiet rental cabins ($50–175).

Wood's Gulf Breeze Campground & Marina (352-498-3948; www.woods gulfbreeze.com), Second Ave N, has shady sites ($23) overlooking the estuary, including some prime tent spots along the marshes of Deadman's Bay.

Forty RV sites, eight tent sites with electric, and a dump station.

✳ Where to Eat
DINING OUT

Mayo
The Golden Pear (386-294-2332; www.lechateaumayo.com), Bloxham and Fletcher streets. Serving up steak, and local seafood favorites ($8–17) such as 'gator tail and grouper, the classy dining room of the Le Chateau de Lafayette B&B (see

Dancing Waters Chapel provides a lovely natural nondenominational setting for weddings and other special events. This family-friendly venue hosts many reunions, including get-togethers of the Carter clan of Plains, Georgia, and caters to newlyweds with romantic Honeymoon Cottages, each with fireplace and hot tub. Rates start at $120 off-season for a one-bedroom, one-night stay in one of the Spice Cottages, modeled after old Florida seaside village homes; discounts apply to stays of weekends and longer.

THE GEORGIAN COTTAGE

Steinhatchee Landing

Bed & Breakfasts) opens to the public Tue–Sat 11–2 for lunch, and 5–9 for fine dining. Sides include Southern favorites like fried green tomatoes, acre peas, sweet potato fries, and three kinds of greens. Reservations recommended.

Steinhatchee
Fiddler's Restaurant (352-498-7427), 1306 Riverside Dr, is set in a giant fishpond (complete with koi) overlooking the river. Kick back and enjoy the view out the picture windows as you feast on specialties like grilled grouper with caper sauce, caprice chicken, and Greek shrimp with feta over linguine. Entrées run $11–18 for fresh local seafood, from mullet and shrimp to crab claws, and the steaks are fantastic: Delmonico, prime rib, and filet mignon, $16–22. The lunch menu offers salads and sandwiches, $5–8, including grouper, shrimp salad, and pecan chicken salad on a croissant. Stop in the lobby on your way out and look over the great selection of Guy Harvey T-shirts. Open daily.

ORIGINAL FLORIDA

Mayo

At 3 PM on a Monday, the parking lot at the **Mayo Cafe** (386-294-2127), 850 Main St (US 27), is packed. That's because everyone in the tri-county area knows Belinda Travis and Shirley Watson, and knows that these ladies dish up great home cooking, buffet style. Try the tempting salads at the salad bar, and Southern comfort foods like fried chicken, fried okra, and collard greens. Breakfast served 5–10:30; lunch and dinner until 9 (10 on weekends).

Perry

✎ I popped into **Pouncey's** (850-584 9942), 2186 S Byron Butler Pkwy, on my last trip through Perry, and wow, what a flashback—it's a real 1950s family restaurant serving up comfort food that feels so good after a long trip. Their burgers are exactly what they claim: the best. Dinners under $10. Don't miss it!

Sisters' Tea Room & Gallery (850-838-2021; www.sisterstearoom.com), 121 E Green St, pours on the charm with your choice of three formal teas ($6–12): a cream tea with scones and fresh fruit; a light afternoon tea including sandwiches, tea breads, and pastries; or a full afternoon tea adding on quiche and desserts. Offering themed teas and unique varieties of tea, they're an unexpected find in downtown Perry.

Steinhatchee

Bridge End Café Restaurant (352-498-2002), 310 10th St. In a cozy little Cracker cottage at the south end of the bridge that spans the Steinhatchee River, look for local seafood favorites and comfort food served with a smile. The baked goods will catch your eye on the way in—leave some room for favorites like cherry pie, coconut cake, and the Steinhatchee Mudslide, a concoction involving brownies, ice cream, and chocolate syrup. Breakfasts include omelets made with fresh shrimp; a selection of salads and sandwiches dominates the lunch menu, and dinner entrées with heaping helpings of sides and a salad bar run $7–12, including the unique Steinhatchee Steamer Pot of fresh steamed clams, potatoes, corn-on-the-cob, onions, broccoli, and celery. If you need a box lunch for a scalloping trip, stop in the night before!

Everyone raves about **Roy's** (352-498-5000; www.roys-restaurant.com), 100 First Ave SW, a fixture since 1969 with a killer view of a Steinhatchee sunset. Their mashed potato salad goes down smooth as silk, and the barbecue attracts folks from several counties. Offering a wide variety of steaks and seafood, Roy's is a place for fresh locally caught specialties, including bay scallops, shrimp, oysters, and tender mullet. Entrées $13–20; open for lunch and dinner. When you can tear your eyes away from the entrancing view of the estuary, enjoy the many regional scenes painted by local artist Linda K. Della Poali. They're for sale, as are the goodies in **Gold N' Gifts** (352-498-0202), with jewelry and local art inside a niche in the restaurant.

✳ Selective Shopping

Perry

You'll find both old and new books at the **Book Mart** (850-584-4969), 1708 S Byron Butler Pkwy, where I was enthralled with the collection of Florida books out front and was pointed toward an essential book for learning about this region, *Along the Edge of America* by Peter Jenkins.

Michelle's Bull Pen (850-584-3098), 3180 US 19 S, is a great westernwear shop with moccasins, boots, hats, and jewelry as well as tack for your steeds.

Perry Flea Market (850-838-1422), US 27 S, held Fri–Sun, is a good, old-fashioned flea market featuring antiques, collectibles, and tools.

In addition to jewelry, **Rebecca's Gold & Gifts** (850-584-2505), 117 E Green St, has a nice selection of home decor items and gifts, including candles and potpourri.

Sisters' Tea Room & Gallery (see *Eating Out*) has an adjoining shop with arts and crafts from regional artists and general gift items.

Steinhatchee
The Goldfish Gift Shop & Café (352-498-0277), 800 First Ave. This sweet little shop showcases nautical gifts and local art on consignment, as well as light breakfasts and tea. Open Thu–Sun 9–6.

The Sea Witch, 12th St and Riverside, carries nautical items, local arts and crafts, and T-shirts.

PRODUCE AND FRESH SEAFOOD Old Hickory (352-498-5333), FL 51, Steinhatchee, has fresh seafood you can't do without, including fresh crabmeat, jumbo crab, and, of course, scallops. Don't pass up the smoked mullet dip.

Produce Place Farm Market, US 19, Perry. Fresh local produce and good Georgia peaches in-season.

✳ Special Events

October: **Pioneer Day Festival,** Mayo, second Sat. This pioneer-themed event mixes up history and fun: Southern belles drift through town as staged gunfights rage; the crowd whoops and hollers at the rodeo while more sedate visitors amble through hundreds of craft booths and an arts show.

THE UPPER SUWANNEE

BAKER, COLUMBIA, HAMILTON, MADISON, AND SUWANNEE COUNTIES

As settlers trickled into the new territory of Florida in 1820, they found the red clay hills and deep ravines of North Florida reminiscent of the terrain they'd left behind in Georgia and the Carolinas. Building farms and plantations along the Suwannee River and its tributaries, they founded villages and cities with a Deep South feel. **Fort White** grew up around a frontier fortress from the Second Seminole War, while **Branford** was once an important steamboat-building town. Antebellum homes grace **Madison, Lake City, Greenville,** and **White Springs.** A post-1900s building boom associated with railroad commerce sets the tone for **Jasper** and **Live Oak.** Covering only 1 square mile, **Lee** is one of the state's smallest incorporated towns. Established in 1913 by the Advent Christian Church, **Dowling Park** remains a religiously oriented retirement

DOWNTOWN LAKE CITY

Sandra Friend

village with a beautiful slice of waterfront on the Suwannee River. **Macclenny,** the seat of rural Baker County, dates back to 1886 and was once known as the horticultural capital of Florida; the Glen St. Mary Nursery, established 1907, was responsible for the citrus industry's standardization of orange varieties. **Lake City,** the heart of the region and the seat of Columbia County, was first known as Alligator Town, a Seminole village ruled by the powerful chief Alligator in the 1830s, and was to have been the home of the University of Florida, but political supporters in Gainesville wooed the college down their way.

Imbued with the grace of the Old South, the towns of the Upper Suwannee offer a reflection on Florida's start as a state during a period of national up-heaval. This is a part of Florida that's remained almost untouched since Recon-struction. The economy is based on agriculture, not tourism. Amber waves of grain wave along the highways, and barefoot youngsters walk the clay roads down to the springs. You'll encounter many postage-stamp-sized towns as you pass through vast swaths of beautiful rural Florida: Stop and sit a spell.

GUIDANCE When you arrive in the region, stop at the **State of Florida's Nature & Heritage Tourism Center** (386-397-4461), FL 136 and US 41, White Springs 32096. As Florida's official outdoor recreation tourism center, it provides a bounty of information on activities throughout the state. Browse their library of guidebooks, or pick up a handful of brochures and a state parks guide. Open daily 9–5. If you're headed out on the rivers, you'll want a map showing boating access and springs: Contact the **Suwannee River Water Management District** (386-362-1001; www.srwmd.state.fl.us), 9225 CR 49, Live Oak 32060; you can also download their recreational guide from the web site. For an over-view of the region, contact **Original Florida** (1-877-746-4778; www.original florida.org or www.springs-r-us.org), which can put in you in touch with anyone in the region. Visit the **Hamilton County Tourism Development Council** (386-792-6828; www.hamiltoncountyonline.com) for details about White Springs, Jasper, and Jennings, and walk into the **Madison County Chamber of Com-merce** (850-973-2788; www.madisonfl.org) for walking tour brochures and more.

GETTING THERE *By air:* The nearest commuter service comes into **Tallahassee** (see the Capital Region chapter) and **Gainesville** (see the Alachua and the His-toric Lake District chapter); however, **Jacksonville International Airport** (see the Jacksonville chapter) provides a broader choice of carriers and is only a two-hour drive away via Interstate 10.

By bus: **Greyhound** (1-800-229-9424; www.greyhound.com) makes stops in Lake City, Live Oak, and Madison.

By car: **I-75** and **I-10** provide quick access to most of the region, but you'll want to wander the back roads to see the sights. Heading north from High Springs, **US 41** passes through downtown Lake City before becoming Hamilton County's "Main Street," running through its three major towns—White Springs, Jasper, and Jennings. **US 129** also runs north–south, linking Branford, Live Oak, and Jasper. For the scenic east–west route, take **US 90** from Olustee west to Lake

City, Live Oak, Lee, Madison, and Greenville; US 27 takes a more southerly route, tying together High Springs, Fort White, and Branford on its way to Tallahassee.

By train: **Amtrak** (1-800-USA-RAIL) has regular service along the main line running through Olustee, Lake City, Live Oak, Lee, Madison, and Greenville.

MEDICAL EMERGENCIES Regional hospitals include **Shands at Lake Shore Hospital** (386-755-3200), 560 E Franklin St, Lake City; **Shands at Live Oak** (386-362-1413), 1100 11th St SW, Live Oak; and **Madison County Memorial Hospital** (850-973-2271), 201 E Marion St, Madison.

✳ To See

DE SOTO TRAIL In 1539 Spanish explorer Hernando de Soto and his troops crossed Florida in pursuit of gold. **Roadside markers** along US 90 interpret his route.

EQUESTRIAN EVENTS **Suwannee River Riding Club, Inc.** (386-935-0447), US 129 north of Branford. Stop by their arena to watch team roping (first and third Fri) and speed events (first and third Sat) each month.

GHOST TOWNS The towns of **Columbus** and **Ellaville** vanished not long after steamboats stopped chugging up the Suwannee, supplanted by railroads. You'll find the **Columbus Cemetery** within Suwannee River State Park (see *Green Space*). Directly across the Suwannee, the remains of Ellaville (primarily foundations and loose bricks) lie along the Florida Trail through Twin Rivers State Forest just north of the former site of the **Drew Mansion** off old US 90, on the west side of the Suwannee River bridge. An interpretive trail loops this historic governor's mansion site.

HISTORIC SITES

Falling Creek
First established as a Baptist congregation in a log cabin prior to 1866, the current **Falling Creek Methodist Church and Cemetery,** Falling Creek Rd, dates back to the 1880s, the land donated to the church after 1855 by heirs of one of the original settlers of the area, Thomas D. Dicks from South Carolina. Wood frame weathered by age, original water glass, shaded by ancient live oaks and southern magnolias; the deep gorge of Falling Creek rings the property (see *Green Space—Waterfalls*).

Jasper
Built in 1893, the **Old Jail** (386-792-1300), 501 NE First Ave, functioned as a prison until 1984 but now serves as the **Hamilton County Historical Society Museum** (see *Museums*) and gives a glimpse into what it was like on both sides of the bars—the sheriff and his family occupied living quarters connected to the jail. Visit the living quarters and walk through the creepy jail cells. Saved from the wrecking ball by a determined group of women, the structure is still undergoing restoration, as is the adjoining **Heritage Village** complex, where Jasper

holds its annual cane-grinding festival (see *Special Events*), and a cotton gin, a small church, and two shotgun houses await restoration.

Lake City

In downtown Lake City, check out the old **Columbia County Courthouse,** circa 1902. The **Columbia County Historical Society** (see *Museums*) sits in a neighborhood dominated by beautiful 1890s Victorian houses, including the **Chalker-**

Sandra Friend

THE LIVE OAK POST OFFICE

Turner House, 104 E St. Johns. Stop at the historical society for information on walking tours in the city's antebellum neighborhoods.

Live Oak

Take a look at that **Wrigley's ad** painted on the side of a building on W Howard St: It's been there since 1909. Glance at Sperring's Muffler and Lube, and you'll realize it's a **1960s Sinclair gas station.** That's the way history is in Live Oak: all around you, but transformed into something utilitarian, from the 1890s downtown block filled with businesses to the pillared **Thomas Dowling** house on FL 136, renovated into a community center. There's plenty of interest for the history buff who's willing to poke around. Stop first at the **Suwannee County Historical Museum** (see *Museums*) to get your bearings for a walking tour of downtown.

Macclenny

Now serving as the town's library, the original **Baker County Courthouse** is an architectural landmark at the corner of Fifth and McIver streets. The old **Baker County Jail,** built 1911–1913 (see *To Do—Genealogical Research*), is next door. The sheriff's family lived on site and prepared food for inmates. Stop in at the **Macclenny Chamber of Commerce,** 20 E Macclenny Ave, to browse through their book of historic sites and get directions to see the town's historic homes from the late 1800s, all privately owned.

FOUR FREEDOMS, MADISON

Sandra Friend

Madison

With more than 30 buildings from the 1800s and nearly 50 historic sites dating to 1936, downtown Madison has the highest concentration of historical architecture in the region. Start your walk by picking up the **Walking/ Driving Tour of Madison County** brochure from the chamber of commerce; it contains a map and detailed

information on each historic site. The **Wardlaw-Smith-Goza Mansion** (850-973-9432), 103 N Washington St, is a Classical Revival mansion built in 1860, once known as Whitehall. North Florida Community College uses the mansion as a conference center, and tours are offered Tue–Thu 10–2 (closed mid-Dec to mid-Jan). Other historic homes of note include the **W. H. Dial House,** 105 E Marion St, a Victorian mansion circa 1880; the **J. E. Hardee House,** 107 E Marion St, a two-story Mediterranean villa from 1918 designed by Lloyd Barton Greer (who also designed the classy Madison County Courthouse); and the **Livingston House,** 501 N Range St, Madison's oldest home, from 1836. In continuous use for worship services since 1881, the small wood frame **St. Mary's Episcopal Church** (850-973-8338), 108 N Horry St, permits tours by appointment.

Dedicated in memory to Captain Colin P. Kelly Jr., a Madison resident and the first American casualty of World War II on December 9, 1941, at Clark Field in the Philippines, the **Four Freedoms Monument,** downtown, reflects on the "Four Freedoms" speech made by President Franklin Delano Roosevelt prior to the outbreak of the war.

Near the old **Madison Depot,** a giant steam engine sits along Range Rd at 109 W Rutledge. It's a relic of what was once **the largest cotton gin in the world,** combing through Sea Island cotton at the Florida Manufacturing Company in the 1880s.

Olustee

Olustee Battlefield Historic State Park (386-758-0400; www.floridastate parks.org/olustee), US 90, is the site of Florida's largest and bloodiest Civil War battle, a patch of hallowed ground beneath the pines, preserved as a memorial by the 1899 Florida legislature to the men who fell during the four-hour conflict. Sparked by a push by Union general Truman A. Seymour, whose success at capturing Baldwin tempted him to send his troops toward the railroad bridge at Columbus without orders from his superiors, the Union forces were met by the largest Confederate buildup to defend Florida—thanks to Florida's crucial role as a beef supplier to the Confederate army. On February 20, 1864, more than 10,000 met in combat in these pine woods; casualties topped 2,000. An annual reenactment (third weekend of February, see *Special Events*) re-creates the battle and encampments; with nearly 10,000 participants, it's one of the South's largest encampments. It's an excellent educa-

OLUSTEE MONUMENT

Sandra Friend

tional experience, especially for those unschooled in Florida's Civil War history. Interpretive center open daily 9–5; an interpretive walk takes you through the battlefield stations. Free.

White Springs

White Sulfur Springs Spa. Behind the Nature & Tourism Center, follow the wooden staircase down to the original White Sulfur Springs Spa, built in the late 1800s. Standing on the balcony, you can look down into the spa, and down along the rapid flow of the Suwannee River. During World War II the spa and its grounds served as an internment camp for German prisoners of war.

MUSEUMS After you learn about Florida's most significant Civil War battle at the visitors center at **Olustee Battlefield** (see *Historic Sites*), stop in the **Olustee Visitor's Center and Museum** at the old railroad depot (off US 90) for an interactive walk through life in this logging and railroad community. In downtown Lake City, the **Columbia County Historical Museum** (386-755-9096) offers exhibit rooms with furnishings that capture the period of this southern Italianate manor circa 1870, including artifacts from the Civil War.

Housed in the former Atlantic Coast Line freight depot from 1903, the **Suwannee County Historical Museum and Telephone Museum** (386-362-1776), 208 Ohio Ave N, Live Oak, presents dioramas and an extensive collection of historic objects—including a working telephone switching station—to bring history alive. At the Old Jail in Jasper (see *Historic Sites*), the **Hamilton County Historical Society Museum** shows off historical documents, display cases with exhibits, and photos of historical structures throughout the county, along with a small gift shop with local art.

A repository of Madison County history, with information on long-lost historic sites like the San Pedro Mission and the Drew Mansion, is the **Treasures of Madison County Museum** (850-973-3661), 194 SW Range Ave, across from Elmer's Genealogical Library. Open Mon–Sat 10–2.

RAILROADIANA Many settlements of the Upper Suwannee started as railroad towns, so their railroad history remains. You'll find turn-of-the-20th-century **railroad depots** still standing in Fort White, Live Oak, and Madison, and restored depots at Olustee (housing a beautiful visitors center with regional railroad history) and Macclenny (with a red caboose outside the depot). A **historic iron boxwork bridge** crosses the Suwannee River at Dowling Park. The east–west main line paralleling US 90 through the region remains a busy thoroughfare (great **train spotting for rail fans**); its Suwannee River crossing (as seen from within Suwannee River State Park, or from

OLUSTEE DEPOT

Sandra Friend

OLUSTEE

the old US 90 bridge, now a walking trail (see *To Do—Hiking*)—is fairly dramatic and has significant historic import—the military objective of the Union troops stopped at Olustee (see *Historic Sites*) was to blow up the original railroad bridge here, severing commerce between North Florida and the Panhandle. Stop in the Suwannee County Historical Museum (see *Museums*) for information on **Live Oak's railroading history.** Live Oak grew up around the Seaboard Air Line railroad, which came through in 1903, and the locally owned **Live Oak, Perry & Gulf Railroad,** affectionately known as the "Lopin' Gopher." Railroad shops in Live Oak once turned out steam locomotives and parts for the Plant System.

✳ To Do

BEACHES While none of the counties in this region touches either the Atlantic or the Gulf, you'll find beautiful white-sand beaches suitable for sunning, swimming, and camping along the Suwannee River at **Suwannee Springs** and **Big Shoals** (see *Green Space*), at **Spirit of the Suwannee Music Park** (see *Lodging*), and along the **Florida Trail** (see *Hiking*).

BICYCLING Mountain bikers have a blast on rugged riverside trails built and maintained by the **Suwannee Bicycle Association** (386-397-2347), P.O. Box 247, White Springs 32096. Stop by their office to pick up maps of local biking routes, including the popular **Swift Creek, Gar Pond, Disappearing Creek,** and **Big Shoals** routes. Each provides challenges to bikers with the undulating terrain along the Suwannee River and its tributaries; trails are posted for three levels of difficulty, from beginner to gung-ho. **American Canoe Adventures** (see *Paddling*) rents mountain bikes in White Springs. For a tamer outing, a paved rail-trail runs along the **Suwannee River Greenway** (see *Green Space*) from Little River Springs County Park in Suwannee County to Ichetucknee Run in Columbia County, passing through the town of Branford. Madison County boasts **The Loop,** a 100-mile marked bike route running down paved rural byways; pick up a map from the chamber of commerce (see *Guidance*).

BIRDING Top sites in the region include **Alligator Lake** (see *Green Space*), where colonies of nesting egrets occupy the islands, and the ♿ **Nice Wander Trail** in the Osceola National Forest, where an early-morning visit lets you watch rare red-cockaded woodpeckers, marked with white bands, emerging from their holes in longleaf pines. Part of the **Florida Trail** (see *Hiking*), which also affords access to red-cockaded woodpecker colonies much deeper in the forest, the 2-mile accessible-with-assistance Nice Wander Trail starts at a trailhead at the Olustee Battlefield Historic State Park entrance. At the **Ladell Brothers Environmental Center** in Madison you can borrow a pair of binoculars from the Hamilton Library and go birding in this lush oasis of hardwoods in the middle of the North Florida Community College campus.

BOATING Most of the rivers in this region have shallows, sandbars, and rapids. Unless your craft has a very shallow draft, don't take it any farther up the Suwannee River than its confluence with the **Withlacoochee**—snags and sandbars are very real hazards and have flipped many a Skidoo. See *Paddling* for details on the best river routes in the region.

DIVING Where the Santa Fe meets the Suwannee, the town of **Branford** calls itself the "Spring Diving Capital of the World." Stop in at the Steamboat Dive Inn (see *Lodging*) for information about open-water dive sites. Cave divers also flock here for both spring diving in the Suwannee River and the extensive underwater cave system at **Peacock Springs** (see *Green Space*). For cold air, gear rentals, instruction, and a friendly chat with Cathy about cave diving, stop at the **Dive Outpost** (386-776-1449; www.diveoutpost.com), 20148 180th St, en route to the park. *Important note:* Many open-water divers have died in this region while attempting cave diving. Do not enter an underwater cave or spring unless you are a certified cave diver. Most springs must be accessed by boat, and a DIVER DOWN flag is necessary while diving the river.

FAMILY ACTIVITIES One of the favorite pastimes of local families is to get the kids in the van and head on down to **Suwannee Springs** (see *Green Space*) for some freebie swimming and sunning on the natural white-sand beaches of the Suwannee River, or to the **water park at Jellystone Campground** (see *Lodging*) in Madison, where a 60-foot-tall, 300-foot-long spiral water slide splashes down into a small lake lined with kids' activities, from playground equipment, boats, and water sprinklers to the nearby mini golf, tractor-train rides to a ghost town in the woods, and cartoons in the Yogi Theatre. $8 person for day use; water park and other kids' activities open weekends and for special events only.

FISHING From **Ocean Pond** at Olustee to **Lang Lake Public Fishing Area,** north of White Springs on US 41, you'll find plenty of stillwater opportunities as well as more than 100 miles of the **Suwannee River** to explore. Don't miss **Cherry Lake,** a WPA reservoir north of Madison popular for bass fishing. Looking for bream? Head for the **Aucilla River** west of Greenville.

GENEALOGICAL RESEARCH In Madison, **Elmer's Genealogical Library** (386-929-2970; www.elmerslibrary .com), 115 W Base St, caters to researchers digging into their family roots, with more than 1,700 rolls of microfilm, 3,000 books, and 4,000 genealogical newsletters to review. Open weekdays 10–4, or by appointment. Housed in the old Baker County Jail in Macclenny, the **Baker County Historical Society Family History Library** (904-259-0587), 42 W McIver, opens Tue 1–8, Sat 1–4 for folks doing historical and genealogical

FISHING FRIENDS

Madison CVB

BIG SHOALS

Sandra Friend

research; you can also make an appointment to visit. Both sites provide fabulous resources for people researching their local connections to the Civil War.

GOLF **Pineview Golf and Country Club** (904-259-3447), 1751 Golf Club Rd, Macclenny, offers golfing in an open, uncluttered environment with pleasing landscaping under the Florida pines. Eighteen holes $21–26, includes golf cart when available.

HIKING Starting at Olustee Battlefield, you can backpack more than 100 miles of the **Florida Trail,** following the Suwannee River for nearly 70 miles from the southern shore of Big Shoals through White Springs to Mill Creek. To pass through sections of private land along the river, you must be a member of the Florida Trail Association (1-877-HIKE-FLA; www.floridatrail.org). One easily accessible public section is the **Big Oak Trail,** starting at the ranger station in **Suwannee River State Park** and crossing the old US 90 bridge to meet the main Florida Trail. You can also find excellent hiking at **Alligator Lake, O'Leno State Park,** and numerous other locations detailed in *50 Hikes in North Florida* (Backcountry Guides). Don't miss the easy 2-mile round-trip to **Big Shoals** from Big Shoals Public Lands north of White Springs, where you can watch the rapids froth like cola, and the easy 0.25-mile walk down to **Falling Creek Falls** (see *Green Space—Waterfalls*). Pursue your Florida State Forests Trailwalker patch with several qualifying trails in **Twin Rivers State Forest,** or take an easy amble along the Suwannee River waterfront on the **Milford Clark Nature Trail** at Dowling Park, a 4-mile round-trip starting behind the Village Lodge (see *Lodging*).

PADDLING The **Suwannee River** is one of the top paddling destinations in

PADDLING SUWANNEE RIVER
WILDERNESS TRAIL

Sandra Friend

Florida, thanks to its length and lack of commercial boat traffic—it has enough shoals and sandbars to discourage most motorboats from heading any farther north than Ellaville. It takes two weeks to paddle the river from its headwaters in the Okeefenokee Swamp in Georgia to the town of Suwannee on the Gulf of Mexico. With its broad sand beaches and beautiful springs, the Suwannee is a perfect choice for a long-distance canoe outing. To read about one man's adventure on the river, check out

Madison CVB

A MARE AND HER COLT

From the Swamp to the Keys: A Paddle Through Florida History by Johnny Molloy (University Press of Florida, 2003); a dated but useful guidebook is *Canoeing and Camping the Beautiful Suwannee River*, written and published by William A. Logan (1998).

To guide you down the river, the new **Suwannee River Wilderness Trail** (see *Green Space*) outlines the 170-mile route, providing riverside cabins and hubs from which you can explore the river bluffs on foot along the Florida Trail and other hiking trails.

Several outfitters provide rentals and shuttles along the Upper Suwannee. In White Springs stop in at **American Canoe Adventures** (1-800-624-8081; www.aca1.com), 10610 Bridge St, where they can set you up with a canoe or kayak and shuttle service, or arrange a multiday outing. Where US 129 crosses the Suwannee north of Live Oak, the **Suwannee Canoe Outpost** (1-800-428-4147; www.canoeoutpost.com) provides canoe and kayak rentals and shuttles out of Spirit of the Suwannee Music Park (see *Lodging*). Canoeists putting in on the Ichetucknee and Santa Fe rivers near Branford can contact the **Santa Fe Canoe Outpost** (386-454-2050), US 441, for rentals.

SWIMMING Swimmers have plenty of choices in the region: from the **water park** at Jellystone Campground in Madison (see *Family Activities*) to the many **springs** open for swimming along the Suwannee River and its tributaries (see *Green Space—Springs*).

TRAIL RIDING Rent horses and tack at **Spirit of the Suwannee Stables** (386-364-1683) inside the Spirit of the Suwannee Music Park (see *Lodging*) to ride the many miles of equestrian trails along the south side of the Suwannee River in Holton Creek Wildlife Management Area. Trail rides run $35 per hour and $30 each additional hour; stall rentals and riding lessons are available. Equestrian trails also wind through **Twin Rivers State Forest** in Madison County and crisscross the **Osceola National Forest** (see *Green Space*), with opportunities for overnight camping.

TUBING ON THE ICHETUCKNEE RIVER
Visit Florida

TUBING The most popular tubing route in the state, the **Ichetucknee River** flows forth from Ichetucknee Springs to create a 6-mile crystalline stream that winds through deep, dark hardwood forests. Pick up a rental tube ($2 a day) at any of the many small shops along US 27; **Joanne's Tubes** is the closest to the park's south entrance, off US 27. A shuttle takes you up to the north end of the park for launch; leave your rental tube in the tube corral at the end of the day for the outfitters to reclaim. Tubing season runs from the end of May through early September.

WALKING TOURS In Lake City, the **Lake Isabella Residential District** covers 30 blocks, and the downtown historic district encompasses another 15 blocks. Pick up a walking tour brochure at the Columbia County Historical Museum (see *To See—Museums*). At **White Springs** grab a walking tour brochure at the State of Florida's Nature & Heritage Tourism Center (see *Guidance*); interpretive signs add to your understanding of the town's history as you walk. The **Madison County Chamber of Commerce** can also provide you with a walking tour brochure for their extensive historic downtown.

✳ Green Space

GARDENS O'Toole's Herb Farm (850-973-3269), Rocky Ford Rd (CR 591). Culinary herbs and flowers grown organically—that's the mainstay of Jim and Betty O'Toole's lovely gardens, and their greens garnish platters in fine restaurants around the region. Their 150-year-old family farm also has a gift shop and tearoom. Mon–Fri 9–6, Sat 9–4; closed Jan, Jul, and Aug.

GREENWAYS Running between Little River Springs County Park and Ichetucknee Run, the **Suwannee River Greenway** provides a paved bicycle path with limited shade along an old railroad route; parking area in downtown Branford. Ten miles north of Madison, the 3-mile **Four Freedoms Trail** starts at Pinetta and heads to the state border at the Withlacoochee River. Now unpaved but providing a pleasant hike, this new greenway project will eventually link the Georgia border to Madison with biking, hiking, and equestrian trails.

O'TOOLE'S HERB FARM

Madison CVB

NATURE CENTER Tucked away in the middle of the North Florida Community College campus west of Madison, the **Ladell Brothers Outdoor Environmental Center** (850-973-1645), 1000 Turner Davis Dr, is a little hard to find: Park on campus near the Hamilton Library and walk between Building 5 (Biology) and the Student Success Center to reach the green space beyond. Follow the lakeshore to the trees, where you'll find the trailhead to this shaded network of hiking trails perfect for wildlife-watching.

PARKS

Branford
On the east shore of the Suwannee River at US 27, **Ivey Memorial Park** has a bait-and-tackle shop, a boat ramp, picnic tables with an expansive view of the Suwannee River, and a swimming hole at Branford Spring accessed via a boardwalk near the park entrance. It also provides parking for people using the Suwannee River Greenway.

© Rob Smith, Jr.

THE CARILLON AT STEPHEN FOSTER STATE PARK

High Springs
One of the oldest state parks in the system, **O'Leno State Park** (386-454-1853), US 41, has two campgrounds with 64 spaces, and 17 stone-and-log cabins nestled along the Santa Fe River, which vanishes into a riversink and flows underground for several miles. A network of hiking trails winds through shady hardwood forests, leading to the river rise.

Lake City
Alligator Lake Recreation Area (386-755-4100), SE Country Club Rd. More than 6 miles of hiking trails surround Alligator Lake and its adjacent impoundments, where colonies of herons nest in the willows. Paddle a kayak across the placid water, or walk the gentle trails with your family.

Lee
Behind city hall, the historic **McMullen Farm House** forms the centerpiece of a small city park with a fishpond, picnic tables, and walking trail. Drive 10 miles east of Lee on US 90 to reach **Suwannee River State Park** (386-362-2746), 20185 CR 132. Although this beautiful riverfront park boasts a pleasant campground, gentle and rugged nature trails, historic Civil War earthworks, and some of the best views you'll get of the Suwannee River, you're missing out if you

don't visit its wild side along the north shore of the Suwannee, accessible only via the Florida Trail (see *To Do —Hiking*).

Macclenny

♿ Along US 90 west of town, **Glen St. Mary River Park** affords access for boaters and canoeists to the Little St. Mary River, with several fishing decks on a dredged channel out to the river.

White Springs

The mission of **Stephen Foster Folk Culture Center State Park** (386-397-2733; www.floridastateparks.org/ stephenfoster), US 41, is to preserve Florida's folk culture heritage, with the State Folklorist on staff, a permanent craft village, and the **Florida Folk Festival** (see the sidebar of the same name), the state's premier venue for cultural preservation. In addition to the cultural exhibits, there is a pleasant campground, and the Florida Trail passes through the park, following the Suwannee River.

Sandra Friend

THE SPA BUILDING AT SUWANNEE SPRINGS

SPRINGS Imagine a mirror-smooth surface of clear water reflecting hues of robin's-egg blue. That's **Ichetucknee Spring,** found at the north end of Ichetucknee Springs State Park (386-497-2511; www.floridastateparks.org/ ichetuckneesprings), 8294 SW Elim Church Rd. In addition to swimming and diving at the spring, visitors grab tubes and float down the placid spring run (see *To Do—Tubing*) or take to the stream with canoes and kayaks for a serene trip down one of Florida's purest rivers.

Contact the **Suwannee River Water Management District** (see *Guidance*) for a map of spring locations in the Suwannee River for diving and swimming; most can only be accessed by boat. In Suwannee County, small county parks provide access to **Charles Spring** (south of Dowling Park), **Little River Springs, Royal Springs** (north of Branford), and **Branford Spring** (at Ivey Park in Branford), all of which invite swimmers and divers to plunge into their chilly depths.

♿ 🐾 At **Peacock Springs State Park** (386-497-2511; www.florida stateparks.org/peacocksprings), 180th

MADISON BLUE SPRING STATE PARK

Madison CVB

St (follow signs east from FL 51), a one-lane dirt road winds through deep woods past pulloffs leading to sinkholes that interconnect underground, forming a karst playground for cave divers. $10 dive fee. You *must* be cave certified to dive in these springs. No solo diving. Swimming is permitted in Orange Grove and Peacock Springs. A new nature trail traces aboveground the route that divers are following below. Leashed dogs only.

Madison Blue Spring State Park (386-362-2746; www.floridastateparks.org/madison) provides visitors a cool natural pool along the Withlacoochee River at FL 6. $10 dive fee for cave divers. Along US 90 near Suwannee River State Park, **Falmouth Springs** creates a popular swimming area. ✐ At **Suwannee Springs** (north of Live Oak off US 129 before the river bridge), a warm sulfur spring pours into a turn-of-the-20th-century spa building before flowing out into the river. Expansive beaches make this a cool weekend hangout (see *To Do— Family Activities*).

WATERFALLS Although Florida isn't known for its waterfalls, the Upper Suwannee boasts a high concentration of scenic spots with waterfalls along streams feeding the Suwannee River basin. Start your tour with a peek at **Falling Creek Falls,** located north of Lake City off US 41 just north of I-10. Turn right on Falling Creek Road (CR 131) and follow it 0.8 mile to the trailhead parking area. It's a 0.2-mile walk to the spectacular, root-beer-colored cascade, which plummets more than 10 feet over a deep lip of limestone and flows away over limestone boulders at the bottom of a ravine. Continue your drive along US 41 through White Springs and turn off on CR 25A. Look for the small CAMP BRANCH sign on the left, and park at the trailhead. Follow the broad bike trail down to **Disappearing Creek,** where Camp Branch drops through a churning set of hydraulics before plunging down into a deep sinkhole. Feeling adventuresome? A blue-blazed trail of less than a mile leads up and around the creek to give you optimal views and a total hike of about 2 miles.

FALLING CREEK FALLS

Sandra Friend

The Florida Trail crosses US 129 north of Live Oak, presenting two more waterfall-viewing opportunities. Park on the northbound shoulder of the road and follow the orange blazes east for less than 0.25 mile to the log bridge crossing over **Sugar Creek,** which cascades a couple of feet between the cypress knees as it flows down to the

Suwannee River. Members of the Florida Trail Association (www.floridatrail.org) can also take the trail west through private lands on a round-trip hike of 7 miles to visit scenic **Mill Creek Falls,** which plunges in a double cascade of more than 15 feet over a limestone escarpment into the river.

WILD PLACES Osceola National Forest (386-752-2577; www.fs.fed.us/r8/ florida) is the smallest of Florida's three national forests. For an orientation to recreation in the forest, stop at the ranger station on US 90 at Olustee (open Mon–Fri 7:30–4) or at the Olustee Depot Visitors Center (open 9–4:30, closed Tue) at CR 231; the railroad depot dates back to 1888. Walk the short nature trail at **Mount Carrie Wayside** for an introduction to the longleaf pine and wiregrass habitat, then head to Olustee Battlefield Historic State Park to walk the & Nice Wander Trail, a 2-mile accessible loop along the **Florida Trail** through red-cockaded woodpecker habitat. Ocean Pond is one of the most beautiful camping areas in North Florida, especially as the sun sets over the cypresses. To see the wildest side of the forest, visit the **Big Gum Swamp Wilderness,** where the Florida black bear roams. A new access point is from the Sanderson Rest Area on the westbound side of I-10, where the accessible-with-assistance & **Fanny Bay Trail** leads you a half mile to a boardwalk into Fanny Bay, a floodplain forest with giant cypresses.

Along CR 135 north of White Springs, **Big Shoals State Park** (386-397-2733; www.floridastateparks.org/bigshoals) encompasses river bluffs and uplands overlooking the roughest whitewater on the Suwannee River.

Linking all of the wild lands along the Suwannee River, the new **Suwannee River Wilderness Trail** (www.floridastateparks.org/wilderness) starts at White Springs and follows the river for 170 miles, offering hubs from which to explore the surrounding wilderness by paddling, biking, hiking, and horseback riding. If you're paddling the length of the river, or hiking through areas where the Florida Trail intersects with a take-out, you have the option of reserving river camps along the route, and cabins at the state parks. Call (1-800-868-9914) to reserve tent sites ($4) or sleep platforms ($20) at Woods Ferry and Holton Creek; more river camps are planned.

Spanning both sides of the Suwannee at its confluence with the Withla-coochee, **Twin Rivers State Forest** (386-208-1462; www.fl-dof.com/state_forests/twin_rivers.html) covers nearly 15,000 acres of thick hardwood forest and timberlands. In addition to seasonal hunting, it provides access to the Suwannee River for anglers and boaters, and hosts an extensive network of biking, equestrian, and hiking trails, including the Florida Trail.

GRACE MANOR

Madison CVB

❋ Lodging

BED & BREAKFASTS

Greenville 32331

🐾 🐾 At the peaceful **Grace Manor** (850-948-5352 or 1-888-294-8839; www.gracemanorinn.com), 117 SW US 221, you'll fall in love all over again. In this 1898 Victorian with a genteel Old South feel, each of the four guest rooms has a private bath and lavish furnishings, $85–125; pets are permitted in a two-bedroom cottage ($135) near the swimming pool and gardens. Full gourmet breakfast, dietary restrictions honored.

Madison 32340

🐾 ♿ ⊙ A newcomer to town, Rae Pike took it upon herself to do some hands-on historic preservation, including the purchase of a 1850s church with the oldest stained-glass windows in Florida and another historic home that was to be torn down. She now operates **Four Freedoms B&B** (850-973-4343; www.madisonfourfree doms.com), 199 NE Range Ave, offering elegant lodging in a converted 1950s minister's home adjoining the church, now used as a private wedding chapel. With three bedrooms upstairs and one down, it's a romantic getaway with spacious rooms, perfect for the wedding party or your anniversary. I was drawn to Sarah's Room with the clawfoot tub, but honeymooners might prefer Margaret Glen's Room, with its canopied bed and heart-shaped spa for two. $125–175. Keep an eye on the web site as work progresses with the three 1800s homes that Rae has moved to the property for restoration into more accommodations.

White Springs 32096

🐾 ⊙ **Sophia Jane Adams House** (386-397-1915 or 1-866-397-1915),

16513 River St. Perched above the Suwannee River on a street lined with historic landmarks, the Sophia Jane Adams House offers a respite for those who want to relax. I feel at home here, reading a book and looking out over the Suwannee River from what is one of the most elegant and *real* B&B experiences in Florida. Built in 1893, this home was commissioned for Sophia Jane by her sons and is now run as a B&B by her great-grandson Watkins Saunders, whose devotion to the property and his guests is apparent. His extensive renovations in the 1990s permitted him to open the family home to the public, and how lucky we are! The now-enclosed back porch, with its polished pine walls and brick floor, overlooks the Suwannee River and is a gathering place for guests to enjoy a movie or borrow a book from the library. Breakfast is served in the formal dining room. Guests can choose from four rooms, $85–115, all tastefully decorated. The Garden Room opens up onto the porch, and the

SOPHIA JANE ADAMS HOUSE

Sandra Friend

cozy Wicker Room, in which we spent our anniversary, looks out over the river. The massive Wisteria and Magnolia Rooms have access to the grand front balcony overlooking the town. Choose any, and you'll be delighted.

HOTELS, MOTELS, AND RESORTS

Branford 32008
Cave divers visiting Branford stay at the **Steamboat Dive Inn** (386-935-2283), corner of US 129 and US 27, providing basic motel accommodations ($40) with dive instructors and "ice cold air" on site.

Dowling Park 32060
🌿 ♿ In the Advent Christian Village, the **Village Lodge** (1-800-371-8381) at Village Landing, CR 136 and CR 250, provides something I haven't found anywhere else on the Suwannee

THE TELFORD HOTEL

Sandra Friend

Telford Hotel
Est. 1903
Restaurant
Bed & Breakfast

River—large, immaculate riverfront motel rooms in a tranquil setting. Rocking chairs outside each room await your arrival; sit and enjoy the view. Follow the walkways (where you can lounge in a porch swing and watch the river) to the Milford Clark Nature Trail, a gem of a hike along the river bluffs. Two rooms are enhanced for wheelchair use. No pets. Rooms and suite, $60 and up.

Lake City
For the traveler on a tight budget, **Lake City** offers a wide variety of older motels just east of the US 90/ I-75 interchange, with rates below $50 a night. Quality and cleanliness vary, so ask to see a room before checking in. Rates in good quality major chains at the same interchange tend to stay below $80 per night.

Madison 32340
🌿 ♿ **Deerwood Inn** (850-973-2504), St. Augustine Rd, is just off I-75 at exit 258, with spacious rooms ($50 and up) featuring a large work space for business travelers, although modem connections must be arranged through the front office. Located in Madison Campground (see *Campgrounds*), it shares amenities such as the pool, game room (classic Pac-Man and pinball lurk here!), tennis, and shuffleboard.

White Springs 32096
The **Historic Telford Hotel** (386-397-2000), P.O. Box 407, on River Rd, dates back to 1903 and continues to welcome guests. Downstairs, enjoy a meal at the Telford Hotel Restaurant, renowned for its Southern cooking (see *Eating Out*). The top floor is anchored by a long corridor on which all rooms ($65) open. They are high-ceilinged and sized for the period,

reminiscent of railroad hotel rooms, each with antique furnishings and a washbasin; shared baths are down the hall. A breakfast room for guests sits at the end of the corridor, and there is a common area with books and games. Some of the rooms interconnect, and some offer multiple beds.

☕ The friendly **Suwannee River Motel** (386-397-2822), P.O. Box 412, on US 41, provides older basic, clean, 1950s-style accommodations for $29 except during the annual Florida Folk Festival (see sidebar). Each room contains a small microwave and refrigerator, and some have full kitchenette. Small dogs permitted.

CAMPGROUNDS

Fort White 32038
Ichetucknee Family Canoe & Cabins (386-497-2150 or 1-866-224-2064; www.ichetuckneecanoeand cabins.com), CR 238, just west of the state park. Primitive cabins and tent camping ($16–45) just upstream from one of the region's most beautiful springs; full-hook-up sites, too. Offers float trips with pickup at take-out.

Live Oak 32060
☕ ♪ **Spirit of the Suwannee Music Park and Campground** (386-364-1683; www.musicliveshere.com), 3076 95th Dr, off US 129 at the Suwannee River. It's a campground. It's a concert venue. And it's so much more. Spread out across 700 thickly wooded acres along the Suwannee River, the Spirit of the Suwannee holds events that draw up to 20,000 people—and they still don't run out of space. You can pitch your tent ($15–17) anywhere, including the soft white-sand banks of the Suwannee River. RVs and campers have their choice of

spaces along four separate loops ($20 and up), and a wide range of rentals (from the cozy but popular "Possum" trailer to the virtual skybox "Treehouse" overlooking the concert grounds) suit everyone's needs ($30–140). There's even a special horse camping area with stables ($17–22). Some visitors come for a weekend; others stay for six months. Canoe rentals, horseback riding, mini golf, swimming, pontoon boat rides, and a classy private floating dining room are just a few of the on-site offerings, along with the camp store and Heritage Village shops (weekends). Rates increase during special events.

Madison 32340
☕ ♪ ♿ ☕ **Jellystone Park Campground** (850-973-8269 or 1-800-347-0174; www.jellystoneflorida.com), Old St. Augustine Rd. This family-oriented camping resort (see *To Do—Family Activities*) has a little something for everyone, with campsites and cabins to accommodate all needs and special events held almost every weekend. $34 for sites; $65–222 for cabins, which range from a playful chuck wagon with bunk beds to comfortably refurbished portable classrooms with enough space for the entire family. No bathrooms provided in low-end cabins; nearby bathhouses are shared with campers. Pets permitted, but not in cabins.

☕ **Madison Campground** (850-973-2504), St. Augustine Rd. Eighty sites set under the trees, suitable for tents or campers, providing picnic tables, grills, and shared amenities such as shuffleboard, tennis, horseshoes, a spacious adult-oriented game room, and an inviting pool. Thirty- and 50-amp service. All major club discounts. Leashed pets permitted. $12–18.

White Springs 32096

🏵 **Kelly's RV Park** (386-397-2616; www.kellysrvpark.com), 142 NW Kelly Lane, off US 41 south of town, has sites for RVs and tents ($25), and roomy rental cabins ($55) with screened porch, air-conditioning, and heat set in a deeply shaded park with nature trails that lead to the adjoining Gar Pond Tract.

🐾 **Lee's Country Campground** (386-397-4132), I-75 and FL 136, has more than 30 sites in an open field, suitable for RVs, vans, and tents. $20 for six people per site includes use of dump station; hot showers and laundry facility available. Overnight stays only. Pets permitted.

🐾 **Stephen Foster Folk Culture Center State Park** (904-397-2733 or 1-800-326-3521; www.floridastate parks.org/stephenfoster), P.O. Drawer G, US 41. Set up your tent at one of 45 sites under the ancient live oaks, $16, or rent one of their beautiful new two-bedroom cabins with screened porch, $90. Leashed pets welcome.

🏵 ✐ 🐾 **Suwannee Valley Campground** (386-397-1667; www .suwanneevalleycampground.com), Rt 1 off FL 136, P.O. Box 1860. Perched well above the Suwannee River, this peaceful campground provides a special primitive tenting area ($12) as well as full-hook-up pull-through sites ($28) and cabins with private bath ($39–59). Amenities include a large clubhouse with general store, canoe and kayak rentals, swimming pool, hiking trails, wireless Internet (extra charge), and a special dog activity area.

✳ Where to Eat

DINING OUT

Lake City

We celebrated our anniversary at **Tucker's** (386-755-5150), 212 N Marion Ave, an intimate hideaway set in the historic Hotel Blanche downtown, the circa 1901 hangout of Al Capone and Governor Cone. With original brick walls and wooden floors, Tucker's candlelit tables made for a romantic dinner—I enjoyed the bacon-wrapped shrimp supreme. Steak and seafood entrées $11–27; closed Mon.

Madison

Enjoy fine dining at the **One Eleven Grill** (850-973-4115), 307 S Pinckney St, which uses fresh veggies and herbs from O'Toole's family farm (see *Green Space—Gardens*) for their tasty preparations, such as Shiitake basil green beans and Thai sizzling snapper with basmati rice and asparagus. It's Southern gone upscale—heck, you can even order grouper cheeks and fried green tomatoes with black-eyed-pea salsa. Appetizers $5–9, entrées $15 and up. Leave room for the fudgy cola cake!

EATING OUT

Branford

Gathering Café (386-935-2768), 100 Suwannee Ave. Western-themed restaurant open daily at 7 AM, serving breakfast (under $4), lunch (sandwiches and salads, $4–6), and dinner favorites like rainbow trout and lemon-pepper chicken.

Nell's Steak and Bar-B-Q House (386-935-1415), 403 Suwannee Ave. Serving up good Southern cooking for more than 30 years, Nell's is a regional favorite with breakfasts under $4 and big buffet spreads. Buffet daily 10–2:30, breakfast buffet on weekends 6–10:30 ($5.50 or $6.50). Lunches $2–4.

Dowling Park

The Village Café (386-658-5777) at Village Landing serves breakfast 7–11 ($3–5). Lunch and dinner options range from hot dogs to crabcakes ($4–7). Open until 8 most evenings.

Fort White

Good food en masse draws the masses to the **Goose Nest Restaurant** (386-497-4725), US 27, with daily lunch buffets ($7) Tue–Sun 11–2; dinner buffets ($9) Fri and Sat 5–8. Stop in for breakfast, too, with cinnamon French toast, grits and eggs, and other favorites for under $6. Closed Mon.

Jasper

Covered in barnyard murals, **Roosters Diner** (386-792-2800), 108 NE First St, is a popular local hangout for good Southern cooking. Breakfast under $4, served anytime; sandwiches and subs $2–5; daily blue plate special $4 or $6 (all you can eat). Open 6–3; closed Sun.

Lake City

Chasteen's (386-752-7504), 204 N Marion Ave. Sandwiches, salads, and daily lunch specials ($5–9); don't miss the homemade pimiento and cheese spread! Serving lunch Mon–Fri.

Ken's Barbecue (386-752-6725), US 90. Mmmm . . . barbecue. This regional chain offers simply the best. Additional locations at South Oak Square on US 129, Live Oak; FL 100 in east Lake City; S First St in Lake City; and US 90 (near the college) in Madison. Closed Sun.

Ruppert's Bakery and Café (386-758-3088), 134 N Marion Ave. For breakfast, enjoy a fresh orange muffin at Ruppert's, served up in a former

drugstore soda fountain on the square downtown. Tempting bakery items include coconut macaroons, fruit turnovers, and a chocoholic's selection of brownies. Lunches $3–5; frozen cappuccino slush and old-fashioned fountain drinks, too!

Lee

Everyone eats at **Archie's** (850-971-5567), US 90 and FL 255, where they serve up huge burgers and country favorites between 11 and 2. On Thu, dinner (5–8) features premium Black Angus prime rib; Fri (noon–9) brings out the popular seafood buffet ($14). Sun buffet.

Live Oak

⚘ **Dixie Grill & Steer Room** (386-364-2810), 101 Dowling Ave. With mouthwatering pies on display when you walk in, you know you'll save room for dessert. This is *the* in place in Live Oak, where the politics of Suwannee County get resolved over coffee. Daily specials ($5 and up) offer heaping helpings of home-cooked favorites like fried chicken and meat loaf.

Live Oak Sub Shop (386-362-6503),

LADYBUG CAFÉ

Madison CVB

603 S Ohio Ave. Boasting "World Famous Subs," this Live Oak landmark piles it on with massive sandwiches good for a picnic on the Suwannee River. Open 10–6 daily.

Macclenny

Pier 6 Seafood & Steak House (904-259-6123), 853 S Sixth St. Pier 6 has a loyal clientele devoted to their heaping seafood platters for two: Order fried, which comes with a lot of 'gator tail, or steamed, my preference, with shrimp, crabs, and clams. Lunch ($5–7) and dinner ($9–14) daily, 11–9.

Madison

Food for Thought (850-973-4248), 683 W Base St, serves up entrées so huge you can easily split one into dinner for two. Their "world famous burgers" ($5–7) run from 5 to 16 ounces, and dinner selections ($9–16) include Southern favorites like grilled pork chops, country-fried steak, butterfly shrimp, and a 16-ounce rib-eye steak. Open Mon–Fri 11–8.

For an old-fashioned soda fountain with quick counter service, try the **Ladybug Café** (850-973-2222) inside the Norris Pharmacy, 110 S Range St, where you can pick up a grilled panini sandwich ($3) or egg salad ($2) to go with your vanilla Coke and hot fudge sundae ($2). Serving breakfast and lunch.

Now *this* is an all-you-can-eat. I'd heard rumors about it for years, but only just lately had a chance to stop in with my husband. **O'Neal's Country Buffet** (850-973-6400), 904 W Base St, offers a $7 spread that boggles the mind with great Southern cooking. Start with ribs, catfish, whitefish, or fried chicken and pile on the creamed corn, yams, cheese grits, sour cream potatoes, and baked beans. Your wait-

ress will bring you crystal-clear homemade lemonade or perfect sweet tea, and you can finish up with cherry cobbler or banana pudding. There are dozens of other choices, too, but come early or late—this place is packed at noon!

White Springs

Country Café (386-397-2040), 16750 Spring St. It's a down-home place with great country cooking—enjoy eggs and grits in the morning, chicken gizzards for lunch, and all-you-can-eat mullet for dinner. Call ahead, and you can pick up your order at the drive-through window! Breakfast options start at $2 for a short stack of pancakes; fish dinners run $5–10, steak entrées $9–18, and all-you-can-eat snow crab legs are $21 on Fri and Sat nights.

🌹 **Suwannee River Diner** (386-397-1181), 16538 Spring St. It's a work of art outside and in, with a vivid wraparound mural depicting the journey of the Suwannee River from the Okeefenokee Swamp to the Gulf of Mexico. Owners Rose and Wayne Stormant handcrafted the wooden booths as well, each of which have historical postcards laminated inside. Try one of their cooked-to-order breakfasts or omelets, or stop in for the all-you-can-eat lunch and dinner bar with daily specials served up with salad bar, hot biscuits, corn bread, dessert, and a beverage. For something offbeat, go for the quail platter. Dinner entrées include vegetables (often collard greens or black-eyed peas), corn bread, beverage, and dessert; you'll be full for under $12. Open at 5 AM for breakfast; $4 and up.

After a few years of absence, the **Telford Hotel Restaurant** (see *Lodging*) is back to serve up their Southern buffet in a comfortable, down-home setting. Stop in Thu–Sun for fried chicken and corn bread, ribs and fried fish, green beans with bacon, and so much more.

✳ Selective Shopping

Dowling Park
In the shops of **Village Landing** on CR 136, the **Rustic Shop** (386-658-5273) stands out with its mix of antiques, import items, and crafts, including fine quilts, pillows, and crocheted baby sets made by local residents. Open 10–5; closed Sun.

Glen St. Mary
Franklin Mercantile (904-259-6040), CR 125 S, is an old-time general store and post office in this once thriving citrus town. Step back a century as you browse through antiques, local crafts, and gifts. Open Fri–Sat 10–5.

Jasper
The Lemon Tree (386-792-1527), 202 NW Central Ave. A distinctly feminine shop hidden inside the Jasper Ace Hardware, it's a real counterpoint to the rest of the merchandise in the store, with country gift and home decor items.

Stephanie's (386-792-2233), SW Central Ave, next to the chamber of commerce. In a century-old building with an original stamped-tin ceiling and bricks made locally with a brick-making machine picked up in trade for a tank of gas, this 30-year landmark offers brassware, figurines, a smattering of antiques, and other home decor items, as well as a wide selection of ladies' attire in the back room.

Lake City
Antiques North-South Connection (386-758-9280), I-75 and US 441, exit

Sandra Friend

FRANKLIN MERCANTILE

414. Five thousand square feet. One owner. Loads of antiques. Literally: A new truckload comes in every week. Look for beaded Victorian lamps, quilts, milk bottles and country kitchen implements, Christmas decor, and, my favorite, row upon row of funky saltcellars.

Creative Stitches Quilting and Embroidery (386-754-3741), 318 E Duval St. Looking for a new frock to wear to the Confederate ball at Olustee? This popular local quilting shop carries a broad stock of Civil War reproduction fabrics and a nice complement of fat quarters, as well as supplies for embroidery and appliqué and specialty sewing machines.

Webb's Antique Mall (386-758-5564; www.webbsantiquemalls.com), US 441-41 and I-10. With 300 dealer booths to roam, you can get lost in here for days, checking out items from vintage tools and golf clubs to fine china, collectible Barbies, and church pews. Plan a day—you'll need it to absorb everything!

North Marion Avenue: With small antiques and artsy venues lining the avenue, downtown Lake City offers a good afternoon's worth of shopping, complete with several pleasant eateries.

A Company of Angels (386-752-5200), 313 N Marion Ave. Uplifting gifts, from spiritual books, candles, and new age music to wind chimes, custom-recipe aromatherapy, and, of course, angel-themed items.

The General Store (386-752-2001), 308 N Marion Ave. A Chippendale escritoire stands next to statues of King Tut: That's the nature of this unique shop, with its mix of country and exotic items, gourmet goodies, teapots, and kitchen decor.

For fine art in stone, visit **Lake City Lapidary & Jewelry** (386-755-9665), 174 N Marion Ave, where I discovered intricately carved and inlaid pelicans and parrots as well as fine gemstones cut and awaiting your choice of setting.

WHITE SPRINGS FOLK ART

Sandra Friend

Linda's Antiques & Collectibles (386-755-6674), 318 N Marion Ave. Dealer booths with a little bit of everything: glassware, dishes, furniture, primitives, and local arts and crafts.

Nana's Antiques & Collectibles (386-752-0272), 327 N Marion Ave. Lovely antique oak china cabinets, country gifts and antiques, collectible Heritage Lace, and Boyds Bears—a little bit of collectibles, a lot of home decor.

Rowand's Mall (386-752-3350 or 1-888-904-9045), 261 N Marion Ave. A bit of everything in this multidealer mall, from collectible coins, stamps, baseball cards, and postcards to minerals, matchbooks, Depression glass, and a smattering of books. Sift through even more antiques at **Yesterdays Once More** (386-288-8575), as well as more modern collectibles and china, just across the hall.

Live Oak
Antique Gallery (386-362-3737), 227 W Howard St. Fine antiques and collectibles; look for classic glassware.

Early Bird Collectibles (386-364-4120), 215 W Howard St. Browse for books (if you don't, I will) and paintings amid the antiques and collectibles; you'll find antique pottery here!

Macclenny
Glass Menagerie, College St. Depression glass, fine china, and collectibles adorn the shelves of this little shop just off US 90.

Rachel's Farmhouse, 238 Macclenny Rd. Step inside this old-time mercantile set in a historic home to browse primitives, local crafts, and old-time farm implements. Antique furniture in various stages of restora-

Florida Folk Festival (1-877-6FL-FOLK; www.floridastateparks.org/folkfest), Memorial Day weekend, Stephen Foster State Folk Culture Center, White Springs. If you truly want to know Florida and its people, plan your vacation around this incredible Memorial Day weekend extravaganza of folk music and Florida culture, now more than half a century old. The Folklife Area brings together Florida's melting pot of cultures, and 14 concert stages scattered throughout the park host more than 250 concerts daily. Each evening the spotlight shifts to the main stage, where Florida troubadours continue the tradition of Will McLean and Gamble Rogers with their haunting ballads of our state, its history, its beauty, and its troubles. Nationally acclaimed folk acts perform on Sat evening, and the Florida State Fiddle Contest brings on a hoedown atmosphere Sun night. As the weekend unfolds, follow the orange blazes in search of the Seminole Camp and homemade churned-on-site ice cream, or join in one of the 75 music, dance, and storytelling workshops. And don't forget the ethnic-food vendors! It's your annual opportunity to touch the soul of Florida. Daily admission costs $20 adults, $5 children; weekend pass $40 adults, $50 families. For optimum comfort, bring your own folding chair.

THE ASHLEY GANG PLAYS THE FLORIDA FOLK FESTIVAL

tion is scattered throughout the house and the porches. Open Wed–Sat.

Madison

It's a nice meld of vintage glass and new art glass at **Jackie's Then and Now** (850-973-8500), 173 N Range Ave, where jazz drifts through the store as you look over Imperial glass, antique pottery, and fine china.

The Old Bookstore (850-973-6833), 115 W Pinckney. Bring your life list! Heavily stocked with out-of-print fiction, especially vintage paperbacks, The Old Bookstore is a bibliophile's dream, a place to spend hours browsing the narrow aisles. Their Florida section includes both used and new books. Record collectors—ask about 78s and other vinyl.

White Springs

Cousin Thelma's is the gift shop at Stephen Foster Folk Culture Center State Park, and thanks to the focus of the park, it's a shop full of Florida folk music and craft. There are turquoise-inlaid fine wood turnings by Tony Cortese, pine needle baskets, painted window folk art, and quilts by "Artist Lady" Ann Opgenorth. I find new treasures here on every visit!

Spring Street Antiques (386-397-4385), Spring St. Housed in a restored 1890s cottage and focusing primarily on glassware and dishes, Spring Street Antiques displays its wares on fine period furniture. Look for a good complement of Fiestaware and saltshakers worth poring over. Specializing in matching antique silverplate patterns. Open Wed–Sat 10:30–4:30.

FARMER'S MARKETS AND U-PICK

Lake City

K. C.'s Produce (386-752-1449), 2275 SE Baya. The most popular spot in Lake City to pick up a bunch of bananas or a pound of peppers—a great selection of fresh fruits and vegetables sold wholesale and retail. Closed Sun.

Live Oak

Suwannee County Farmer's Market (386-776-2362), 1302 SW 11th St. Fresh produce from local farms every Sat 9:30–1 at the Suwannee County Agricultural Colosseum, year-round.

Pinetta

At **Emmolyn Gardens** (850-929-4580), 3344 NE Oak Hill Rd, you can pick your own seasonal vegetables and have peas and butter beans shelled on the spot. Open all year.

Wellborn

Scott's Blueberry Farm (386-963-4952), US 90. Watch for the sign that says FOLLOW THE YELLOW DIRT ROAD and do just that to one of the region's most popular U-picks.

✳ Entertainment

Spirit of the Suwannee Music Park (see *Campgrounds*), Live Oak. Hosting everything from the Suwannee River Gospel Jubilee to the Further Festival, this massive music venue has concerts on an ongoing basis in both indoor and outdoor locations. Check their web site (www.musicliveshere.com) for the current schedule of events, which also range to antique car shows, national trail riding meetings, and other large gatherings.

At **Thayer's Grove** (www.southwest floridabluegrass.org/fljams.cfm) enjoy free bluegrass and folk music jams on Wed at 1 PM and Sat at 6 PM, off FL 18 just west of I-75.

✳ Special Events

February: The **Battle of Olustee,** Olustee, third weekend. It's the largest Civil War reenactment in the Southeast, featuring living history encampments, a large sutler's (period shopping) area, and battle reenactments on Sat and Sun.

"Just Because" Herb Festival, O'Toole's Herb Farm (see *Green Space—Gardens*), brightens up a winter's day betwixt the solstice and equinox. Come out for live music, workshops, and vendors; fee.

March: **Wild Azalea Festival** (386-397-2310), third Sat, White Springs. Celebrate the fragrant blossoms that usher in spring on the Suwannee with arts, crafts, music, and food.

Suwannee County Fair (386-362-7366; www.suwanneecountyfair.com), 1302 11th St, at the Suwannee County Fairgrounds, held the last week of March. A traditional, old-time county fair with judged livestock and vegetables, quilting, fine arts, and other crafts; commercial and educational exhibits, a popular midway, talent show, and the "politician bake off" (this, I've gotta see!).

April: **Lee Days,** Lee, first Sat. A celebration of the heritage of this tiny Florida town, with arts and crafts and food vendors at the park.

May: **Hamilton County Rodeo** (386-792-1415), first weekend, Hamilton County Arena, Jasper.

Down Home Days, Madison, third weekend. Step back to pioneer days in downtown Madison with traditional crafts and foods.

November: **Cane Grinding Festival** (386-792-1300), second weekend, at Jasper's Heritage Village. Learn how sugarcane becomes molasses at this annual celebration of agricultural history.

December: **Christmas on the Square,** featuring arts and crafts and entertainment in Live Oak's historic downtown.

Festival of Lights, Live Oak. A drive-through wonderland of light in Spirit of the Suwannee Music Park (see *Campgrounds*), including a miniature Victorian Christmas Village and Santa's workshop. $5 per car.

Eastern Panhandle 3

CAPITAL REGION

APALACHICOLA REGION

Visit Florida

Eastern Panhandle

ALABAMA

GEORGIA

27

19

84

Lake
Seminole

Jackson
County

Thomasville

84

Marianna

Wash.
County

Exit 130

90

Gadsden
County

Havana

319

Jefferson
County

Monticello

Exit
192

Exit
199

Exit 203

10

Exit 225

Exit
241

231

Tallahassee

Exit 209

19

To
Jacksonville

Bay
County

20

Apalachicola R.

Calhoun
County

Liberty
County

Leon
County

Wakulla
County

CAPITAL
REGION

19

27

221

Taylor
County

Panama City

Wakulla

319

98

APALACHICOLA
REGION

APALACHICOLA
NATIONAL
FOREST

ST. MARKS NATIONAL
WILDLIFE REFUGE

Apalachee
Bay

Gulf
County

Franklin
County

319

98

Apalachicola

ST. VINCENT NATIONAL
WILDLIFE REFUGE

N

Gulf of
Mexico

0   25   50
Miles

© The Countryman Press

CAPITAL REGION
LEON, JEFFERSON, GADSDEN, AND WAKULLA COUNTIES

On March 4, 1824, Florida's politicos decided on a meeting place half-way between the thriving cities of Pensacola and St. Augustine, and dubbed it **Tallahassee**—a corruption of the Creek word for "abandoned village." A log cabin served as the first capitol, replaced by a more grandiose structure completed just in time for Florida's induction into the Union in 1845. Tallahassee's classy downtown, a mix of old brick buildings and modern architecture with side alleys just wide enough for a horse and carriage, has incredible hills for a Florida city—you'll think you're in New England.

Atop the tallest hill in **Monticello,** the Jefferson County Courthouse evokes déjà vu: It's a replica of Thomas Jefferson's famous home. The namesake of **Havana** is indeed Cuba, as the Red Hills region supplied the Cuban cigar industry with tobacco until Fidel Castro came to power. The old tobacco drying barns and downtown infrastructure now make up the region's top antiquing town. Two generations ago folks in the nearby tobacco community of **Quincy** invested in a young company called Coca-Cola, and their dividends show in the Victorian homes that dominate this artistic town.

As you head toward the Gulf of Mexico, red clay hills give way to the densely forested Woodville Karst Plain, a wonderland of sinkholes and springs defining **Wakulla County.** It's a green, wet place, with lushly canopied roads edged by floodplain

THE OLD CAPITOL

Sandra Friend

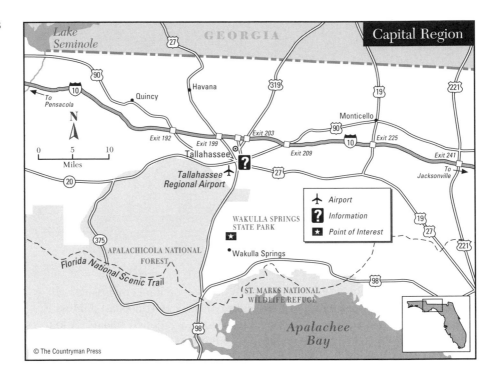

forests and salt marshes. The medicinal qualities of the sulfur and magnesium springs near **Panacea** lead to its unusual name, but this coastal town is best known for its seafood. Buy it roadside direct from the fishermen, or have it fried or broiled at one of the local eateries. Also renowned for seafood, the fishing village of **St. Marks** sits along the St. Marks River and the vast estuaries where it meets the Gulf of Mexico. The U.S. Congress created this town in 1830 as a port of entry to the United States before Florida's first major railroad, the Tallahassee & St. Marks, joined the two cities in 1837.

GUIDANCE The **Tallahassee Area Visitor Information Center** (850-413-9200 or 1-800-628-2866; www.seetallahassee.com) has a delightful walk-in storefront at 106 E. Jefferson St, downtown, with a wall of brochures and a gift shop serving free iced tea Mon–Fri 8–5, Sat 9–1. Parking may be tricky, so head to nearby Kleman Plaza. You'll find the **Wakulla County Chamber of Commerce** in the county seat of Crawfordville along US 319, housed in the historic old County Courthouse (behind the new courthouse), open Mon–Fri 8–noon, 1–5, and a new **Wakulla Welcome Center** along US 98 in Panacea.

GETTING THERE *By air*: **Tallahassee Regional Airport** (850-891-7800; www.talgov.com/airport/index.cfm), 3300 Capital Circle SW, has commuter service on Atlantic Southeast, Continental, Delta, Northwest, and USAirways.

By bus: **Greyhound** (850-222-4240) pulls into 112 W Tennessee St, downtown Tallahassee.

By car: **I-10** is the major east–west corridor through Florida's Panhandle, with US 98 providing the scenic route connecting coastal villages and US 90 running through the northerly Red Hills region.

By train: **Amtrak** (850-224-2779 or 1-800-872-7243) connects Tallahassee via New Orleans with Los Angeles with the transcontinental Sunset.

GETTING AROUND *By car*: With its many one-way streets, downtown Tallahassee can be a bit confusing: Watch for signs that direct you to points of interest. Roads radiate out of Tallahassee like spokes on a wheel: **US 27** leads northwest to Havana, southeast to Perry; **US 319**, north to Thomasville, Georgia, and south to Crawfordville; **FL 363** south to St. Marks; **US 90** northeast to Monticello, northwest to Quincy. Capital Circle defines the wheel's rim.

By bus: Weekdays, catch a free ride between downtown Tallahassee points of interest on the **Old Town Trolley**, every 20 minutes, 7–6. **StarMetro** (850-891-5200), the public bus service, runs routes to suburban neighborhoods; fares $1.25, or $3 for a one-day pass.

By taxi: **Ace Taxi** (850-521-0100), **City Taxi** (850-562-422), **Red Cab** (850-425-4606), **Yellow Cab** (850-580-8080).

PARKING Havana, Monticello, and Quincy have free street parking for shopping But in busy Tallahassee, metered on-street spaces have time limits from 30 minutes to 10 hours. If you're visiting a museum or restaurant, it's best to pop into a parking garage. Kleman Plaza, between Bronough and Duval, is roomier than the Eastside Parking Garage on Calhoun and offers easy access to museums and downtown historic sites; $1 an hour, $10 a day.

MEDICAL EMERGENCIES Tallahassee Memorial Hospital (850-681-1155; www.tmh.org), 1300 Miccosukee Rd, Tallahassee. In outlying areas, call 911; it may take up to an hour to reach the emergency room.

✳ To See

ANTEBELLUM PLANTATIONS Most of Florida's remaining antebellum plantations are found in the Capital Region—the visitors bureau lays claim to 100 plantations between Tallahassee and Thomasville, many still working farms, some owned by folks like Ted Turner. Although specifically noted for its formal gardens, the

INSIDE THE GOODWOOD PLANTATION
Sandra Friend

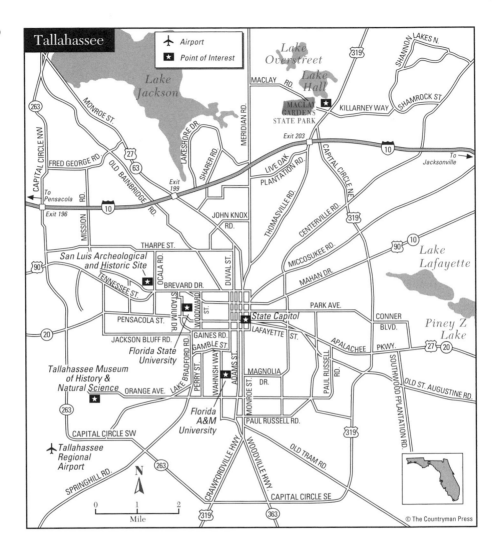

Tallahassee

✈ Airport
★ Point of Interest

© The Countryman Press

grounds of **Alfred B. Maclay Gardens State Park** (see *Green Space—Botanical Gardens*) encompass an antebellum quail hunting plantation.

A corn-and-cotton plantation dating back to the 1830s, **Goodwood** (850-877-4202), 1600 Miccosukee Rd, is the most accessible of the region's grand antebellum plantations. With period furnishings (including many European antiques) dating back to the home's ownership by Senator Hodges circa 1925, the classy interior is beautiful to behold. Crystal chandeliers dangle from the ceilings, velvet drapes add a touch of Europe, and the ornate ceiling in the salon is considered the oldest existing fresco in Florida. Traditional dogtrot architecture is broken up by a half-curved stairway in the center of the building leading up to the bedrooms, which are extremely roomy for their period. An ornate canopied alabaster bed frame sports an original lace bedspread; the medallion above the master bed is painted with delicate roses, as is the bath. It is a place of romance and history, where Granny slyly smiles like Mona Lisa from the picture frame. Step inside, and touch a Florida long gone. Sixteen buildings make up the complex, but the main house is truly the crown jewel. Fee.

Tallahassee Area CVB

BROKAW-MCDOUGALL HOUSE

In 1896 the **Hickory Hill Plantation** encompassed 2,800 acres along the Georgia border. Architect Henry Beadel designed a grand home overlooking Lake Iamonia, now known as the Beadel House. With four rooms upstairs, and four downstairs decked out in original furnishings, this unique plantation home reflects the sensibilities of its New York owners, who added an Adirondack-style hunting lodge in 1923. A skilled photographer and painter (whose watercolors are signed with the number of minutes it took to complete each piece), Henry Beadel was an avid sportsman who felt that the lack of controlled burns of plantation fields limited quail populations. In 1958 Beadel founded the **Tall Timbers Research Station** (850-893-4153; www.ttrs.org), 13093 Henry Beadel Dr, which occupies much of the original plantation and serves as a facility for the study of fire to regenerate habitats. Tall Timbers, with walking paths above Lake Iamonia, is open daily; the plantation home opens for docent-led tours once monthly on the third Sun (except on holidays). Fee.

Evoking *Gone with the Wind*, the **Brokaw-McDougall House** (850-891-3900), 329 N Meridian Ave, shows off its 1850 Classical Revival charm with its balcony and verandas behind the Corinthian columns. Nearby, **The Grove,** home of Florida's first territorial governor, Richard Keith Call, isn't open for tours, but you can drive by (100 E First Ave) and admire this 1825 beauty, dubbed the finest Greek Revival building in Florida. The current **Governor's Mansion** (850-488-4661) is not an antebellum plantation, but it looks like one—it's patterned after Andrew Jackson's Hermitage and is open for tours.

ARCHEOLOGICAL SITES Two extraordinary earthen temple sites in the region are the **Lake Jackson Mounds Archeological State Park** (850-922-6007; www.floridastateparks.org/lake jacksonmounds), 3600 Indian Mounds Rd, and **Leitchworth Mounds** (www.floridastateparks.org/letch worthmounds) off US 90 west of Monticello. On the north shore of Lake Jackson, the temple complex of Lake Jackson Mounds consists of six earthen temple mounds and a burial mound, part of an A.D. 1200–1500 village. At Leitchworth Mounds you

LEITCHWORTH MOUND

Sandra Friend

To step far back into Florida's history, head for **Mission San Luis** (850-487-3711; www.missionsanluis.org), 2020 Mission Rd, the site of the first Spanish mission in this region, which oversaw the operation of more than 100 missions throughout Spanish Florida from 1656 to 1704. Managed by the Department of State, this is Florida's *only* reconstructed Spanish mission. History comes alive as you stroll along the walkways between mission buildings, Spanish residences, and the mighty Apalachee council house, a full-sized replica complete with palm thatch. When you duck inside, take in the proportions—the enormous original could hold up to 3,000 people, one of the largest indigenous structures in the southeastern United States. When you finish your walk through time, stop and take a look at the ongoing archeological dig, and follow the Ravine Trail, a nature trail showcasing the natural habitats of Tallahassee's steep-sided hills. Open Tue–Sun 10–4; free.

A SPANISH SETTLER TALKS ABOUT HER DAY AT THE MISSION   *Mission San Luis*

can walk around the base of the tallest and most complex ceremonial mound in Florida, 46 feet high, from the Woodland Period circa A.D. 500.

One of the more unique ways to tour the region's archeological treasures is to paddle the **Apalachee Archeological Boat Trail** along Ochlocknee Bay, with 11 points of interest, including middens, ceremonial mounds, and fisheries. Pick up a tour brochure from the Wakulla County Chamber of Commerce (see *Guidance*).

ART GALLERIES

Havana
First Street Gallery (850-539-5220), 204 First St NW, is a local fine-arts co-op with sculpture, paintings, and photography by area artists. Open Fri–Sun.

Florida Art Center and Gallery (850-539-1770), 208 First St NW, handles consignments from area artists in a large, open gallery space, showcasing ceramic tiles, paintings, photography, and other fine art.

Quincy
Gadsden Art Center (850-875-4866; www.gadsdenarts.com), 13 N Madison St, showcases fine visual arts in a historic 1910 hardware store; this is one of North Florida's top collections. Massive wood sculptures by Mark Lindquist dominate the lobby. Climb upstairs to see the Bates Children's Gallery, with the fine works

of local schoolchildren, and don't miss the gift shop, with its one-of-a-kind works of art. Open Tue–Sat 10–5, Sun 1–5; closed holidays.

Tallahassee
The Le Moyne Art Foundation (850-222-8800), 125 N Gadsden St, encompasses a complex of three major buildings connected with a sculpture garden, where fine arts from local, regional, and national artists fill the galleries and gardens. Closed Mon and major holidays; fee. Near Florida State University, **Railroad Square** (850-224-1308), 567 Industrial Dr, contains a cluster of art galleries and gift shops surrounding a sculpture garden and a diner inside a railroad caboose. The **Museum of Fine Arts at Florida State University** (850-644-6836; www.mofa.fsu.edu), 250 Fine Arts Bldg, features changing exhibits from students and national artists, and the **Foster Tanner Art Center** (850-599-3161) at Florida A&M focuses on world art, with an emphasis on African American artists.

GHOST TOWNS There isn't much left of **Port Leon,** founded in 1838 as the terminus of Florida's first railroad, the Tallahassee Railroad. Located southeast of San Marcos de Apalache (see *Historic Sites*), scattered bricks and the outlines of streets are all that remain in the salt marsh. In 1843, soon after Port Leon became the seat of the newly formed Wakulla County, a hurricane obliterated the town; water covered the streets up to depths of 10 feet. The survivors decided not to rebuild and moved inland to establish the village of Newport.

HISTORIC SITES

Chattahoochee
Since the early 1900s, the historic **Chattahoochee Arsenal,** site of Florida's first arsenal in 1839, has been part of the grounds of the Florida State Hospital, a sanitarium.

Crawfordville
The original **Wakulla County Courthouse** houses the chamber of commerce and has exhibits on regional history. Across the street, the **Old Jail** is undergoing renovation for use as a county history museum.

Greensboro
Dating back to 1875, the picturesque **Shepard's Mill** (850-875-2694), CR 12 on Telogia Creek, is Florida's last working water-powered gristmill. Stop by on Fri or Sat, 10–5, to see how meal and grits are ground from corn.

Monticello
A Florida Heritage downtown, Monticello has more than 40 historic buildings, including the **1908 county courthouse** that mimics Thomas Jefferson's grand home. Since 1890, the **Monticello Opera House** has dominated the town square; peer in the windows of the office to see historical artifacts, including a 1928 Greta Garbo poster found under the stage. Built in 1852, **Monticello High School**, west on US 90, is Florida's oldest brick school building. Walk around downtown to enjoy other residential and business structures with fine

Classical and Greek Revival architecture, including the 1833 **Wirick-Simmons House.**

Newport

One of the most photographed structures in the region is the **St. Marks Lighthouse** at the end of the road in St. Marks National Wildlife Refuge (see *Green Space—Wild Places*), which dates back to 1842. During the Civil War, the Fresnel lens was removed and hidden in the salt marsh to make the lighthouse useless to the Union Blockading Squadron. Lighthouse keepers and their families lived in the structure until 1960, when the U.S. Coast Guard automated the beacon.

Quincy

Quincy has an extraordinary number of historic buildings in excellent condition; all are privately owned but can be viewed from the sidewalks. Stop by the **United Methodist Church** to see the handiwork of Louis Comfort Tiffany, who also installed windows in homes around town. Around the corner, the **White House,** constructed in the early 1840s, became the home of Pleasants Woodson White, chief commissary officer for the Confederate army in Florida. Both the **Allison House** and **McFarlin House** (see *Lodging—Bed & Breakfasts*) offer glimpses into Quincy's storied past; many more structures are explained in the walking tour handbook available at the Gadsden Art Center (see *Art Galleries*).

St. Marks

good birding

San Marcos de Apalache (850-922-6007), 148 Old Fort Rd. Significant as the site of the first coastal fortress along Florida's Panhandle, this historic site protects several generations of battlements, from the faint tracings of the original wooden stockade fort completed by the Spanish in 1679 at the confluence of the St. Marks and Wakulla rivers to the remains of the masonry structure occupied up through the Civil War. Visit the small museum before walking the interpretive trail along the rivers. Open 9–5; closed Tue and Wed. Fee.

DIG AT MISSION SAN LUIS

Tallahassee Area CVB

Tallahassee

There are more than 100 historic sites in the Tallahassee area; pick up a copy of *Tallahassee Treasures* and *Touring Tallahassee* from the visitors center to start your exploration. The downtown contains many historic treasures, including some narrow old brick alleyways reminiscent of those in New England cities. The **First Presbyterian Church** (850-222-4504), 102 N

Adams St, built in 1838, is Tallahassee's only church remaining from territorial days, complete with frontier accoutrements like rifle slits in the basement. The massive pipe organ was built to fit the building, and the North Gallery served as a segregated congregation for plantation owners' slaves. Across the street, the **Old U.S. Courthouse** (850-224-2500) has murals depicting great moments in government—honest! At **The Columns** (850-224-8116), 100 N Duval St, the Greek Revival columns say it all: It was built for the first president of the Bank of Florida. The **Old Capitol Building** dates back to 1845, and the 1843 **Knott House** is one of several houses in town built by George Proctor, a free black man (see *Museums* for both). Both the **Park Ave and Calhoun St historic districts** are lined with antebellum and early-1900s homes. Tallahassee's two universities, **Florida A&M and Florida State,** also merit their own historic districts.

Sandra Friend

NATURAL BRIDGE HISTORIC STATE PARK

Woodville

Natural Bridge Historic State Park (850-922-6007; www.floridastateparks .org/naturalbridge), 7502 Natural Bridge Rd. An important site in Florida's Civil War history, Natural Bridge speaks to a time when the Confederacy was close to collapse. On March 6, 1865, Union troops marching north from their landing point at the St. Marks Lighthouse met the Florida 5th Cavalry and cadets from the West Florida Seminary (now Florida State University). The Confederate troops routed the Union attack and are credited with keeping Tallahassee the only Confederate capital east of the Mississippi that did not fall into Union hands during the war—although some historians surmise that the Union objective was to capture the key port of St. Marks rather than invade the capital city, and they came to this spot to utilize the Natural Bridge, a place where the St. Marks River dives underground at a river sink and reemerges less than 0.25 mile south at a spring. Free.

MARINE CENTER At the **Gulf Specimen Marine Lab** (850-984-5297; www .gulfspecimen.org) along US 98, Panacea, you can interact with the native marine life of the Gulf estuary. You'll find no sharks or dolphins here: The center has a special focus on the small side of Florida sea life—scallops and crabs, snails and lobsters, sea fans and sea urchins, shrimp and oysters, and other tiny denizens of the coastline. Open daily; fee.

MUSEUMS In addition to commemorating the former senator's accomplishments, the **Claude Pepper Center** (850-644-9309), 636 W Call St, Tallahassee, contains research materials dating back to the New Deal era and an art gallery with a focus on political activism. A true believer in liberalism, Senator Pepper received the Presidential Medal of Freedom while working to improve life for his fellow Americans. Open Mon–Fri 8:30–5; free.

At the **Knott House** (850-922-2459), 301 E Park Ave, Tallahassee, step into 1928 and learn about the lives of William Knott, a former state treasurer, and his wife, Luella, a temperance advocate and whimsical, published poet who wrote about and attached short poems to virtually every piece of the home's original furnishings, earning the home the nickname "The House that Rhymes." The home was designed by George Proctor, a free black man, in 1843, commissioned as a wedding gift for Catherine Gamble from her husband-to-be, attorney Thomas Hagner; on May 20, 1865, the Emancipation Proclamation was read from its front steps. Tours on the hour Wed–Fri 1–3, Sat 10–3; free.

✒ At the **Museum of Florida History** (850-245-6400), 500 S Bronough St, Tallahassee, prepare to have your eyes opened about Florida's rich and colorful past. In addition to rotating thematic exhibits, the state's official history museum includes a climb-aboard replica of an early steamboat, tales of buried treasure, a citrus-packing house from the 1930s, information on Florida's role in the Civil War, and much more—interactive exhibits that'll keep the kids hopping. The adjoining History Shop contains classy reproductions and a great selection of Florida books. Open Mon–Fri 9–4:30, Sat 10–4:30, Sun noon–4:30. Free.

Old Capitol Museum (850-487-1902), 400 S Monroe St., Tallahassee, Construction began in 1839 to replace the old log cabin used as a meeting place for Florida's first legislators. Although the new capitol opened in 1845, a hurricane damaged it in 1851. Restoration and expansion followed; the building continued to sprawl until the 1970s, when the state replaced it with a tall modern structure next door. Saved from the wrecking ball by public support, the Old Capitol, restored to its 1902 Classical Revival glory, is now a museum devoted to Florida's legislative history.

John G. Riley Center and Museum of African-American History & Culture (850-681-7881; www.tfn.net/Riley), 412 E Jefferson St, Tallahassee. In this 1890 home designed by John G. Riley, a black architect, you'll find a museum of regional African American history from Reconstruction through the civil rights movement, with a special focus on historic cemeteries. Mon–Wed and Fri 10–4; fee.

✒ **Tallahassee Antique Car Museum** (850-942-0137; www.tacm.com), 3550 US 90 E, Tallahassee. From the first steam-powered car ever built (the 1894 Duryea) to prop vehicles from several Batman movies, Devoe Moore has a car collection to put Jay Leno to shame. But it's not just about the autos. Moore is a collector of collections, and his grand display (in addition to the top antique-car collection in the nation) includes more than 80 classic vehicles, sports memorabilia, children's pedal cars, brass fans, antique toys, and the finest collection of antique outboard motors in the world. $7.50 adults, $5 students, $4 children under 10.

✔ **Tallahassee Museum of History & Natural Science** (850-575-8684), 3945 Museum Dr, Tallahassee, isn't at all what you'd expect from a museum. Gentle footpaths blend into the natural surroundings, winding through Florida habitats alive with native wildlife like bald eagles, alligators, Florida panthers, and river otters; I looked up in a tree and saw a gray fox peering calmly down at me. In the Discovery Center, interactive natural science exhibits change every four to six months. Kids were busy in a fossil dig as I continued on to the Big Bend Farm, a living history area that shows Florida as it used to be: Workshops demonstrate shucking corn and pressing cane for sugar. On the opposite side of the main building (with a gift shop full of fun toys for the kids) are several historic structures, including the 1897 Concord School, the first post-Reconstruction school where blacks were taught, and Catherine Murat's 1850s manor home, moved here from the Bellevue cotton plantation. To truly enjoy the historic exhibits on display, rent the audio tour, which lets you plug codes into a cellphone-like device to get audio clips from the Florida State Archives—oral histories, music, interviews, and narrations. What impressed me the most? Inside the 1924 Florida East Coast Railroad caboose, I pressed a button and heard a recording from the 1940s of Zora Neale Hurston singing a railroad lining chant. Now *that's* bringing history to life. $7 adults, $6.50 seniors, $5 ages 4–15.

The **Union Bank Museum** (850-487-3803), Apalachee Pkwy, Tallahassee, is Florida's oldest surviving bank building, dating back to 1841. Mon–Fri 9–4, Sat and Sun by appointment; free.

RAILROADIANA In addition to Tallahassee's **Railroad Square** near FSU, be sure to see the railroad exhibit at the Tallahassee Museum of History & Natural Science (see *Museums*) and make a stop at the **Sopchoppy Railroad Depot,** currently under renovation. The Tallahassee–St. Marks Historic Railroad Trail State Park (see *Green Space—Greenway*) traces the route of Florida's earliest lengthy railroad, circa 1837, and in downtown Chattahoochee, Heritage Park has a **red caboose** parked next to a beautiful mural of the John W. Callahan steamboat on the Apalachicola River.

WINERY Monticello Vineyards & Winery (850-294-WINE; www.fgga.org/monticello.htm), 1211 Waukeenah Hwy, is a small operation at Ladybird Organic Farm on CR 259 south of Monticello. All wines are certified organic, processed from muscadine grapes grown on site. Call to arrange a visit.

✳ To Do

BEACHES The vast salt marshes of the Gulf estuary yield to several small beaches, found off the side roads south of US 98; look for signs to **Shell Point** and **Wakulla Beach** near Wakulla, and **Mashes Sand Beach** at Panacea.

BICYCLING The **Tallahassee–St. Marks Historic Railroad Trail State Park** (see *Green Space—Greenway*) is the region's longest bike trail, ideal for overnight trips. Or follow FL 12 through Gadsden County on the North Florida Art Trail; signs lead the way.

BIRDING St. Marks National Wildlife Refuge (see *Green Space—Wild Places*) can't be beat for the number of species to spot during the winter migration. Stop by the Henry M. Stevenson Memorial Bird Trail at **Tall Timbers Research Station** (see *To See—Antebellum Plantations*), open Mon–Fri 8–4:30, for prime birding along Lake Iamonia.

DIVING The Woodville Karst Plain draws cave divers from all over the world for exploration of the interconnecting underground waterways at **Leon Sinks Geological Area** (see *Green Space—Wild Places*); cave diving certification required. *Important note:* Many open-water divers have died in this region while attempting cave diving. Do not enter an underwater cave or spring unless you are a certified cave diver.

FAMILY ACTIVITIES ✔ **The Mary Brogan Museum of Art and Science** (850-513-0700; www.thebrogan.org), 350 S Duval St, Tallahassee, an associate of the Smithsonian Institution, offers an interesting mix—science for the kids, art for you. And it works! Rotating first-floor exhibits feature colorful hands-on play stations; the second floor showcases permanent science exhibits such as the Ecolab (check out the Florida watershed map), WCTV weather station, and the Early Childhood Area for the smallest of small fry. Third-floor exhibits celebrate the merging of art and science; I enjoyed a stroll through the History of Photography, which kicked off with Matthew Brady's classic photo of Abraham Lincoln. Special stations focused on the science behind photography. Stop in the Museum Store for a delightful selection of creative gifts to spark any budding artist. Open Mon–Sat 10–5, Sun 1–5; closed Thanksgiving and Christmas; fee.

✔ At the **Challenger Learning Center and IMAX Theatre** (850-644-IMAX; www.challengertlh.com), 210 S Duval St, Tallahassee, most folks are there for the big-screen IMAX with 20,000 watts of sound and the incredibly crisp digital planetarium in its 50-foot dome, where dazzling graphics immerse you into space like no other planetarium show I've ever seen. But with reservations, your kids can also spend three hours taking over Mission Control and become astronauts on a space station mission to collect data on a comet in two realistic training laboratories (minimum age 10). This collaborative effort between the FSU College of Engineering and NASA is a living memorial to the *Challenger* crew. Open Mon–Thu 10–8, Fri–Sat 10–1, Sun 1–7; fee.

ST. MARKS RIVER

Sandra Friend

🐟 At **Cross Creek Driving Range & Par 3 Golf** (850-656-GOLF), 6701 Mahan Dr, Tallahassee, practice your putts on the driving range, or challenge the kids to a round of par 3. Open daily at 8 AM.

🐟 **Tallahassee Rock Gym** (850-224-ROCK), 629-F Industrial Dr, Railroad Square, Tallahassee, offers a popular climbing wall in a historic railroad warehouse; take lessons, or practice your skills!

FISHING Saltwater anglers head for St. Marks, the region's launch point into the Gulf of Mexico; ask after guides at **Shell Island Fish Camp** (see *Lodging— Fish Camps*). Inland, **Lake Talquin,** a hydroelectric reservoir on the Ochlocknee River, has plenty of speckled perch, sunfish, and the tantalizing, trophy-sized largemouth bass for the patient angler. There are numerous **fish camps** off FL 267 and several off FL 20 on the Upper Ochlocknee River. Use **Chattahoochee Landing** off US 90 as your access point to the Upper Apalachicola River.

GAMING **Greyhound racing** is the focus of the Jefferson County Kennel Club (850-997-2561), US 19 north of Monticello, but I'm told their dining room offers good old-fashioned Southern hospitality; dress for the occasion!

GENEALOGICAL RESEARCH You'll hit the jackpot for all sorts of historical research at the **Florida State Archives** (850-245-6700; http://dlis.dos.state.fl.us/ barm/fsa.html), 500 S Bronough St, but most folks who quietly sit at the long tables inside are digging through their ancestors' roots. *Tip:* Use their online resources first, and then come to Tallahassee to look through manuscripts and letters you couldn't otherwise view.

GOLF In Tallahassee enjoy a round at **Hilaman** (850-891-3935), 2737 Blair Stone Rd, with 18 holes and driving range; **Jake Gaither** (850-891-3942), 801 Tanner Dr, nine holes, reservations on weekends; **Seminole** (850-644-2582), 2550 Pottsdamer St, an 18-hole course with lighted driving range, reservations required; and the semiprivate **Players Club** (850-894-4653), Meridian Rd, 18 holes.

For nine-hole par-3 fun, head to Cross Creek (850-656-4653) on US 90 at I-10 to play on the rolling greens. Wakulla County boasts **Wildwood Country Club** (850-926-4653), a par-72 semiprivate club with lush landscaping along US 98 in Medart (see *Lodging*).

HIKING The **Florida Trail** (www.floridatrail.org) winds its way from St. Marks National Wildlife Refuge through the entire width of the Apalachicola National Forest: One of the trail's wildest and most remote sections is through the Bradwell Bay Wilderness, a watery swamp forest with ancient trees. For a close-up look at the wondrous world of the Woodville Karst Plain, a place where water vanishes underground to flow through caverns into springs, hike 6 miles of trails at **Leon Sinks Geological Area** (850-926-3561), US 319 in the Apalachicola National Forest. Lake Talquin State Forest (see *Green Space—Wild Places*) has several excellent hiking trails, as do **Eleanor Klapp Phipps Park** (see *Green Space—Parks*) and the **Lake Overstreet Trails** at Maclay Gardens

WAKULLA RIVER

Sandra Friend

(see *Green Space—Botanical Gardens*) in Tallahassee.

PADDLING With the **Sopchoppy, Aucilla, Ochlocknee, St. Marks,** and **Wakulla** rivers sluicing through this region (and goodness knows, I've forgotten others I haven't yet explored), paddlers will find plenty of challenges. The Aucilla offers rapids, while the Sopchoppy is a twisting, winding, blackwater river. The Ochlocknee, St. Marks, and Wakulla rivers pour out into the Gulf of Mexico through a mazy meander of salt marshes, much fun for kayakers. In Crawfordville, **Williams BP Home & Garden** (850-926-3335), 3215 Crawfordville Hwy, rents canoes for $25 per day, including paddles and PFDs. Take 'em with you to a nearby put-in, and return them at the end of the day. You can also set up float trips (including pickups) through **The Wilderness Way** (850-877-7200; www.thewildernessway.com), 4901 Woodville Hwy, an outfitting shop that offers paddling instruction and ecotours. Check in at Backwoods Bistro (see *Eating Out*) to connect with **Sopchoppy Outfitters** for Sopchoppy and Ochlocknee expeditions. Along US 98 you'll find **Hide Away Rental** at the Wakulla River Bridge and **Lighthouse Center Canoe and Bait** (850-925-9904) at the St. Marks River Bridge; the **Riverside Café** (see *Eating Out*) in St. Marks rents canoes, too. For a trip on the Wacissa River, the **Canoe Man** (850-997-6030) rents canoes and runs shuttles Mar–Nov.

SCENIC DRIVES In addition to cruising Tallahassee's many "official" canopy roads, such as **Meridian Road**—which is wonderful in late March when azaleas and wisteria are in bloom—you'll want to pick up the **North Florida Art Trail** brochure and follow rural CR 12 and FL 269 across Gadsden County from Havana through Quincy, Greensboro, and Chattahoochee to enjoy the rolling farmland and stops for art aficionados along the way.

SKYDIVING Seminole Skydiving (850-297-2127; www.seminoleskydiving.com), US 98 at the Wakulla County Airport, Medart, offers extraordinary scenery for skydive training and tandem dives, as well as helicopters and airplane rides over the Gulf estuaries.

SWIMMING At **Wakulla Springs State Park** (see *Green Space—Springs*), dive into Florida's deepest spring and paddle back to the sandy shoreline; stay within the ropes, since the 'gators cruise just outside them!

WALKING TOURS In **Tallahassee,** grab *Touring Tallahassee* at the visitors center and hit the bricks for a self-guided walk around more than 60 historic sites

downtown. You can watch the Florida legislature at work by hooking up with a
walking tour at the capitol; don't miss the view from the 22nd-floor observation
deck! **Quincy** also offers *On the Trail in Historic Quincy,* a self-guided walking
tour booklet of 55 historic homes and churches; drop by the Gadsen Arts Center
for a copy. **Monticello** offers a historic walking tour following numbered posts
in front of significant buildings; drop in at the chamber of commerce for a guide.

✳ Green Space

BOTANICAL GARDEN **Alfred B. Maclay Gardens State Park** (850-487-4556;
www.floridastateparks.org/maclaygardens), 3540 Thomasville Rd. Walk through
the iron gate and up the brick path—the azaleas are in bloom, and the air is
strong with their sweet fragrance; a thousand shades of green march down the
hill to Lake Hall. It's spring, and it's just as New York financier Alfred Maclay
envisioned—his retirement home surrounded by blooms. When Maclay purchased an antebellum quail-hunting lodge in 1923, he turned his landscape
design skills to the surrounding hills. Several years after he died, his widow
opened the formal gardens as a tourist attraction, turning it over to the state a
decade later. The flow of form is subtle: As you approach the house, the grounds
yield from wild woodlands to formal Italianate walled gardens, with burbling
fountains and stands of cypress. Prime blooming months run from December to
early summer, but the gardens are a joy to explore any time of year; adjacent
Lake Overstreet is a wild, wooded addition to the park with miles of hiking and
biking trails. The antebellum home, furnished in antiques bought and used by
the family, is open for tours 9–5 Jan.–Apr. Fee.

GREENWAY **Tallahassee–St. Marks Historic Railroad State Trail** (850-922-
6007), 1022 Desoto Park Dr. Although the trail runs up into the southern suburbs of Tallahassee, the trailhead along FL 363 provides ample parking, restrooms,
picnic tables, and a historic marker that explains it all: The Tallahassee–St. Marks
Railroad began operation in 1837 with mule-drawn cars and switched to steam
locomotives in 1839, connecting ships coming into Port Leon with Tallahassee.
This paved bike trail runs through
wilderness areas along its 23-mile
route to its southern terminus in St.
Marks, so take plenty of water and
ride with a friend if possible. An
equestrian trail runs parallel to the
forested right-of-way.

PARKS Lake Jackson, the largest lake
in Tallahassee, is one of those oddball
geological mysteries: Every 25 years
or so, the lake's waters vanish "down
the drain" into a sinkhole, and it takes
a few years for the lake to brim with
water again. Bordering Lake Jackson's

THE BRICK WALK AT MACLAY GARDENS
Maclay Garden Tallahassee Area CVB

east shore on Meridian Road, **Eleanor Klapp Phipps Park** (850-891-3975) has an excellent hiking loop as well as biking and equestrian trails; on the west shore of Lake Jackson, **J. Lee Vause Park,** 6024 Old Bainbridge Rd, has a boardwalk along the lake and nature trails as well as picnic shelters. Off to the west along FL 20, **River Bluff State Picnic Area** gives you a scenic panorama of Lake Talquin with a fishing dock and nature trail. In downtown Tallahassee, folks like to stroll around Lake Ella in **Fred O. Drake Jr. Park,** Monroe St, where you can picnic under the pines, or at **Dorothy B. Oven Park,** 3205 Thomasville Rd, a 1824 land grant

Sandra Friend

THE ENTRANCE TO THE TALLAHASSEE–ST. MARKS TRAIL

with a manor house and formal azalea and camellia gardens. For a longer stroll, visit **Lake Munson Preserve,** just south of Capital Circle on US 319.

In Panacea the **Otter Creek Unit** of St. Marks National Wildlife Refuge (see *Wild Places*) has a boat launch, fishing area, hiking trail, and shady picnicking along the shores of Otter Lake. **St. Marks River City Park,** with restrooms, picnic tables, a fishing pier, and a boat ramp on the St. Marks River, marks the southernmost terminus of the Tallahassee–St. Marks Historic Railroad Trail (see *Greenway*).

Ochlocknee River State Park (850-962-2771) sits just south of Sopchoppy on US 321 and has hiking trails, camping, and plenty of waterfront for fishing the estuary. The riverfront trail is especially scenic for an afternoon stroll, and all of the picnic pavilions come with a cool river breeze.

SPRINGS ✐ **Edward Ball Wakulla Springs State Park** (850-224-5950), 550 Wakulla Park Dr. Showcasing Florida's deepest spring, where the water is so clear you can see the bones of mastodons and giant sloth resting at the bottom of the 180-foot pool, Wakulla Springs State Park offers swimming facilities (69 degrees year-round) with a high diving platform, nearly 3 miles of shady nature trails, and daily boat tours (choose the river tour or glass-bottomed boat; fee), where you're bound to see dozens of alligators and innumerable waterfowl. At the center of it all is the classic Wakulla Lodge (see *Lodging*); don't miss the marble-topped soda fountain in the gift shop! Fee.

[handwritten: good birding]

WILD PLACES The **Apalachicola National Forest** (850-643-2282; www.fs .fed.us/r8/florida) is the wildest place on the Florida Panhandle. Sweeping around the southern edge of Tallahassee, it's also Florida's largest national forest. Some of its special spots include **Leon Sinks Geological Area,** popular for hiking and cave diving (see *Hiking* and *Diving* under *To Do*); Bradwell Bay, a wild and lonely wilderness area along the Florida National Scenic Trail; and the cypress-lined Sopchoppy River, a great paddling route.

Encompassing more than 16,000 acres, **Lake Talquin State Forest** (850-627-9674) is spread across 10 tracts on the shores of the Ochlocknee River and Lake Talquin. You can hike through forests of magnolia and beech along trails on the Fort Braden Tract and Bear Creek Tract, or ride horses on the equestrian trails. Bicycling is permitted on forest roads, numerous boat ramps allow access for anglers, and there is seasonal hunting on some of the tracts.

EXPLORING LEON SINKS

Established in 1931 to protect the fragile Gulf estuaries, **St. Marks National Wildlife Refuge** (850-925-6121; http://saintmarks.fws.gov), 1255 Lighthouse Rd, spans three counties. Monarch butterflies rest here in October on their annual migration to Mexico, carpeting the saltbushes in shades of orange and black. Although the refuge is broken up into several units, most folks arrive at the visitors center south of Newport off US 98. Browse the exhibits and learn about this mosaic of habitats before setting off down the road. The Florida Trail crosses the entire width of the refuge. Shorter nature trails give you a taste of the salt marshes, pine flatwoods, and swamps. Drive to the end of the road to visit the historic St. Marks Lighthouse (see *To See—Historic Sites*).

✳ Lodging
BED & BREAKFASTS

Monticello 32344
✐ 🐾 The **John Denham House** (850-997-4568; www.johndenham house.com) is a classic piece of history, built by a Scots immigrant in 1872. Luxuriate in the silky sheets under a down comforter, or relax in a clawfoot tub. Each of the five large rooms has a fireplace accented with candles. $80–150; children and pets are welcome in a safe, family-friendly environment.

Tallahassee 32312
At the **Little English Guest House** (850-907-9777; www.littleenglish guesthouse.com), 737 Timberlane Rd, you'll step right into London in the company of Thom and Tracey Cochran, who re-created a slice of Tracey's homeland with two roomy guest rooms with four-poster beds topped with fluffy duvets from England, comfy whirlpool tubs, English towel warmers, and a pretty English garden. Share time with guests in the common dining and living areas, where the *Union Jack* newspaper is on prominent display. Oh yes, and there's tea. Two rooms, $85 and up, in a quiet house in the suburbs.

Quincy 32351

🦐 ♪ 🐾 **Allison House Inn** (1-888-904-2511; www.allisonhouseinn.com), 215 N Madison St. The former home of General A. K. Allison, who stepped into office as governor of Florida at the end of the Civil War, this 1843 Georgian-style house is one of the oldest in North Florida. Extensive renovation in 1925 added a story to the house and gave it an English country look. Step into Florida's genteel past and enjoy one of the six spacious guest rooms ($95–140) and fine crumpets and orange marmalade offered by innkeepers Stuart and Eileen Johnson; many of the rooms have multiple beds in this family-friendly inn.

🦐 ∞ **McFarlin House** (1-877-370-4701; www.mcfarlinhouse.com), Love St. Decorated with Tiffany windows original to the home and 11,000 square feet of imported Italian tile, this century-old Queen Anne Victorian showcases the good life that Quincy's well-to-do gentry enjoyed. With renovations completed in 1996, this was a finalist for an award as one of the top homes in the United States. The three-story mansion has nine elegant rooms, each unique in size, shape, and decor, offering romantic amenities such as Jacuzzi and fireplace as well as cable TV, phone, and Internet access; $90–200.

🦐 ♪ **Millstone Farms** (850-627-9400; www.millstonefarms.com), 3895 Providence Rd. Off the beaten path in the rolling farmlands west of Quincy, this unique B&B offers a stay on a peaceful 78-acre working beef cattle ranch (tours available on request). Settle into a truly country atmosphere in this grand farmhouse with three large guest rooms ($90–100) and a hot tub and pool out back; enjoy the big-screen TV, walk the nature trails, or sit under the pines and read a book. A camping cottage plus multibed rooms make this a good choice for families, especially when the kids meet pet goats Lucy and Ethel or find the Secret Garden.

St. Marks 32355

🦐 ∞ **The Sweet Magnolia** (850-925-7670; www.sweetmagnolia.com), 803 Port Leon Dr, offers an interesting meld of old-fashioned charm and updated facilities; it's a former railroad boardinghouse from 1923, but the interiors are sparkling new. I picked this place to kick off my honeymoon. Of the seven roomy bedrooms ($95–175), five offer a Jacuzzi for two. I especially like the beautiful water gardens behind the home, a perfect place to settle in and read a book, and the comfy back porch for just hanging out. Gourmet breakfasts served; dinner on request.

SWEET MAGNOLIA'S PORCH

Sandra Friend

Crawfordville 32327

👷 ♿ 🐾 ⊙ For a getaway in the heart of the region's outdoor recreation, head to the new **Inn at Wildwood** (850-926-4455 or 1-800-878-1546; www.innatwildwood.com), 3896 Coastal Hwy. Art reflects nature in details throughout the common areas, from the etched-glass doors to the large breakfast area with fireplace in wood and stone. Each of its comfortable guest rooms ($89 and up) features a writing desk (with free high- speed Internet access), luxury linens, and coffeemaker. Certified a "green" accommodation for its energy-efficiency and reuse practices, the inn offers deals with local outfitters so you can get out and play and return and relax—from paddling and guided photography trips to golf packages. Included in your room rate is access to the pool and tennis courts at the adjacent golf course (see *To Do— Golf*). A gazebo out back is popular for small weddings.

Tallahassee

As the hub of regional activity, Tallahassee boasts a large number of hotels and motels, primarily major chains such as **Homewood Suites** (850-402-9400; www.tallahasseehomewood suites.com), 2987 Apalachee Pkwy, Tallahassee 32301; **Quality Inn and Suites** (850-877-4437), 2020 Apalachee Pkwy, Tallahassee 32301; and **Wingate Inn** (850-553-4400), 2516 Lakeshore Dr, Tallahassee 32303. Despite the many choices, it can still be hard to find a room in town—lobbyists and football fans often book the place full. Your best bet is to call the **Hotel Hotline** (850-488-BEDS); they update availability hourly during peak occupancy periods.

♿ **Cabot Lodge** (1-800-223-1964; www.cabotlodgenorthmonroe.com), 2735 N Monroe St (US 27), Tallahassee 32303. The lobby and room decor are reminiscent of a Maine lodge, including a spacious wraparound porch with rocking chairs overlooking the swimming pool. Each large, comfortable room ($59–85) has special touches for business travelers: a pinewood desk with lamp; a hair dryer, an iron, and an ironing board in the vanity area. Mingle with other guests over free cocktails every evening in the great room, or in the morning as you enjoy a continental breakfast with fresh fruit and pastries. An additional location on Thomasville Rd (1-800-255-6343) features interior hallways.

🍴 **The Governors Inn** (850-681-6855 or 1-800-342-7717; www.thegovinn .com), 209 S Adams St, Tallahassee 32301. This intimate boutique hotel (rooms, $159–239; suites, $189–309), created in the heart of a historic warehouse and stable in the shadow of the capitol, showcases the finest that Tallahassee has to offer, with complimentary valet parking, breakfast, and cocktail hour. Learn a little history, too—each room is named for one of Florida's former governors. The refined atmosphere extends from the common spaces into the rooms, where you'll enjoy a large bath, writing desk, and terry robe for lounging.

Wakulla Springs 32305

👷 ✏ ⊙ Dating back to 1937, **Wakulla Lodge** (850-224-5950), 550 Wakulla Park Dr, overlooks the fabulous springs at Wakulla Springs State Park (see *Green Space—Springs*). This is Florida's only state park lodge, a true step back in time, with gleaming Tennessee marble floors and period furnishings in each of the 27 rooms

Sandra Friend

WAKULLA LODGE

($85–105), and no television—except in the lobby, where guests mingle as they enjoy checkers, cards, and conversation at the marble tables in front of "Old Joe," an 11-foot alligator shot by a poacher in 1966. Look up and take in the artistic beauty of the hand-decorated wooden beams, completed by a Bavarian artist, or thumb through the album of clippings that spell out the history of the lodge and its builder, Edward Ball, once the wealthiest philanthropist in Florida, who donated up to $27,000 a day to charity at age 93! As night falls, a soft mist rises from the springs, and alligators crawl up onto the beach as you peer from the windows of the Ball Room (see *Dining Out*) during dinner. In the morning head out on a boat tour or a hike, or hit the 33-foot diving board for a jump into Florida's deepest spring.

FISH CAMPS Six fish camps cluster around Lake Talquin off FL 267,

offering anglers a place to retreat from busy Tallahassee. The busiest is **Whippoorwill Sportsman's Lodge** (850-875-2605), 3129 Cooks Landing Rd, Quincy 32351, which has cottages, two rooms in the lodge, a campground, and a marina. For saltwater fishing, visit **Shell Island Fish Camp** (850-925-6226), St. Marks 32355, on the Wakulla River. They offer basic, clean motel rooms ($60) with a small fridge, cable TV, no phones; cottages and mobile homes also available. Boat ramp $3, overnight docking $5.

CAMPGROUNDS

Chattahoochee 32324

⚓ Perched on a high bluff above the Apalachicola River off US 90, the county-owned **Chattahoochee RV Resort** (850-663-8000; www.fcn.state .fl.us/chattaho/rv&fishing.html) offers flat spaces ($12–14, full hook-up), older cabins ($50), a playground, fishing pond, and nature trails, and easy access to the river for your boat. No credit cards. Near I-10, the **Chattahoochee KOA** (850-442-6657), 2309 Flat Creek Rd, is just what the family needs—camping cabins and shady spaces ($22 and up) clustered around a playground and swimming pool.

Newport

Newport Recreation Area (850-925-6171), US 98, Wakulla, with picnicking, playground, and deeply shaded campsites in the forest along the St. Marks River, sits just outside St. Marks National Wildlife Refuge (where camping is not permitted).

Panacea 32346

🦐 ⚓ 🏕 **Holiday Campground** (850-984-5757; www.holidaycampground .com), US 98 at the Panacea Bridge, is a large family campground with a steady breeze off Ochlocknee Bay; great views from many of the sites. They can accommodate anything from a tent to a big rig ($27–36) and offer full 30- and 50-amp service, nice bathhouses, playground, 200-foot pier for fishing the bay, a swimming pool, and camp store. Dump station available.

Sopchoppy

Set along the Sopchoppy River, the **Myron B. Hodge Sopchoppy City Park** (850-962-4611) has campsites and hot showers at the bathhouse, nature trails, a boat ramp, and fishing docks, and is a great put-in for explorations of the river.

Tallahassee

☙ **Big Oak RV Park** (850-562-4660; www.bigoakrvpark.com), 4024 N Monroe St, Tallahassee 32303, offers shady spaces under grand old oaks just north of Tallahassee, perfect for antiquing excursions and a favorite for legislators living on a budget, offering a mix of back-in and pull-through full-hook-up sites ($33, 50 amp) for self-contained RVs only. Wifi available throughout the park!

Tallahassee RV Park (850-878-7641; www.tallahasseervpark.com), 6504 Mahan Dr, Tallahassee 32301, has azalea-lined roads with shaded spaces, picnic tables and full hook-ups ($34) at each site, and a swimming pool. Travelers have use of the central modem hook-up at the clubhouse; cable and phone lines available for long-term stays.

✳ Where to Eat

DINING OUT

Havana

🍴 🐾 ♿ It's not just a meal. **Nicholson's Farmhouse Restaurant** (850-539-5931; www.nicholsonfarmhouse.com), 200 Coca-Cola Ave, is a destination. Dr. Malcolm Nicholson's plantation lives on with a collection of four historic buildings centered on the old family home. High-raftered, country-style dining halls inside the renovated buildings set the stage for tasty steaks, quail, lamb, and seafood entrées, $14–30. The meat is guaranteed fresh—they have their own butcher on the premises. I can attest to the perfect sweet tea, the homemade buttermilk ranch dressing, famous "twice baked" potatoes, and green beans—but my husband's word on the steaks means more than mine, and he didn't leave a bite. Leave room for the homemade pies! (Sadly, we didn't.) Enjoy wagon rides on weekends; walk around the farm and visit the horses, chickens, and peacocks; or settle down to listen to a hoedown on the porch of the old filling station. Open Tue–Sat 4–10; reservations suggested.

Monticello

Three Sisters Restaurant (850-342-3474), 370 S Jefferson St, serves up Angus beef and other fine cuisine in a comfortable, home-style atmosphere.

NICHOLSON'S FARMHOUSE RESTAURANT
Sandra Friend

Lunch Wed–Sat 11–2, dinner Fri and Sat 5–8. Reservations suggested.

Panacea

Angelo's Seafood Restaurant (850-984-5168), US 98 at the bridge, stretches out over Ochlocknee Bay into the next county, providing gorgeous waterfront views while you dine on dishes with a Greek flair. Unfortunately, they took a serious beating in the 2004 hurricanes. It's my understanding they'll reopen by 2007, so I'm not scratching their listing. We'll both discover what the new menu is like, but since it's still the family business, I expect the quality to remain superb.

Tallahassee

Andrew's 228 (850-224-2935; www.andrewsdowntown.com/andrews228.html), 228 S Adams St. The upscale big brother to Andrew's Capital Grill & Bar (see *Eating Out*) presents a very different face than its neighbor, featuring fine continental cuisine, with entrées $14–33.

Bahn Thai Restaurant (850-224-4765), 1319 S Monroe St. Melding Chinese and Thai cuisine, Bahn Thai presents a wide array of fresh Asian food for discriminating palates in an unassuming locale. Nothing is precooked, save the items on the nightly all-you-can-eat buffet, and there are more than 126 menu options, including 15 different soups and an extensive selection of vegetarian dishes; entrées $10–19. The convivial staff can be caught breaking into traditional song and dance in honor of their patrons' birthdays. Serving Tallahassee for more than 20 years, Chef Sue deserves her many top ratings from local reviewers. Open for lunch on weekdays, dinner daily.

Carlos' Cuban Café (850-222-8581; www.carloscubancafe.com), 402 E Tennessee St, takes high marks from local reviewers for their excellent presentation of authentic Cuban cuisine ($11–30) such as *pollo asado, bistec Annie,* and *media noche.*

☙ **Chez Pierre** (850-222-0936; www.chezpierre.com), 1215 Thomasville Rd, is French, as the name indicates —but with a Southern twist. Chalk paintings greet you along the walk, and flamboyant modern impressionism dresses up the tasteful maroon walls, setting a festive mood that spills over to Chef Eric's parade of fresh French cuisine—hors d'oeuvres ($8–14) include crabcakes and escargot, sandwiches and a quiche du jour are available, and entrées ($19–32) feature *magret de canard* and shrimp and grits. Save room for a selection from the elegant pastry tray! The wine selection, of course, is broad, and **Le Piano Bar** hosts jazz weekends. Stop in on Bastille Day, and find yourself surrounded by festivity —more than 1,000 people show up for dancing, arts and crafts booths, and wine tastings.

☙ Always reserve ahead at the **Cypress Restaurant** (850-222-9451; www.cypressrestaurant.com), 1350 W Tennessee St, as it's a favorite of the local politicos; and can I blame them? Chef-proprietor David Gwynn serves up creations like sugar cane mopped rib eye and low country boil; entrées start around $20. Open Tue–Sat for dinner, Tue–Fri for lunch 11–2.

The Silver Slipper (850-386-9366; www.thesilverslipper.com), 531 Silver Slipper Lane, a Tallahassee institution since 1938, is the classy place to bring a date for dinner. Overseen by executive chef John Rich, the entrées ($12–

40) range from a vegetable platter to a 22-ounce porterhouse and are accompanied by an extensive wine list.

Wakulla Springs

🐾 Large windows open out onto a view of the Wakulla Springs as you settle back into a fine-dining experience at **The Ball Room at Wakulla Lodge** (see *Lodging*). With backlit photos of the park, it feels a little like an interpretive center, although period music drifts through the air and your food comes served on vintage dishes with signature dogwood blossom pats of butter. And what food! Breakfast brings fluffy stacks of pancakes and eggs with grits, and after you spend a day out on the water, it's tough to choose between the fresh-as-can-be Apalachicola fried oysters for lunch or and the traditional "Old South" fried chicken for dinner ($12 and up), a patrons' favorite since 1946; their world-famous navy bean soup is a must.

EATING OUT

Crawfordville

💕 **Myra Jean's Restaurant** (850-926-7530), 2669 Crawfordville Hwy. For nearly 20 years this fun family restaurant and ice cream parlor has entertained kids young and old with its model railroad; order some comfort food like a gravy dip sub and a chocolate shake ($2–8) and settle in to hear the whistles blowing. Don't miss the adjoining bakery, **Myra Jean's Cakes Etc.,** with its great selection of fresh-baked confections.

Panacea

Posey's Up the Creek (850-984-5243), 1506 Coastal Hwy. I stopped here for dinner late one day and ate a mess of shrimp and a slice of Key lime pie . . . yum. Next time I came through, they were closed (Wed). Great dinners for under $20.

Quincy

Gucchidadi's (850-627-6660), 7 N Madison St, serves up tasty tomato, onion, and bacon pie (the family's variant on quiche) each morning, and a selection of pasta and garden salads for lunch, $3–6. Open Mon–Fri 8:30–2.

St. Marks

🐾 The cheese grits are great at **Nichols Restaurant** (850-925-4850), 785 Port Leon Dr, where the shrimp comes fresh from Panacea to get boiled in Tabasco and butter, and the crispy fried chicken is as Southern as can be. A proper salad bar accompanies your meal. Prices are more than reasonable for this unpretentious family food, with dinners under $15.

Riverside Café (850-925-5668), 69 Riverside Dr, is the epitome of Old Florida waterfront dining—open air, the breeze coming right in off the

DINING COMPANIONS AT THE RIVERSIDE CAFÉ

Sandra Friend

river. Chow down on a variety of sandwiches from oyster to BLT, or savor a dinner of stone crab claws in-season, or any of several vegetarian specialties. They rent canoes as well; ask at the front counter. Breakfast served daily 9–11, lunch and dinner thereafter, $8 and up.

Sopchoppy

Backwoods Bistro (850-962-2220), 106 Municipal Ave. You won't miss the full-sized gorilla outside, nor the barnacle-encrusted bicycle in the front window of this classy pizza parlor, housed in the renovated 1912 drugstore that served this once bust-ling railroad town. Choose from spe-cialty pizzas like the Extreme, Veggie Garden, or Carnivore, $7–17, or try a gourmet Greek or Mexican pizza; sandwiches, salads, and lasagna, too, with a side of music on Fri evening. Ask about canoe and kayak rentals via Sopchoppy Outfitters.

Spring Creek

Spring Creek Restaurant (850-926-3751), 33 Ben Willis Rd. Tended by the Lovel family since 1977, this off-the-beaten-path seafood restaurant draws folks from all over for fresh,

locally caught seafood, including grouper, mullet, and soft-shell crabs. Landlubbers can choose from fried chicken or rib eye. Lunch and dinner; sandwiches $5–7.50, entrées $9.95–27.50.

Tallahassee

At **Andrew's Capital Grill & Bar** (850-224-2935; www.andrewsdown town.com/capitalgrill.html), 228 S Adams St, the sandwiches come named for Florida politicos—try the "Jeb"" or the "Bob Gra-HAM" burg-ers for lunch ($8–9). Looking for something more substantial? G.O.P. (Grand Old Pastas) start at $10, and the Executive Branch features entrées like cedar-planked salmon, lemon grouper, and wasabi tuna with wilted greens ($11–23). Open daily at 11:30.

Big-band music drifts into the **Black Dog Café** (850-224-2518), 229 Lake Ella Dr, from the adjoining American Legion, filling this hangout where friends chat and singles tap on their laptops, hoping to be noticed. Be the scene: Order up a latte and settle into a comfortable chair. Anywhere that hosts Scrabble Nights is all right by me!

El Chico (850-386-1133; www .elchico.com), 2225 N Monroe, offers Mexican combo platters ($8–11) and à la carte. After a basket of light, crisp chips appeared (and disappeared), my Juarez came with two enchiladas and beans flanked with stripes of rice, accompanied by a second plate with a taco and fresh-made guacamole. Extensive dessert menu, including brownie sundaes.

Higher Taste (850-894-4296), 411 St. Francis St, offers vegetarian fare with flair inside a historic Tallahassee home. The lunch buffet (Mon–Fri), $7, features organic salads, curried

BACKWOODS BISTRO

Sandra Friend

vegetables, Indian-style soups, and more. Buffet dinner served Wed and Fri, $11.

Metro Deli (850-224-6870), 1041 S Monroe St. Since 1942, this tiny downtown sub shop packs 'em in at lunchtime with its full slate of deli sandwiches, hot subs, melts, and grinders, $4–7. The aroma of cheddar bacon soup will draw you in!

Paradigm Restaurant & Lounge (850-224-9980), 115 W College Ave, draws in the lunch crowd with tasty wraps (including a wrap of the day, $7); a dressy BLT with baby spinach, Roma tomatoes, and provolone ($5); and fresh fruit salad ($6).

Po'Boys Creole Café (850-224-5400; www.poboys.com), 224 E College Ave, dishes up more than 20 types of po'boy sandwiches (from crawfish to tuna salad, $3–7) and authentic Creole favorites like crawfish roll and Southern pork for dinner ($8–9). Stop in on Sun for the Bayou Brunch, 10–2, with omelets stuffed with crabmeat and shrimp, soufflés with andouille sausage, and more.

San Miguel (352-385-3346), 200 W Tharpe St. Authentic Mexican in a comfortable atmosphere, with à la carte items $1–3, and entrées $5–8, like the tasty enchiladas verde, smothered in spicy green tomatillo sauce. Murals brighten the intimate spaces; I couldn't help but notice the Aztec warrior carting off a maiden toward a raging volcano!

Shell Oyster Bar (850-224-9919), 114A Oakland Ave, is a hot spot for the capitol crowd, where the raw and steamed oysters are the talk of the town. It's a small, family-owned business focused on fresh seafood—and I enjoyed a heaping plate of peel-and-

eat on my last visit. All fish, lunch and dinner, $7–14, with sides like cheese grits and homemade onion rings. No credit cards.

The Soul Vegetarian Restaurant (850-893-8208) is a weekday lunchtime pushcart on Kleman Plaza that's served up vegan specialties for nine years. Try a spicy jerk tofu platter, lentil soup, or a slice of sweet potato pie.

Uptown Café (850-218-9800), 1325 Miccosukee Rd, moved away from downtown but still serves breakfast and lunch (under $7) made from scratch, including buttermilk biscuits and hearty blueberry pancakes.

Vintage Lace Tea Parlor (850-561-6944), 917 N Monroe St, is a haven of elegant Victoriana, a meld of a tearoom with a gift shop filled with antiques, where frilly hats decorate walls throughout the house and I found my childhood Mother Goose book on display. Open for lunch, afternoon tea, and dinner; call to reserve teatime, which ranges from a simple children's or cream tea to a full tea with finger sandwiches.

Woodville

☙ No matter the hour, **The Seineyard** (850-421-9191), 8159 Woodville Hwy, is a busy dining spot—I have friends who'll drive two hours to have dinner here. Fresh Gulf shrimp is featured prominently on the menu; have your seafood fried, broiled, or blackened to taste. Entrées run $9–14, including combination platters; this is one of the rare places where you can have a mullet sandwich for lunch.

COFFEE SHOP & ICE CREAM PARLOR It's a tradition to have an ice cream sundae on the **marble-topped soda**

fountain at Wakulla Springs State Park (see *Green Space—Parks*), but for a relaxing coffee break, head to **Coffee Break** (850-997-9996), 190 N Jefferson, Monticello. There are books to browse and sandwiches available at lunchtime.

✳ Selective Shopping

Centerville
A drive up Centerville Rd from Tallahassee will take you to **Bradley's Country Store** (850-893-1647; www .bradleyscountrystore.com), 10655 Centerville Rd, a general store in continuous operation since 1927. Stop in for their signature country-smoked sausage and milled grits, tasty coffee, local history books, and country-themed gifts.

Crawfordville
Simple Things Antiques and Collectibles (850-926-9617), 3299 Crawfordville Hwy. Decked out with Coca-Cola signs, wind chimes, and other ephemera, this little Cracker home houses a nice mix of arts and crafts; the shelves and antique furnishings are crowded with baskets,

BRADLEY'S COUNTRY STORE

Sandra Friend

pottery, old-time tins, and paintings with a regional flair.

Tattered Pages Books & Espresso Bar (850-926-6055), 2807 Crawfordville Hwy. The hub of this shop, its small café, serves cappuccino, lattes, and smoothies, but the big attraction here is the books—all new. There's an excellent selection of new releases, literature, and fiction, books of regional interest, and an entire room devoted to titles just for kids.

Havana
Havana is the Panhandle's antiques hub, with more than 20 shops filling the downtown buildings, old railroad station, and tobacco barns to overflowing with a little bit of everything country. Prices are great, too. Here's a selection—but spend a day and see them all!

Furniture shopping? **Custer's Last Stand** (850-539-1902), 101 SE Second St, had some of the nicest writing desks I've seen, as well as other fine furnishings in dark, rich woods.

Little River General Store (850-539-6900; www.littlerivergs.com), 308 N Main St, is a page from the past, where kids gaze at the penny candy while Mom picks up a bar of Fels-Naptha soap; mixed in are comfy throws, old-fashioned toys, and gourmet foods.

Mirror Image Antiques (850-539-7422; www.havanaflorida.com), 303 First St NW, is a sprawling complex with an eclectic selection of items—it's not just antiques. You'll find an art gallery, a gourmet food room stocked with British imports, rooms filled with books, and intriguing items from the Far East, like a Vietnamese Buddha. Since it's all in the family, they absorbed a great deal of the

HAVANA'S SHOPPING DISTRICT

Sandra Friend

Beare's Historical Bookshelf, and these antiquarian tomes are offered along with the Peterson Asian Collection and other vintage items.

With a female backpacker gracing their sign, how could I not visit **Wanderings** (850-539-7711; www.thewanderings.com), 312 First St NW. This roomy shop, part of the 1906 Havana depot, deals in exotic home decor and primitives—arts, crafts, and furnishings.

Medart
Just Fruits & Exotics (1-888-926-7441), 30 St. Francis St. Along US 98 east of Medart, this sprawling native plant and exotic fruit emporium has everything from ferns and *Sarracenia* (carnivorous pitcher plants) to persimmon and guava trees. A must-stop for the serious gardener.

Monticello
Stroll downtown Monticello and you'll find more than a dozen funky little

shops, old-fashioned drugstores, and mercantile shops filled with collectibles and not-so-antiques, like the **Old Bank Antique Mall** (850-997-8163), 100 N Jefferson St.

I found perfect Christmas gifts at **Great Adventure Outfitters** (850-997-8675), 225 N Jefferson St, where you can buy mosquito head nets, Nalgene bottles, hiking boots, and technical clothing as well as fun Life is Good logo items, retro lunchboxes, and local crafts.

Imagine Interiors (850-997-4408; www.imagineantiques.net), 168 E Dogwood St, has fine antique furniture and a smattering of collectibles.

It feels like the '50s inside **Jackson's Drug Store** (850-997-3553), 166 E Dogwood, where local art spruces up the walls along the corridor off Jefferson Street.

The Southern Friends Antique Mall (850-997-2550; www.southern friends.net), 235 N Jefferson St, recently moved into more cozy digs downtown, still featuring dealer booths with lots of Coca-Cola memorabilia and china. The owner specializes in postcards and vintage paper collectibles.

Town Square Antiques (850-997-2127), 220 W Washington St, is an open, roomy shop with plenty of room for browsing their selection of saltcellars, glassware, and plates; look for larger items like fine furniture, primitives, and old washing machines in the back.

Sopchoppy
The Book and Art Tea Room (850-962-1900), 114 Municipal Ave. Featuring Florida titles and a nice concentration of books of regional interest, it's a place to kick back, relax, and browse while sipping a cup of tea.

George Griffin Pottery (850-962-9311), 1 SunCat Ridge Rd. It's a rough road back to George's place, a little cabin in the woods where he's practiced his craft for more than 30 years. But you'll be glad you made the detour to his tin-roofed gallery, as George's pottery is a wonderful, fluid thing; it's natural sculpture in a very natural setting, reflective of his inherent love of the craft. Stroll the shaded grounds and enjoy the outdoor art; sculptures rise along the fishpond, looking like the pitcher plants that grow in the surrounding forest. Little sheds contain earth-toned treasures, and inspirational quotes (along with Polaroids of folks who've come to learn at the studio) are interspersed among pieces with form and function inside the main gallery. Open Tue–Sun.

The Petunia Patch (850-567-2100), 118 Municipal Ave, showcases the creative output of the Sopchoppy Arts Association, including watercolors and ceramics, amid a good array of antiques and collectibles like playbills, matchbooks, and fine china. Stop

GEORGE GRIFFIN POTTERY

Sandra Friend

here for your official Worm Grunting T-shirts (see *Special Events*)!

The scent of clean fills the air at **Rose's Botanicals** (850-962-7830; www.rosesbotanicals.com), 57 Rose St, where their soaps, medicinal creams, and salves are made in small batches, by hand, from local herbs. In addition to their mainstays, they offer gourmet foods, gift baskets, and vitamins and supplements. Open Tue–Sat.

Tallahassee
Artworks (850-224-2500), 110 S Monroe St, offers the finest in local art on consignment from artists creating original oils, dichrotic glass and glass bowls, sculpture, and literature.

Stop by the shops of **Betton Place** at 1950 Thomasville Rd to browse through the Museum Shop (850-681-8565), filled with unique educational gifts for all ages; continue down a few doors to **My Favorite Things** (850-681-2824), where Tallahassee brides walk into the faux Southern mansion to register for fine china, elegant home decor, and Swarovski crystal.

At Lake Ella (1650 N Monroe St), it's fun to browse the historic tourist cottages that now make up the **Cottages at Lake Ella.** My favorites include **Quarter Moon Imports** (850-222-2254) and their new Quarter Moon Annex, filled with exotica like lush tapestries from India, sensuous sushi platters, and Moroccan tea sets; **Barb's Southern Style Gourmet Brittles** (850-385-9839), for a sweet treat; **Glasswork by Susan** (850-222-5095), a stained-glass studio with supplies and original art; and **Lofty Pursuits** (850-521-0091; www.lofty pursuits.com), where you can buy a kite, a yoyo, or a board game.

At **The Mary Brogan Museum of Art and Science** (see *To Do—Family Activities*), the Museum Shop offers creative and fun science toys, a great selection of children's books and art books, and beautiful works of art—art glass tables, bowls, limited-edition baskets, and more.

✿ **Native Nurseries** (850-386-8882), 1661 Centerville Rd. It's a nursery for nature lovers, a shop where you'll learn about native plants and animals as you browse. Be sure to check out the Children's Nature Nook and the Wren's Nest Nature Shop, and if you're in town for a while, sign up for one of the many free workshops on native creatures and gardening.

Offering both new and used titles, the **Paperback Rack** (850-224-3455), 1005 N Monroe St, has been around for more than 20 years and shines with an incredible diversity of titles (I found Alison Lurie, Gerald Durrell, and Jack Kerouac all in a few minutes' search), with an especially deep selection in fine literature but also a great variety in travel, Black studies, and children's books. An extensive genre paperback section fills the front of the store.

Funky castoffs and mod art fill **Remember When** (850-425-4755), 115 W Sixth Ave, an antiques and collectibles shop focusing on the 1930s through the 1960s, where lava lamps sit side by side with Parisian hats and lingerie.

Someone's in the Kitchen (850-668-1167; www.someoneskitchen .com), 1355 Market St. A fun stop for culinary items: gourmet foods and wines, plus kitchen accessories that would make a chef proud.

Something Nice (850-562-4167), 5019 Metzke Ln. The former Metzke

Pewter Designs building is now a collection of gallery shops filled with antiques, collectibles, and handcrafted children's furniture; they also hold a flea market the first Sat monthly.

The Tallahassee Area Visitor Information Center (see *Guidance*) has its own shop featuring art, books, and CDs from Tallahassee artists, including photo cards, primitives, bold acrylics, fiber arts, paintings on slate, and more.

With more than 30 years serving Tallahassee, **Trail & Ski** (850-531-9001), 2748 Capital Circle NE, is the shop where backpackers and campers head when they're gearing up for a trip. The store features a fine selection of outdoor guidebooks, travel items, and technical clothing; rental gear available.

FARMER'S MARKETS, FRESH SEAFOOD, AND U-PICK

Havana
Get your hands dirty at **Beare Blueberry Farm U-Pick,** 1.7 miles west of Havana on FL 12, where organic berries are the name of the game. Open May 15–Jul 15.

Lamont
A 1960s-style roadside stand, **Robin Hood's Pecan House** on US 19 (south of I-10 at Monticello) sells fresh fruit, jumbo pecans, and country-smoked sausage.

Medart
Captain Hook's, along US 98 in Medart near the junction with US 319, features "Hot Boiled Green Peanuts," watermelon, and other seasonal fruits. Pick up your fresh fish and smoked mullet at nearby **Fishbonz** on US 98.

Monticello

Turkey Hill Organic Farm (850-216-4024), 3546 Baum Rd. Organically grown veggies on an 89-acre family-run farm; holds an annual open house but otherwise sells produce every Sat at Market Square Shopping Center, Timberland Rd. Get your peaches and grapes in-season at **Windy Hill Farm,** 1 mile west of FL 59 on US 90.

Newport

Where FL 267 meets US 98, you'll find a longtime local vendor selling tupelo honey, mayhaw jelly, and cane syrup out of the back of his pickup truck on weekends year-round.

Panacea

Known for its fresh fine seafood, the fishing village of Panacea boasts the largest number of roadside seafood stands in Wakulla County. In addition to folks selling shrimp and oysters out of the backs of their trucks, some of the old standbys with storefronts on US 98 include **Rock Landing Seafood,** featuring "live crabs when light is flashing"; **D. L. Thomas Seafood,** the oldest outlet in town; and **My Way Seafood.**

Quincy

Davis Farm Fresh Fruits & Vegetables, a large farm stand on FL 65 S, sells direct from this family grower; you'll always find green boiled peanuts and vine-ripe tomatoes in-season.

St. Marks

Lighthouse Seafood Market (850-925-6221), Port Leon Dr, features fresh fish caught daily.

Tallahassee

🎵 Don't miss the **Downtown Marketplace** (850-980-8727; www.downtownmarket.com) in Ponce de Leon Park (Park Ave between Monroe and Adams), where vendors haul in the freshest of local produce while local musicians play on stage, poets and authors offer readings under the grand live oaks, and kids can join in fun activities like pumpkin carving, sidewalk chalk art, and other hands-on arts and crafts. Sat 8–2, Mar–Nov; free.

A community co-op, **New Leaf Market** (850-942-2557; www.newleafmarket.coop), 1235 Apalachee Pkwy, is more than 30 years old and invites the public in to shop for organic produce, ecofriendly household goods, alternative diet foods, and more.

✳ Entertainment

Watch your representatives at play: Legislators hang loose at **Clyde's and Costello's** (850-224-2173), 210 S Adams, a city pub with pool tables. But Tallahassee has a classy side, too: 25 years old, the annual **Tallahassee Bach Parley** features classical music in venues like Goodwood; the **Tallahassee Symphony Orchestra** (850-224-0461; www.tsolive.org), 1345 Thomasville Rd, has a decade of concert series behind them, playing Sep–May. The **Big Bend Community Orchestra** (850-893-4567) offers Sun-afternoon classical and "pops" in area parks, and the Artist Series (850-224-9934) brings in philharmonic orchestras and soloists from around the globe. **Theatre A La Carte** (850-224-8474; www.theatrealacarte.org) bills itself as North Florida's premiere musical company, putting on two musicals each year, and the **Tallahassee Film Society** (850-386-4404; www.tallahasseefilms.com) shows indie, art, and retro films twice monthly at the EFC Miracle 5 Theatre.

More off the beaten path, you'll find live music (bluegrass, country, and classic rock) on the waterfront at **Riverside** in St. Marks on Fri and Sat nights (see *Eating Out*) and at the **Sopchoppy Opera,** a country music and bluegrass jam venue along US 319 where country legend Tom T. Hall hangs out. The **Apalachee Blues Society** meets at the Bradfordville Blues Club (850-906-0766), Moses Lane off Bradfordville Rd, where you can catch live blues concerts on Fri and Sat evenings.

✳ Special Events

March: **Natural Bridge Civil War Re-enactment** (850-922-6007), first weekend at National Bridge Historic State Park, Woodville (see *To See— Historic Sites*).

❧ **Red Hills Horse Trials** (850-893-2497; www.rhht.org), Eleanor Klapp Phipps Park, Tallahassee. A nationally recognized equestrian competition with Olympic riders, educational exhibits, and special activities for the kids. Fee.

April: **Gold Cup Antique Car Race and Show** (850-653-9419), Tallahassee, first Sat. Nearly two decades old, this special event features classic automobiles winding through the city's streets.

❧ **Sopchoppy Worm Grunting Festival** (850-962-5282), first Sat. If you didn't know how to grunt an earthworm out of the ground, you will by

the end of this festival, which also features live bluegrass, arts and crafts, and the annual worm grunters' ball. No jokes, folks—this is an honest profession in the Apalachicola woods!

May: **Panacea Blue Crab Festival** (850-227-1223), first weekend. A parade and craft booths are an adjunct to seafood, seafood, and more seafood from the folks who know crabs!

October: ❧ Celebrated at St. Marks National Wildlife Refuge (see *Green Space—Wild Places*), the **Monarch Festival,** last weekend, offers guided naturalist tours to view butterflies along hiking trails, environmental exhibits (including a great butterfly tent for the kids), arts and crafts, and the opportunity for you to volunteer to tag butterflies for research. (I couldn't believe it was possible until I saw it done!) During the same weekend, the **St. Marks Crab Festival** draws visitors to the riverside restaurants with massive fixed price feeds, live bluegrass, and a small arts and crafts festival.

November: ❧ **North Florida Fair** (850-878-3247), Tallahassee, is the region's largest agricultural fair, featuring major country music acts, midway rides, agricultural competitions, and food vendors. Fee.

December: **Just One More Invitational Art Festival** (850-980-8727), second Sat, Park Ave, Tallahassee. Featuring live music, food, children's activities, and works from selected southeastern artists.

APALACHICOLA REGION

LIBERTY, FRANKLIN, GULF, CALHOUN, JACKSON, AND WASHINGTON COUNTIES

History runs deep along the Apalachicola River, the meandering 108-mile watercourse that defines the boundary between the Eastern and Central Time Zones in Florida. Spanish traders and British seafarers fought over commerce here in the 1700s, and merchants established the town that is now **Apalachicola,** the vibrant heart of the region, in 1829. Soon after, Carrabelle and Port St. Joe grew up around Florida's first railroad connections with the sea; along with Eastpoint, these coastal towns are defined by their working shrimpers and oystermen, who provide a bounty enjoyed in local restaurants and elsewhere—Apalachicola harvests 90 percent of Florida's oysters. White-sand beaches and rolling dunes define the barrier islands of **St. George, St. Vincent, Dog Island,** and **Cape San Blas,** where spectacular public lands like St. Joseph State Park let you enjoy the beauty of the "Forgotten Coast."

In the northerly counties along the watershed, expect pine-topped ridges and high bluffs above the rivers, where Old Florida thrives in settlements like **Wewahitchka, Blountstown,** and **Bristol.** Working downtowns characterize these small towns—islands in a sea of cotton fields and cattle ranches. **Marianna** anchors the northern corner of the region, with genteel historic homes and outstanding outdoor recreation. The Apalachicola region is a friendly place, where you can share small talk with shopkeepers and innkeepers, or hoist a beer with the locals down at the waterfront. And don't be surprised to see the sheriff wave hello as he drives past on US 98!

GUIDANCE You'll easily find the **Apalachicola Bay Chamber of Commerce** (850-653-9419; www.apalachicolabay.org), downtown on Market St, but the **Carrabelle Chamber of Commerce** (850-697-2585; www.carrabelle.org) and the **Gulf County Tourist Development Council** (1-800-482-GULF; www.visitgulf.com) are best contacted in advance. Take time to visit the **Jackson County Chamber of Commerce** (850-482-9633; www.jctdc.org), 4318 Lafayette St, in the beautifully restored Russ House in Marianna (see *To See— Historic Sites*).

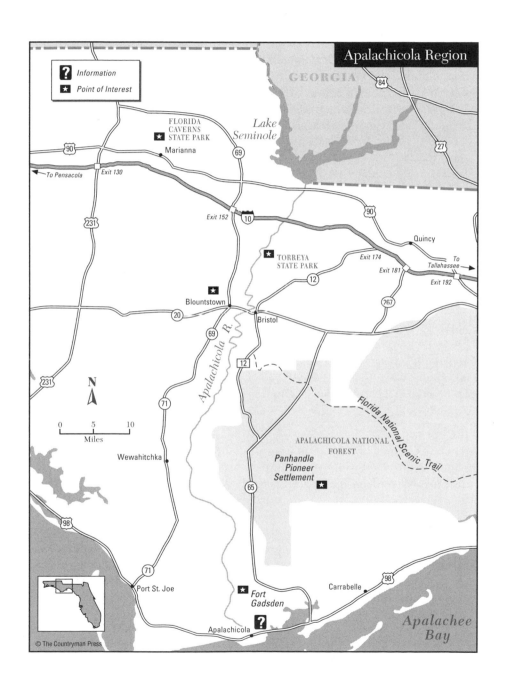

GETTING THERE US 98 is "Main Street" for the coast, running east–west through Franklin and Gulf counties. Use scenic **FL 65, 67, and 71** to parallel the Apalachicola River to reach the northern part of the region, where **I-10** and **US 90** provide access to towns near the Georgia–Alabama border.

MEDICAL EMERGENCIES Emergency treatment can be received at **George E. Weems Memorial Hospital** (850-653-8853), 135 Ave G, Apalachicola, and at **Jackson Hospital** (850-526-2200), 4250 Hospital Dr, Marianna. *Important note*: Most of this region is extraordinarily remote, and cell phone service isn't guaranteed in the vast wilderness areas between I-10 and US 98.

✳ To See
ART GALLERIES

Apalachicola
I am in love with Apalachicola's artists and can't wait for the day when my checkbook says I will patronize them properly. At the **J. E. Grady & Co. Market** (see *Selective Shopping*), visit **Richard Bickel Photography** (850-653-4099; www.gradymarket.com/bickel.htm) for black-and-white images that capture the soul of this region. The **Alice Jean Art Gallery** (850-653-3166), 29 Ave E, showcases Alice Jean Gibbs's haunting coastal scenes, Jane Tallman's pastels, and the photography of Alecia Ward. See *Selective Shopping* for other outlets for local artists.

Carrabelle
Carrabella Cove (850-697-8984), 1859 US 98, across from the beach, showcases coastal art, pottery, and sculpture, all by local artists who love the estuaries they call home.

St. George
Sea Oats Gallery (850-927-2303; www.forgottencoastart.com), 128 E Pine St, has four rooms filled with scenes of Apalachicola and the Panhandle, featuring artists like Ellen Sloan and Roger Leonard, who deftly capture the coastal light. The sculptures of Cass Allen Pottery are joyful figures of angels in flight. Don't miss this place!

GHOST TOWNS Off FL 65 in the Apalachicola National Forest at New River, **Vilas** has little more to note its passing than some scattered building materials and a long-unused railroad siding; the Florida Trail (see *What's Where*) meanders through the remains of this turn-of-the-20th-century turpentine town.

HISTORIC SITES Driving through this rural region, you'll uncover Florida's pre–Civil War plantation history, where cotton grows on lands handed down through the generations. Most of the small towns have an old-time county courthouse, and sometimes the entire downtown district is a Florida Heritage Site. Here are a few of the most significant stops along the way.

Apalachicola

Downtown Apalachicola is a Florida treasure. Pick up a walking tour map at the chamber of commerce (see *Guidance*) and explore the many unique sites, such as the **1836 Greek sponge exchange,** the **1831 Chestnut Street Cemetery,** the **Greek-built shrimp boat** *Venizelos,* and this port city's **Customs House** from 1923, now the post office. On a high bluff above the river, the **Orman House** (850-653-1209; www.floridastateparks.org/ormanhouse), 177 Fifth St, was built by early settler and shipping magnate Thomas Orman with wood shipped from Syracuse, New York, in 1838. It's now a state park with history-packed tours on the hour (9–11, 1–3) led by ranger John Winfield Thu–Mon. Fee.

Carrabelle

Although the police force has outgrown its old digs, the **World's Smallest Police Station,** a phone booth downtown, remains, with a squad car always parked next door. It dates back to 1963, and I was going to ask the officer on duty about it, but he was busy giving a ticket to a speeder. I crept past and headed on to the **Crooked River Lighthouse** along US 98, built in 1895 to replace a lighthouse destroyed in a hurricane on Dog Island. A citizens' group is working on its restoration.

Greenwood

Established in 1869, **Pender's Store** on Bryan St is one of the oldest continuously operated stores in Florida, retaining its original shelving and heart pine floors. On the way there, you'll pass stately **Great Oaks,** known as Bryan Plantation during the Civil War. The **Erwin House** on Fort St is perhaps the oldest structure in Jackson County, circa 1830. All three structures are on the National Register of Historic Places.

Marianna

First settled in the 1820s, **Marianna** formed the commercial center for a hub of busy plantations, including Sylvania, the home of Civil War–era governor John Milton, now the grounds of **Florida Caverns State Park** (see *Green Space—Parks*). During the war, Marianna became a target because it was the governor's hometown. On September 17, 1864, the **Battle of Marianna** pitted the Home Guard (a militia of old men and teenagers) against invading Union

THE WORLD'S SMALLEST POLICE STATION
Sandra Friend

Fort Gadsden (850-643-2282). Constructed during the War of 1812 to defend British colonial interests, the original fortress encompassed a 7-acre tract along the Apalachicola River as a base to recruit runaway slaves and Indians to the British cause of wresting control of Florida from the Spanish. In 1815 the British abandoned the effort but left behind a force of 300 former slaves and Seminoles to watch over the river from what was then dubbed the "Negro Fort." When American colonel Duncan Clinch sailed upriver under the auspices of General Andrew Jackson in 1816, the inhabitants of the fort fired on his gunboats. Clinch returned fire. A single cannonball hit the ammunition pile inside the fort, causing a massive explosion that blew apart the fort and its defenders. Only 30 survived, and Clinch had several of them executed. Jackson ordered a new fortress erected on the spot as a base of operations for his missions during the First Seminole War. Lieutenant James Gadsden and his men held the fort until Florida became a U.S. territory in 1821. The fort fell into disrepair, although it was briefly occupied by Confederate troops guarding the gateway to the Apalachicola River. Reached by dirt roads from FL 65 south of Sumatra, a mile-long interpretive and nature trail showcases the key points. Open sunrise–sunset; fee.

INTERPRETIVE KIOSK AT FORT GADSDEN

Sandra Friend

troops. They fought in and around **St. Luke's Episcopal Church,** which was burned during the conflict. A Union officer preserved and returned the Holy Bible to the church, where it remains on display. Faced with surrendering the state to the Union army, Governor Milton returned home on April 1, 1865, and shot himself, eight days before Lee surrendered the Confederacy. Milton is buried at St. Luke's.

Down the street, the distinctively rounded **Russ House,** built 1895 by prominent merchant Joseph W. Russ, had its fancy neoclassical pillars added in 1910. It now houses the Jackson County Chamber of Commerce (see *Guidance*), where you can pick up a walking tour guide to Marianna's many other historic structures.

MUSEUMS

Apalachicola
Apalachicola Maritime Museum (850-653-8700), 71 Market St. Learn about the Gulf Coast's long and storied maritime history through the permanent and changing exhibits at this museum, including the fully restored 1877 schooner the *Governor Stone,* moored along the waterfront. It's considered the oldest operating sailing vessel in the American South.

John Gorrie Museum State Park (850-653-9347; www.floridastateparks.org/johngorriemuseum), 46 Sixth St. Living in malaria-stricken Florida in the 1850s, Dr. John Gorrie had a problem: how to keep his recovering patients cool? With a great deal of engineering savvy, Gorrie found a way to use compressed air and condensation to make ice, then ran a fan across the ice to keep his infirmary cool. By doing so, he developed the world's first system for mechanical refrigeration, patented in May 1851: an icemaker. At the time, ice for refrigeration was cut from frozen northern lakes and packed in sawdust for transport. Gorrie died in obscurity, his achievement too "far out" for his time. It wasn't until the 1890s that ice merchants discovered the magic of Gorrie's system, which led to the design of air-conditioning. In 1911 Gorrie was honored with a statue as one of two representatives of Florida history in the U.S. Capitol in Washington, DC. The museum is open 9–5; closed Tue and Wed. Fee. Across the street, Gorrie is buried in Gorrie Square.

Blountstown
Hidden behind the Sam B. Atkins Recreation Complex off Silas Green Street, the **Panhandle Pioneer Settlement** (850-674-3050; www.panhandlepioneersettlement.com) brings together vintage buildings from towns along the Apalachicola. Outfitted with period furnishings, each tells a story of Florida's frontier days. Volunteer docents lead informative tours, Tue and Thu–Sat, noon–4 (summer 9–1). Fee.

Carrabelle
Bet you didn't know that the first amphibious landing craft didn't land at Utah Beach on D-Day: They tried them out in Carrabelle first! From 1942 to 1946, the Gulf Coast from Ochlocknee Bay to Eastport was Camp Gordon Johnston, a

training facility for more than 250,000 amphibious soldiers as they practiced storming beaches. **The Camp Gordon Johnston Museum** (850-697-8575; www.campgordonjohnston.com), 302 Marine St, honors the World War II troops who trained here and preserves the history of that important effort that clinched the Allied liberation of France, with artifacts and archives of special interest to vets and history buffs. Mon–Tue, Thu–Fri 1–4; Wed 10–4; Sat 10–1. Donation.

Port St. Joe

At the **Constitution Convention Museum State Park** (850-229-8029; www.floridastateparks.org/constitutionconvention), 200 Allen Memorial Way, interpretive exhibits and artifacts put a face on Florida's frontier days, with a special focus on St. Joseph. Established by homesteaders who were kicked out of Apalachicola, thanks to a sneaky 1830 land deal called the Forbes Purchase, St. Joe was Florida's first real tourist destination, a deep-water port that was the Las Vegas of its day. Some said the hand of God wiped out Sin City in 1841 with a triple whammy of yellow fever, hurricane, and wildfire. A stone marker, cemetery, and this museum are all that's left. In 1838 St. Joe hosted Florida's Constitutional Convention. A replica meeting room has bios of all of the delegates and gives a nice glimpse into a time when Mosquito County took up most of the southern peninsula. Thu–Mon 9–noon, 1–5. Fee.

RAILROADIANA Inside the Constitution Convention Museum you'll find a **scale replica of Florida's first steam engine,** which ran on an 8-mile route, the St. Joseph & Lake Wimico Canal & Railroad, between St. Joseph and Depot Creek in 1836. Outside the museum, look for a 1915 steam engine that belonged to the St. Joe Lumber Company. In Marianna, the **L&N Railroad Depot** dates back to 1881.

✳ To Do

BICYCLING A dedicated **bicycle path** runs down the middle of St. George Island; rent bikes at **Journeys of St. George Island** (see *Ecotours*). The brand-new Blountstown Greenway (see *Green Space—Greenway*) offers a paved path from the Panhandle Pioneer Settlement (see *To See—Museums*) to the Apalachicola River. The region's scenic rural roads lend themselves to long-distance excursions as well.

Chipola River N of Marianna

BIRDING On nearly 100 miles of back roads in the **Apalachicola River Wildlife and Environmental Area** (see *Green Space—Wild Places*) look for hundreds of bird species, including swallow-tailed and Mississippi kites roosting in tall cypresses. Shorebirds abound on the tidal flats of the barrier islands.

BOAT EXCURSIONS To get to the remote barrier islands, you'll need a shuttle, such as **St. Vincent Island Shuttle Services** (850-229-1065; www.stvincentisland.com), **Dog Island Water Taxi** (850-697-3989), or **Journeys of St. George Island** (see *Ecotours*). Or kick back and enjoy a pleasurable sail on a 1950s sloop **Wind Catcher** (850-653-3881), which offers daily trips and can be chartered out to the islands.

BOATING Located at the Port St. Joe marina, **Seahorse Water Safaris** (850-227-1099; www.seahorsewatersafaris.com) rents everything from a kayak to a 23-foot pontoon boat. Bringing your own boat? Look for public ramps at Carrabelle, Eastpoint, Apalachicola, and Indian Pass.

DIVING Offshore wrecks make exploring this region exciting. **Carrabelle Fish & Dive** (850-697-8765; www.cbellefishdive.com) runs deep-sea trips and has cold air on the premises; **Burkett's Diving** (850-647-6099), 212 Gulf St, Port St. Joe, can set you up in style, as can **Seahorse Water Safaris** (see *Boating*) and **The Moorings Dive Shop** (see *Lodging*) in Carrabelle.

ECOTOURS Apalachicola Estuary Tours (850-653-TOUR; www.apalachicola tours.com) runs informative two-hour cruises on a 40-foot, 32-passenger boat out of Scipio Creek Marina; $20 adults, $10 children. **Journeys of St. George Island** (850-927-3259; www.sgislandjourneys.com) has a complete menu of tours, ranging from guided paddling trips to ecotours to St. Vincent and Dog islands, to deep-sea and bay fishing. They also rent sailboats, motorboats, and kayaks, and run environmental summer camps and special kid-oriented trips; call for details.

FAMILY ACTIVITIES ✔ **Putt-N-Fuss Fun Park** (850-670-1211), 236 US 98. Mini golf, bumper boats, and an arcade clustered around a miniature mountain at the gateway to St. George Island. Open daily, hours vary by season; adults $8, children $7.

FISHING No matter whether you prefer deep-sea excursions or casting a line off a bank, the entire Apalachicola River watershed is a huge destination for sport fishing, with tournaments held nearly every month. In Carrabelle ask about fishing guides at the **Dockside Marina** and **C-Quarters Marina** (850-697-8400), US 98. **Top Knot Charters** (1-800-446-1639; www.topknotcharters.com) is one of the long-established services in the area. Ask around Apalachicola and Port St. Joe for top guides like the **Robinson Brothers** (850-653-8896; www.floridaredfish.com), or **Boss Charters** (850-853-8055) for deep-sea fishing on *Miss Emily*. Depending on the guide, length of trip, and location, you'll pay $250–700 for a trip. To fish the Apalachicola River on your own, put your boat in the river at any of many ramps along FL 71 or FL 67. Stop in at **Forgotten Coast Outfitters** (850-653-9669), 94 Market St, Apalachicola, for fly-fishing tackle and homespun advice.

ST. VINCENT ISLAND

Visit Florida

Trophy-sized lunkers lurk along the **Dead Lakes** at Dead Lakes State Park and in **Lake Seminole** at Three Rivers State Park (see *Green Space—Parks*). You won't want to miss the serenity of cypress-lined **Merritts Mill Pond** along US 90, Marianna, and **Spring Creek** for fly-fishing.

GOLF Built by the CCC in the 1930s, the **Florida Caverns Golf Course** (850-482-4257), 3309 Caverns Rd, has nine holes under the tall pines adjoining the state park. Off US 90 east of Marianna, **Indian Springs Golf Club** (1-800-587-6257), 5248 Club House Dr, offers 18 holes, par 72.

HIKING The **Florida Trail** (www.floridatrail.org) passes through true wilderness in the Apalachicola National Forest between Porter and Camel lakes, with rare pitcher plant savannas (best seen during their blooming period in March) west of Camel Lake and around Memery Island. For more pitcher plants, hike the **Wright Lake Trail** around Wright Lake Recreation Area. See *Green Space* for other excellent backpacking and day-hiking locales in the region.

HORSEBACK RIDING Several outfitters offer horseback riding on the shifting sands of St. George Island and Cape San Blas, including **Broke-A-Toe** (850-229-WAVE). Expect to pay $40 and more for a ride along the surf.

PADDLING Along FL 65 you'll find numerous put-ins for **paddling adventures** into Tate's Hell and on the Apalachicola River; watch for the yellow and black signs at places like Graham Creek. Eleven such routes are outlined in the free **Apalachicola River Paddling Trail System** map available from the **Apalachicola River Wildlife and Environmental Area** office (850-488-5520; www.myfwc.com/recreation/apalachicola_river/default.asp). The **Chipola River Canoe Trail** starts at Florida Caverns State Park (see *Green Space—Parks*) and flows 50 miles south to Dead Lake at Wewahitchka, a three-day trip with a stretch of whitewater (portage recommended) near the FL 274 bridge. For canoe rentals and shuttling, check with **Scott's Ferry Landing** (see *Lodging*) or **Bear Paw Adventures** (850-482-4948; www.bearpawescape.com), Magnolia Rd off FL 71, which runs half-day, full-day, and overnight trips Mar 16–Sep 30. For day trips on the Upper Chipola, rent a canoe at **Florida Caverns State Park,**

PITCHER PLANTS AT WRIGHT LAKE
Sandra Friend

$10–25. On St. George Island, **Journeys of St. George Island** (see *Ecotours*) runs guided kayaking trips and rents and sells kayaks. Explore the needlerush marshes along St. Joseph Bay by launching in the state park or at the public launch. Rent kayaks at **Happy Ours** (850-229-1991; www.happyourskayak.com), 775 Cape San Blas Rd, or at **The Entrance** (850-227-PLAY; www.escapetothecape.com) in front of St. Joseph State Park.

Apalachicola Bay CVB

EXPLORING IN APALACHICOLA BAY

SCALLOPING **St. Joseph Bay** is scalloping central on the coast, July 1–Sep 10. You can wade in at the public beaches and sift through the shallows for free, or book a charter—check in at **Port St. Joe Marina** (850-227-9393; www.brandymarine.com/psjmarina), or drop in at **Scallop Cove** (850-227-7557; www.scallopcove.com), 4310 Cape San Blas Rd, where they also rent canoes and run ecotours.

SCENIC DRIVES One of Florida's best scenic drives is a little-known treasure through Liberty and Franklin counties. Start at FL 20 in Bristol; head south on CR 12 into the Apalachicola National Forest. This designated scenic route merges with FL 65 and continues south through nearly 50 miles of unspoiled old-growth longleaf pine forest as the road parallels the Apalachicola River. When the road ends, turn left. Atop a high sand bluff, US 98 offers sweeping views of St. George Sound for the next 22 miles. At Carrabelle, head north on FL 67 through the national forest to return to FL 20 at Hosford. Total drive time: three hours. Alternatively, CR 379 south of Bristol is the Apalachee Savannahs Scenic Byway, which dovetails into the above route onto FL 65 at Sumatra. Along this route, you'll see vast pitcher plant savannas blooming each spring.

APALACHEE SAVANNAS

Sandra Friend

SWIMMING In addition to the region's many beaches (see *Green Space—Beaches*), swimmers flock to pristine **Blue Hole** at **Florida Caverns State Park** (see *Green Space—Parks*) and to **Blue Spring** in Marianna (see *Green Space—Springs*).

TUBING **Bear Paw Adventures** (see *Paddling*) sets up 4-mile tubing trips down crystal-clear, cypress-lined Spring Creek; Mar–Sep, $12.

WALKING TOURS Stop at the **Apalachicola Bay Chamber of Commerce** (see *Guidance*) for a copy of their historic walking tour booklet that highlights 34 sites, most within seven blocks of Market St. In Marianna, **Main Street Marianna** (850-482-6046), 2880 Green St, has a 44-page self-guided tour of historic sites in Jackson County, which you can use to explore downtown on foot.

WATER SPORTS Check on the beach in front of the **Blue Parrot** (see *Eating Out*) on St. George Island for summer season stands with Hobie Cat rentals and parasail rides.

✳ Green Space

BEACHES East to west, you can sample public beaches off US 98 at **Bald Point State Park** (see *Parks*), **Carrabelle Beach** (used for D-Day invasion practice in 1942), **St. George Island State Park, Cape Palms Park** and **Salinas Park** at Cape San Blas, and **Beacon Hill Park** at St. Joe Beach. Don't miss **St. Joseph Peninsula State Park** (see *Parks*) with its stunning tall dunes and beaches, voted best in the nation by *Condé Nast Traveler* magazine. If you have the time and inclination, kayak out or catch a charter to the unspoiled coasts of **Dog Island, Cape St. George State Reserve,** and **St. Vincent Island,** where you can sun without the crowds.

BOTANICAL GARDENS The small **Chapman Botanical Garden** on Martin Luther King Jr. Ave, Apalachicola, honors native son Dr. Alvin Wentworth Chapman (1809–1899), an internationally renowned botanist. Sidewalks wind through green space; boardwalks carry you over wetlands. The park seems somewhat neglected; it would be nice to see it with blooming beds again, especially since clouds of butterflies stop here on their fall migration. Free.

DOG ISLAND

Visit Florida

GREENWAY The ribbon was cut in April 2007, and now the **Blountstown Greenway** provides a new way to explore this historic riverside community. Park your car at the Panhandle Pioneer Settlement and walk, bike, or rollerblade this 5-mile paved trail that connects to a park along the Apalachicola River. The Blountstown Greenway is a new section of the statewide Florida Trail.

NATURE CENTER ✍ At the end of Market St, the **Apalachicola Nature**

Center (850-653-8063) at Apalachicola National Estuarine Research Reserve gives a great introduction to the estuary, with interpretive and hands-on exhibits, microscopes for examining sea critters, a little-kid corner with games and puzzles, open tanks with turtles and fish, and a popular boardwalk to an overlook on the estuary. Mon–Fri 8–5; free.

Sandra Friend

BALD POINT STATE PARK

PARKS **Apalachicola Bluffs and Ravines Preserve** (850-643-2756; www.tnc.org), CR 12, Bristol, provides hikers with a look at unique natural areas along the bluffs of the Apalachicola River along the extremely rugged 3.5-mile Garden of Eden Trail, where the world's most endangered conifer, the torreya tree, grows along with rare varieties of magnolias and the showy Florida anise—look for bright red blooms in spring!

Bald Point State Park (850-349-9146; www.floridastateparks.org/baldpoint), 146 Box Cut Rd, provides Alligator Point with its only sandy beaches along a peninsula of scrub oaks and pines. Nature trails and bicycle paths following old roads wind through the hammocks.

Dead Lakes (850-639-2702), FL 71. This strangely beautiful, 6,700-acre lake with dark tannic waters is located on the Chipola River near the town of Wewahitchka. The lake is accessible off FL 71 just north of Wewahitchka on State Park Rd and south off Land Rd. There are fish camps located along the shore. Care should be taken when operating a motorboat in this lake—it's filled with cypress snags and stumps. This spot enjoys a wide reputation for its bluegill (bream) and redear (shellcracker) fishing in spring.

FLORIDA CAVERNS STATE PARK

Sandra Friend

Florida Caverns State Park (850-482-9598; www.floridastateparks.org/floridacaverns), 3345 Caverns Rd. Built by the Civilian Conservation Corps' "Gopher Gang" from 1938 to 1942, this park's gem is the state's only show cave tour. Active features glisten with calcite crystals:

good birding

ST. JOSEPH PENINSULA STATE PARK

Shimmering rimstone pools, translucent soda straws, and rippling cave bacon underscore the delicate world inside Florida's limestone karst as you walk, duck, and squeeze through places like the Wedding Room, the Cathedral, and the Catacombs. For the claustrophobic, a video tour plays constantly in a big theater at the visitors center, where informative exhibits explain the unique habitats found in the park. Hikers, bikers, and equestrians share the 6.7-mile Upper Chipola Trail System, and hikers enjoy rugged limestone bluffs along the 1.5-mile Caverns Trail System, where the Bluff Trail goes right through a cave once used for shelter by ancient peoples! Campground, picnic pavilions, canoe rentals, and adjacent state-run golf course. Fee. Additional fee for cave tour; go directly to the visitors center to buy your ticket, as tours frequently sell out.

& **Rish Park** (850-227-1876), Cape San Blas Rd, deserves special note as Florida's only state park designated specifically for and limited to wheelchair-bound residents and their families. Boardwalks and tunnels allow access to swimming, cabins, the beach, fishing piers, and nature trails on both sides of the highway. Only Florida residents with developmental disabilities may utilize the facilities; call in advance of your visit.

St. George Island State Park (850-927-2111; www.floridastateparks.org/st georgeisland/default.cfm), 1900 E Gulf Beach Dr, has a pleasant campground nestled in among the pines at the east end of the island, and primitive camping for folks who hike the Gap Point Trail. But the big draw here is the miles and miles of unspoiled beach. Enjoy! Fee.

St. Joseph Peninsula State Park (850-227-1327; www.floridastateparks.org/ stjoseph), 8899 Cape San Blas Rd, has the distinction of having the top beach in the United States, according to Stephen Leathermann, "Dr. Beach." Is it the white-sand beaches or the tall sand dunes? You decide. The campgrounds are spectacular, as are the hiking trails—this is one of the few places you can really get away from it all on a backpacking trip to the western tip of the cape. There are well-appointed cabins, too. It's an excellent state park experience.

& In Marianna, tiny **Spring Creek Park** on US 98 provides a wheelchair ramp right down to the water for fishing.

& **Three Rivers State Park** (850-482-9006; www.floridastateparks.org/three rivers), 7908 Three Rivers Park Rd, Sneads. Defined by the confluence of the Chattahoochee and Flint rivers creating the Apalachicola, this expansive recreation area includes Lake Seminole, a top-notch bass fishing destination, as well as a large lakeside campground ($8–10) with a new wheelchair-accessible rental cabin, picnic pavilions, two hiking trails, and canoe rentals.

good birding

Torreya State Park (850-643-2674; www.floridastateparks.org/torreya), FL 271 between Bristol and Greensboro. From the 150-foot bluffs above the Apalachicola River, you can see for miles. An 1849 mansion, the Gregory House, dominates the skyline. The star attraction, however, is the 11.5-mile hiking trail system, offering one of the most rugged backpacking experiences in the state as you pass earthen battlements built during the Civil War and walk through ravines with the aroma of the rare torreya tree, also known as the stinking cedar. Enjoy the peaceful, scenic, developed campground, where you can try out a yurt!

SPRINGS Marianna's **Blue Spring Park** (850-482-9637; www.jacksoncountyfl .com), 5461 Blue Springs Hwy, offers a sandy beach, diving boards, and playground fringing a 70-degree, first-magnitude spring bubbling more than 64 million gallons of water daily. Open Memorial Day–Labor Day. Fee.

WILD PLACES Apalachicola National Forest (850-643-2282) encompasses more than half of Liberty County, with some of the world's finest pitcher plant savannas on its western edge. Walk the Florida Trail west from Camel Lake Recreation Area for an immersion into this unique marshy environment; the brightest blooms occur in late March. Adjoining the forest, the **Apalachicola River Wildlife and Environmental Area** protects thousands of acres of floodplain forests and marshes along both sides of the river, with more than 10 boat ramps and an interpretive trail at Sand Beach Recreational Area. Primitive camping (no permits, no fees required) is permitted in the upland areas of the preserve.

Several of the region's wild places are barrier islands, accessible only by boat. **Cape St. George Island,** a 9-mile stretch of beach sheltering Apalachicola Bay, has a historic lighthouse and plays host to families of red wolves being acclimated to the wild, as does adjacent **St. Vincent National Wildlife Refuge** (850-653-8808). Off Carrabelle, **Dog Island Preserve** can only be reached by boat. Coastal scrub and coastal pine forests are the predominant ecosystems on these barrier islands, where day-use visitors are welcome to roam the beaches and watch for birds; no overnight visits are permitted.

♿ **Tate's Hell State Forest** (850-697-3734; www.fl-dof.com/state _forests/tates_hell.html), 1621 US 98, Carrabelle. With nearly 150,000 acres of mostly wetlands, this is one helluva swamp. It's an important chunk of land, a giant natural filtration system

GREGORY HOUSE

Sandra Friend

for water flowing out of the swamps of the Apalachicola National Forest and into the bay and estuaries. Hunting, fishing, and paddling are the main recreation here, but hikers have two spots to explore: the short wheelchair-accessible Ralph G. Kendrick Dwarf Cypress Boardwalk (look for signs on FL 67) leading out over a rare (for North Florida) dwarf cypress swamp, and the High Bluff Coastal Nature Trail along US 98.

✳ Lodging

BED & BREAKFASTS

Apalachicola 32320
✿ **Bryant House** (1-888-554-4376; www.bryanthouse.com), 101 Sixth St. European elegance infuses this grand 1897 home, where Brigitte (enjoying her dream job) brings a touch of Germany to Florida, and Einstein, the resident blue and gold macaw, will call out a cheery greeting on your arrival. Period antiques (with price tags attached—buy one if the mood strikes!) embellish each of the three lavish rooms: Blue, Gold, and Red. Business travelers will appreciate free DSL access, while the romantically inclined will fall in love with this very grand setting. Brigitte's traditional German breakfast of thinly sliced smoked meats, cheeses, fresh fruit, and a soft-boiled egg is simply superb. $87–227.

✿ ⓓ **Coombs House Inn** (850-653-9199; www.coombshouseinn.com), 80 Sixth St. One of the grandest restored mansions in the South (circa 1905) and one of the nation's top inns, the pride of lumber baron James Coombs will amaze you. Step inside the doorway into a grand hall lined with black cypress walls and a high-beamed ceiling. Each room offers spacious Victorian elegance with careful restorative touches, such as the gleaming colored tile on the coal-fired fireplaces (a relic of the days when ships from Liverpool swapped coal ballast for cotton) and built-in cabinets moved into the bathrooms. You'll feel like royalty amid the lush furnishings and art, and the aroma of home-baked breads will ensure you come to the breakfast table. Eight rooms, each with en suite bath, $79–225.

The **Witherspoon Inn** (850-653-9186; www.witherspooninn.com), 94 Fifth St, was the home of a 19th-century sea captain—now it's yours. Settle in under the oaks and relax in your comfortable room or suite, $95–109.

Cape San Blas 32456
✿ Along a tiny finger of St. Joseph Bay, the **Cape San Blas Inn** (1-800-315-1965; www.capesanblasinn.com), 4950 Cape San Blas Rd, offers five spacious guest rooms ($95–150) with DVD and VCR, phones, small refrigerators, and extraordinarily comfort-

COOMBS HOUSE INN

Apalachicola Bay CVB

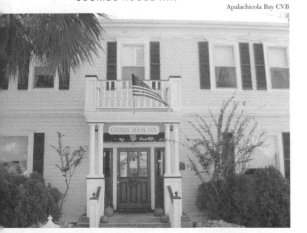

able beds. Stroll down to the dock and put in your kayak for a paddle, or head up the road to one of the top beaches in the United States.

Carrabelle 32322

🦐 🐢 The **Old Carrabelle Hotel** (850-697-9010; www.oldcarrabelle hotel.com), 201 Tallahassee St, circa 1890, is a former railroad hotel, lovingly restored by Skip and Kathy Frink in 2000. Like a sea captain's home (which it once was), it's filled with treasures from abroad, fine art from the tropics and from Florida's coasts, reflecting the owners' exotic and artistic tastes. Kick back and read the morning paper in the Monkey Bar, or curl up with a good book in the Hemingway Room, which certainly appealed to me with its literary theme and decor evoking dreams of Africa. Each room is a quiet, private retreat, or you can mingle with your fellow guests in the parlor or on the veranda and watch the sunset shimmer on the Carrabelle River. $77–97, includes full breakfast Fri and Sat. New in 2006— the Oyster Cabin, a remodeled early-1900s oyster-shuckin' cabin that can sleep a crowd, $107 for four.

Marianna 32446

🦐 🗡 ♿ It's always Christmas at the **Hinson House** (1-800-531-4786; www.phonl.com/hinson_house), 4338 Lafayette St, a Victorian gem in Marianna's historic residential district. Choose from two regular rooms or three spacious suites (including the Home Guard Suite, which looks over the site of the Battle of Marianna), with your choice of multiple beds— great for friends and relatives traveling together. $55–85; Judy welcomes well-behaved children.

Port St. Joe 32456

Turtle Beach Inn (850-229-9366; www.turtlebeachinn.com), 140 Painted Pony Dr. Along a relaxing stretch of remote Gulf beachfront at Indian Pass, the inn features four comfy modern rooms ($165–195) and several cottages; enjoy a full breakfast with an ocean view. The large wooden sea turtles set amid the pines and palms remind you that in the proper season, you can watch loggerheads nesting or hatching. Walk by moonlight—no lights, please!

GUEST HOUSES

Apalachicola 32320

As the historic hub of the region, Apalachicola is blessed with several guest houses, where you're left to your own devices after checking in. The settings are just as comfy as the B&Bs, with rates to match. Your selections include the **1835 Raney Guest Cottage** (850-653-9749; www .apalachicola-vacation.com), 46 Ave F, at $125; and the **House of Tartts** (850-653-4687; www.houseoftartts .com), Ave F and Fourth St, $95–135. The new kid on the block is a restored 1886 home, the **Wind-de-Mer Guest House** (850-653-1675), 102 Fifth St, $75–95.

HOTELS, MOTELS, AND RESORTS

Apalachicola 32320

🐢 At the **Apalachicola River Inn at Oystertown** (850-653-8139; www.apalachicolariverinn.com), 123 Water St, all of the pleasant, large rooms come with a river view and boat slips (excepting Fri and Sat). Kick back on your riverfront balcony and watch the shrimpers come in. $95–150.

GIBSON INN

🦞 ✿ 🐾 The **Gibson Inn** (850-653-2191; www.gibsoninn.com), 51 Ave C, dominates downtown with the classic charm of 1907. This three-story restored beauty offers 31 moderate rooms and spacious suites (check out Room 209!), each different, decorated in period antiques (I love the shawl canopied beds) but with full bath and television, $85–195. Wraparound porches let you sit back and watch the world go by. Best of all—and rare for a historic property like this—they love kids and pets. Downstairs, Avenue Sea is open Wed–Sun for fine dining.

Carrabelle 32322
🐾 **The Moorings** (850-697-2800; www.mooringscarrabelle.com), 1000 US 98. This popular full-service marina overlooking the Carrabelle River offers large waterfront condolike suites with docking slips just outside your door, $90–150; more for multi-bedroom units. Swimming pool, dive shop, and charter captains on site.

Marianna 32446
Chain motels such as **Holiday Inn Express** (850-526-2900), **Microtel** (850-526-5005), **Hampton Inn** (850-526-1006), and **Comfort Inn** (850-526-5600) cluster around I-10, exit 142, at FL 71.

Port St. Joe 32456
🦞 ♿ **Port Inn** (850-229-PORT; www.portinnfl.com), 501 Monument Ave. This snazzy new motel resurrects the original, circa 1913, with 20 spacious rooms ($69–149) reflecting modern sensibilities such as cable TV, Internet access, and a sparkling pool. But you can still sit on the front porch rocking chairs and dine on the complimentary breakfast while watching the fishing boats on St. Joseph Bay.

St. George 32328
♿ **The Inn at Resort Village** (1-800-296-9518), 1488 Leisure Ln, has an unparalleled setting for a hotel: It's nestled into the coastal scrub, peering over the dunes to the sea. Resort Village (see *Beach Rentals*) surprised the heck out of me by showing good eco-friendly sense in the way its buildings share the natural environment, peering out from beneath centuries-old pines along rolling dunes covered in Florida rosemary. The 24-room inn shares these sensibilities, with a beautiful pool hidden in the natural habitat, boardwalks to carry you over the dunes to the beach, and a minimalist parking area. All rooms have a great view. Some come with Jacuzzi or kitchenette, and there are three large rooms outfitted for wheelchairs. Full of amenities like writing desks, dataports, and private balconies, this seaside hotel offers serenity for $99 and up.

♿ **St. George Inn** (1-800-332-5196; www.stgeorgeinn.com), 135 Franklin Blvd. Built to look like a turn-of-the-20th-century hotel, this pleasant, modern inn is a short walk from beach and bay and features large well-appointed rooms, a wraparound porch with rockers, and a swimming pool. Weekly rentals only, starting at $856 in low season and $1,098 in high season.

BEACH RENTALS Anchor Vacation Properties (1-800-624-3964; www.florida-beach.com) manages classy properties like *Casablanca,* a well-appointed two-story beach home that tips its hat to Bogey. Traveling solo, I felt a little lonely kicking around this four-bedroom rental at Resort Village on St. George Island, but borrowing someone's lifestyle is the fun of a beach rental. You'll find it cost-effective if you split the tab with enough people to fill the house. Anchor's properties run from Carrabelle to Mexico Beach. Other rental agencies in the region include **Ochlocknee Bay Realty** (850-984-0001; www.obrealty.com), with a focus on Alligator Point; and **Collins Vacation Rentals** (1-800-423-7418; www.collinsvacationrentals.com) and **Prudential Resort Realty** (1-800-332-5196; www.stgeorgeisland.com), both covering St. George Island.

CABINS

Port St. Joe 32456
🐾 🦴 🐾 If you loved to play "fort" as a kid or are a history buff, don't miss

the **Old Saltworks Cabins** (850-229-6097; www.oldsaltworks.com), CR 30A. Hidden in a pine forest at the historic St. Joseph Saltworks, the cabins share a big play fort and a nice slice of St. Joseph Bay. Look for artifacts and Civil War dioramas at the office—the Confederates produced salt here, after all. Eleven upscale cabins with various configurations of bedrooms, perfect for families. Minimum two-night rental, starting at $163.

FISH CAMPS

Wewahitchka 32465
Fish camps are clustered around **Dead Lakes** (see *Green Space—Parks*), catering to anglers looking for peace and quiet amid the cypresses. Your choices include **Gate's Fish Camp** (850-639-2768), FL 71; **Lakeside Lodge** (850-639-2681), just 1 mile north of Wewahitchka on FL 71; and **Dead Lakes Sportsman Lodge** (850-639-5051) at the old Dead Lakes Dam, 2001 Lake Grove Rd.

CAMPGROUNDS

Blountstown 32424
Scott's Ferry Landing and General Store (850-674-2900), 6648 FL 71, along the Chipola River, offers a back-to-nature campground under the pines along the Chipola River, with RV and tent sites ($18 and up), and cabins ($55) built on stilts above flood level. A restaurant is under construction. They also rent canoes (see *To Do—Paddling*), and there's a fish-cleaning station and boat launch.

Carrabelle 32322
Carrabelle Palms RV Park (850-697-2638), 1843 US 98, sits right across from the public beach, with

CARRABELLE BEACH

Sandra Friend

nice views and sea breezes from the sunny spaces; full hook-ups, $23. Shaded by tall pines and with a view of the Gulf of Mexico, **Ho Hum RV Park** (850-697-3926 or 1-888-88-HO-HUM; www.hohumrvpark.com), 2132 US 98, offers free cable and wireless Internet with their sites, $26–29.

Indian Pass 32456
☙ At the end of CR 30A, **Indian Pass Campground** (850-227-7203; www.indianpasscamp.com), 2817 Indian Pass Rd, encompasses a small peninsula surrounded by estuary, with sites set under gnarled oaks. There's plenty to do, with the newly renovated pool, fishing charters (they'll set you up with a local guide), excursions to St. Vincent Island, canoe and kayak rentals, and bike rentals. Choose from RV sites with water and electric for $38–42, waterfront tent camping, or the new Stewart Lodge camping cabins (I love 'em!) for $95 and up.

Marianna 32446
On beautiful, cypress-lined Merritts Mill Pond, **Arrowhead Campground** (850-482-5583; www.arrowheadcamp.com), 4820 US 90, has several rental cabins ($45–55) in addition to its full-hook-up spaces ($26 and up) shaded by tall pines. Swimming pool and general store; canoe rentals available. The sites at **Dove Rest RV Park & Campground** (850-482-5313), FL 71 S, are nicely tucked under the pine trees. $10 tents, $20 full hook-ups.

✴ Where to Eat
DINING OUT

Apalachicola
After I saw the VW "staff car" outside **Chef Eddie's Magnolia Grill** (850-653-8000; www.chefeddiesmagnolia grill.com), 99 11th Ave, I was especially sorry I'd missed meeting Eddie Cass—he's bound to be a personality. Hailing from Boston, he takes Apalachicola's fruits of the sea and gives them an upscale twist in bisques and gumbo, or fried and broiled with select sauces. There's even a gourmet kids' menu. Honest! You can view his superbly presented entrées ($15–24) on the web site. Serving dinner daily.

Owl Café (850-653-9888), 15 Ave D, treats your taste buds with fun dishes like Apalachicola Bay oyster salad, the blue crab Café Quesadilla, and grilled chicken with grapes, berries, and red onion. Richard Bickel's scenes of Apalachicola add moodiness to the room. Serving lunch and dinner, $12 and up.

Tamara's Café Floridita (850-653-4111; www.tamarascafe.com), 17 Ave E, serves up funky fusion foods orchestrated by its South American owner. Look for tapas, paella, pecan-crusted grouper, and grouper tacos with fresh cilantro sauce. Trust me, they're fabulous! Lunch and dinner with most entrees under $20; closed Mon.

Marianna
Pesce's (850-482-8005), 2914 Optimist Dr. Off I-10, exit 136, this newcomer to the region has captured locals' palates with Maine lobster, Ipswich clams, and snow crab. Featuring Italian and seafood entrées. Lunch and dinner; closed Sun.

Port St. Joe
Sunset Coastal Grill (850-227-7900; www.sunsetcoastalgrill.com), 602 Monument Ave. Settle back and watch the sun set over the bay in this New Orleans–influenced restaurant, where fresh, local seafood has a twist of Cajun spice and hand-cut steaks

sate the hungry landlubbers. Dinner served nightly, $13–25.

St. George Island
Finni's Grill & Bar (850-927-3340; www.finnisgrillandbar.com), 200 Gunn St, is the island's bayside hot spot, serving the only sushi in Franklin County. Enjoy the view of Apalachicola Bay while feasting on ahi tuna, fresh grouper, and crabcakes served up with their signature garlic mashed potatoes, $11–25.

EATING OUT

Apalachicola
🐚 **Apalachicola Seafood Grill** (850-653-9510), 100 Market St. With the best people-watching view in town (big picture windows and an unobstructed view down to the shrimp boats) and fabulous fresh fish, this is a century-old (yes, century) landmark in a city best known for its seafood. I sampled the oysters and of course they were perfect, but you won't go wrong with shrimp, grouper, or "the world's largest fried fish sandwich." Lunch and dinner; closed Sun.

🐚 Kick back and enjoy the view of Cape St. George Island at **The Hut** (850-653-9410), 426 US 98, where the fried mullet and stuffed grouper come with a heap of cheese grits and an AYCE salad bar. Daily seafood specials; closed Mon.

Blountstown
The Callahan (850-674-3336), 19900 FL 20 W, named for one of the grand steamboats of the Apalachicola River, serves up home-style cooking in a comfy café with pecky cypress walls and a country-dining atmosphere, open 10–8; sandwiches $3–6, entrées $6–12. Live entertainment Fri and Sat, no alcohol served—bring the kids!

Carrabelle
Carrabelle Station (850-697-9550), 88 Tallahassee St, feels like an old-time eatery, thanks to Ron Gempel's eye for antique signs and ephemera adding to the original 1940s soda fountain decor. Grab a sundae or a sandwich ($3–6), or enjoy one of his nicely done salads or made-from-scratch soups ($3–5).

Indian Pass
Indian Pass Raw Bar (850-227-1670; www.indianpassrawbar.com), 8391 CR 30A, looks like an old general store, where folks hang out drinking cold beer while chowing down on some of the freshest seafood in these parts. And geez, according to their web site, they've dudified since my visit! Grab oysters and shrimp by the dozen, steamed crab legs, or get the kids a corn dog. Lunch and dinner Tue–Sat.

Marianna
Bobbie's Waffle Iron (850-526-5055), 4509 Lafayette St, is your best bet for a cheap, hearty breakfast, starting at $3; don't miss the home-cooked hash browns! Open 6–3 daily.

Gazebo Coffee Shop & Deli (850-526-1276), 4412 Lafayette St, is a popular downtown coffee and lunch stop. Open Mon–Fri 7–3.

At the **Old Ice House** (850-482-7827), 4829 US 90, I dined on catfish while watching an egret spear his dinner along cypress-lined Spring Creek. Housed in the original icehouse circa 1900, it's a simple family restaurant with a herd of deer on the wall and an extensive Weight Watchers menu. Lunch and dinner $5 and up; closed Sun.

Port St. Joe

Dockside Café (850-229-5200), at the marina, offers a nice selection of local seafood, including some creative entries like crab-stuffed grouper, mandarin spinach salad, and sea scallops Alfredo. Lunch and dinner; watch for AYCE mullet on Wed evening.

St. George Island

The Blue Parrot Café (850-927-2987), 68 W Gorrie St, offers the island's only oceanfront dining; feast on oyster and grouper while the sea breeze blows in your face. I loved the fact that I could have gumbo instead of fries with my sandwich, but watch out for the tropical drinks—they're potent! Serving lunch and dinner, when entrées are $25 and under.

St. George Island Gourmet (850-927-4888), 235 W Gulf Beach Dr, feeds the famished with deli delights and salads ($6–8); don't miss the fancy desserts, like coconut gelato. Gourmet foods and imported beers and wines, too. Daily 9–6:30.

✳ Selective Shopping

Alford

Old School House Antique Mall (850-579-3915), Park Ave, off US 231. Browse this massive (17,000 square feet!) selection of dealer booths housed in the town's old school, and you're bound to come away with a bargain; adjoining flea market. Open daily 9–5.

Apalachicola

You can spend hours wandering the downtown shops and never see everything. It's tough to narrow down choices—there's not a bad apple in the bunch. Here's my short list, but don't miss the others!

Chez Funk (850-653-3885), 88 Market St, captured my eye straightaway with their gleeful sign, and the shop is filled with Florida funk, including way-cool lamp shades and light-switch plates celebrating Florida's past through postcards, created by artist Nanci Kerr. And who couldn't love Nunzilla?

At **All That Jazz** (850-653-4800), 84 Market St, I love the local arts and crafts, especially the clever coin catchers—socks topped with open-mouthed ceramic faces. Crème brûlée coffee tempts, too.

Looking for nautical antiques? **The Tin Shed** (850-653-3635), 170 Water St, has everything from portholes and ship's bells to lobster traps, buoys, and even a ship's binnacle or two.

Gaily painted scenes decorate the floors of **Betsy's Sunflower** (850-653-9144), 14 Ave D, where you can pick up splashy enamelware, fine linens, and gourmet foods.

Step through the back door into busy **Downtown Books** (850-653-1290), 67 Commerce St, which features an excellent range of literary fiction, Florida books, and a small newsstand; Mon–Sat 10–5:30. I knew Apalachicola was my kind of town when I discovered there are two independent bookstores to browse. At 54 Market St, **Hooked on Books** (850-653-2420) focuses mainly on used books but has a good Florida selection.

✿ **Avenue E** (850-653-1411; www.avenuee.biz), 15 Ave E, features home decor worthy of any coastal home, with a nice mix of antiques, contemporary items, and local art (paintings, photography, and pottery). You'll find unique toys for the kids, too.

On the waterfront, the renovated **J. E. Grady & Co. Market** (850-653-4099), 76 Water St, Apalachicola's ship's chandlery circa 1884, is now a department store with tin ceilings and its original wooden floor. Browse for everything from dressy apparel, classic reproduction toys, and "Wild Women" gear to the photographic art of Richard Bickel.

I'm an outdoorsy gal, but **Riverlily** (850-653-2600), 78 Commerce St, caught my feminine eye with the wedding gown of my dreams and other delightful items—dresses, scarves, purple satin slippers, aromatherapy, incense, and candles—to uplift a woman's spirit.

Blountstown

The **Bargain Corner** (850-674-1000), FL 20 and FL 71, is a large antiques shop dominating the downtown corner, furnishings and glassware their stock-in-trade.

Carrabelle

At the **Beach Trader** on US 98, ALL OUR DUCKS ARE IN A ROW says the yellow sign with concrete ducks beckoning you into this collection of driftwood art, lawn ornaments, seashells, and more. Open Thu–Sat.

Two Gulls (850-697-3787), corner of US 98 and Marine St. You'll find nautical gifts, inspirational items, toys, candles, and local art—a little bit of everything. Closed Sun.

Marianna

Our Secret Garden (850-482-6034; www.secretgardenrareplants.com), US 90 E and Turner Rd, has been in business for 35 years selling both native and unusual plants, including bonsai, water gardens, ferns, and bog plants. Mon–Sat 8–5.

P. C. Oak & Brass (850-482-5150), 2859 Mc Pherson Street, can take hours to explore—it fills a three-story Victorian hotel and overflows with garden items and antique signs out into the yard. Every room brims with goodies, from antique walking sticks and Oriental swords to primitives and kitchenware. Open daily.

Port St. Joe

Bay Artiques (850-229-7191), 301 Reid Ave, displays classy coastal art from local and Panhandle artists, interspersed with antiques. Thu–Sat 10–5.

Portside Trading Company (850-227-1950), 328 Reid Ave, has home decor and goodies with a nautical flair—painted stemware, glass sea horses, and gourmet foods from the Blue Crab Bay Company. Closed Sun.

St. George Island

At **Hooked on Books** (850-927-3929), Judy Shultz hangs out in an old Cracker beach house with cats draped everywhere and a great selection of books. Check out the Florida authors corner, or browse the used-book shelves. Closed Sun.

J. E. GRADY & CO. MARKET

Sometimes It's Hotter (1-888-468-8372; www.sometimesitshotter.com), 37 E Pine St. Showcasing spicy, unusual foods, including boutique beers, private-label hot sauces, and their own award-winning seasonings. Open daily.

Wild Woman Mall (850-927-3259), 240 E Third St, at **Journeys of St. George Island,** is part outfitter, part beach shop, with kayaks for sale under one roof and sarongs, teeny dresses, and Hawaiian shirts in the next room. Closed Sun and in Feb.

PRODUCE AND SEAFOOD MARKETS

Apalachicola
At **Seafood-2-Go Retail Market** (850-653-8044), 123-A Water St, buy today's catch direct from the fishermen —it doesn't get any fresher! Overnight shipping available; closed Sun.

Marianna
Operating Apr–Aug, the **Jackson County Farmers Market** (850-592-5848) at the county administration building is an open-air fete starting every Tue, Thu, and Sat at 7 AM.

Port St. Joe
St. Patrick's Seafood Market (850-229-0070) along FL 71 packs your shrimp, oysters, and other seafood treats for travel.

Sneads
Along US 90, **Buddy's Picked Fresh Produce** stand offers farm-fresh fruits and vegetables all year long.

Two Egg
This tiny town amid the cotton and cane fields of northern Jackson County has a dozen explanations for its very odd name; take away a piece of its history from **Robert E. Long**

Cane Syrup, a roadside stand along CR 69 selling fresh cane syrup by the quart and gallon. If you stop in at the crack of dawn on the first Saturday of December, you'll catch the crew grinding cane and cooking up a big breakfast for visitors.

✳ Entertainment
Apalachicola
The restored **Dixie Theatre** (850-653-3200; www.dixietheatre.com) on Ave E hosts musicals, plays, jazz and folk concerts, and ballroom dancing.

Carrabelle
Catch the spirit of the Gulf at **Harry's Bar** (850-697-3420), 306 Marine St, an old-time fisherman's hangout; shoot some pool and shoot the breeze 7 AM–10 PM daily. Up the street, **Carrabelle Station** (see Eating Out) hosts live jazz on Wed night, and the **Tiki Hut** on Carrabelle Island is a favorite hangout at the marina.

Marianna
Chipola Junior College (850-718-2301), 3094 Indian Circle, sponsors an annual performing arts series that includes Broadway shows, musicians, choral groups, and opera; Sep–Jan, Fri and Sat evenings.

✳ Special Events
April: **Panhandle Folk Life Days** (850-674-3050). Demonstration of traditional arts and crafts at the Panhandle Pioneer Settlement. First weekend, 9–3. Free.

Apalachicola Classic & Antique Boat Show (850-653-9419), last Sat. Free.

Carrabelle Riverfront Festival (850-697-2585), last weekend, features arts and crafts, lots of fresh seafood, and an open house at the FSU Turkey Point Marine Lab.

May: On the **Apalachicola Annual Spring Tour of Historic Homes** (850-653-9550), tour up to 20 historic private homes on a guided walking tour; $10 donation.

Tupelo Festival (850-227-1223), mid-May. They've been making tupelo honey in Wewahitchka for more than a century, and the town celebrates this heritage with food, crafts, and entertainment at Lake Alice Park. Free.

August: **St. Joseph Bay Scallop Festival** (850-227-1223), Port St. Joe,

last weekend. It's educational and entertaining—learn all about scallops and scalloping along the bay. Free.

October: **Florida Panhandle Birding & Wildflower Festival** (850-229-9464; www.birdfestival.org), Port St. Joe. Tours and lectures held at various locations along the coast. Varying fees; check web site for details.

November: **Florida Seafood Festival** (1-888-653-8011; www.florida seafoodfestival.com), Apalachicola. The granddaddy of seafood festivals is now more than 40 years old and simply shouldn't be missed—from oyster shucking to the annual blessing of the fleet, it's a huge event.

Central Panhandle 4

PANAMA CITY

THE EMERALD COAST & THE
BEACHES OF SOUTH WALTON

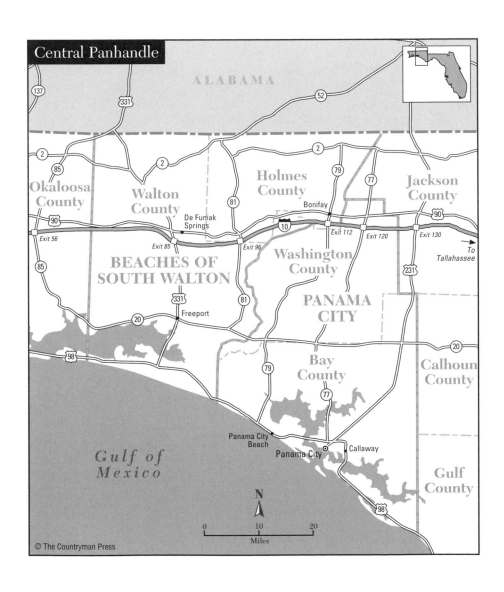

PANAMA CITY

MEXICO BEACH, ROSEMARY BEACH

In the beach area of Bay County, you can experience the lively hustle and bustle of Panama City and Panama City Beach, the quiet and solitude of down-home Mexico Beach, and the plush accommodations at the resort-style Rosemary Beach. Farther north, away from the beach into Washington County, you'll pass through the country towns of Chipley and Ebro.

Panama City Beach and **Panama City** are two separate municipalities connected by the Hathaway Bridge, which crosses St. Andrews Bay. Panama City is the seat of Bay County and the largest municipality between Tallahassee and Pensacola. It was recently named one of the best places to invest in real estate; property values have soared, and new developments are popping up everywhere. Also actively developing and expanding, the 7 square miles of Panama City Beach is known as an active vacation mecca, with crowds peaking during spring breaks. While developers sought many of the Panhandle beach areas during the 1920s' land boom, Panama City and Panama City Beach didn't really take off until the construction of Tyndall Air Force Base in 1941. After World War II, the base was demobilized and made part of the USAF Tactical Air Command. Today it is home to the 325th Fight Wing, focusing on air education and training. Over the years, many service personnel who served at Tyndall returned to the sugary sand beaches and emerald green waters to make Bay County their home.

After a 30-minute drive west of Panama City Beach you'll find the 3-mile long waterfront community, **Mexico Beach,** which is so small that you may drive through without taking notice. The 35–45 mph speed limit should help. Felix DuPont, who used the local pine trees for turpentine production, bought the land around 1900. As vacationers traveled across US 98, along the Panhandle coastline from Panama City to Pensacola, the area was often overlooked. With only a few hundred residents by the mid-1950s, the town continued to grow slowly, finally incorporating in 1966. By then many beaches along the Panhandle were under full development, causing the townsfolk to take interest in preserving their Emerald Coast homestead. Mexico Beach's first mayor, Charlie Parker, happened to be a developer, but he recognized that the town had something

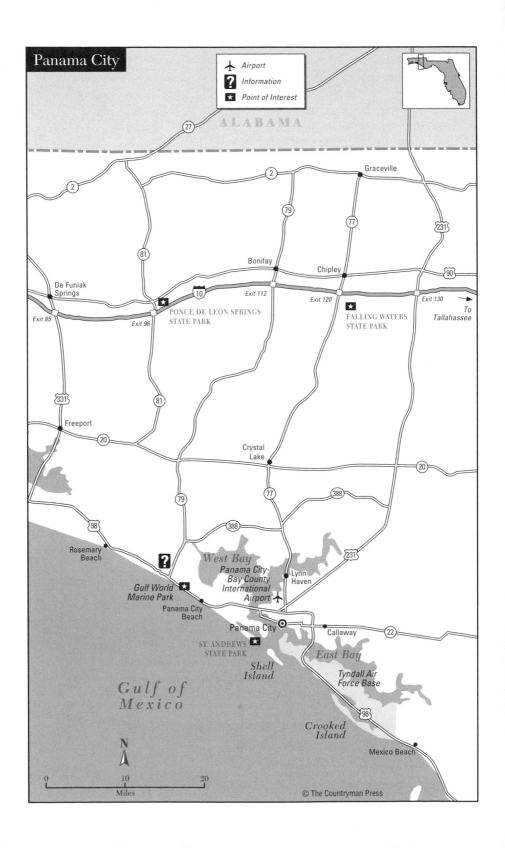

Panama City

Airport
Information
Point of Interest

ALABAMA

27

2 · Graceville

79

77

231

2

81

Bonifay · Chipley

90

De Funiak
Springs

10

Exit 112

Exit 120

Exit 130 →

Exit 85

Exit 96

PONCE DE LEON SPRINGS
STATE PARK

FALLING WATERS
STATE PARK

To
Tallahassee

331

81

Freeport

20

Crystal
Lake

20

79

77

388

388

231

98

Rosemary
Beach

West Bay

Panama City-
Bay County
International
Airport

Lynn
Haven

Gulf World
Marine Park

Panama City
Beach

Panama City · Callaway

22

ST. ANDREWS
STATE PARK

East Bay

Shell
Island

Tyndall Air
Force Base

Gulf of
Mexico

Crooked
Island

N

Mexico Beach

0   10   20
Miles

© The Countryman Press

special and should remain a small, quiet, getaway destination. Since that time many developers have tried to expand into the area, and local politicians have remained steadfast, enacting zoning restrictions and establishing town ownership of the entire beach. Today, with about 1,000 permanent residents, the beachside community retains much of its small-town appeal and is a great destination for families and romantic couples to wind down. Building height is restricted to 4 stories, and you'll find no chain-style establishments as all of the shops, eateries, and lodgings are owned locally. If you should you require a faster pace, head only 26 miles east to the towering condos and high-octane activities of Panama City.

Rosemary Beach, established in 1995, was named for wild Florida rosemary, which is native to this area. In fact the town's developers took great care to land-scape all properties using native species. Lush and plush, this self-contained re-sort village on the eastern edge of Bay County offers a quaint town center and exclusive vacation rentals (see *Lodging—Vacation Homes*). You'll relax as you wander down charming paths that lead you through a maze of gardens, past lawns of soft Bermuda grass, and down secluded nature trails. This is the place where pristine beaches and four world-class pools are never jam-packed.

In 1825, frontier farmers created Washington Country, growing pears, water-melons, sweet potatoes, and cotton. By 1882, the Pensacola & Atlantic Railroad was completed near present-day **Chipley,** 60 miles north of Panama City, and the small community was renamed to honor Colonel W.D. Chipley, the builder of the railroad. In 1927, Chipley became the county seat; its first post office was located in one of the boxcars. With just a few hundred residents, **Ebro,** just 16 miles northwest on FL 79 from Panama City Beach, provides a quiet natural area for camping, hiking, and canoeing. Since 1899, the entire county has pro-hibited the sale or manufacture of alcohol. The close-knit farming community welcomed the revivalist influence that spread the nation in 1916, holding one of the largest religious revivals in the Florida Panhandle. Today, the religious influ-ence remains strong with Baptist, Methodist, and Presbyterian churches found countywide. You'll find more than two dozen churches dating from the turn of the 20th century in Chipley alone.

GUIDANCE **Panama City Beach Convention and Visitors Bureau** (850-233-5070; www.800pcbeach.com), P.O. Box 9473, Panama City Beach 32417, covers the main beach area along with smaller beach and inland townships. For more information on Mexico Beach, contact the **Mexico Beach Community Devel-opment Council** (1-888-723-2546; www.mexicobeach.com/cdc), 102 Canal Pkwy, Mexico Beach 32456. Connections to everything in **Rosemary Beach** is at 1-888-855-1551; www.rosemarybeach.com; P.O. Box 611040, Rosemary Beach 32461. For the towns of Chipley and Ebro, contact the **Washington County Chamber of Commerce** (850-638-4157; www.washcomall.com), 685 Seventh St, Chipley 32428.

GETTING THERE *By air*: **Panama City/Bay County International Airport** (850-763-6751).

By bus: **Greyhound** (1-800-231-2222).

By car: **I-10** and **FL 90** run east–west along the Panhandle. Chipley is at the intersection of **FL 90** and **FL 77**. A few miles west of Chipley, take **FL 79** south a few miles to reach Ebro. **FL 231** will take you from **I-10** south to Panama City. **US 98** also runs east–west and will take you along the beaches of Panama City, Panama City Beach, Mexico Beach, and Rosemary Beach, continuing all the way west to Pensacola.

GETTING AROUND Local transportation can be found in Panama City and Panama City Beach. The **Bay Town Trolley** (850-769-0557; www.baytowntrolley.org), 1116 Frankford Ave, Panama City, is the local public transportation service in and around Panama City and Panama City Beach, covering hundreds of stops for shopping, dining, and fun in the sun. Buses are equipped with bicycle racks and wheelchair lifts. The trolley operates Mon–Fri 6 AM–6:30 PM. Full fare for bus or trolley is $1; 50¢ for seniors, persons with disabilities, and students; children under 5 ride free. During special events, a free beach trolley runs along the 3-mile stretch of Mexico Beach. On New Year's Eve, the shuttle transports you across Eastern and Central time zones so you can ring in the New Year twice; contact the Mexico Beach Community Development Council (see *Guidance*).

MEDICAL EMERGENCIES In the Panama City area, **Bay Medical Center** (850-769-1511) and **Gulf Coast Medical Center** (850-769-8341). Those staying farther west in Bay County may find Destin and Fort Walton area hospitals more convenient: **Fort Walton Beach Medical Center** (850-862-1111) and **Twin Cities Hospital** (850-678-4131).

✳ To See

AQUARIUM ✿ ♿ Spend a day exploring the creatures of the sea at **Gulf World Marine Park** (850-234-5271; www.gulfworldmarinepark.com), 15412 Front Beach Rd, Panama City Beach, where you can see a wide variety of shows. Marvel as spectacular bottlenose dolphins leap and flip, and streamlined rough-toothed dolphins display great speed; laugh at the comical California sea lion shows; and learn about loggerhead and sea turtles at the reptile show. Wander through the lush tropical gardens where colorful macaws greet you with a loud squawk or touch slippery stingrays in the petting pool. The well-kept facility, open since 1969, exhibits a variety of sharks, alligators, sea turtles, flamingos, and even penguins. Later on see the colorful and musical Splash Magic Laser Show with 16 fountains reaching sky high and laser lights projecting on 50-foot screen. Open daily 9 AM–sunset. The admission price of $24 adults, $11 ages 5–11, includes all shows. As an add-on adventure you can swim with a dolphin ($150) or be a trainer for a day ($199).

ART GALLERY AND MUSEUM The **Visual Arts Center of Northwest Florida** (850-769-4451; www.vac.org.cn), 19 E Fourth St, Panama City. The building itself is a piece of art. Built in the 1920s, the Spanish Revival facility also reveals art deco influences, combining neoclassical, Gothic, and baroque features.

Inside, it's the only museum of its kind for more than 100 miles. Permanent and rotating exhibitions from local and nationally acclaimed artists in a variety of media are shown in the Main, Higby, and Permanent Galleries. The Impressions Gallery is a hands-on experience for children. Open Mon, Wed, Fri 10–4; Tue and Thu 10–8; Sat 1–5; museum admission, donation. Some classes are free; others are $65–130 for six-week sessions.

ATTRACTION ✈ The curious and weird can be found at cartoonist's Robert **Ripley's Believe it or Not! Museum** (850-230-6113; www.ripleyspanamacity beach.com), 9907 Front Beach Rd, Panama City Beach. The pirate ship counterpart to the original in St. Augustine will have you walking through spinning tunnels and displays of the bizarre. On the new 4D movie ride you'll experience a mineshaft or cosmic galaxy—a great roller coaster experience for those wanting a virtual thrill without the physical dips and turns. Open daily 8 AM–1 AM; museum admission $15 adults, $12 ages 4–12; theater admission $12 adults, $10 for children; a combo pass includes both museum and movie, $17–23.

HISTORIC SITES

Chipley
Take a walk through the **South Third St. Historic District** (circa 1887–1938) and reminisce about the old days. The affluent neighborhood contains 16 private residences of historical interest, built in the frame vernacular style.

The 1857 **Moss Hill Church** at the corner of Vernon and Greenhead Rd is another fine frame vernacular construction. The one-story church is the oldest unaltered building in Washington County and is an excellent example of local preservation efforts.

Panama City
The **Robert L. McKenzie House** (also known as the Belle Booth House) features one and a half stories under a gabled roof. The private residence at 17 E Third Ct is not open to the public, but you can gaze at the frame vernacular architecture circa 1909.

MUSEUMS You'll have hands-on fun and learn about science, history, and culture at the **Junior Museum of Bay County** (850-769-6128; www.jrmuseum.org), 1731 Jenks Ave, Panama City. See northwest Florida pioneer life portrayed through a gristmill, cabin, barn, smokehouse, and 1943 Bay Line Engine. The nature boardwalk winds through 12 acres of hardwood swamp. Open daily, except Sun. Fee, but no charge for Florida residents.

Divers will want to visit the **Museum of Man of the Sea** (850-235-4101), 17314 Panama City Beach Pkwy, Panama City Beach, which showcases the history of work in the ocean. The small museum contains artifacts such as diving suits, military equipment, remote submersibles, and submarines. Open daily 10–4; adults $5, ages 6–16 $2.50.

ZOOLOGICAL PARK At **ZooWorld Zoological and Botanical Park** (850-230-1243; www.zooworldpcb.net), 9008 Front Beach Rd, Panama City Beach, you'll get closer to the animals at than at any other zoo. With more than 260 animals, including big cats, giraffes, and orangutans, this zoo is also one of the cleanest. Through the glass windows at the Tilghman Infant Care Facility you can view the care and feeding of newborn baby animals. *Your* little ones will enjoy the friendly Gentle Jungle Petting Zoo. Open daily 9–4:30; adults $14, seniors $12, ages 4–11 $9.

✳ To Do

BICYCLING The 9-mile **Crooked Creek Trail** in Pine Log State Forest (see *Green Space—Wild Places*) was built with mountain bikers in mind; access the trailhead off FL 79, 1 mile south of the main entrance of the forest's recreation area.

BOAT TOURS The **Glass-Bottom Boat Cruise** (850-234-8944), 3605 Thomas Dr, Panama City, takes you to Shell Island, where you can swim or search for shells along the sugar-sand beach. This unique trip also explains shrimp nets and crab trap operations. Located at Treasure Island Marina.

Swashbucklers will want to step back in time aboard Captain Memo's 85-foot authentic pirate ship, the **Sea Dragon** (850-234-7400; www.piratecruise.com), 3601 Thomas Dr, Panama City. You'll enjoy cruising the Gulf while pirates blast cannons, hang from the rigging, and then have a sword fight, which you might be asked to join! $32 adults, $27 seniors and juniors ages 13–17, $22 ages 3–12.

SEA DRAGON

Panama City Beach CVB

DIVING The waters off Panama City are known as the **"Wreck Capital of the South"**; you can swim among sea turtles, rays, catfish, flounder, grouper, and curious puffer fish in a half dozen historic wrecks in natural reefs reaching 100 feet a few miles offshore, or in 50 artificial reefs set just offshore. The famous 465-foot *Empire Mica* is there; dive down 75 feet to reach a 184-foot-long naval mine sweeper. Or inspect a 100-foot aluminum Hovercraft, also sitting under 75 feet of water. A favorite dive is the *Black Bart*. The intact 185-foot oil-field supply ship offers an abundance of fish and turtles and is a great spot for underwater photography. Explore cargo holds, wheelhouse, galley, and even the heads. Sitting in 75 feet of water, the bridge is at 40 feet; the main deck at 66. Certified divers have several charter options:

You'll never feel crowded with **Wild Goose Diving Charters** (850-896-3304; www.wildgoosepcb.com), 3304 Treasure Cir, Panama City Beach, where, for more than 20 years, Coast Guard–licensed captain Terry "Captain Cranky" McNamer has taken small parties to natural reefs at secret dive spots in search of spiny lobsters. His inshore dives, 5 to 6 miles out, take you to 60–80 feet for $70; offshore dives, 10–12 miles out, take you to depths of 80–120 feet for $80–90.

Whether diving inshore or offshore on wrecks or natural and manmade reefs or in the crystal clear waters of a natural spring, **Dive Locker/Panama City Dive Charters** (850-230-8006; www.divelockerpcb.com), 106 Thomas Dr, Panama City Beach, takes you on an unforgettable dives. Dives 5 to 6 miles offshore take you to 60–80 feet for $74; dives 10–12 miles offshore take you from 80–120 feet for $84–104. A three-day dive class in a freshwater spring certifies you for up to 60 feet ($285). Rental equipment available.

DOLPHIN SWIM You've seen dolphins at the parks; you may have even taken a dip with them in the constraints of a pool or lagoon. Now you want to swim in the open water with them—because this is what true dolphin lovers *really* want to do. At **Water Planet** (850-230-6030; www.waterplanetusa.com), 5605 Sunset Ave, Panama City Beach, your dream is realized. One-day, three-day, and weeklong programs teach you about ecology, dolphin physiology, and how to interact with wild dolphins both socially and legally. Only six guests per excursion; you'll travel on a 24-foot pontoon boat around Shell Island for an unforgettable experience with wild bottlenose dolphins. Later the team will take you on a walk in the shallows for a marine ecology wet lab, where you'll learn about crustaceans and local fish. A one-day excursion is $98; three days $430; weeklong trip $750 (five days, plus one replacement day if needed). Snorkeling equipment is available to rent for $5.

FAMILY ACTIVITIES ✍ One of the country's most challenging mazes is at the **Coconut Creek Family Fun Park** (850-234-2625; www.coconutcreekfun.com), 9807 Front Beach Rd, Panama City Beach. Longer than a football field, the Gran Maze has doors that are changed often so you can never really memorize the routes. When you've completed the maze, head over to the South Pacific Island–style mini golf park and bumper boats for more family fun. See the Web site for a discount coupon. Play a game of mini golf at **Barnacle Bay Mini Golf** (850-234-7792; www.barnacle-bay-mini-golf.panamacitybeachfanatic.com), 11209 W US 98, Panama City Beach, which has two tropically landscaped 18-hole golf courses with rope bridges, waterfalls, and dark caves. Drive extreme go-carts at **Cobra Adventure Park** (850-235-0321), 9323 Front Beach Rd, where 9-horsepower go-carts race up and down three-story coils. Experience the Alien Arcade, bungee bounce, and bumper boats at **Emerald Falls Family Entertainment Center** (850-234-1049), Thomas Dr at Joan Ave. Play 1950s mini golf at the original 1959 **Goofy Golf** (850-234-6403), 12206 Front Rd. Race on the longest go-cart track in North Florida at **Hidden Lagoon Super Racetrack & Super Golf** (850-233-1825), 14414 Front Beach Rd, or on a winged Sprint Track at **Great Adventures Family Entertainment Center** (850-230-1223), 15236 Front Beach Rd. Swashbuckling adventurers will want to head **Pirate's Island Golf** 850-235-1171; www.piratesislandgolf.com), 9518 Front Beach Rd, Panama City.

FISHING A quiet place to drop a line is off the Mexico Beach Fishing Pier at 37th St. Bait, licenses, and gear can be purchased nearby at **Cathey's Ace Hardware** (850-648-5242), 3000 US 98, which also rents some equipment.

GOLF Always at the top of any golfer's list, Panama City offers five challenging courses with greens fees averaging $50 or less. The area's first golf course, built in 1962, is **Signal Hill** (850-234-3218; www.signalhillgolfcourse.com), 9615 N Thomas Dr, originally designed on dunes. An inexpensive 18-hole public course, it is the best value in the area. The second-most challenging course in the United States is the intimidating par 72 **Nicklaus Course** (850-235-6397; www.bay pointgolf.com), 4701 Baypoint Rd. Measuring more than 7,100 yards and with a slope rating of 152, the former Lagoon Legend was completely overhauled in 2005 and is the first Nicklaus course in the Florida Panhandle. If the Nicklaus Course is too much to handle, you'll never be bored at county club–style **Club Meadows** (850-235-6950; www.baypointgolf.com), 4701 Baypoint Rd. Easy enough for beginners, the course still offers enough challenge for experienced golfers. The 18-hole, par 72 course at

ONE OF THE REGION'S MANY GOLF COURSES

Panama City Beach CVB

Holiday Golf Club (850-234-1800; www.holidaygolfclub.com), 100 Fairway Blvd, is only 1 mile from the beach and is the only night nine-hole executive course in the county. At **Hombre Golf Club** (850-234-3673; www.hombregolfclub.com), 120 Coyote Pass, wetlands and waterholes are favorites.

good birding

HIKING St. Andrews State Park (see *Green Space—Beaches*) offers two excellent nature trails through coastal scrub and pine flatwood habitats. The

0.6-mile Pine Flatwoods Trail starts at a replica of an old-time turpentine processing plant and loops through scrub and coastal flatwoods along the bay side of the park, while the Gator Lake Nature Trail offers a 0.4-mile loop with views of both a freshwater pond and the distant dunes.

One of the most intriguing walks in Florida is the **Sinkhole Trail** at Falling Waters State Park (see *Green Space—Park*), a boardwalk that carries you above and between a series of deep sinkholes leading to the state's highest waterfall.

Sandra Friend

ST. ANDREWS BEACH

As it crosses the Central Panhandle, the statewide **Florida Trail** (see *What's Where*) provides opportunities for backpacking and day hiking on two distinct segments. The 18-mile stretch paralleling scenic **Econfina Creek** can be accessed from FL 20 and off Scott Rd in Fountain; another 6.1-mile segment passes through the Sand Pond Trailhead at **Pine Log State Forest** (see *Green Space—Wild Places*). This trailhead is the nexus of three hiking trails on which you can explore the cypress-lined ponds and dense pine flatwoods of Florida's oldest state forest.

SHELLING Shelling can be good on any beach, especially after a storm. Several tours will take you to **Shell Island** across from St. Andrews State Park (see *Boat Tours* and *Dolphin Swim,* and *Green Space—Beaches*). Paddling across is not recommended due to rough open water, submerged rocks, and treacherous shipping lanes. **Mexico Beach** offers a quiet place to search for sand dollars, fragile paper fig shells, and the rare brown speckled junonia. Removal of live shells is prohibited. To clean your stinky shells before your trip home, soak them overnight in a 50:50 solution of bleach and water, rinse with fresh water, and then shine them up with a bit of baby or mineral oil. Sand dollars require more delicate handling. Let them dry naturally outside in the shade for a few days (sunlight will make them brittle). While not as smelly, some people still like to give them a dip in a pan of bleach.

SHELL ISLAND BEACH

Panama City Beach CVB

SPA THERAPY Moisturize your body after a day in the sun at **Solace Day Spa & Salon** (850-0231-6801; www.solacesalonspa.com), 8 Georgetown Ave in Barrett Square, Rosemary Beach. The full-service oasis offers pampering in a tropical setting. You'll experience treatments with nature-based and organic products in this Aveda concept salon.

SURFING Surf's often up at **St. Andrews State Park** (see *Green Space—Beaches*), where wave action is almost guaranteed along the zone between the jetty and fishing pier.

WATER PARK Families will love swimming around the Great Shipwreck or riding the White Knuckle Rapids at **Shipwreck Island Waterpark** (850-234-3333; www.shipwreckisland.com), 12201 Middle Beach Rd, Panama City Beach. Little ones will delight at Tadpole Hole, where they can slide down a toad's tongue into a few inches of water, while the thrill seekers will scream as they descend the 65-foot Tree Top Drop. Those needing to relax can float on tubes down the scenic Lazy River. For the most part, fees are measured in inches, not age. Guests 50 inches and above $29, 35 to 50 inches $24, under 35 inches are free. Seniors over age 62 get in for $18, regardless of height.

✳ Green Space

BEACHES Camp Helen State Park (850-233-5059; www.floridastateparks.org/camphelen), 23937 Panama City Beach Pkwy, Panama City Beach. A peninsula that once served as a vacation getaway in the 1940s, the new Camp Helen State Park borders the Gulf of Mexico, Phillips Inlet, and Lake Powell, and is an excellent site for birding. Hike along the trails and beaches, or cast your line from the shore. Employees of an Alabama textile mill enjoyed the lodge and cottages from 1945 until 1987 as their getaway; the structures are in the process of being restored. Fee.

FUN ON THE BEACH

Visit Florida

St. Andrews State Park (850-233-5140; www.floridastateparks.org/standrews), FL 392, Panama City Beach, is the one pristine getaway on the coast that you won't want to miss. Encompassing 1,200 acres of undisturbed forests and sand dunes, the park has miles of beaches; you can swim and snorkel in the protected pool behind the jetty or cast a line off one of two fishing piers. It's the only place along Panama City Beach where condos won't be staring you in the face. Two beautiful natural campgrounds under the pines have sea breezes as a bonus, and two hiking trails introduce you to the splendor of

Sandra Friend

FALLING WATERS STATE PARK

one of Florida's most threatened habitats, the coastal scrub. I was entranced by my first visit, since it is truly an escape from the overpopulated mass that is Panama City Beach. The nature trail through the coastal pine flatwoods is a delight, and I was surprised to see an alligator in a freshwater pond less than a quarter mile from the beach. This is Surfer Central, too—catch big waves near the jetty; camping, fishing, and picnicking round out the activities at this park at the end of FL 392. Fee.

PARK **Falling Waters State Park** (850-638-6130; www.floridastate parks.org/fallingwaters), 1130 State Park Rd, Chipley. On my first visit to the park, I was disappointed that Florida's tallest waterfall wasn't falling—it drops 67 feet into a perfectly cylindrical sinkhole. But the Sinkhole Trail, on boardwalks over the rugged fern-lined karst, was a delight. Stop by in the rainy season to get the full feel of this unusual geological site. The park offers camping, hiking, and picnicking; fee.

SPRINGS **Pitt Spring,** along FL 20 at Econfina Creek west of Fountain, offers a crystalline venue for swimming; my hiking buddies stopped there to fill their water bottles from the chalky-blue water.

WILD PLACES Florida's oldest state forest is **Pine Log State Forest** (850-872-4175; www.fl-dof.com/ state_forests/pine_log.html), FL 79, Ebro. Established in 1936, it covers 6,911 acres of sandhills, flatwoods, cypress-lined ponds, and titi swamps, with several extensive trail systems introducing you to this variety of habitats; the Florida Trail passes through here as well. A campground with electric and water hook-ups, showers, and restrooms provides respite beneath the pines. Bring your canoe and paddle across East Lake, or fish in the natural streams and ponds. Trail riding is permitted on numbered forest roads.

THE RE-CREATED TURPENTINE PROCESSING PLANT AT ST. ANDREWS STATE PARK
Sandra Friend

✳ Lodging

INNS

Mexico Beach 32456

☀ You'll find a simpler way of life at the **Driftwood Inn** on the beach (850-648-5126; www.driftwoodinn .com), 2105 US 98, where relaxation is the number one activity. The Victorian-style inn is more like a bed & breakfast with a beachy twist. You'll note the grand architecture, spacious verandas, and luscious lawns and think you have gone back in time. Families will enjoy the slower pace as they barbecue on back decks that overlook the Gulf of Mexico. Stay in the main house or the spacious duplex and quad-plex cottages next door. Each air-conditioned room comes with fully equipped kitchen and cable TV. If you'd like more privacy, you can stay at one of their Victorian houses located across the road behind the inn. The two-bedroom, one-and-a-half-bath homes will accommodate six guests. This is a pet-friendly establishment; warm fuzzies abound. Your own pets are welcome with prior arrangements for an additional $15 per night. For those who miss their best friend, the innkeepers' friendly 140-pound Great Dane, Dufus, meanders through the property, providing lots of love. Rooms nightly in-season (Apr–Sep), $140–170; off-season (Oct–Mar), $110–135; weekly $980–1,085 in-season, $770–840 off-season. Victorian homes nightly $175–190 in-season; $130–145 off-season, weekly $1,225 in-season; $840 off-season. Monthly rates available. No food is served at the inn, but you can grab a cup of coffee or tea, then take a short walk to a couple of local eateries (see *Eating Out*.)

Rosemary Beach 32461

♿ You can't miss the carnelian red stucco as you drive up to the Italian-style **Pensione Bed & Breakfast Inn** (850-231-1790; www.thepensione .com), 78 Main St. The quaint inn has only eight rooms; two are wheelchair accessible. Rooms are decorated in contemporary simplicity with many furnishings from local artisans. Take notice of the tiniest details, such as the tiles in the bathroom, which not only look like a sparrow's speckled egg, they feel like one, too. Located directly across the street from the Gulf of Mexico; each room offers one queen-sized bed and breathtaking views of the emerald green water. Nightly rates $138–198, depending on season, and includes a light continental breakfast buffet. The Onano Neighborhood Cafe (see *Dining Out*) is on the main floor.

HOTELS

Rosemary Beach 32461

The newest addition to Rosemary Beach, the **Hotel Saba** (850-231-2973; www.rosemarybeach.com), 63 Main St, is located in the heart of town. Opened in 2007, the full-service luxury hotel features 56 rooms and suites, along with fine dining, boutiques, pool, and on-site spa. Call for rates.

CONDO HOTELS

Panama City Beach 32408

On the beach, overlooking the Gulf of Mexico, the **Boardwalk Beach Resort** (850-914-8484; www.board walkbeachresort.com), S 9450 Thomas Dr, features a tropical paradise with lots of water activities. Relax as you float down the lazy river pool, lounge around the lagoon pool, or let the kids splash in the kiddie pool. Then head to the beach, where you can splash in the surf or hunt for shells. Simple efficiencies to deluxe one-, two-, and three-bedroom suites are all uniquely decorated according the taste of the unit's owners; $99 to $299, with weekly and monthly rates available.

You can spend your entire vacation on site at the **Edgewater** (850-235-4977 or 1-800-331-6338; www.edgewater beachresort.com), 11212 Front Beach Rd, where you'll find everything from water sports, such as windsurfing, banana boats, Jet Skis, parasailing, tropically landscaped pools, and lazy river, to land sports, such as tennis on 11 all-weather Plexicushion-surfaced courts and golf on the nine-hole executive course at the 18-hole Hombre Golf Club (see *To Do—Golf*). One-, two-, and three-bedroom suites ($99–650) are located oceanside and across from the beach. An on-site trolley takes you all over the property.

VACATION HOMES Ocean Reef Resort Properties (850-837-3935; www.oceanreefresorts.com) offers furnished cottages, beach homes, condos, town homes, luxury homes, and resorts by the day, week, or month.

One of the largest suppliers of fully furnished homes, the folks at **Resort-Quest** (www.resortquest.com) can select which home will be right for you—from condos in resort-style settings to portfolio homes with private pools. By the day, week, or month.

Mexico Beach
Rent a beachfront home from **Anchor Vacation Properties** (1-800-624-3964; www.florida-beach .com), an agency based in Apalachicola that manages oceanfront home

rentals up and down this coast. Properties range from old-fashioned beachfront cottages to mega-mansions.

Sand Bucket B Townhouse (850-647-3882; www.sandbucket.net), 100 S 39th Street; Unit B is located beachside at the corner of US 98 and 39th St. This townhome is elevated, providing spectacular views of blue green waters of the Gulf of Mexico. Stretched over two floors above the carport, the two-bedroom unit has one queen bed and two twin beds, along with a queen sofa bed and three full bathrooms. It is also has a fully equipped kitchen, a laundry room, an outdoor shower, and beach wagon. Weekly Apr–Sep $850; monthly only Sep–Mar, $1,000.

✍ 🐾 One of the few street-level properties, **Tropic Garden Suites** (www.beachscent.com) is a simple duplex home just across from the 28th St beach. Each apartment features a family area, two bedrooms, one bath, a full kitchen, cable TV, VCR, washer, dryer, outside showers, and BBQ grill. Great for families, it also allows pets. Rates during season $625 per week; off-season $525. Call Paradise Coast Vacation Rentals at 1-888-227-2110 for reservations.

Rosemary Beach 32461
In the tiny village of **Rosemary Beach** (1-888-855-1551; www .rosemarybeach.com), you can rent upscale cottages and carriage houses by the night or week. Some even allow pets. Carriage Houses are 400–1,000 square feet with rates from $155 a night to $2,100 a week. Cottages run 1,000–5,000 square feet, with rates from $250 a night to $8,000 a week.

Ebro 32437

Ebro Motel (850-535-2499), 5312 Captain Fritz Rd, offers nine clean, comfortable rooms ($34–40) in a family-owned motel with a swimming pool, just around the corner from acres of outdoor recreation at Pine Log State Forest.

Mexico Beach 32456

Every room at the beachfront **El Governor Motel** (850-648-5757; www.mexicobeach.com/elgovernor), 1701 W US 98, overlooks the blue green waters of the Gulf of Mexico. Take in the fresh air from your own private balcony, curl your toes in the sugary sand, take a dip in the ocean or pool, and then sip a cool drink at the beachside pool bar. The spacious rooms ($129 and up), with double or king-sized beds, offer cable TV and kitchenettes. Daily and monthly rates available. RVs park across the street (see *Campgrounds*).

☙ Across from the beach, the **Gulf View Motel** (850-648-5955) 1404 W US 98 and 15th St, offers an affordable option. Rates are $55–65 per night in the off-season; $129 per night in-season.

CAMPGROUNDS

Chipley 32428

At **Falling Waters State Park** (see *Green Space—Park*), 24 campsites are nestled in a dense pine forest and offer easy access to all of the park's amenities. Each site offers a picnic table, ground grill, and clotheslines; electric and water are available, and there is a dump station on site. Reserve in advance online or by phone through Reserve America, 1-800-326-3521.

Ebro 32437

Twenty campsites await beneath the pines at **Pine Log State Forest** (see *Green Space—Wild Places*), each with electric and water hook-ups. No reservations accepted; sites are first-come, first-served.

Mexico Beach 32456

For those with their own campers, the **El Governor Campground** (850-648-5432; www.mexicobeach .com/elgovernor), 1701 W US 98, is just across from the El Governor Motel (see *Motels*) and the sugar-sand beach. The full-service campground offers spacious shady sites with full hook-ups ($31), showers, and laundry.

Panama City Beach 32408

Catch a sea breeze through the windows of your RV at **St. Andrews State Park** (see *Green Space—Beaches*), where 176 campsites with water and electric hook-ups give you the opportunity to park your rig or pitch your tent within walking distance of the beach. Reserve in advance online or by phone through Reserve America, 1-800-326-3521.

MARINAS

Mexico Beach 32456

Marquardt's Marina (850-648-8900), 3904 US 98, has been around since 1977. Whether you need fuel for yourself or your craft, the knowledgeable staff will help you stock up on supplies for your day of fishing or cruising the emerald green waters of the Gulf of Mexico.

You can also get bait, tackle, licenses, diesel, and gasoline at the **City of Mexico Beach Public Boat Ramp/ Hide-A-Way Harbor Marina** (850-648-5407), 3700 US 98. The pump out is located at the City Pier, where you can also find public toilets.

✳ Where to Eat

DINING OUT

At **Amanda's Bistro** (850 648-5102), 2904 US 98, Mexico Beach, you'll love the special touch that Amanda Reeves provides in the relaxed Euro-American setting. Healthy, creative meals are served daily at breakfast and lunch, as well as a classic after-noon tea. Dinner is served on week-ends; there is a new menu each week. You'll enjoy such sumptuous delights as châteaubriand au Artichaut, served with a creamy artichoke au gratin and spinach fettuccine, or the scallops Asi-ago, made with fresh local bay scal-lops and served with a velvety cheese sauce and roasted garlic mashed pota-toes. For dessert, you may find such devilish delights as banana Amaretto mousse or chocolate Key lime pie with Toad Sweat (a must-try dessert hot sauce).

Relax after a long day of fishing or sightseeing at **Toucan's Restaurant** (850-648-8207), 812 US 98, enjoying a breathtaking view of the Gulf of Mexico. The fine-dining establish-ment features fresh locally caught seafood and Apalachicola oysters.

Onano Neighborhood Cafe (850-231-2436; www.rosemarybeach.com), 78 Main St, Rosemary Beach, is locat-ed in Pensione Bed & Breakfast Inn (see *Lodging*). The northern Italian cuisine features local seafood served with Tuscan flair.

For fine seafood dishes, head to **Blue by Night** (850-231-6264; www .rosemarybeach.com), 60 N Barrett Sq. Open for dinner in-season (May–Sep) only Tue–Sun, 5:30–9:30.

During the day, Summer Kitchen occupies the space, serving breakfast and wholesome lunches (see *Eating Out*).

EATING OUT

Mexico Beach

Gourmet pizzas and specialty subs with the finest ingredients are found at **Beach Pizza** (850-648-4600), 3200 US 98, and they'll even deliver!

Known to serve the freshest seafood on the Gulf of Mexico, the **Fish House Restaurant** (850-648-8950), 3006 US 98, is also a great place for breakfast.

Ever have a seafood or fish taco? The folks at **Killer Seafood** (850-648-6565), 820 US 98, will be happy to introduce you to this unique sand-wich, along with tasty hamburgers for landlubbers.

On hot days, head to the local ice creamery at **Scoops Up** (850-648-5118), 2802-A US 98, where you can cool down with a quick cone while you shop in their cute gift shop.

Locals love **Sharon's Café** (850-648-8634), 1100 US 98, for breakfast and lunch. This is the place to meet and greet. Kids of all ages love their gigantic Happy Face pancakes.

Panama City

Bayou Joe's Marina Grill (850-763-6442; www.bayoujoes.com), 112A E Third Ct, serves all three meals daily—homemade jam in the morn-ing, Cajun cookin' in the evening—with a side order of a blissful view of Massalina Bayou.

Since 1978, the Old English–style **Boars Head Restaurant & Tavern** (850-234-6628; www.boarshead restaurant.com), 17290 Front Beach Rd, has been serving up great prime rib and fresh Gulf seafood at a casual eatery. Open daily at 4:30 with live music on the weekends.

The **Boatyard** (850-240-9273; www.boatyardclub.com), 5323 N Lagoon Dr. Executive chef Doug Shook of Key West's Louie's Backyard fame spent the better part of a year developing the menu here, which features fresh seafood treasures along with many of his renowned recipes. Sit back and relax in the Key West tradition with live entertainment and tropical dishes at the base of the beach's only lighthouse. Lunch $5–16, dinner $15–24.

Grab dessert and a hot cup of joe at the eclectic **Panama Java Coffee Bar** (850-747-1004), 233 Harrison Ave.

The top dog in town is at **Tom's Hot Dogs** (850-769-8890), 555 Harrison Ave, where they are consistently voted best hot dog year after year.

Take a break from shopping at the charming English tea shop **Willows** (850-747-1004), 207 E Fourth St.

Rosemary Beach

Take your laptop to the **Courtyard Wine & Cheese** (850-231-1219; www.rosemarybeach.com), 66 Main St, where you can connect to wireless Internet while enjoying wine by the glass from more than 50 varietals. Add a nice piece of imported and domestic gourmet cheese and enjoy the fresh air of the open courtyard. Open daily 11–11.

Get your sweet tooth on at the **Sugar Shak** (850-231-3655; www.rosemary beach.com), 46 N Barrett Sq, where you can indulge in ice cream, shakes, candies, and baked treats.

Grab breakfast or a healthy lunch of wraps, salads, or sandwiches at **Summer Kitchen** (850-231-6264; www.rosemarybeach.com), 60 N Barrett

Sq. At night the restaurant turns into Blue by Night (see *Dining Out*). Open daily for breakfast 8–10:30 and lunch from 10:30–3.

At the **Wild Olives Market** (850-231-0065), 29 Canal St, you can shop for specialty groceries or order lunch salads, sandwiches, pizza, and hot meals to go. The tapas menu is a great for a late-afternoon snack.

✳ Selective Shopping

Mexico Beach

A nice selection of gifts and beachwear can be found at **Beachwalk** (850-648-4200), 3102 US 98.

A great place to pick up beach and fishing supplies, **Cathey's Ace Hardware** (850-648-5242), 3000 US 98, also rents some equipment.

You'll enjoy browsing antiques and fine gifts at the **Driftwood Inn Gifts Shop** (850-648-5126), US 98, as much as you'll enjoy the ambience of this grand Victorian Inn.

Kitschy souvenirs and beach necessities can be found at the beachside gift shop inside the **El Governor Motel** (850-648-5757; www.mexicobeach.com/elgovernor).

Inside Toucan's Restaurant (see *Dining Out*), the **Gift Shop** (850-648-5861), 812 US 98, carries a great line of beachwear, including bathing suits—in case you forgot yours.

If you are into nautical and beachy decor, then head to **The Grove** (850-648-4445), 2700 US 98, where you'll find accessories for both and outside the home.

All your grocery needs are fulfilled at **Gulf Foods & Gifts** (850-648-5129), 900 US 98, which also has a nice selection of beach items and souvenirs.

Whether beachy or preppy, ladies will be sure to find just the right ensemble at **LadyFish** (850-648-4847), 2802 US 98, which features such boutique wear as Lacoste and Lilly Pulitzer. Open Wed–Sun.

Named after fruit native to the area, a must-stop is **Prickly Pears Gourmet Gallery** (850-648-1115; www.prickly pears.net), 101 S 36st St (set back off US 98), where owner Dolores Lowery offers up a unique collection of gourmet food, organic spices, coffee, hand-dipped chocolates, and exotic cheeses, such as the Drunken Goat Cheese from Spain, or my favorite, the blueberry Stilton from England. The eclectic gallery also exhibits a wide variety of art crafted by local artisans. Check the schedule for her wonderful wine tastings and creative cooking classes, where she'll teach you how to cook with the prickly pears. Open Tue–Sat 10–5:30.

You'll find great shelling on the beach, but fabulous shell jewelry at **The Shell Shack** (850-648-8256), 3800 US 98, which also houses a seafood market.

The chic shopper will enjoy **Two Gulls at the Beach** (850-648-1122), 2802 US 98, which offers resort wear for both men and women along with a nice line of Brighton jewelry.

Panama City

🐾 Don't forget Fluffy and Rover while you're on vacation. They'll want to go to the **Downtown Pet Salon** (850-769-9786), 547 Grace Ave, for conditioning and grooming after the dog days of summer.

The gallery and studio of internationally known watercolor artist **Paul Brent** (850-785-2684), 413 W Fifth St, features originals and prints of coastal scenes and wildlife art, along with pottery, jewelry, and glassware from other talented artists.

The **Gallery of Art** (850-785-7110), 36 W Beach Dr, houses original art, sculpture, and pottery by local artists.

Vision Quest Gallery and Emporium (850-522-8552), 230 W 15th St, displays art, antiques, and jewelry and offers classes.

Along Harrison Ave, you'll find an extensive selection of antiques, jewelry, and collectibles at the **Antique Mall** (850-763-9993), along with a nice art collection. For more antiques, fine furniture, and collectibles, seek out **Second Edition Antique and Uniques** (850-215-1420). Grab a new or used book to read on the beach at **Books by the Sea** (850-784-8100). Fine women's clothing, including plus sizes, can be found at **DeHerberts** (850-769-0592), while **Elegante Heirs** (850-769-0245) has nice clothing and gifts for your little ones. Learn some new recipes and then pick up a fine wine to complement your new culinary skills at **Somethin's Cookin'** (850-785-8590).

Rosemary Beach

Cool threads are found at **Dunes** (850-231-3602; www.rosemarybeach .com), Lofts West, featuring the latest in island wear for the entire family. You'll find island-inspired Tommy Bahama shirts for Dad, comfortable Ella Moss garments for Mom, and Fresh Produce coastal wear for the kids. Open Mon–Sat 10–6; Sun 11–5.

Be sure to stop into **Flavours of France** (850-231-9016; www.flavours offrance.com), 54 Main St, if you love 18th- to mid-20th-century French antiques, then browse through their extensive selection of interior design books and cookbooks.

Take the little tykes to **Gigi's Fabulous Kids Fashions and Toys** (850-231-0110 or 1-888-353-6161; www.gigisfab kids.com), 62 Main St, for fun toys and cool clothes. You'll also find education al and craft supplies to keep the little ones busy on rainy days. Open daily 10–7.

At **The Gourd Garden Courtyard Shop** (850-534-0070), www.gourd garden.com), 66 Main St, you'll find lots of natural items such as clay cookware, hand-woven baskets, and beeswax candles, along with their signature gourd birdhouses.

Shabby Slips (850-231-4164), 58 Main St, is known mainly for its custom slipcovers and pillows, but you'll also enjoy browsing their fine collection of original abstract art.

You'll want to remember this beach paradise; your best bet for Rosemary Beach logo items is at the **Trading Company** (850-231-2410; www .rosemarybeach.com), Lofts East, 34 N Barrett Sq, which also features other nifty souvenir items.

✱ Entertainment

The art-deco-style **Ritz-Martin Theatre** (850-763-8080; www.martintheatre .com), 409 Harrison Ave, Panama City, first opened in 1936 as part of a movie house chain. During the 1950s, the Martin family purchased the aging facility and operated it for more than 20 years. It then sat dormant for more than a decade; only in the late 1980s were major renovations brought about by the Panama City Downtown Improvement Board. With the historic theater gracefully restored to life, the state-of-the-art facility now serves the community as an intimate venue for comedy, plays, and musical performances.

✱ Special Events

February: Chefs from all over the United States compete annually at the Mardi Gras–style Mexico Beach **Gumbo Cook Off** (1-888-723-2546; www.mexicobeach.com/cdc); proceeds subsidize the town's Independence Day celebration.

May: ✍ The Mexico Beach **Spring Fling and Fishing Tournament** (1-888-723-2546; www.mexicobeach .com/cdc) offers thousands of dollars in cash prizes. Families will enjoy the children's fishing tournament and live entertainment in a wholesome party atmosphere.

The **Gulf Coast Triathlon** (850-282-8573; www.gulfcoasttriathlon.com) kicks off in Panama City Beach, where athletes from all over the United States and 15 countries compete in a celebratory weekend.

July: ✍ Touted as the **Best Blast on the Beach** (1-888-723-2546; www .mexicobeach.com/cdc), the Fourth of July fireworks display is partially subsidized by the Mexico Beach's Gumbo Cook Off in February. Expect a fun beach party with lots of entertainment for the kids. A beach trolley runs up and down the 3-mile stretch of town for easy transportation from your hotel or campground.

In Panama City Beach, the **Bay Point Invitational Billfish Tournament** gives anglers top dollar awards for fishing billfish, dolphin, wahoo, and tuna, such as the 998.6-pound billfish that landed Barry Carr the $100,000 prize in 2006. Invitations are by nomination or by application to Bay Point Marina Company (850-235-6911; www.baypointbillfish.com).

August: A family favorite! Anglers of all ages will want to compete in the largest kingfish tournament in the area. Sponsored by the Mexico Beach Artificial Reef Association, the annual **King Mackerel** event (1-888-723-2546; www.mexicobeach.com/cdc or www.mbara.org) is held the weekend before Labor Day. There's lots of music, fun, and food, including a fish fry. Cash prizes awarded for the largest king mackerel, Spanish mackerel, and wahoo. Proceeds benefit artificial reef and fisheries habitat education and research and local fishery habitat improvements.

October: Don't miss the annual **Mexico Beach Art & Wine Festival** (1-888-723-2546; www.mexicobeach.com/cdc), when the tiny town presents a juried artists, fine wines, unusual beers, and live jazz and blues at the Driftwood Inn.

Join in the ecofun at the Panama City Beach **Nature's Gallery** (850-233-5117; www.friendsofstandrews.org), featuring Civil War reenactments amid an arts and crafts festival.

December: A highlight of the holiday season, the **Holly Fair,** features crafts, choirs, and culinary delights at the Boardwalk Beach Resort (850-785-7870; www.boardwalkbeach resort.com) in Panama City Beach.

THE EMERALD COAST & THE BEACHES OF SOUTH WALTON
HOLMES, OKALOOSA, AND WALTON COUNTIES

L ocated in the extreme northwest section of Florida, the Emerald Coast in the Western Panhandle is an area filled with miles of white-sugar-sand beaches, emerald blue green water, fine museums, historic towns, and outdoor adventure. Second only to the theme-park mecca—Orlando, Kissimmee–St. Cloud—**Destin** and **Fort Walton Beach** in **Okaloosa County** surprisingly eclipse all other areas of Florida as a tourist destination, attracting 4.5 million people each year. The main allure is the beach, covered in pure Appalachian quartz. The tiny crystals resemble powdered sugar, are baby-powder soft, and are surprisingly cool to walk on with bare feet. You'll want to keep your sunglasses handy when collecting the plentiful seashells; the sand is as white and bright as newly fallen snow.

The history of the region is showcased at the Indian Temple Mound and Museum in Fort Walton Beach, where you'll discover a unique ceremonial mound and artifacts from five distinct Native American periods. European settlers arrived 1538, Spanish explorers who first surveyed the land. Many pioneers tried to settle here, but it wasn't until 1845 that the first permanent settler, Connecticut shipmaster Captain Leonard Destin, took hold of the land. Instrumental in creating a rich and prosperous fishing community, Captain Destin, for whom the town is named, laid the groundwork for present-day town, which is now home to Florida's largest charter fishing fleet. Chartered in 1916, **Crestview** is the county seat for Okaloosa County, 30 miles north of Fort Walton Beach. In the late 1800s, Crestview was a stop on the Pensacola & Atlantic Railroad, a trading center for farmers, timbermen, and ranchers on a crest between the Yellow and Shoal rivers.

In 1931, Eglin Air Force Base was built on 137 acres north of Destin to test non-nuclear weaponry. Today, the base covers 384,000 acres of the Choctawhatchee National Forest, wrapping around Fort Walton Beach and Destin to the north, thus restricting further development. Hikers will enjoy nearly 50 miles of trails through the national forest's pine flatwoods. A favorite pastime of tourists and residents alike is sitting on the beach or at a local waterfront eatery watching

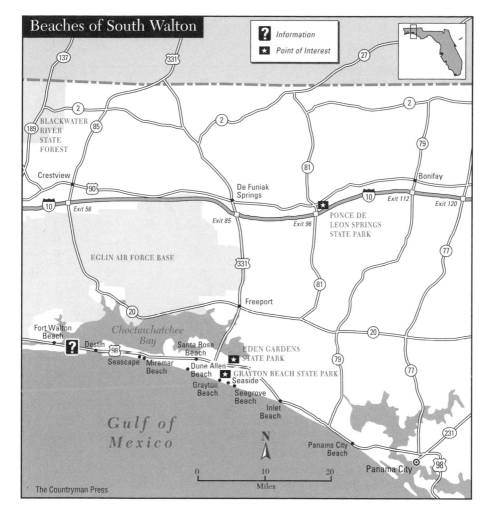

pods of dolphins greet a variety of seafaring craft—it's almost impossible to look out on the water without seeing one. There are more than 100 vessels moored at the Destin Marina, so you'll be sure to find just the right charter boat to fish the open waters of the Gulf of Mexico or the backwater flats of Choctawhatchee Bay. Paddlers will especially love exploring the bay's calm backwater, where they can pull up on isolated sandy beaches and bask in the solitude. From Destin, a scenic drive east along US 98 will take you through areas teaming with shops, restaurants, attractions, beaches, and coastal natural areas.

The Beaches of South Walton community stretches along 26 miles of coastline and includes 14 diverse hamlets. In **Destin** you'll find luxury resorts; in quaint towns such as **Grayton,** great opportunities for antiquing or finding an electric piece of art; and in **Seaside,** where the movie *The Truman Show* was filmed, you'll find a picture-perfect beachside Victorian town dotted with white

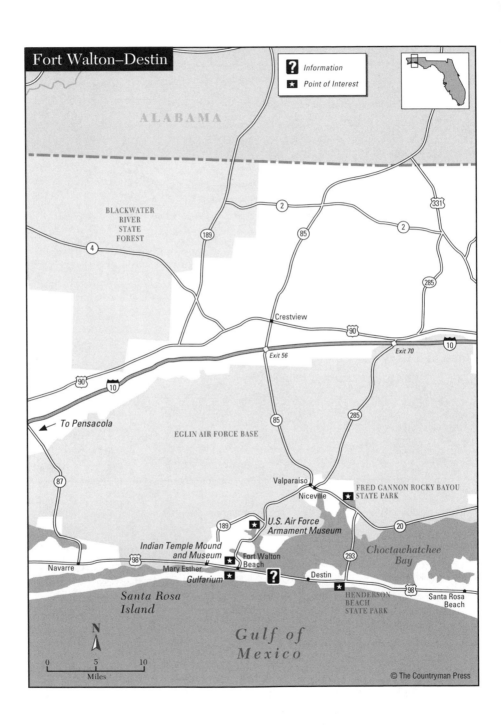

Fort Walton–Destin

? Information
★ Point of Interest

ALABAMA

BLACKWATER
RIVER
STATE
FOREST

2

331

189   85   2

4

285

Crestview   90

Exit 56   Exit 70   10

90
10

← To Pensacola

EGLIN AIR FORCE BASE   85   285

Valparaiso   FRED GANNON ROCKY BAYOU
★ STATE PARK
Niceville

87

189 ★   U.S. Air Force
Armament Museum

20

Indian Temple Mound
and Museum   293   Choctawhatchee
Bay

Navarre   98   Fort Walton
Mary Esther ★   Beach
Gulfarium ★   ?   Destin   98   Santa Rosa
Beach
Santa Rosa   ★
Island   HENDERSON
BEACH
STATE PARK

N
↑   Gulf of
Mexico

0   5   10
Miles

© The Countryman Press

picket fences. For a unique paddling experience, head to one of 17 coastal dune lakes in Walton County: The rare ecosystem is found only in Africa and this part of Florida. As you travel west to east along scenic highway CR 30A, the first lake you will see is Stalworth Lake in **Dune Allen.** The lake has significant historic interest: In the 1800s it was home to turpentine laborers, one of the earliest successful integrated societies in the state. A full marina is located at the popular 220-acre Western Lake in Grayton Beach State Park (see *Green Space—Beaches*).

Founded in 1881 as a railroad town along the Louisville and Nashville Railroad, **DeFuniak Springs** is the county seat of Walton County, its historic residential district clustered around a perfectly round spring-fed lake exactly a mile in circumference. The town is named after Fred R. DeFuniak, General Manager of the railroad, and it truly came to life when the Florida Chautauqua Association organized and held its first assembly here in February 1885, establishing one of the first grand cultural centers of the Southeast. After the 1920s post-boom crash, the town retreated into a quiet rural community with a grand Victorian heart and the oldest continually operating library in Florida. The historic district surrounding Lake DeFuniak is a delight to visit, its classical architecture evoking old New England.

In adjacent rural Holmes County, **Ponce de Leon** has no traffic light, but it's a center of summer fun thanks to its three major springs—Ponce de Leon, Vortex, and Morrison—open for swimming and diving.

GUIDANCE **Walton County Chamber of Commerce** (850-892-3191; www.waltoncountychamber.com), 95 Circle Dr, DeFuniak Springs 32435, covers all of Walton County. Contact the **Beaches of South Walton** (800-822-6877; www.beachesofsouthwalton.com), P.O. Box 1248, Santa Rosa Beach 32459-1248, for information on the the 14 beachside towns of South Walton.

For vacation planning in towns in Okaloosa County, including Destin, Okaloosa Island, and Fort Walton, contact the **Emerald Coast Convention & Visitors** welcome center (850-651-7131 or 1-800-322-3319; www.destin-fwb.com), 1540 Miracle Strip Pkwy SE, P.O. Box 609, Fort Walton Beach 32549. In Crestview, stop in the **Crestview Chamber of Commerce** (850-682-3212), 502 S Main St. You'll also find valuable resources at the **Greater Fort Walton Beach Chamber of Commerce** (850-244-8191; www.fwbchamber.org), 34 Miracle Strip Pkwy SE, Fort Walton 32549, and the **Destin Chamber of Commerce** (850-837-6241; www.destinchamber.com), 1021 US 98 E, Suite A, Destin 32541. In DeFuniak Springs, the **Walton County Chamber of Commerce** (850-892-3191; www.waltoncountychamber.com), 95 Circle Dr, is part of the grand Chautauqua Hall along Circle Dr; pick up pamphlets and walking tour brochures here. For explorations of Ponce de Leon and Bonifay, see the **Holmes County** Web site (www.holmescountyonline.com).

GETTING THERE *By air:* **Okaloosa Regional Airport** (850-651-7160), **Panama City/Bay County International Airport** (850-763-6751), **Pensacola Regional Airport** (850-436-5005).

By bus: **Greyhound** (1-800-231-2222).

By rail: **Amtrak's** Sunset Limited Line stops in Crestview.

By car: **I-10** and **FL 90** run east–west along the Panhandle. **FL 85** will take you from Crestview down past Eglin AFB and into Fort Walton; **CR 87** will take you from Milton to Fort Walton and Navarre Beach. **US 98** also runs east–west and will take you along the beaches from Panama City right up to Pensacola.

GETTING AROUND ♿ **The Okaloosa County Transit/The WAVE** (850-833-9168; www.rideoct.org) is the local public transportation service in and around Destin and Fort Walton. The **Wave** operates only in Fort Walton and connects to the Okaloosa Island and Destin **Beach Shuttle,** which runs in sections along US 98 from Fort Walton to the Silver Sands Factory Stores. All vehicles are equipped with wheelchair lifts. No charge to bring a bicycle, which gets loaded on the front rack. The Wave operates Mon–Fri 6–6. The Beach Shuttle operates seven days, 7–10. Full fare for both is 50¢, 25¢ for seniors, and free for children under 12 traveling with an adult and for military personnel.

PARKING **DeFuniak Springs** offers ample free parking in the downtown shopping district and in the historic district around the lake.

MEDICAL EMERGENCIES In the Destin and Fort Walton area, **Fort Walton Beach Medical Center** (850-862-1111) and **Twin Cities Hospital** (850-678-4131).

✳ To See

ALLIGATOR SPOTTING The best place to spot alligators is **Gator Beach** at Fudpucker's on US 98 in Destin, where you can see more than 75 2- to 4-foot alligators at the entrance to the popular eatery.

ART GALLERIES The Mimi Bash collection is housed at the **Fort Walton Beach Art Museum,** 38 Robinwood Dr SW, Fort Walton Beach, along with other American paintings, sculptures, and pottery. You'll also find Chinese, Thai, and Cambodian art objects and relics. Donations welcome.

View international and national exhibitions at the **Arts Center at Okaloosa–Walton College** (850-729-6000; www.owcc.cc.fl.us/arts), 100 College Blvd, Niceville. The center houses two galleries: the Holzhauer and the McIlroy. Between the two sits *The Sculpture of the Seven Dancers,* an exquisite example of the creative talents of internationally famous sculptor Esther Wertheimer. Open Mon–Thu 9–4; Sun 1–4.

HISTORIC SITES

Crestview

Built in 1947, the **Fox Theatre,** Main St, premiered the movie *12 O'Clock High,* filmed in and around the area with Gregory Peck. A recent sign on the building says that renovations are under way to reopen it as a cinema.

The city of **DeFuniak Springs** boats more than 250 buildings on the National Register of Historic Places, most clustered around circular Lake DeFuniak. They are privately owned but can be enjoyed from Circle Dr or the sidewalk on a walking tour (see *To Do—Walking Tours*). You'll find the **DeFuniak Springs Historic District** roughly bounded by Nelson and Park Ave and Second and 12th streets.

The 1890 **St. Agatha's Episcopal Church,** with its beautiful stained-glass windows, is the oldest church building in the city.

Several notable homes include **The Verandas,** 262 Circle Dr, a 1904 "steamboat" style folk Victorian with wraparound porches; the **Dream Cottage,** 404 Circle Dr, built in 1888 for poet Wallace Bruce, former U.S. Consul to Scotland; and the turreted **Thomas House,** 188 Circle Dr, an elaborately decorated 1895 three story Queen Anne. Florida's oldest continually operating library, the **Walton-DeFuniak Library,** 3 Circle Dr, opened in 1887. It has many rare books as well as a medieval armor collection.

Built in 1909, the **Chautauqua Hall of Brotherhood,** 95 Circle Dr, remains an imposing structure along Lake DeFuniak. Seating more than 4,000, it attracted visitors for its broad slate of cultural programs, which were discontinued during the Great Depression. In 1976, local citizens revived the Chautauqua tradition (see *Special Events*), and this hall (undergoing renovations) is used for major events.

Although many North Florida towns have monuments to honor their Confederate soldiers, the **Confederate Monument** at the Walton County Courthouse in DeFuniak Springs was the first such memorial in the state, installed in 1871.

Destin and Fort Walton Beach Area

In downtown Fort Walton, take in a picture show at the historic 1940 **Tringa's Theatre**, 174 Miracle Strip Pkwy SE. Shows are 4:30 and 7 daily for only $3 (see *To Do—Family Activities*).

The 1912 **Camp Walton School House** (850-833-9596), 107 First St, was in use until 1936 and is now restored and maintained by the Junior Service League, which has fully furnished it with desks, chairs, and chalkboards of the period, even a dunce cap! Open by appointment only.

Listed as a National Historic Landmark, the **Indian Temple Mound** (850-243-6521), 139 Miracle Strip Pkwy, built between A.D. 800 and 1400, is now a monument to Native Americans. Climb 15 feet to the top of the ceremonial mound, which measures 223 by 220 feet at the base and 90 by 150 foot at the top. Next door, in the museum, more than

CHAUTAUQUA HALL OF BROTHERHOOD
Sandra Friend

Emerald Coast CVB

INDIAN TEMPLE MOUND MUSEUM

4,000 artifacts, some as much as 10,000 years old, describe the history of Native Americans. Open Sep–May, Mon–Sat 10–4; Jun–Aug, Mon–Sat 9–4:30, Sun 12:30–4:30; fee.

Tour the **Wesley House** and gardens at **Eden Gardens State Park** (850-231-4214), CR 395. The seven-bedroom mansion, built in 1898, showcases different time periods, cultures, and the second largest collection of Louis XVI furniture in the United States. Guided tours through the home begin on the hour, Thu–Mon 10–3.

On the water you'll want to take your boat over to **Crab Island** (www.destin crabisland.com) in Choctawhatchee Bay off Destin. Originally two, created in the 1930s when the Corps of Engineers dredged the Destin East Pass Road, the island once teaming with natural wildlife is now submerged after decades of erosion. During the season boats anchor together around a snack and ice cream boat at this popular meet and greet spot.

One of only five surviving two-masted schooners in the United States, the 1877 **Governor Stone** Schooner is moored at the Village of Baytowne's dock inside Sandestin Resort. The 66-foot-long wooden-hulled vessel has masts made of longleaf yellow pine.

MUSEUMS

Baker
The **Baker Block Museum** (850-537-5714; www.rootsweb.com/~flbbm/baker .htm), 1307 Georgia Ave (corner of FL 189 and CR 189), provides a pictorial history of rural Okaloosa County's cotton and lumber heritage with a dramatic mural; inside, browse through artifacts and archives, including extensive genealogical records. Historic farm buildings brought in from their original rural settings surround the museum. Open Tue–Fri 10–3:30 and third Sat of the month. Free; donations appreciated.

DeFuniak Springs
You'll find the **Walton County Heritage Museum** (850-951-2127 or 1-800-822-6877; www.waltoncountyheritage.org), 1140 Circle Dr, inside an 1882 L&N Railroad depot. The museum provides a great overview of the history of the area along with a vignette showcasing Allison's Grocery. The exhibit features songs and memorabilia of Feenie Allison, the woman who owned it for 61 years, retiring in 1992 at the age of 89. You'll also enjoy the collection of general store items from the 1930s and 1950s.

Destin and Fort Walton Beach Area
At the **Eglin Air Force Armament Museum** (850-882-4062, www.eglin.af.mil/museum), 100 Museum Dr, you'll find an impressive selection of U.S. aircraft

Sandra Friend

AN L&N CABOOSE AT DEFUNIAK SPRINGS
DEPOT

and weaponry, along with similar items from around the world. Outside, walk or drive on a tour past two dozen aircraft, including a SR-71A Blackbird and a Soviet MIG-21. Inside the museum, you can walk around carefully restored planes representing several war periods, such as the P-51 Mustang and F-105 Thunderchief. The history of Eglin AFB is shown throughout the day in a 32-minute movie. Don't miss the balcony exhibits; at one point you'll step inside the Airborne Battlefield Command Control Center (ABCCC) for a rare view of the high-tech, automated airborne command center. On a sidewall, an exquisite watercolor by Val Williamson was created in memory of the crew of the AC-130H Spectre gunship lost in action during Desert Storm on January 31, 1991. The Shipman Model Collection, showcasing more than 105 1:72 scale model planes, was painstakingly and accurately detailed by Major Ernest Shipman. A fighter pilot, Major Shipman was a POW from 1944 to 1945 in Germany's Luftwaffe Prison Camp. His dedication to this project has spanned nearly two decades. In the gift shop you can purchase a wide variety of model planes to take home and assemble yourself. Open daily 9:30–4:30; donations welcome.

✍ For rainy day activities, head to the **Emerald Coast Science Center** (850-664-1261; www.ecscience.org), 139 Brooks St, where you can learn about tropical birds, Florida snakes, and more in the Critter Room or watch a model airplane fly through a wind tunnel in the Electricity Room. Lots of hands-on activities. Open Mon, Wed, Fri 9–2; Tue and Thu 9–4; Sat and Sun 11–4. Adults $5, seniors $4, age 4–17 $3.50, age 3 and under free.

RAILROADIANA Along Crestview's Main Street, watch for the **railroad mural** fronting the railroad tracks that cross the street.

An **L&N caboose** sits on a siding adjoining the **DeFuniak Springs Depot,** where trains still fly through on an adjacent working track. Built in 1882, the depot was expanded in 1909 and once hosted more than 4,000 passengers a day.

WILDLIFE REFUGE At **On the Wild Side Wolf & Wildlife Ranch** (850-836-4600), 2654 Wolf Hollow Dr, Ponce de Leon, the emphasis is on

CRESTVIEW'S RAILROAD MURAL

Sandra Friend

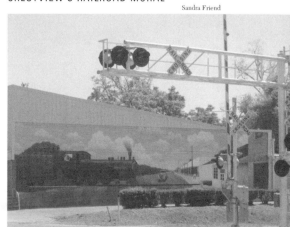

the caretaking of wolves, tigers, and other wildlife born in captivity. Visitors will see timber wolves, arctic wolves, a Siberian tiger, and other mammals that cannot be released to the wild. Visits by appointment only; donations appreciated.

WINERIES Learn about grape growing and winemaking at **Chautauqua Vineyards** (850-892-5887; www.chautauquawinery.com), 364 Hugh Adams Rd, De-Funiak Springs, just off I-10. Planted in 1979 and opened in 1989, the winery has the largest vineyards in Florida and has won more than 140 awards internationally for its vintages. One of their specialties is a barrel-aged port. Take the tour and enjoy the tasting, and then browse their gift shop for goodies like grapeseed cooking oil, made right on the premises. Harvest time is late Aug through early Sep, but the shop and tasting room are open year-round.

The master winemakers at the unique **Destin Winery** (850-654-0533; www.destinwinery.com), 36150 Emerald Coast Pkwy, Destin, take tropical fruits and marry them to unusual ingredients with award-winning expertise. Sample a unique wine, maybe the chardonnay-like 40 Karat, made with Florida carrots, the refreshing Category 5 Florida sangria, or the distinctive Cocoa Beach, which marries chocolate with Florida orange juice. Located 1 mile east of Destin Commons (see *Selective Shopping*) in the City Market Shopping Plaza; open Mon–Sat 10–6.

ZOOLOGICAL AND MARINE PARK The **Florida Gulfarium** (1-800-243-9046 or 1-800-247-8575; www.gulfarium.com), 1010 Miracle Strip Pkwy SE, Fort Walton Beach, is the oldest continuously operated marine show aquarium in the world. A true gem of the Emerald Coast, the facility has been teaching the general public about marine life since 1952, and in the process has undergone a great deal of growth and renovation, today featuring a 400,000-gallon dolphin tank and 60,000-gallon living sea aquarium. Despite several hurricanes that pummeled the coast, the dedicated staff and supporters have continued to keep the facility in great shape with extensive rebuilding. Visit places like Dune Lagoon, which has a large variety of marine fowl, or Fort Gator, where you'll see a pair of American alligators; compare seals and sea lions at the Seal and Sea Lion Rookery; watch the unique eating habits of lemon and nurse sharks; and enjoy colorful tropical birds and unique tropical penguins, which are native to near-equatorial regions in South America. You'll keep cool under the comfortably shaded exhibits and from occasional splashes from playful dolphins. Open daily 9–6, last admission at 4; $18 adults, $16 age 55 and over, $11 age 4–11.

THE DOLPHIN SHOW AT THE FLORIDA GULFARIUM

Emerald Coast CVB

✳ To Do

BICYCLING The Eastern Lake Bike/Hike Trail in Point Washington State Forest offers up to 10 miles of doubletrack riding through natural areas accessed via Grayton Beach State Park; the trailhead is on CR 395 (see *Green Space—Beaches*).

The **Timberlake Mountain Bike Trail System** (850-882-4164; www.eglin .af.mil), 107 Hwy 85 N, Niceville, is located in the Eglin Air Force Base Recreation Area, where you can travel through 21 miles of narrow rolling trails to elevations up to 50 feet. Before using the trail, you must stop by the Eglin Natural Resources office to get a permit ($7); Mon–Thu 7–4:30, Fri 7–6, Sat 7:30–12:30, closed Sun.

BOAT TOURS Lots of family fun can be found on the glass-bottomed boat at **Boogies** (850-654-4497; www.boogieswatersports.com), at the foot of Destin Bridge, Destin, which features dolphin encounters, bird feedings, and an eco-talk on a narrated cruise ($22 adults, $10 children 2–12).

Take a relaxing sunset cruise aboard **Moody's *Emerald Magic*** (850-837-1293; www.moodysinc.com), 194 US 98, Destin, to see dolphins and birds in their natural habitat ($15 adults, $7.50 children 3–11).

To truly enjoy the "dancing dolphins" of the Emerald Coast, take a sail aboard a 64-foot luxury schooner. The legendary ***Silent Lady*** (850-837-1166; www .harborcovecharters.com), 116 US 98 E, Destin, slips quietly across Destin Harbor and, weather permitting, into the Gulf of Mexico for unforgettable day and sunset sails.

DIVING In Ponce de Leon, spring diving awaits. At **Vortex Spring** (see *Lodging—Dive Resort*), diving classes and certifications are offered at all levels, from PADI to cavern. The 25-million-gallon spring is a beautiful place for open-water divers to explore. If you're cavern certified, you can go deep to see the spring basin 50 feet down, lit well through the crystalline water. Gear rentals are available, and off-site excursions to other springs are offered. Non-diving visitors are welcome to snorkel the spring and lengthy spring run. Open 7–dusk daily except Christmas.

FAMILY ACTIVITIES ⚓ Rent Jet Skis and Waverunners at **Bayside Watersports** (850-664-0051 or 850-302-0021; www.bayside-watersports.com), 1310 US 98, Fort Walton Beach, or **Boogies Watersports** (850-654-4497; www.boogieswatersports.com), 2 Harbor Blvd, Destin, which also offers parasailing.

⚓ Part water, all adventure, **Big Kahuna's Adventure Park** (850-837-8319; www.bigkahunas.com), 1007 US 98 E, Destin, offers days of activities. The tropical setting touts the largest man-made waterfall, with clear water descending 250 feet. There's something for everyone, with high adrenaline pipeline speed slides, spectacular splash fountains, a lazy river, and a pirate ship splash zone for the little ones. At the adventure side of the park you can race in Grand Prix go-carts, play mini golf on a tropically landscaped course, or try your skill on a wide variety of arcade games.

⚓ You won't break your wallet at the original 1950's **Goofy Golf** (850-862-4922), 401 Eglin Pkwy NE, Fort Walton Beach, where mini golf is only $2.

⚓ At the **Track Recreation Family Fun Center** (850-654-5832; www.destin track.com), 1125 US 98 E, Destin, you'll find thrill rides like the skyflyer and bungee jumping, along with mini golf, bumper cars, and go-carts. They even have mini go-carts for five-year-olds. At Kids Kountry, little ones will want to ride the Rio Grande Train and Red Baron Plane Ride over and over.

⚓ On rainy days, get a blast from the past while watching today's movies at the 1940s **Tringa's Theatre** (listed under Cinema Plus, 850-302-0129), 174 Miracle Strip Pkwy SE, Fort Walton. And dine on beer and pizza! Daily shows at 4:30 and 7; movie tickets $1–3; beer and pizza extra.

⚓ If you want to race a few laps, fire it up at **Vortex Spring Speedway** (www.vortexspring.com/public/promo/speedway.htm), Ponce de Leon, a five-turn modified oval go-cart track where 20 laps run $10. The complex also includes paintball and video games, and it adjoins Vortex Springs (see *Diving*).

FISHING Captains Paul and Cathy Wagner of **Back Country Outfitters** (850-654-5566) will take you into the shallow flats to fish for speckled trout, redfish, and tarpon day or night on their four-, six-, or eight-hour charters.

Go bottom fishing for snapper, triggerfish, sea bass, flounder, and grouper aboard **Moody's *American Spirit*** (850-837-1293), 194 US 98. $35 for a half-day, half price for ages 3–12 and riders.

Drop a line from the "ultimate fishing machine," the *Swoop* (850-337-8250; www.harborwalk-destin.com), 66 US 98, Destin. This 65-foot-long fishing boat, with air-conditioned cabin, takes up to 49 passengers for half- or full-day charters, $40 and up.

If bottom fishing is your game, Captain Jim Westbrook on the 85-foot *New Florida Girl* (850-837-6422; www.newfloridagirl.com), 314 US 98, Destin, E brings in the catch. Search for red snapper, flounder, and grouper. $40 adults, $20 children under 12.

For those wanting a private deep-sea charter with only a few people, **Harbor-Walk Charters** (850-837-2343 or 1-800-242-2824; www.harborwalkfishing.com), located at Harbor Walk, Destin, will match you with up to eight passengers for half-or full-day excursions. $94–187 per person.

GOLF You'll enjoy the scenery at Fred Couple's signature par 72, 18-hole golf course at **Kelly Plantation** (850-650-7600 or 1-800-811-6757, www.kelly plantation.com), US 98 just west of Mid Bay Bridge, covering a challenging, 7,099-yard course complete with satellite yardage system. At **Indian Bayou Golf Club** (850-837-6192, www.indianbayougolf.com), One Country Club Dr, tee off on the 18-hole par 72 course or play a quick game on the nine-hole, par 36 course.

HIKING Pick up an Annual Recreation Pass ($7) at the Jackson Guard Station, Eglin Air Force Base, to enjoy more nearly 50 miles of the **Florida Trail** (www.floridatrail.org) complete from DeFuniak Springs at US 331 to Crestview at FL 85, with beautiful backcountry campsites set in old-growth forests.

Unusual scenery and salt breezes make for pleasant hikes at **Topsail Hill Preserve State Park** (see *Green Space—Beaches*), where more than 7 miles of hiking along the Campbell Lake and Morris Lake Trails leads you to hidden freshwater lakes behind the dune line. At **Grayton Beach State Park** (see *Green Space—Beaches*), the nature trail loops through a variety of coastal habitats, while at **Eden Gardens State Park** (see *Green Space— Botanical Garden*), a short trail leads you to a hidden bayou. The **Seven Runs Trail,** starting along FL 81 at Seven Runs Park, follows Seven Runs Creek for 7 miles to its confluence with the Choctawhatchee River. **Ponce de Leon Springs** (see *Green Space—Springs*) offers an excellent short nature trail through lush hardwood river bluff habitat.

Sandra Friend

TOPSAIL HILL STATE PARK

KITE SURFING You'll enjoy watching adventure enthusiasts kite surf off the bay side of Gulf Islands National Seashore (see *Parks*). To learn how, contact Liquid Surf & Sail for lessons (see *Surfing/Sailboarding*).

PADDLING Follow scenic **Holmes Creek** as it flows from Alabama to the Choctawhatchee River, edged by cypresses. An easy 12-mile route runs from Cypress Springs (3 miles north of Vernon) to Live Oak landing off CR 284.

Go paddling with **The Kayak Experience** (850-837-1577 or 850-837-1579; www.kayakexperience.com), 600 US 98E, Destin, where you can rent a open kayak and launch right into the blue-green waters of Destin Harbor for fun in the surf. Then explore the calm waters of Choctawhatchee Bay. Rentals from two hours to all day includes all safety equipment, $30–75; Mon–Fri 10–5, Sat 10–4.

PARASAILING At **Sun Dogs Parasailing** (850-244-3647 or 850-664-7872), 1310 Miracle Strip Pkwy, Okaloosa Island, you can float effortlessly high above gulf or bay on single, double, or triple parasails. Rent out a 24-foot pontoon boat or go on a guided dolphin excursion. Three-seater Waverunners are also available for rent. A second location is directly across from the Emerald Coast Convention & Visitors (see *Guidance*). **Boogies Watersports** (850-654-4497; www.boogies watersports.com), 2 Harbor Blvd, Destin, also offers parasailing.

SCENIC DRIVES Take a drive along scenic highway CR 30A for a great view of rare **coastal dunes lakes,** an ecosystem that only exists here and in Africa.

When the freshwater lakes become too full, they naturally dump run-off into the ocean. At that time seawater seeps back into the lakes, creating a unique, biodiverse ecosystem. There are 17 dune lakes along this route, starting at the western end with Stalworth Lake, the focal point in Dune Allen. Oyster Lake, also in Dune Allen, once filled with oysters, is actually named after its oysterlike shape. At Deer Lake in Santa Rosa Beach, you'll discover rare pitcher plants. A walk around Eden Gardens State Park will reward you will views of beautiful gardens and a historic home (see *Green Space—Botanical Garden*). The highest point on the Gulf of Mexico in the United States is at Blue Mountain Beach at 62 feet above sea level. It is named for the beautiful, rare blue Gulf lupine.

SURFING/SAILBOARDING Located away from the beach in downtown Fort Walton Beach, **Liquid Surf & Sail** (850-664-5731 or 1-888-818-9283; www.liquid surfandsail.com) is the tops for all your surfing and sailing needs for beginner or experienced water lovers. Lessons by qualified instructions will get you up surfing, sailing, or kite boarding in no time. Rentals by the half or full day: windsurfers ($45–65), foam and glass surfboards ($20–30), sit-on-top kayaks ($35–60), and Hobie mirage pedal kayaks ($45–75). Lessons start at $150 for two hours.

WALKING TOURS Check in with the Fort Walton Beach Main Street Organization (850-664-6246; www.fwbmainstreet.org), 12 SE Miracle Strip Pkwy, for information on architectural and archeological sites on the **Fort Walton Historic Walking Tour.**

Take a nice leisurely stroll through **Grayton Beach,** one of the oldest towns on the Emerald Coast. Dating back the turn of the 20th century, the main street area is flush with quaint shops and eateries. Take note that driving on the beach is for residents only.

Pick up *A Walking Tour of Historic Circle Drive* at the visitors center in DeFuniak Springs (see *Guidance*) for an appreciation of the architecture found around Lake DeFuniak, and follow the mile-long route to enjoy the historic homes (see *To See—Historic Sites*).

✳ Green Space

BEACHES The rare coastal flatwoods ecosystem in **Deer Lake State Park** (850-231-0337; www.floridastateparks.org/deerlake), 357 Main Park Rd, on CR 30A just east of Seagrove Beach in Santa Rosa Beach, provides many opportunities to view Gulf Coast lupine and stately magnolias. The dune crossovers at this park provide sweeping views of tall sand dunes.

& Reserve beach wheelchairs in advance at the Emerald Coast Convention & Visitors welcome center for a view of the Gulf from Beasley Park, 1550 Miracle Strip Pkwy (US 98), and **Fort Walton Beach,** located next door to the welcome center (see *Guidance*).

Grayton Beach State Park (850-231-4210; www.floridastateparks.org/grayton beach), 357 Main Park Rd, Santa Rosa Beach. With more than 2,000 acres of coastal dunes, coastal scrub, pine flatwoods, and beachfront, this is one of the

Western Panhandle's most beautiful state parks. Resembling a romantic scene from *Lord of the Rings,* it is a great place for hiking, with a nature trail winding through dunes and pines to end up along a scenic stretch of beach. Canoeists and kayakers find this lake especially appealing, and the campground offers access to it all. Fee.

Emerald Coast CVB

GRAYTON BEACH LAGOON

& Overlooking the Gulf of Mexico, **Henderson Beach State Park** (850-837-7550; www.floridastateparks.org/hendersonbeach), 17000 Emerald Coast Pkwy, Destin, is a coastal oasis amid the sprawl of condos; you can get back to nature on more than a mile of scenic shoreline backed by coastal dunes topped with scrub vegetation. Fish for pompano, camp in the full-service campground, or walk the nature trails. A handful of beach wheelchairs are available on a first-come, first-served basis. Fee.

A favorite of locals, on Old Scenic US 98, the quiet **James Lee County Park,** near the Walton County line, features 300 feet of waterfront along emerald green seas.

Topsail Hill Preserve State Park (1-877-232-2478; www.floridastateparks.org/topsailhill), 7525 W CR 30A, Santa Rosa Beach, Hike the 2.5-mile Morris Lake Nature Trail, or swim along more than 3 miles of beautiful beaches. The campground is a destination in itself, with 156 sites near the ocean. Fee.

BOTANICAL GARDEN **Eden Gardens State Park** (850-231-4214), CR 395, Point Washington. A century ago this grand plantation belonged to the William Henry Wesley family. Tour the manor by candlelight, picnic at the old mill, or come out and enjoy the fragrant camellia blooms each spring. Walk under a canopy of moss-draped oaks and pause for a moment by a tranquil reflection pool. Gardens surrounding the home include a rose garden, azalea garden, camellia garden, and a "hidden garden" in the forest. Note the unusual monkey puzzle trees near the ranger's office; they are native to Chile.

PARKS **Fred Gannon Rocky Bayou State Park** (850-833-9144), 4281 FL 20, Niceville. Scenic nature trails and great fishing on the tidal bayou draw visitors to this beautiful park on an

FORT WALTON BEACH

Emerald Coast CVB

arm of Choctawhatchee Bay; enjoy camping in one of their 42 spacious, shaded sites.

✄ You'll love **The Landing Park,** 139 Brooks Street SE, Fort Walton Beach, for quiet picnics after your visit at the Emerald Science Center. Enjoy the cool breeze from the Intracoastal while the kids play on jungle gyms under shady trees. In the summer, free movies are shown every Fri night.

SPRINGS Surrounded by the town that bears its name, **DeFuniak Springs** is a perfectly circular spring-fed lake more than 60 feet deep. **Pitt Spring,** along FL 20 at Econfina Creek west of Fountain, offers a crystalline venue for swimming; my hiking buddies stopped there to fill their water bottles from the chalky blue water. Privately owned **Vortex Spring** (see *Lodging—Dive Resort*) is surrounded by lush forests; fee.

South of I-10 off FL 81 and CR 181, **Morrison Springs** was purchased by the state in 2004 and turned over to Walton County to manage. The 161-acre county park is a destination for divers, with three major vents in the spring descending to 50 feet; cave diving extends 300 feet underground. For the less adventuresome, the clear water makes this second-magnitude spring pleasant for swimming and snorkeling as well. Fee.

Ponce de Leon Springs State Park (850-836-4281; www.floridastateparks.org/poncedeleonsprings), 2860 Ponce de Leon Springs Rd, Ponce de Leon. Chalky blue 68-degree water tempts swimmers in for a chilly dip in this first-magnitude spring, gushing forth 14 million gallons of water daily. Fish, picnic, or walk the nature trails through the lush hardwood forest. Fee.

PONCE DE LEON SPRINGS

Sandra Friend

WILD PLACES Established as the Choctawhatchee National Forest in 1909 by Theodore Roosevelt, **Eglin Air Force Base** encompasses 300 square miles and offers public recreation along its fringes.

Point Washington State Forest (850-231-5800), 5865 E US 98, Santa Rosa Beach. Sea breezes filter through the pines in this state forest protecting a vast swath of southern Walton County; access the forest for nature study, biking, and hiking via the Eastern Lake Bike/Hike Trail. Fee.

✴ Lodging
BED & BREAKFASTS

Bonifay 32425
Built in 1919 by local timber baron

George Waits, the 10,000-square-foot **Waits Mansion** (850-547-0321; www.waitsmansion.com), 209 W Kansas Ave, is constructed of heart cypress and features oak flooring milled at Caryville. Renovated by Frank Barone, who purchased the property in 2005, it is now open as an elegant bed & breakfast with four picture-perfect roomy suites evoking the 1920s, even though they include wireless Internet ($110–149).

DeFuniak Springs 32433

🦆 In the heart of downtown, the **Hotel DeFuniak** (1-877-333-8642; www.hoteldefuniak.com), 400 E Nelson Ave, dates back to 1920 and was painstakingly restored to its original glory in 1997, evoking the rich ambience of the Florida boom years, with 19th-century antique furnishings throughout. Centrally located for your exploration of the historic downtown and residential districts, it offers three large suites and seven rooms (each uniquely themed), plus a massage therapist on staff who can see you in a private massage room, and wi-fi throughout the building. Rates start at $90–110, an amazing value for such luxury; breakfast is included with your stay.

Grayton Beach 32459

♿ Tucked off the beaten path, the **Hibiscus Coffee & Guesthouse** (850-231-2733; www.hibiscusflorida.com), 85 Defuniak St, has a room for everyone ($95–225). Lovers will want to check into the Romance Room with king-sized bed and super-sized Jacuzzi for two. In the Hibiscus Room, you'll find an antique claw-foot tub in the bathroom. Those with special needs will feel right at home in the Big Easy cabin. Formerly the home's kitchen, the room is equipped

with a small refrigerator, microwave, and coffeemaker. The new Wood-pecker Cottage is a mini suite, which also has a small refrigerator and microwave. And unlike most other B&Bs, a crib or cot can be provided if you have a small child. A hot breakfast is included each morning 7:30–11:30, with the coffeehouse also open to general public. Check out the BE sign posted out front. Each day it has a different saying. The day I was there it said BE CHEERFUL.

Santa Rosa Beach 32459

The re-created antebellum-style home **A Highlands House Bed & Breakfast** (850-267-0110; www.ahighlandshousebbinn.com), 4193 W Scenic CR 30A, is situated west of Destin directly off the sugar-sand beach. It's private and peaceful, and you'll enjoy sitting on the porch overlooking the beautifully landscaped lawn, sand dunes, and emerald green water. A healthy breakfast includes warm homecooked breads, and since there are only seven bedrooms, tranquility is ensured. Queen- and king-sized beds in most rooms; one room has two double beds ($130–200).

Seagrove Beach 32459

The cheerfully decorated **Sugar Beach Inn Bed & Breakfast** (850-231-1577; www.sugarbeachinn.com), 3501 E Scenic CR 30A, is only a short walk from the picturesque town of Seaside. Rooms have queen and king brass canopied and poster beds; some offer Jacuzzi and fireplace ($110–200).

Seaside 32459

Josephine's Bed & Breakfast (850-231-1940 or 1-800-848-1840; www.josephinesinn.com), 38 Seaside Ave, the Georgian-style plantation home surrounded by a white picket fence, is where you'll find all the comforts of home and then some. Rooms and suites are named after a historic French character, such as the romantic Madame Bovary Room with wrought-iron queen-sized poster or the Juliet Suite with queen-sized mahogany poster. Rooms are beautifully appointed with beds dressed in crisp white linens and Battenberg skirting; most rooms feature a fireplace ($175–450). It's nestled in a quiet section of town, but you're never too far from all the activities— 900 feet from the beach and only a few feet to the center of town. The hot country breakfast is included, and requests for seconds are never a problem, often encouraged.

HOTELS AND MOTELS

Destin 32541
Two chain-style accommodations stand out due to their extra friendliness and close proximity to the beach and golf courses. **Country Inn & Suites** (850-650-9191 or 1-800-456-4000; www.countryinns.com), 4415 Commons Drive E, is the best choice for those wanting to be near the greens at Kelly Plantation Golf

THE INN AT CRYSTAL BEACH

© Dale E. Peterson

Course (see *To Do—Golf*). The home-style motel offers both guest rooms and suites with a wet bar and mini fridge ($101–185). High-speed Internet access is free, so you can plan your activities around town or to destinations beyond.

At the **Comfort Inn Destin** (850-654-8611; www.comfortinn.com), 19001 Emerald Coast Pkwy, Henderson Beach State Park (see *Green Space—Beaches*) is located directly across the street. Or sit out by the pool where palm trees sway in warm Gulf breezes. Enjoy the complimentary breakfast in the bright and cheery breakfast room. Standard rooms have two queen beds; king and family suites also available ($119–169).

CONDO HOTEL RESORTS

Destin 32541
Situated directly on the Gulf, all condo accommodations face the ocean at the **Inn at Crystal Beach** (850-650-7000), 2996 US 98. Providing premiere service, the resort features celebrity chef Tim Creehan (see *Dining Out*). While this is a condo-hotel (meaning each room is decorated by individual owners), all decor is governed by strict guidelines. You'll find each unit uniquely decorated, typically with a tropical theme. The resort web site allows you to virtually tour most rooms, so you'll know what to expect before you get there. And the 24-hour front desk ensures a pleasant greeting when arriving late. My favorite unit is the tastefully decorated I607, with a South Seas Island theme. The owner of this three-bedroom condo has artistic talent; many walls are covered in stylish murals and accents complementing the furnishings. Another fine unit is

1410, furnished in white wicker throughout. The floor-to-ceiling mirrored walls in the Florida-themed two-bedroom unit makes the already spacious abode seem even larger. You'll find all units have washers and dryers along with Jacuzzis in most master suites. For resort-quality amenities, what better way to exercise than by looking out over the Gulf at the state-of-the-art fitness center, or taking a dip in the heated pool. Condos have two to six bedrooms ($219–1,382 per day; $1,473–9,351 per week). Expect a reservation and housekeeping fee in addition to the regular room taxes. All reservations are booked through Dale E. Peterson Vacation Resorts, not through the property (1-800-336-9669; www.destinresorts.com).

© Sandestin Resort

SANDESTIN GOLF AND BEACH RESORT

Destin 32550

✍ Centrally located between Pensacola and Panama City, the resort destination **Sandestin Golf and Beach Resort** (850-267-8000 or 1-877-622-1038; www.sandestin.com), 9300 Emerald Coast Pkwy W, is only 8 miles from downtown Destin. Pools, lakes, beaches, golf, tennis, shopping, and dining can all be found within the boundaries of the resort. Kids will enjoy parks and playgrounds throughout the property, with the three-and-a-half-story Sooper water slide and the beachside rock-climbing wall always favorites. Choose from several types of accommodations grouped in five unique "neighborhoods": beachside condos, villas overlooking a picturesque lake, cottage-style homes just off the fairways, and penthouse suites overlooking the Gulf and Choctawhatchee Bay; one will surely suit your taste and budget ($105–900). On the bay side, the Grand is their signature luxury hotel with hotel rooms and condos decorated in the Old South style. Shoppers will want to be near the restaurants and boutiques in the village of Baytowne Wharf. Nature lovers can nestle in to quiet cottages overlooking the saltwater marshes of the 5-acre Jolee Island Nature Park. Gulfside, you'll find Mediterranean-inspired town homes and villas in a quaint neighborhood setting or towering condos overlooking the beach. A free trolley links the resorts, beaches, and village shopping.

VACATION HOMES Ocean Reef Resort Properties (850-837-3935; www.oceanreefresorts.com) and **Dale E. Peterson Vacation Resorts** (1-800-336-9669; www.destinresorts.com) both offer furnished cottages, beach homes, condos, town homes, luxury homes, and resorts by the day, week, or month.

One of the largest suppliers of fully furnished homes, the folks at **ResortQuest** (1-800-GO RELAX; www.resortquest.com) can select which home will be right for you—from condos in resort-style settings to portfolio homes with private pools. By the day, week, or month.

CENTRAL PANHANDLE

DeFuniak Springs 32433

♂ 🐾 **Sunset King Lake RV Resort**
(850-892-7229 or 1-800-774-5454;
www.sunsetking.com), 366 Paradise
Island Dr, with direct access to King
Lake, is a favorite of folks seeking big
bass from their boat. Campsites are
set in a forested area, with all hook-
ups (including cable) and pull-
through sites available ($27). Rental
units include beautiful log cabins and
cottages, fully furnished, starting at
$65. Discounts for military, Good
Sam, and Coast to Coast members.
Enjoy the clubhouse with pool and
wi-fi, playground, game room, and
general store.

Santa Rosa Beach 32459

At **Grayton Beach State Park** (see
Green Space—Beaches), camp with a
sea breeze in the 37-site campground
(or rent one of 30 fully furnished cabins). Reserve in advance online or by
phone through Reserve America, 1-
800-326-3521.

Topsail Hill Preserve State Park
(see *Green Space—Beaches*) offers
one of the top campgrounds in the
nation—the Gregory E. Moore RV
Campground. The 156 sites have 30
or 50 amp electric, water, sewer, and
cable, and are set in a diminutive
coastal scrub forest and pine flatwoods. Amenities include a heated
swimming pool, shuffleboard, and private tram access to the beach. If you
don't have a big rig, consider renting
one of their modern bungalows, each
with living room, dining room, bed-
room, screened porch, and carport
(by week or month). Reserve in
advance online or by phone through
Reserve America, 1-800-326-3521.

Ponce de Leon 32455

Vortex Spring (850-836-4979;
www.vortexspring.com), 1517 Vortex
Spring Ln, opened in 1972 and is the
largest privately owned diving facility
in Florida, owned and operated by
active divers. The complex includes
the 68-degree spring, a campground,
and three lodges. The Pinewood
Lodge has male and female dorms,
each with 26 bunk beds, and eight
four-person rooms upstairs with private bath and television. Otter Creek
Lodge offers six kitchenettes and a
variety of large rooms sleeping up to
six, with private baths. The new
Grandview Lodge has rooms with
queen beds, full kitchens, and dive
gear lockdown cages. All three lodges
are nestled in lush woods and require
that you bring your own linens (sleeping bag or sheets, pillow, towels).
Rates start at $64, or $15 per night
per person for the dorm (minimum
$135).

✳ Where to Eat

DINING OUT

Destin/Fort Walton Beach

On the first floor of the Inn at Crystal
Beach (see *Lodging—Condo Hotel
Resorts*), you can look out at the
emerald waters at the **Beach Walk
Café** (850-650-7100; www.beachwalk-
cafe.com), 2996 Scenic US 98 E, and
enjoy an elegant culinary experience.
Award-winning chef Tim Creehan
dazzles your palate with fresh Gulf
seafood and meats accented with
French, Italian, and Asian flair, such
as pepper-crusted tuna with sautéed
spinach and a soy ginger sauce
(entrées $29–49). Chef Creehan,
author of several cookbooks, presents

a cooking class once a month. Open for lunch Sun–Fri 11–2, dinner nightly 5:30–10, and Sun brunch 9–2:30.

🐚 Head downtown to **Big City, an American Bistro** (850-664-0664; www.bigcitybistro.com), 171 Brooks St, for a bubbly Sun brunch buffet featuring a live jazz vocalist and cello. Owner and executive chef James Garrison, a graduate of the Culinary Institute of America, has received numerous awards and television notoriety for his culinary imagination. You'll enjoy both common and creative dishes, from old-fashioned meat loaf with cream onion gravy to curry dusted char-grilled salmon "steak" with whole-wheat couscous tabouleh salad and red wine shellfish sauce. Open for lunch 11–2:30, dinner 5–close, and Sun brunch 10:30–2:30; closed Mon. For the cool character and quintessential quality of this place, you'll find dinner entrées very reasonably priced between $10–19.

It's easy to spot the **Crab Trap Seafood & Oyster Bar** (850-654-2722) on US 98 at the lively boardwalk, but if you want to find their second location, veer west off the beaten path to 3500 Old Scenic US 98, where you'll be greeted by friendly staff as you gaze out over the white sand and emerald green seas of the Gulf of Mexico. Crab entrées are the main attraction, so you'll want to start with the rich and creamy she crab soup, loaded with crab. The restaurant is also a great place to try a wide variety of locally caught fish, such as light and flaky red grouper and red snapper, and the meatier amberjack ($8–26). Open 11–9.

At **The Lucky Snapper Grill & Bar** (850-654-0900; www.luckysnapper .com), 76 US 98 E, go ahead and spoil your appetite with one of their signature drinks, such as the Snapper Sensation, which blends tropical rum with cool and creamy raspberry ice cream. The open-air restaurant caters to an upscale crowd without all the stuffiness. It overlooks Destin Harbor, and you'll sit inside at comfortable wood-grained booths or high-top tables and stools on the deck, watching dolphins swim by. For hungry appetites, dig into the Crystal Beach grouper, a house favorite, stuffed full of crabmeat and blanketed with a creamy white cheese sauce. If you can't decide between sea and shore, order it with a half rack of ribs smothered in honey-glaze barbecue sauce for a few dollars more. Open daily 11–10; entrées $9–25.

Enjoy great gumbo in the historical 1910 Florida home at **Magnolia Grill** (850-302-0266; www.magnolia grillfwb.com), 157 Brooks St. The house was one of many of the period that were mail-ordered and shipped by train in a complete kit ready for assembly, bricks for the chimneys and cupboards for the kitchen. The home is still in pristine vintage condition with many original components, such as the brick fireplace and left and right bookcases, windows that still open with ropes and pulleys, and cupboards still containing the wavy glass typical of that period. You'll also want to take note of the board marked DR. G.G. FRENCH, CAMP WALTON, FLA., which was the mailing label for the assembly kit. The fine-dining eatery features dishes such as steak magnolia, served with green peppercorn and mushroom sauce, and blackened amberjack, a local fish, served with rice on a crawfish étouffée ($13–26). You'll also find more than a dozen

Italian entrées on the menu. Lunch 11–2 weekdays; dinner Mon–Thu 5–8, Fri and Sat 5–9.

A must-stop for any Irish gal, the lively Irish folk music and traditional fare at **McGuire's Irish Pub and Brewery** (850-654-0567; www.mcguiresirish pub.com), 33 US 98, will keep you going till after midnight. You'll find healthy portions of traditional Irish pub fare along with a wide selection of seafood, steaks, and chops ($10–27); the senate bean soup is still only 18¢. Sing-alongs are encouraged, and at times mandated. And if you don't learn the words, you'll have to kiss the moose, and that's no blarney. Daily 11–11; light fare served until 1:30 AM.

❧ Established in 1913, **Staff's** (850-243-3482), 24 Miracle Strip Pkwy SE, is a true Florida treasure, the second-oldest continually operating restaurant in Florida. Founder "Pop" Staff was one of the area's first pioneers, supplying the Gulfview Hotel with fresh-caught fish and vegetables from his family garden. The tradition continues, with family members serving up

STAFF'S

Rob Smith, Jr.

fish purchased right off the boat, from amberjack to triggerfish; soft-shell crabs, scamp, and shrimp several ways. Meat eaters will appreciate six choices of fine steaks, and the soups are savory. All entrées ($16–44) include salad, fresh-baked wheat bread, German potato salad, corn on the cob, new potatoes, and dessert. Most of the recipes have been handed down from generation to generation, and that's something you rarely encounter these days. Their seafood-okra gumbo recipe is a family secret, and the crab-meat-stuffed green chiles will get your mouth warmed up for the main dish. While you can order a fine steak or a chicken breast, why bother—the heart of this restaurant's business is great seafood, served your way, broiled or fried. Open for dinner daily at 5.

EATING OUT

Bruce

Bruce Café (850-835-2946), corner of FL 20 and FL 81. Generals and lumberjacks rub elbows at this great family café, where Lillie Mae serves up $5 specials like beef tips, fried chicken, and barbecued pork with three country-style veggies on the side. Seat yourself and look over the menu board, which includes burgers and a pork chop sandwich, $2–3. Save room for one of the 10 choices of cakes and pies! Open 6 AM–7 PM; closed Sun and Mon.

Crestview

A 1950s-style lunch counter with a loyal following, **Desi's Restaurant** (850-682-5555), 197 N Main St, offers up a buffet laden with southern favorites like roast chicken, ribs, fried fish, cheese grits, greens, and three kinds of peas—black-eyed, zipper, and field.

Featuring Apalachicola oysters and other local fruits of the sea, the **Destin Seafood Market & Fish Net Restaurant** (850-683-1418), 1260 S Ferdon Blvd, is a popular dinner stop.

Espresso's Coffee Café (850-689-2011), 1676 S Ferdon Blvd, invites you to "try a hazelnut mocha" in their retro digs.

DeFuniak Springs

A 1916 landmark in the historic downtown district, **Busy Bee Café** (850-951-2233; www.busybeecafe .net), 35 S Seventh St, offers an array of entrées sure to please any palate, from grouper almandine to a grilled New York strip smothered in grilled onions, mushrooms, and melted provolone ($11–19). Open for lunch (10:30–2:30) Tues–Sat and dinner (5 9) Fri and Sat.

Since 1947, tiny **H&M Hot Dog** (850-892-9100), 43 S Ninth St, has been a place where you can walk right up to the lunch counter window and place your order. The hot dogs and hamburgers are cooked to order, and the sides are carefully handmade, with the Bodiford family carrying on the tradition that Harley & Margaret Broxson started. Enjoy your meal at the picnic table underneath the adjacent arbor. Open Mon–Fri 9–5:30, Sat 10–4.

After a tiring day hiking and four-wheeling, I adjourned with friends to **McLain's Family Steakhouse** (850-892-2402), 622 Hugh Adams Rd, just north of I-10. You can order from the menu or take the buffet, and given the wide range of foods you'll find on it—good traditional southern food, of course—the buffet is your best bet.

You'll find homespun goodness at **Murray's Café** (850-951-9941), 660

Baldwin Ave, where a mile-high cake turned my head and lured me in. I started off with whisper-thin fried-green tomatoes, some of the finest I've ever had, and delighted in my fresh fried grouper, green beans cooked southern style, and perfect sweet tea. Yum! Their adjacent gift shop carries china and whimsical gifts, baked goods, gourmet cookies, and ice cream.

Destin and Fort Walton Beach

✐ A great photo op can be found right at **Angler's Beachside Grill** (850-790-0260), 1030 Miracle Strip Pkwy SE, located next door to Florida Gulfarium (see *To See—Zoological and Marine Park*). Kids, who are always welcome here, can crawl through a partially submerged sand shark's belly and out through the mouth—definitely one for the scrapbooks. They offer cool drinks, burgers, sandwiches, and baskets, and you'll want to try the

H&M HOT DOG

Sandra Friend

Anglers Elizabeth, a dish made with mahimahi with a shrimp, crabmeat, and pine nut topping.

Shucking fresh oysters since 1984, **AJ's Restaurant & Bimini Bar** (850-837-1913; www.ajs-destin.com), 116 US 98 E, is the place to go for great food, beer, and fun. Try the baked Oyster AJ made with fresh jalapeños, Monterey jack, and bacon. Sensational seafood entrées are broiled, baked, and fried. The broiled seafood platter always includes oysters. The fresh-air restaurant also serves food for land-lubbers. And for fun, AJ's charter fleet will take you on their *Sea Blaster* at speeds up to 55 mph. If fishing is your game, their charter fleet will help you land coastal favorites, such as grouper, amberjack, and wahoo.

Locals travel hours for **Ali's Ciao Bella Pizza** (850-654-9815), 29 US 98 E, with the #10, Ortolana Pizza, a favorite choice. The crunchy thin-crust pizza allows you to really enjoy all the toppings. The menu has more than 70 items, so you'll want to go back again and again, but you'll want to put the Toscana salad, chicken cacciatore sandwich, and portobello mushroom ravioli at the top of your list ($7–16). Open daily 11–9:30.

The top breakfast and lunch spot for locals and tourists alike is at **Another Broken Egg** (850-650-0499; www.anotherbrokenegg.com), 104 US 98 E. With its ambience of pure country comfort, you wouldn't expect gourmet items such as the Pontchartrain, an open-faced crois-sant covered with scrambled eggs, broccoli, tomatoes, mild green chiles, onions, and melted Jack cheese. Dainty appetites will want order the yogurt, fruit 'n granola parfait with strawberries, bananas, kiwi, and gra-nola layered between low-fat vanilla and strawberry yogurts, and served with muffins. The presentation of each dish is worth admiring before you dig in. While the menu reads like a gourmet magazine, you'll find the prices very reasonable ($3–13). The house specialty, Blackberry Grits, is still only $2.39. Burgers, salads, and sandwiches available during lunch hours. Get there early or plan to patiently wait in line. Open Tue–Sun 7–2; closed Mon.

The Candymaker (850-654-0833 or 1-888-654-6404; www.thecandy maker.com), 757 US 98 E. The "Grouchy Old Candymaker," Tom Ehlke, isn't so grumpy after all. Once he decided there had to be a better saltwater taffy, he set his sights and shop up in Destin and since 1992 has been satisfying locals and tourists alike with not only his saltwater taffy but other confections as well. You'll find sumptuous delights like crunchy, rich, south Georgia–style pralines; creamy, buttery fudge; and chewy caramels. So you're never too far from the chocolate, he's got other locations in Sandestin (850-351-1986) and Mystic Port (850-534-0030).

A 12-foot giraffe greets you at the door at **Harry T's** (850-654-4800; www.harryts.com), a souvenir from his circus days. Harry loves to make kids laugh, so every Tue is Kids Night, with lots of clowns and balloons. Moms and dads will enjoy the 99¢ kids menu every day 11–7. But don't be misled: Harry also has grown-up food, like grouper beurre blanc—a char-grilled grouper topped with shrimp, crab-meat, and creamy beurre blanc sauce —and filet mignon kebabs. Open for lunch, dinner, and Sun brunch. After 18 years, the restaurant is moving in spring 2007 to HarborWalk Village on Harbor Blvd in Destin.

Just 1 mile east of the Destin Bridge is the world-famous **Hogs Breath Café** (850-837-5991; www.hogsbreath.com), 541 US 98. Established in 1976, this is the original café to its porcine cousin in Key West. The saloon features live music, restaurant and raw bar, great beer, and even fishing charters. Open daily for lunch and dinner.

For a cool treat on a hot summer day, or even a rainy day, **Shake's Frozen Custard** (850-269-1111; www.shakes frozencustard.com), 1065 US 98 E (tucked a bit back from the roadway), is the place to be. Made fresh every hour, the smooth and creamy frozen concoction contains no fillers or preservatives and is never fluffed-up with air. Any hey, it's 90 percent fat free! For only $5, the Pink Poodle dips up the creamy custard and smothers it with pineapples, bananas, and strawberries. The signature Shake's Bopper contains a monstrous three scoops of creamy frozen custard, caramel, and hot fudge. Open 10 AM–midnight during the summer and 11 AM until close during the winter months.

Can't get to some of these fine eateries? **Emerald Coast Food Taxi** will deliver (850-650-8150; www.emerald coastfoodtaxi.com).

Freeport
Stop in for the freshest seafood at the **Corner Café & Oyster Bar** (850-835-1799), corner of FL 20 and US 331, the place where the locals eat. Seafood specials appear seasonally and almost always include shrimp and oysters; entrées, $5–13.

Grayton
At **Picolo's & The Red Bar** (850-231-1008), 70 Holz Ave, you can lis-

ten to live music while lounging in the red velvet living room. The comfy eclectic restaurant serves some of the best burgers around. Accepts only cash. Serving lunch, dinner, and brunch.

Ponce de Leon
The Red Rooster Café & Grill (850-836-4008), 2972 N FL 81. A popular stop for breakfast just south of I-10, where you can pick up a massive breakfast—try the Rock a Doodle Doo Breakfast Platter with one pancake, two eggs, ham, bacon, sausage, and hash browns, all for $5—and many other options for less. They serve lunch and dinner, too, from burgers to pork chops, seafood, and fried chicken ($4–14).

Seaside
Named after a dog and cat, **Bud & Alley's Restaurant** (850-231-5900; www.budandalleys.com), 2236 CR 30A E, overlooking the beach, is a great place for a quick bite.

✳ Selective Shopping

Baker
In this historic little rural downtown, you'll never know what treasures you'll find at **Baker This & That** (850-537-2003), 1264 Georgia Ave.

Crestview
Walk the aisles at **Emerald Coast Book Haven** (850-682-1956; www .ecbooks.com), 801 W James Lee Blvd (US 90), and you're bound to find something you're looking for. With more than 50,000 books (mostly used, some new) in stock, it's quite the collection! Open Mon–Wed 10–6, Thu and Fri 10–8, Sat 10–4.

The life-sized horse statue out front is a great landmark for the **Gypsy Den**

Antique Mall (850-682-0500), 404 W James Lee Blvd, a large complex of dealer booths.

I couldn't help but notice the full-sized traffic light in the window of **Pappy T's Antique Uniques & Collectibles** (850-689-2323), a small shop stuffed with jewelry, gifts, and collectibles, including dolls, fine china, artwork, glassware, kitchen items, and home decor.

Looking like it plopped down here from Durango, **Ron's Antiques** (850-305-2441), 213 N Main St, draws you in with its turquoise Wild West facade to examine the wares, from beaded lamps and large advertising signs to a vintage stove, cuckoo clocks, and a watch repair counter.

DeFuniak Springs

The Book Store (850-892-3119), 640 Sixth Ave, carries a large selection of

RON'S ANTIQUES IN CRESTVIEW

Sandra Friend

used books, with trades welcome. Look for new titles near the front, and freebie paperbacks on the bench outside. Open Mon–Sat 10–5.

Browse for antiques and gifts at **Heavenly Designs Florist & Gifts** (850-892-4528), 782 Baldwin Ave.

An old-time general store, the **Little Big Store** (850-892-6066), 35 S Eighth St, offers country goodies, gifts, and more.

Destin

The shoe fits everyone but Cinderella at **Allen Edmonds Shoes** (850-654-4790), 10406 US 98 E. The fine footwear establishment has sizes 5–18, widths AAA–EEE, but only for the men.

Great beachwear is found at **Beach Bums** (850-837-7111), 9539 US 98; **Beach Zone** (850-837-4500), 34871 Emerald Coast Pkwy; and **Wings** (850-650-9115), 1115 US 98 E, with brand names from Anne Klein to Tommy Bahama.

The quaint atmosphere at **Destin Commons** (850-337-8700; www .destincommons.com), 4300 Legendary Dr, will satisfy everyone in your family. The small-town main-street layout makes it easy to walk among a bevy of upscale shops, boutiques, galleries, and eateries. Kids will love to ride the mini train that winds its way through the town past the interactive fountain. Open daily.

Fudpucker Trading Company (850-654-4200), 20001 Emerald Coast Pkwy, features "fudnominal" shopping and the world-famous Fudpucker merchandise. You'll also enjoy the eclectic mix of Clay Works pottery, Cow Parade cows, Maryhoonies, raku pottery, neon clocks, and kids' toys.

Potagers Gardens & Verandas (850-269-3211; www.potagers.net), 9755 W Emerald Coast Pkwy, has a nice display of French and Italian pottery, European linens and toiletries, garden elements, and a few select antiques. Oh, and they are also a florist.

At **Silver Sands Factory Stores** (850-654-9771; www.silversands outlet.com), 10562 Emerald Coast Pkwy, you'll find more than 100 designer-name stores.

Wyland's Pardise Galleries (850-650-6240), 51 US 98 E in Harbor-Walk, features limited-edition prints, sculptures, jewelry, and collectibles from the famous marine artist.

Fort Walton Beach

Several antiques stores line the Miracle Strip Pkwy (US 98) along the 100–300 block, such as **Darby Mitchell Antiques** (850-244-4069; www.darby-mitchellantiques.com), 158 Miracle Strip Pkwy SE, and **Baileys Ruth and Son Antiques** (850-224-2424), 136 Miracle Strip Pkwy SE.

As a new grandmother, I couldn't resist checking out **Hugs & Hissyfits** (850-796-4847), 184-2 Miracle Strip Pkwy, which is loaded with cute little girls' dresses, and **Little Bo Feet** (850-314-7400), 174 Brooks, just around the corner, for unique shoes and accessories for kids.

Next door to the Indian Temple Mound Museum is **One Feather** (850-243-9807), 161 Miracle Strip Pkwy, an authentic Native American shop housing an impressive selection of authentic Native American goods from 40 different tribes. Ask to see the tiny kachina dolls. The removable headdress reveals a carefully painted face about the size of a grain of sand.

Grayton

The 2006 Walton County Artist of the Year, Phil Kiser, displays his dimensional mosaics created using recycled materials, including vintage plates and glass, at **Big Mama's Hula Girl Gallery** (850-231-6201; www.big mamashulagirlgallery.com), 1300B CR 283 S. Allison Tanner's dog portraits are also worth close inspection. Exhibiting a wide range of local creative talent, this eclectic gallery is one of the best in the state.

Pick up a CD by artist Nancy Veldman at **Magnolia House Lifestyle Store** (850-231-5859 or 1-888-272-3250; www.magnoliahouse.com), 2 Magnolia St, where this incredible, inspirational woman plays selections of her own music on a white baby grand piano at the entry. In her quaint gift shop you'll find a phenomenal selection of her watercolor art among that of other local artists, custom-designed Diane Katzman jewelry, and unique gifts. A fine selection of inspirational books, her writings on beauty, insight, and inspiration will open your awareness of provide a sense of purpose.

At the **Shops of Grayton** on Grayton Rd (2 blocks north of CR 30A), you'll find home decor, art, antiques, and unique clothing in eight colorful cottages. A great place to go antiquing is at **Grayton Antiques** (850-231-1171), 26-G Logan Lane. While walking around town, note the buildings on Hotz Ave, which date back to the early 1900s, where you'll also find the eclectic home and garden store, **Zoo Gallery** (850-231-0777), 89 Hotz Ave.

Ponce de Leon

A whimsical little shop, **Flutes & Vegetables** (850-836-9996), 2831 N FL 81, has everything from fresh produce and local honey to bamboo poles, natural stone for landscaping, handmade soaps, rock albums, and of course, bamboo flutes.

Old Town Trading Post (850-865-0810), 2988 FL 81, welcomes you to browse its selection of western-themed collectibles and home decor, including carved Native American figurines, dream catchers, and architectural accents; they also sell saddles and other tack.

Sandestin Resort

A must-visit for any Southern gal is the **Magnolia & Ivy Tea Room** (850-267-2595; www.magnoliaivy .com), 147 Tupelo Courtyard, where one can dress up in hats and fluffy boas while sipping diva-licious teas. The elegant gift shop has all you need to create your own tea party at home, from cups and saucers to loose-leaf teas. They even offer conferences if you want to open your own tearoom.

At the **Shoppes of Baytowne Wharf** (850-267-8000; www.baytownewharf .com), 9300 Emerald Coast Pkwy, you'll first need to pass through the

Sandestin Resort guard gate. Tell them you are heading to Baytowne Wharf, then pull into the dock and ride the *Miss Connie* ferry over to the quaint shopping village, open Mon–Sat 10–9, Sun 10–6. Intermingled with restaurants that cater to folks staying at the resort, the boutiques are centered around a lagoon off the bay and offer a variety of interesting themes, from children's toys to seashells, upscale pet supplies, and resort wear.

Santa Rosa Beach

Get the local buzz at **Miss Lucille's Gossip Parlor** (850-267-2522), 45 Town Center Loop in Gulf Place. The artsy boutique also serves great desserts and coffee.

Seaside

Follow CR 30A to the quaint village that served as the backdrop for *The Truman Show,* starring Jim Carrey. More than 40 shops, quaint cafés, and eateries line the storybook streets, some of which are cobblestoned. At the heart of town is the **Ruskin Place Artist Colony** (Ruskin, Quincy, and Central Square area), where you'll find a nice collection of arts, crafts,

and galleries, such as superior blown glass at **Fusion Art Glass Gallery** (850-231-5405), 63 Central Sq. Pieces by Josh Simpson are especially mesmerizing, with entire planetary scenes inside each globe. The local grocer, **Modica Market** (850-231-1214 or 1-877-809-0994), 109 Seaside Central Sq, has everything to outfit your cottage while staying in the area, from fine foods to the dishes from which you eat. And if the market looks vaguely familiar, it might be because you saw it in a scene from the movie. A few doors down, **Sundog Books & Central Square Records** (850-231-5481; www.sundogbooks.com), 89 Central Sq, is a great place to browse, with something for all ages. Breathe in aromatic scents at **Patchouli's Body Bath and Home** (850-231-1447), Four Corners. The beachside open-air market, **Per-spi-cas-ity** (850-231-5829), is only a few steps from the town center. It has something fun for everyone, just say the name three times fast!

FISH MARKET Didn't catch the big one? Or can't take the rolling seas? Just want to cook your own? Then you'll want to stop by **Sextons Seafood** (850-837-3040), 601 US 98 E, for the freshest catch of the day. Open daily 8–7.

✳ Entertainment

PERFORMING ARTS You'll enjoy Broadway shows at the two-tiered, 1,650-seat **Mainstage Theater** at the Arts Center at Okaloosa-Walton College (850-729-6000; www.owcc.cc .fl.us/arts), 100 College Blvd, Niceville. Take particular note of the walls in the lobby, which are covered with fossilized Mexican limestone. The deep theater seating ensures that everyone is within 100 feet of the stage. For smaller performances the square, 195-seat **Sprint Theater** offers options—show seating on two or three sides of the theater or an intimate theater in the round. Outside, the **OWC Amphitheater** houses up to 4,000 on sloping grounds for concerts and shows.

✳ Special Events

January: Don your favorite costume or penguin suit at the **Annual Mardi Gras Ball** (850-244-8191; www .mardigrasontheisland.com), Fort Walton. The fun continues throughout the weekend with the Island Festival and Parade. Sandestin-area restaurants compete at the **Great Southern Gumbo Cook-off** (850-267-8092), with live Cajun music and door prizes.

February: **Mardi Gras on the Island** features a 70-float parade followed by a street festival on Santa Rosa Blvd. Contact the Fort Walton Beach Chamber of Commerce (850-

SEASIDE

Visit Florida

244-8191) for more information (see *Guidance*).

The perfect spot for chocoholics is at the Beverly McNeil Gallery (850-654-4322; www.beverlymcneil.com) in Destin for the **Champagne & Chocolate Extravaganza.** The annual event features food, wine, and crafts, along with the gallery's fine pottery.

Florida Chautauqua Assembly (www.florida-chautauqua-center.org), DeFuniak Springs, is a southern companion to the original New York Chautauqua, offering workshops and classes, lectures and activities.

March: ✆ Take the kids out to the **Annual Kite Festival** (850-796-0102), a two-day event at the boardwalk on Okaloosa Island, sponsored by Kitty Hawk Kites. Free kitemaking, and exhibitions of stunt and giant kite flying.

April: At **Musical Echoes** (850-243-4405; www.musicalechoes.com), held at The Landing (see *Green Space—Parks*) in Fort Walton Beach, you'll experience an authentic Native American flute gathering. The nonalcoholic cultural event is weekend-long festival of music, food, and performances presented by the Muscogee Nation of Florida.

Chautauqua Celebration Day (850-892-9494), held around Lake DeFuniak, is a celebration of a full local slate of cultural activities that revived the Chautauqua spirit, from concerts and theater productions to musical workshops and artists in the schools.

June: If you love wine, you're in the right area for the annual **Chautauqua Wine Festival** (850-267-8092 or 850-892-5887) in DeFuniak Springs (see *To See—Wineries*).

The Billy Bowlegs (Bowles) Pirate Festival in Fort Walton Beach is not to be missed, featuring a torchlight parade with "Captain Billy" and "Queen and the Krewe of Bowlegs" throwing goodies to the kids. The charismatic scoundrel, from 1779, was one of this region's earliest settlers, capturing the shipping lanes and creating a band of pirates out of runaways and renegades. Only one other —the independent Republic of Texas —outlives Captain Bowles' governing body, the Independent State of Muskegee. Three days of activities involve a mock battle between the captain and city militia, which often includes the Fort Walton Beach mayor. Food, fun, music, and unique performances are celebrated in a festival atmosphere for all ages. Contact the Fort Walton Beach Chamber for more information (see *Guidance*).

July: **Biggest All-Night Gospel Sing in the World,** Bonifay, has been held by the Kiwanis Club (www.bonifay kiwanis.com) for more than 50 years. Nationally known singers entertain from sundown to sunup for more than 8,000 appreciative fans; buy tickets in advance online.

September: One of the top five beach volleyball events in the United States takes place in Destin at the **Fudpucker's Fall Classic Beach Volleyball Tournament** (1-800-447-7954).

🐾 How could you miss doggy square dancing at the **Annual Dog Daze** (850-664-6246), Fort Walton Beach Landing? Field events and other doggy delights take place throughout this one-day event.

October: A month-long fishing frenzy goes on at the **Annual Destin Fishing Rodeo** (850-837-2711), one of the most prestigious fishing events in the world.

There's fun for all at the **Boggy Bayou Mullet Festival** (850-678-1615), Niceville, with food, crafts, and national country music stars performing.

Championship Rodeo, Bonifay, is another major event put on by the Kiwanis Club (www.bonifaykiwanis .com). It's been a stable of Walton County life since 1944 and has recently been voted one of the best rodeos in Florida. A three-day-pass costs $30.

November: The **Annual Pow-wow** (850-822-1495) celebrates Native Americans with storytelling and inter-tribal dancing at the corner of FL 85 and College Blvd, Niceville.

Grit & Grace (www.comperf.com/ grit_and_grace.htm), the official folk-life production of Walton County, runs during the second week of Nov annually in Freeport.

December: **Christmas Reflections** (www.christmasreflections.com), DeFuniak Springs. More than three million lights bring a storybook Christmas to the Victorian residential district; free.

Western Panhandle

5

SANTA ROSA COUNTY

PENSACOLA

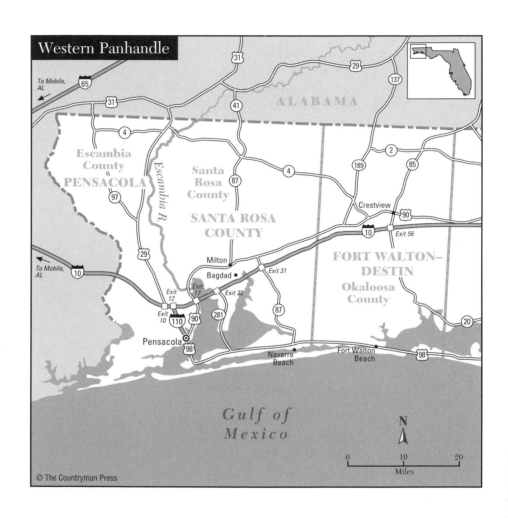

Western Panhandle

To Mobile, AL
65

31

31

41

29

31

137

ALABAMA

4

Escambia County
PENSACOLA

Escambia R.

Santa Rosa County

87

4

189

85

2

97

SANTA ROSA COUNTY

Crestview

90

To Mobile, AL
10

29

Milton

Bagdad

Exit 31

10

Exit 56

FORT WALTON–DESTIN

Okaloosa County

Exit 12

Exit 17

Exit 22

281

87

20

Exit 10

110

90

Pensacola

98

Navarre Beach

Fort Walton Beach

98

Gulf of Mexico

N

0   10   20
Miles

© The Countryman Press

SANTA ROSA COUNTY
NAVARRE BEACH, MILTON, AND BAGDAD

First explored in 1559 by Don Tristan de Luna, this region of powdery beaches, lush forests, broad open prairies, rugged bluffs, and clear, sand-bottomed rivers is a delight to outdoor enthusiasts, with so much to explore. Six flags have flown over this land first claimed by Spain and usurped by France, including the British, West Florida Republic, and Confederate. For the most part, **Santa Rosa County** is off the beaten path and one of the best places to get away from the crowds. **Navarre Beach,** a narrow 3-mile stretch on Santa Rosa Island, was completely washed over during the hurricanes of 2004 and 2005 and buried under several feet of sand for months. As of December 2006, you'll find the quiet beachside community fully recovered and friendlier than ever. **Gulf Breeze,** which also took a beating during Hurricane Ivan in 2004 and Hurricane Dennis in 2005, has recovered as well. You'll want to stop in and take a look at the interesting animals at the Gulf Breeze Zoo on US 98, some of which were born after the storms.

The county seat of **Milton** began as an early-1800s trading post along the Blackwater, a river deep enough to navigate up from the Gulf of Mexico for trade with the indigenous peoples. The bluffs made it tough to get from ships to land, resulting in the town's early names of "Scratch Ankle" and "Hard Scrabble." Thanks to its lush canopy of live oaks and vast longleaf pine forests, Milton became an important shipbuilding and repair center. In 1842, Santa Rosa County was created from parts of Escambia and Walton counties. Milton became the county seat and applied to be an official port of entry. Adjacent **Bagdad** developed as a company town for a new lumbermill in 1840 and grew with the size of the enterprise.

As you drive north from Milton on FL 87 you can see a series of ridges off in the distance, giving the sense of ascending into the mountains, something you'll experience nowhere else in Florida.

GUIDANCE Contact the **Santa Rosa County Tourist and Development Council** (850-748-7317 or 1-800-480-7263; www.beaches-rivers.com) for accommodations, dining, and activities from Navarre Beach to inland areas, including

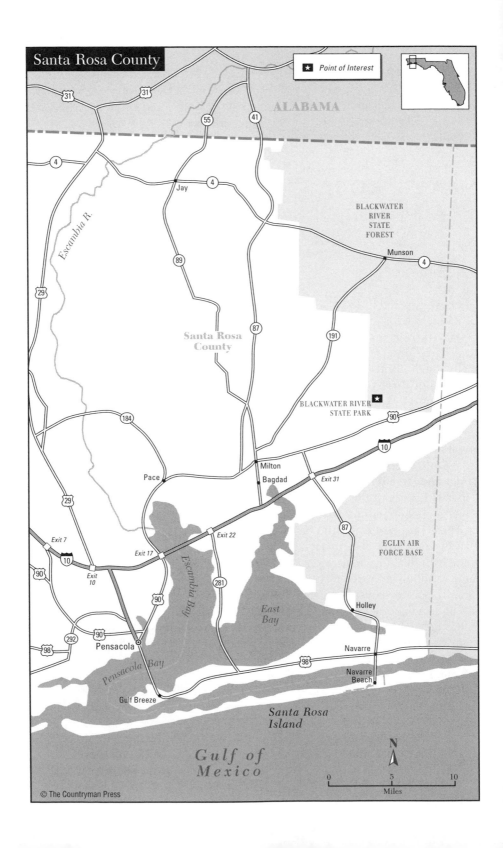

historic Milton and the Blackwater River State Forest. Not to confuse Santa Rosa County with the beach of the same name, you'll find Santa Rosa Beach located in Walton County west of Destin (see The Emerald Coast & the Beaches of South Walton chapter). In Milton, stop at the Santa Rosa County Chamber of Commerce, at the corner of FL 87 and Berryhill, for local information.

GETTING THERE *By air*: **Okaloosa Regional Airport** (850-651-7160), **Panama City/Bay County International Airport** (850-763-6751), **Pensacola Regional Airport** (850-436-5005).

By bus: **Greyhound** (1-800-231-2222).

By car: **I-10** and **FL 90** run east–west along the Panhandle. **FL 29** and **FL 90** bring you through Pensacola, then south to Pensacola Beach. **US 98** also runs east–west and will take you along the beaches from Panama City right up to Pensacola.

GETTING AROUND **US 98** cuts through the center of mainland towns Navarre and Gulf Breeze, where speed traps are notorious. You'll find the hub of Navarre at the junction of **US 98** and **FL 87.** To get to the beach, which is about a mile from the mainland, you'll need to cross over Santa Rosa Sound from **US 98** on the Navarre Beach Causeway. Milton is in the north end of the county, away from beach areas. To get there, head north on **FL 87** from **US 98** or **I-10** until you see the signs for the town center and Blackwater River State Park. For those puzzling over their maps, Santa Rosa *Beach* is not in this county, it's over in Walton County between Destin and Panama City (see The Emerald Coast & the Beaches of South Walton chapter).

MEDICAL EMERGENCIES To the west is **Sacred Heart Hospital** (850-416-7000) in Pensacola and **Baptist Hospital** in West Pensacola (850-434-4011). To the east, in the Destin and Fort Walton area, you find **Fort Walton Beach Medical Center** (850-862-1111) and **Twin Cities Hospital** (850-678-4131).

PARKING Milton has free two-hour parking throughout downtown.

✳ To See

ARCHEOLOGICAL SITES Dating back to 1830, the **Arcadia Mill Complex** (850-628-4438; www.uwf.edu/anthropology/research/arcadia.cfm), 5709 Mill Pond Ln, Milton, was the first and largest industrial complex built in Florida. Excavation of the site began in 1990 under the auspices of the University of West Florida. It includes a silk cocoonery, along with water-powered sawmill, gristmill, cotton mill, and textile mill, all of which turned local resources into trade goods. Now that the land surrounding it has been preserved, it is open to the public for free guided walking tours and a museum has been built on the site.

ART GALLERIES In the historic Faircloth-Carroll House, the **Dragonfly Gallery** (850- 981-1100), 5188 Escambia St, Milton, showcases the creativity of local artists—stained glass, photography, folk art, natural wood sculptures with stone

DRAGONFLY GALLERY

Sandra Friend

accents, and fine paintings in acrylics and oils. Open Tue–Fri 10–4, Sat 10–2.

HISTORIC SITES

Bagdad

At one time, everything you needed to build a house was created in Bagdad, so it's no surprise that so many fine homes remain. Stop in at the Bagdad Village Museum (see *Museums*) for a walking tour brochure and to visit the 1867 post office and New Providence Missionary Baptist Church as well as an original shotgun cottage. The imposing **Thompson House,** 4620 Forsyth St, can't be missed—it's a Greek Revival home that was built in 1847 for timber baron Benjamin Thompson; Union troops camped on the front lawn in October 1864. You'll find it along FL 191, but it is a private residence, so enjoy it from a distance.

Harold

Paralleling US 90 between the Harold Store and CR 87, the **Old Pensacola Highway** is a stretch of historic roadway now used as a footpath for the Florida Trail. Completed in 1921, this early brick highway known as Florida Highway 1 connected Pensacola with Jacksonville, enabling Model Ts to putter across the state.

Milton

Milton boasts 117 buildings of historic significance, from 1850s Victorians to Spanish Mission–style homes erected during the 1920s boom. Listed on the National Register of Historic Places, the Bungalow/Craftsman, Late Victorian, Greek, Gothic, and Colonial Revival styles are evident in structures such as the 1872 **St. Mary's Episcopal Church and Rectory,** 300–301 Oak St, built in the Greek and Gothic Revival styles, respectively. The church is also known as the **McDougall House,** because the town's physician, Dr. Charles E. McDougall, who was also the rector, built it. A little-known fact shared by one of my home-

ONE OF BAGDAD'S MANY HISTORIC HOMES

Sandra Friend

owner friends in Milton pertains to the city's Ringling legacy: In one of his many ventures during the 1920s Florida boom, circus magnate John Ringling built a grand hotel in Milton that never opened. Rather than let the costly materials go to waste, resourceful residents recycled portions of the hotel into their home construction, including doors, mantles, and decorative elements. Pick up *Tour of Milton's Historic Sites and Murals,* a brochure, to discover the city's many landmarks,

Sandra Friend

THOMPSON HOUSE

among them the 1872 **Milligan-Kil-martin House,** 6820 Berryhill St, a gingerbread Victorian from 1872 built by a Confederate veteran who later went on to rename the town of Chaffin, up the road, to Milligan. The steamboat-style **Williams Shields House,** 6810 Berryhill St, dates back to 1887. The **Santa Rosa County Courthouse,** 6865 Caroline St, was dedicated on July 4, 1927, and the Gothic **Olliner-Cobb-Tilghman House,** 6829 Pine St, is a large Gulf Coast cottage dating from 1871. A simple cottage, the **Ollinger-Cobb House** (circa 1870), 302 Pine St, includes Gothic elements. The home was built by Joseph Ollinger, a ship's carpenter and immigrant from Luxembourg. The historic Milton Depot is now a museum (see *Railroadiana*).

MEMORIAL One of the more moving memorials I've encountered is the **Veterans Memorial** at the Riverwalk in Milton. Reflective slabs of black granite hold relief images of warfare, with a roll call of all American wars and their key dates, each with a sidebar of the population of the United States at that time, the Commander in Chief, number of service members, combat deaths, and casualties. It was a history lesson that gave me the chills—especially when I saw the blank panels remaining to be inscribed.

MURALS Five large murals decorate the sides of historic buildings in downtown Milton. Pick up *Tour of Milton's Historic Sites and Murals* (see *Historic Sites*) to track them down.

MUSEUMS

Bagdad

Open the first Sat of the month and by appointment, the **Bagdad Village Museum** (850-623-5771; www.bagdadvillage.org) showcases artifacts of the early logging and shipping history that shaped this riverside town, as well as local architecture and domestic life in the 1920s. The complex includes a shotgun cottage and the original town post office.

Milton

The Santa Rosa Historical Society manages the **Museum of Local His-**

ONE OF MILTON'S MURALS

Sandra Friend

tory (850-626-9830; www.miltonflhistoricalsociety.org/museum.htm), US 90, in the historic Imogene Theatre. Showcasing artifacts and photos from the early days of Milton, it's a volunteer effort open Wed 10–4 or by appointment; free.

RAILROADIANA ✔ Housed in the historic Milton Depot, the **West Florida Railroad Museum** (850-623-3645; www.wfrm.org), 206 Henry St, focuses on the railroad history of the historic logging districts of northwest Florida and southern Alabama, particularly the L&N Railroad. Volunteers continue active restoration of rolling stock (some of which dates back to 1911); their current focus is a dining car. See the live coal-burning miniature steam engine, walk through the Museum of Railroading History, and come for the annual open house, their big event, in October. Open Fri and Sat 10–3, or by appointment.

ZOOLOGICAL AND MARINE PARK Ride the Safari Line train through 30 acres of free-ranging wild animals at **Northwest Florida Zoological Park** and **Botanical Gardens** (850-932-2229; www.thezoonorthwestflorida.org), 5701 Gulf Breeze Pkwy, Gulf Breeze, where you'll see wildebeests, pygmy hippos, capybaras, and more. Then walk along the perimeter enclosures to get an up-close look at lions, tigers, and bears. Oh my! Open daily 9–5 in-season, 9–4 during winter months; $12 adults, $11 ages 62 and up, $8 ages 3–11.

✳ To Do

BICYCLING Love the salt air in your lungs while pedaling? You've come to the right place. The coastal **Navarre Bicycle Path** links Navarre Beach with Gulf Islands National Seashore; the link is almost complete to the **Pensacola Bicycle Path,** which extends through the commercial district out to Fort Pickens. Inside this segment of the national seashore, there are several more miles of hard-packed biking trail between Battery Langdon and Fort Pickens. You can rent beach cruisers on Navarre Beach for $10 a day at **Eco-Beach Store** (850-936-7263; www.eco-beach.com), 8460 Gulf Blvd. Open daily 8–5, with extended summer hours (see also *Paddling*).

The **Blackwater River Heritage Trail** (850-983-5363), 7720 Deaton Bridge Rd, is the region's premier forested cycling venue, a paved rail-trail on the old Whiting Naval Railway. It stretches 8.5 miles, following the Blackwater River north from Milton.

WEST FLORIDA RAILROAD MUSEUM
Sandra Friend

BOATING Boaters can tie up at the **Riverwalk** in Milton to wander into town for a bite to eat or some shopping.

FAMILY ACTIVITIES ✔ Strap on a pair of skates at **Skateland** (850-623-9415; www.skatelandmilton.com), 6056 N Stewart St, Milton, a massive roller rink that's popular with the younger set.

Santa Rosa County TDC

KITE FLYING ON NAVARRE BEACH

GOLF The par 36 and par 72 courses at the **Tiger Point Golf and Country Club** (850-932-1330; www.tiger pointclub.com), 1255 Country Club Rd, Gulf Breeze, feature views of Santa Rosa Sound. The East Course is the favorite, designed in the Scottish style.

Tee off at the spectacular 18-hole, par 72 course at **Hidden Creek Golf Club** (850-939-1939; www.hidden-golf.com), 3070 PGA Blvd, Navarre.

HIKING Blackwater River State Forest (see *Green Space—Wild Places*) is a prime destination for backpackers and day hikers, with a half dozen loop trails and one spectacular segment of the Florida Trail running 38 miles from Deaton Bridge to the Alabama state line. A truly hidden treasure best visited in early April, the **Clear Creek Nature Trail,** just outside the gates of Whiting Air Force Base, is a short loop with spectacular punch—Clear Creek is lined with the densest array of pitcher plants I've ever seen along a stream. At the south end of the county, both **Garcon Point** and **Yellow River Preserves** showcase a stunning display of pitcher plants each spring along their trails. For more ideas, check out the Northwest Florida Interactive Trails Map (www.beaches-rivers.com/trailsmap/index.html).

PADDLING Adventures Unlimited Outdoor Center (850-623-6197 or 1-800-239-6864; www.adventures unlimited.com), 12 miles north of Milton off CR 87, has offered canoeing, tubing, and kayaking down Coldwater Creek, Juniper Creek, and the Blackwater River since 1975. You'll also enjoy land activities such as the ropes course, hiking, biking, and hayrides. Founder Jack Sanborn was stationed at Whiting Field and decided he wanted to start a business that kept him outdoors. He's parlayed the original 12 canoes into a complex where guests can stay in relocated, renovated historic cabins, even a schoolhouse (see *Lodging*), and has earned Milton the title of the "Canoe Capital of Florida." Paddling excursions start at $20 per person and can

HIKERS PAUL & WALLIS MAYO AT BLACK-WATER RIVER STATE FOREST

Sandra Friend

Sandra Friend

PADDLING THE BLACKWATER RIVER

run from 4–18 miles for a day trip. The staff can also arrange overnight trips of up to three days.

Whether you want a short or long canoe or kayak trip or just want to go tubing, **Blackwater Canoe Rental** (850-623-0235), Milton, has several rental packages on the pristine Blackwater River. The snow-white sandbars are graced on each side by magnolias and river cedar. Can't you just smell the fresh air? At **Bob's Canoe Rental** (850-623-5457), FL 191, rent tubes, canoes, and kayaks for a paddle down Coldwater Creek, one of the most beautiful of the Blackwater River's tributaries; shuttles included in price.

& After two major hurricanes, Mike and Caryn Martino's home was completely demolished. You'd think they'd have packed up and headed back to California, but the couple is so in love with the area, I suspect they'll never leave. Go for a paddle with them at **Eco-Beach Store** (850-936-7263; www.eco-beach.com), 8460 Gulf Blvd, Navarre Beach. Kayaks rent for $10 per hour, $35 per day. Their beach store has everything for fun in the sun, and they also rent surfboards, beach chairs, beach wheelchairs, fishing poles, and beach cruisers (see *Bicycling*). Open daily 8–5, with extended hours during the summer season.

SPA THERAPY Step inside the gorgeous **Villa Soleil Day Spa** (850-936-6850; www.villasoleilspa.com), 8006 Navarre Pkwy, Navarre, on mainland US 98, and you will immediately relax. The full-service spa offers full-body treatments, such as aqua facials ($106), hot stone massages, body wraps with aromatic oils (starting at $115), remineralizing body masks ($35–55), hydrotherapy ($35–55), and deep sea salt scrubs (starting at $125). For something different, you'll want to try the unique Ashiatsu Oriental bar therapy ($76–166), which uses deep compression massage using feet, and the thai massage ($76–166), which involves a lot of stretching and assisted Hatha yoga poses. After your treatment, plan to spend a little time in the nature garden or rest in the quiet room, which has a selection of teas and juice. They insist you take a few moments to "come back to the real world." Yoga and belly dancing classes are also available.

ALONG THE BLACKWATER

Sandra Friend

SURFING Catch a wave at **Eco-Beach Store** (850-936-7263; www.eco-beach .com), 8460 Gulf Blvd, Navarre Beach, where Mike Martino will get you up and hanging 10 in no time with individualized surfing lessons and surf clinics; board rentals available. Open daily 8–5, with extended hours in during the summer season.

TUBING Coldwater Creek is *the* destination for floating down a lazy creek in an inner tube. Check with the outfitters listed under *Paddling* for logistics.

WALKING TOURS Talk a stroll along the beautiful banks of the Blackwater River in historic **Bagdad Village** (www.bagdadvillage.org). Listed on the National Register of Historic Places with 143 buildings, the Village's frame vernacular and Greek Revival architecture dates back to the mid-1800s. Built with Creole elements by former slaves, Bagdad Village is located just north of Milton. Maps and guided tours are available by calling 850-623-8493 or through the Santa Rosa County Tourist and Development Council (see *Guidance*).

The **Milton Historic District,** also listed on the National Register of Historic Places, contains a day's worth of exploring, with homes and structures dating from 1850 to 1945 (see *Historic Sites* and *Museums* under *To See*).

✳ Green Space

BEACHES Along CR 399, the public strands at **Navarre Beach State Park** (850-936-6188; www.floridastateparks.org/navarrebeach), 8579 Gulf Blvd, Navarre, protect more than 1,600 acres of vanishing coastal habitats like dune lakes, sand pine scrub, and ancient longleaf pines. The park abuts the easternmost point of **Gulf Islands National Seashore,** Opal Beach.

GREENWAY ⅙ **Blackwater Heritage Trail State Park** (850-245-2052), 5533 Alabama St, Milton, is a paved, linear 8.5-mile biking and hiking trail following the historical route of the Florida & Alabama Railroad, with nice views of the Blackwater River. Free.

PARK Blackwater River State Park (850-983-5363; www.florida stateparks.org/blackwaterriver), 7720 Deaton Bridge Rd, Holt. Bask on a sandy freshwater beach, hike the Chain of Lakes Trail along ancient oxbows in the floodplain, or drop your kayak in for a scenic trip along one of the purest sand-bottomed rivers in the world. The park offers a campground with electric and water hook-ups, plus primitive camping for backpackers along the Juniper Creek Trail, part of the Florida Trail System. Fee.

TWO ANGLERS SHARE NAVARRE BEACH.
Santa Rosa County TDC

WILD PLACES At **Blackwater River State Forest** (850-957-6140; www.fl-dof.com/state_forests/blackwater_river.html), 11650 Munson Hwy, Milton, immerse yourself in the largest state forest in Florida—190,000 acres surrounding the Blackwater River and its tributaries. Fingers of red clay seep down from Alabama, exposed in outcroppings like the tall cliffs above Juniper Creek. With high ground topped with longleaf pine and wiregrass, the undulating landscape seems to stretch on forever. Paddling, hiking, and hunting are the major draws to this vast wilderness: enjoy backpacking 38 miles of the Florida Trail, drop your kayak in at Red Rock, or utilize one of three reservoirs built especially as fish management areas—Karick, Hurricane, and Bear Lakes. With six campgrounds and recreation areas to choose from, you won't run out of things to do!

Sandra Friend

GARCON POINT PRESERVE

Just outside the gates of Whiting Naval Air Station north of Milton off FL 87, **Clear Creek** is protected by military and conservancy lands. Follow the Clear Creek Nature Trail for one of the most spectacular scenes in natural Florida when you arrive in late March–early April in time to see thousands of pitcher plants in bloom along the boardwalk.

Garcon Point Preserve (850-539-5999), FL 191 just north of the Garcon Point Bridge tollbooth, offers more than 4 miles of trails through open prairies and pine flatwoods, providing panoramic views of Blackwater Bay and close encounters with carnivorous pitcher plants. Open sunrise–sunset; free.

CLEAR CREEK FLORA

Sandra Friend

Florida's largest pitcher plant prairie is protected at **Yellow River Marsh Preserve State Park** (850-983-5363; www.floridastateparks.org/yellow river), FL 191 south of Bagdad at Dickerson City Rd. There are no formal trails yet, but there is a parking area as well as plenty of colorful blooms to explore in April—bring your GPS to find your way back. Open sunrise–sunset; free.

✳ Lodging

Because Santa Rosa County is a quiet getaway destination, lodging is limited to vacation properties at the beach and camping inland. You'll also find a few small chain motels along US 98.

CONDO HOTEL RESORTS Stay at any one of four condo hotels, all on Gulf Blvd on Navarre Beach. The stately 19-story **Pearl** with tropical lanscaping, the 12-story **Navarre Towers** with angled balconies, the **Regency** with 9-foot ceilings, and **Summer Wind Resort** with floor-to-ceiling glass overlooking the Gulf of Mexico are all managed Navarre Properties (850-936-1312 or 1-866-936-1312; www.navarrelistings.com). Nestled on a narrow strip on Navarre Beach, each property overlooks the Gulf of Mexico and Santa Rosa Sound. Amenities feature heated swimming pools, exercise rooms, and barbeque areas. One-, two-, and three-bedroom condo units are offered ($108–292 daily, $650–2,625 weekly, $1,350–3,050 monthly, winter only). Vacation town homes are also available. Each unit is owned independently, so decor is of the owners' choosing; you can take a virtual tour of all units on the web site. Check-in is at Navarre Properties, 1818 Alpine Ave, Navarre.

VACATION HOMES Ocean Reef Resort Properties (850-837-3935; www.oceanreefresorts.com) offers furnished cottages, beach homes, condos, town homes, luxury homes, and resorts by the day, week, or month. One of the largest suppliers of fully furnished homes, the folks at **Resort-Quest** (www.resortquest.com) can select which will be right for you— from condos in resort-style settings to portfolio homes with private pools. **Century 21 Island View Realty, Inc.** (850-939-2774 or 1-800-757-2121; www.c21ivr.com), 8510 Navarre Pkwy, Navarre, offers accommodations from quaint villas overlooking the sound to oceanfront condos, such as at The Pearl (see *Condo Hotel Resorts*). Give Sean Golden a call at **Beach House Rentals** for a number of superb vacation homes in and around Navarre Beach (1-800-565-0400; www.beachhouserentals.com). The bonus with these rentals is that Sean lives in the area, so he can be right there if you need assistance.

HOTELS, MOTELS, AND RESORTS
Milton 32570
In the 1930s, it served as a working schoolhouse in Fidelis; now, it provides a retreat in a most restful setting. Tucked away in the forest at Adventures Unlimited (see *Campgrounds*), the **Old School House Inn** showcases original beadboard walls and ceiling and hardwood floors in each of its literary-themed rooms: Poets, Audubon, Faulkner, Dr. Seuss, Hemingway, Mitchell, Rawlings, Twain. My room, Margaret Mitchell,

ROOM AT THE SCHOOL HOUSE INN

Sandra Friend

boasted a set of related books on the mantle, photos from the Civil War period, and a framed image of Tara above the bed. I appreciated being able to sit in a rocking chair on the porch while sipping my morning coffee and reading a novel. No phones, no television, and no Internet access—but you'll appreciate the coffeemaker, microwave, and small fridge. Rates run $79–109 per night with a two-night minimum; weekly rates start at $474, a small price to pay for seven days unplugged.

CAMPGROUNDS

Milton 32570

Adventures Unlimited (850-623-6197 or 1-800-239-6864; www .adventuresunlimited.com), 12 miles north of Milton off CR 87, offers a wide variety of accommodations, including cabins, motel rooms, and camping. Stay in the Old School House Inn (see *Hotels, Motels, and Resorts*) or choose from a variety of fully equipped cottages with country charm and sizes to fit every family, from Granny Peadon's Cottage with period furnishing and a back porch overlooking Wolfe Creek ($109–119) to the Fox Den Bungalow with its fireplace. For something more basic, try the rustic one- and two-room camping-style cabins with air-conditioning and bunk beds ($39–59), some of which are along the creeks. Primitive campsites are $15 ($20 with hook-up).

Blackwater River State Forest (see *Green Space—Wild Places*) has six campgrounds amid its sweep of 190,000 acres between Milton and Alabama. My favorite is **North Hurricane Lake,** a scenic site along the Florida Trail, but the bathhouse at **North Karick Lake** can't be beat.

Each campground is centered on a recreation area along one of the "lakes" (reservoirs, really) and offers electric and water at sites tucked beneath the forest canopy, as well as direct access to hiking trails, paddling, and fishing. The other campgrounds are from South Hurricane Lake (tents only), Krul Recreation Area, South Karick Lake, and Bear Lake Recreation Area.

At **Blackwater River State Park** (see *Green Space—Park*), 30 campsites with electric and water hook-ups offer easy access to paddling and hiking expeditions. The sites book up every weekend, so reserve well in advance.

✳ Where to Eat

DINING OUT

Milton

A gas station revitalized as bistro dining—that's the **Mainstreet Café** (850-626-3376), 6820 Caroline St, the hot upscale spot in downtown Milton, featuring "fine dining in a casual atmosphere." Lunch includes gourmet-style deli sandwiches, wraps, and a classic cheeseburger or grouper sandwich ($6–8). Their dinner menu changes weekly. On my visit, I encountered crabcakes with fried green tomatoes, amberjack, grouper, and duck, $16–21. It's a popular hangout for locals, not just for the food but for live music Thu–Sat nights.

Navarre Beach

The New Orleans–style **Cocodries** (850-939-8777), 8649 Gulf Blvd, is located right on Navarre Beach, just as you cross over the sound. With stellar service, it's a nice place near the beach accommodations. Reasonably priced, it features mainly seafood, with pasta and meat entrées for landlubbers ($6–11 for sandwiches and salads; $12–25 for entrées).

EATING OUT

East Milton

🍴 Savor the view at **Reggie's Seafood & Bar-B-Que** (850-623-3126), 7040 US 90, perched above the Blackwater River across from downtown. Your meal is made to order, be it oyster stew, a seafood platter with fresh fish, or a barbecued pork sandwich, all served up with sides like black-eyed peas, turnip greens, candied yam, fried okra, and corn nuggets ($4–15). All barbecue is smoked with local bay wood and served up sloppy, just the way I like it. Kudos for the perfect sweet tea!

Milton

At **Kwik Burger** (850-623-6942), 5173 Stewart St, "Mama Bass" is a legend, and her homemade pies (apple and egg custard are favorites) and fresh veggies with dinner keep a regular clientele coming back. You'll often see her shelling a pile of peas while she cooks up the best southern fried chicken you've had in years. Open for breakfast, lunch, and dinner; closed Sun.

A manatee mural on the exterior makes **Manatee's** (850-981-1464), 5365 Stewart St, especially distinctive, and inside, they have those Gulf munchies I've grown to love, like fried dill pickle chips, fried green tomatoes, fried shrimp po'boy, and fresh marinated tuna. Platters and sandwiches $8–10, entrées $16–20; and a nice Jamaican banana pie to top it all off.

Munson

Ruth's Country Store (850-957-4463), corner of FL 4 and CR 191.

Established in the 1940s in a onetime timber industry boomtown, this quaint country store has deep local roots—Bobby (Ruth's son) grew up sleeping under the cash register, and his wife, Patty, offers a great little breakfast in the back room. Gather around the picnic table and order up fresh pancakes, omelets, and eggs and bacon, or stop in for burgers and dogs at lunch on your way to Blackwater River State Forest. Open 6–2; meals $1–5.

Navarre Beach

For fresh baked breads and hot coffee, start your mornings at **Sailors' Grill & Bakery/Winery Shop** (850-939-1092), 1451 Navarre Beach Blvd (corner of Gulf Blvd). Cold beer and wine coolers can be found next door at **Juana's Pagoda** (850-939-2130). This meet-and-greet spot is best around sunset.

FARMER'S MARKETS All during the growing season, the **Santa Rosa County Vegetable Growers Association** holds a daily market on US 90 in Milton from noon until all produce is sold. Stop by the **Riverwalk** for a farmer's market Tue, Thu, and Sat 7:30–1.

MAINSTREET CAFÉ

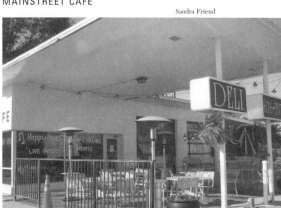

Sandra Friend

✳ Selective Shopping

Bagdad

Just off the I-10 exit for Bagdad, **Stuckey's** (850-623-2522), 3675 Garcon Point Rd, is the last of its breed. Back in the 1960s, I saved up my allowance to buy pecan pralines whenever we'd stop at Stuckey's on a road trip, and I still have an old brochure that shows more than a dozen in Florida in the 1970s. But in Florida today, only this store remains in its original building (shared with a Dairy Queen) and retains the kitschy ambience and southern charm—not to mention all the classic candy I remember from childhood.

HISTORIC DOWNTOWN MILTON
Santa Rosa County TDC

East Milton

With dozens of dealer booths spaciously spread out beneath one roof, **The Copper Possum** (850-626-4492), US 90, is a pleasure to explore. First, it's fully air-conditioned. The booths contain all sorts of treasures, from a 1963 Chevy owner's guide to chewing tobacco molds, quilts, artifacts for historic home restoration like windows and sinks, fine antique furniture, and Floridiana. Since I had little time at the beach, I was glad to see an inexpensive sea shell vendor so I could bring a few goodies home for the kids.

Milton

Browse through a mix of old and new in a rambling historic home at **Camelot Junction** (850-981-1322), 5243 Berryhill St, where I found beaded lamps and birdhouses, candles and mirrors, fine china, antique bottles, art glass, and a pair of vintage water skis. Part of the house is set aside as a coffeehouse, where you can stop in 6–9 PM Fri and Sat for coffee and beignets while listening to local musicians jam.

Navarre Beach

You'll find antiques shops all along US 98 and FL 87, including the fine collections at **Empire Antique Services & Auction Company** (850-916-9833; www.empireantique service.com), 8700 Navarre Pkwy, and **Miss Donna's Antiques & Auctions** (850-939-9040; www.missdonnas .com), 3240 FL 87, in Navarre. Over in Gulf Breeze, you'll browse through more than 100 vendors at **The Flea Market** (850-934-1971; www.flea marketgulfbreeze.com), 5760 Gulf Breeze Pkwy.

"Got Sand?" That's the catch phrase at the Martinos' **Eco-Beach Store**

(850-936-7263; www.eco-beach.com), 8460 Gulf Blvd. The central hub of all activities on Navarre Beach, here you can rent beach equipment, go on paddling tours, and stock up on beach supplies, such as necessities like sunscreen and beer; open daily 9–5. **Caryn's Eco-Beach Shack** is located a few steps down the street at Cocodries (see *Dining Out*), where you can grab quick snacks on Fri, Sat, and Sun.

✳ Special Events

October: **Jay Peanut Festival,** first weekend, Gabbert Farms, Jay. A true farmers' festival, this annual event began more than 15 years ago and continues to delight large crowds that return each year for live music, pig chases, tractor pull, pet parade, and peanuts every way you can dream of eating them. Free.

November: The **Okaloosa County Fair and Fine Arts Show** takes place at the Okaloosa County Fairgrounds (850-862-0211).

✐ The family-friendly **Depot Days Arts and Crafts Festival** (850-623-3645; www.wfrm.org), 206 Henry St, is held the second weekend at the L&N Train Depot/West Florida Railroad Museum (see *To See— Railroadiana*).

PENSACOLA

Founded in 1559, **Pensacola,** nicknamed P'cola, interested Spanish explorers because of its large and easily defended deep-water harbor in Escambia Bay. Located in the extreme northwest section of Florida, it is an area filled with miles of white, sugar-sand beaches, fine museums, and outdoor adventure. The city's name is a corruption of "Panzacola," the name of the now-extinct Native American tribe that inhabited the area when the first European explorers arrived. First sighted by Spanish explorer Juan Ponce de León, the initial attempt at settlement was by Spanish explorer Don Tristán de Luna y Arellano in 1559. Two years later, the 1,400 colonists of the continental U.S.'s first European settlement met a devastating hurricane, and it wasn't until 1698 that more conquistadores arrived. This may be why many people regard St Augustine, which was founded in 1565, as the first official settlement in the United States. Throughout the following centuries, control of the city was passed through five flags: Spain had three reigning periods, 1698–1719, 1722–1763, and 1781–1819, with France taking control in 1719, with yet another hurricane driving the French out in 1722. At the end of the French and Indian War in 1763, England held the city until 1781, when the United States became the governing body. In January 1861, Florida became the third state to secede from the Union, giving control to the Confederate States of America. It wasn't until 1868 that Florida was readmitted to the Union. The people of Pensacola have seen their fair share of hurricanes, with the most recent—Opal in 1995 and category 4 "Ivan the Terrible" on September 15, 2004—causing devastating destruction. News reports around the world showed the damage to the I-10 bridge, which was open to traffic just one month later. Today, the resilient community is fully recovered, and as the locals say, "We're open for business!"

GUIDANCE **Pensacola Bay Area Convention & Visitors Bureau** (850-434-1234 or 1-800-874-1234; www.visitpensacola.com), 1401 E Gregory St, Pensacola 32502.

GETTING THERE *By air*: **Okaloosa Regional Airport** (850-651-7160), **Pensacola Regional Airport** (850-436-5005).
By bus: **Greyhound** (1-800-231-2222).

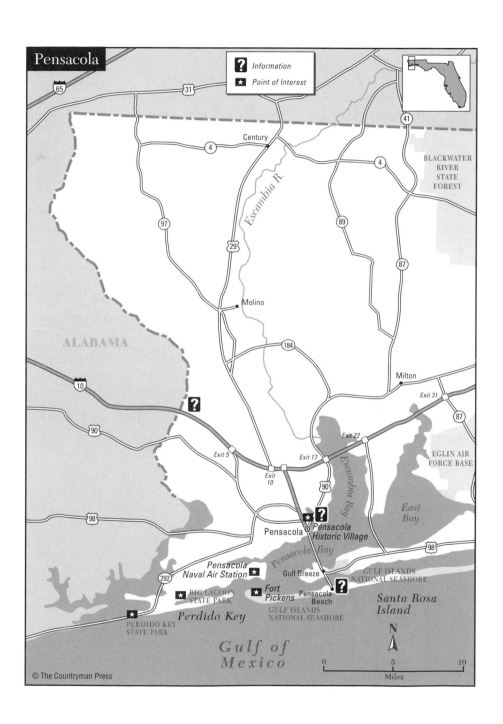

By car: **I-10** and **FL 90** run east–west along the Panhandle. **FL 29** and **FL 90** bring you through Pensacola, then south to Pensacola Beach. **US 98** also runs east–west and will take you along the beaches from Panama City right up to Pensacola.

GETTING AROUND Escambia County's **EGCAT** public transportation system runs 285 miles throughout the Pensacola area ($1.50 adults, 75¢ seniors, children shorter than the fare box ride free). The seasonal **Beach Trolley** operating Fri–Sun from Memorial Day to Labor Day is free for everyone (850-595-3228; www.goecat.com).

MEDICAL EMERGENCIES In Pensacola, **Sacred Heart Hospital** (850-416-7000); **Baptist Hospital** in West Pensacola (850-434-4011).

✳ To See

ART GALLERY AND MUSEUM **Pensacola Museum of Art** (850-432-6247; www.pensacolamuseumofart.org), 407 S Jefferson St, Pensacola. The museum's permanent collection is of 19th-, 20th-, and 21st-century artists, including John Marin and Salvador Dalí, with rotating exhibits by world-renowned artists such as George Rodrigue. The museum also has a superb collection of European and American glass, and African tribal art. From 1910 to the mid-1940s the building was used as a jail. Note original fixtures and hardware on many of the doors and windows. Open Tue–Fri 10–5, Sat and Sun noon–5. Fee.

A Means of Expression (850-434-6300 or 1-888-207-3123; www.ameansof expression.com), 215 E Zaragoza St, Pensacola, offers original works of art and high-quality reproductions in addition to fine crafts such as art furnishings and art glass, pottery, and jewelry.

HISTORIC SITES

Harold

Paralleling US 90 between the Harold Store and CR 87, the **Old Pensacola Highway** is a stretch of historic roadway. Completed in 1921, this early brick highway known as Florida Highway 1 connected Pensacola with Jacksonville, enabling Model Ts to putter across the state. It is now used as a footpath for the Florida Trail.

Pensacola

After Pensacola was selected to be the site of a federal naval yard in the early 1800s, four forts were constructed (or shored up) to protect it. Originally built by the British Royal Navy as a log redoubt in 1763, **Fort Barrancas** sits on a hill above the western shore of Pensacola Bay. The Spanish added their touches in 1797, and the fort went through another update between 1839 and 1844, supervised by Major William H. Chase. The nearby **Advanced Redoubt of Fort Barrancas** was built between 1845 and 1859 to protect the Pensacola Naval Yard but was never used. Accessible only by boat, **Fort McRee** on Perdido Key dated back to 1834, with 128 cannons trained on the entrance to Pensacola Bay.

It succumbed to erosion over the decades; only a single battery modified in 1942 remains. But of the four forts, **Fort Pickens** on Santa Rosa Island has the most storied history. Chase supervised construction between 1829 and 1834. Construction materials came from all over the world, including copper from Switzerland for the drains and granite from Sing-Sing; the fortress contains 21.5 million locally made bricks. The night before Florida seceded from the Union (January 10, 1860), Federal commander Lieutenant Adam J. Slemmer moved his men from the mainland to Fort Pickens to hold what President Lincoln considered a key position in coastal defenses. Confederate troops attempted to rout the entrenched Federals on September 2, 1861, during the Battle of Santa Rosa Island, but failed, and subsequently turned the city over to the Union forces. In 1886 the Apache chief Geronimo was imprisoned at the fort as a tourist attraction. Fort Pickens came into play during World War I with new defensive batteries constructed to protect Pensacola, but no shots were fired. All of Pensacola's forts are now part of Gulf Islands National Seashore (see *Green Space—Beaches*); fee.

The stucco on the circa 1932 **Crystal Ice Company Building,** 2024 N Davis St, conveys the impression of a block of ice. The one-story building is one of the few remaining examples of vernacular roadside commercial architecture in Pensacola.

In the Seville Historic District, the **Old Christ Church** is one of the oldest in the state, circa 1830–1832. Several concerts are performed under the shady trees across from the church in Seville Square. Guided tours at 9 and 2:30; fee.

First lit in 1859, the **Pensacola Lighthouse** stands on a 40-foot hill above Fort Barrancas at the Pensacola Naval Station. Its first-order Fresnel lens was removed during the Civil War for safekeeping, since the lighthouse was an easy target for cannonades, and reinstalled in 1869. Open for tours May–Oct, Sun noon–4; fee.

MEMORIALS The **Florida Vietnam Veterans Memorial** on Bayfront Pkwy near Ninth Ave is the nation's only full-name, permanent replica of the Vietnam Veterans Memorial in Washington, DC.

The historic **St. Michael's Cemetery** (www.stmichaelscemetery.org), at the corner of Alcaniz and Chase streets in Pensacola, dates back to 1822, with 3,200 marked burials. Open daily.

MUSEUMS **Bearheart Gallery** at Native Paths Cultural Heritage and Resource Center (www.perdidobaytribe.org), 400 S Alcaniz St, Pensacola. Learn about the heritage and culture of the Lower Muskogee Creek Indians from the chief of Perdido Bay Tribe.

Civil War Soldiers Museum (850-469-1900), 108 S Palafox Place, Pensacola. A fascinating look into Florida's Civil War history, in which Pensacola played a pivotal role—Abraham Lincoln sent troops to take Fort Pickens before the first shots were fired at Fort Sumter. Don't miss the video *The Civil War in Pensacola* for the details. Browse one of the country's largest displays of Civil War medical artifacts. Open Tue–Sat 10–4:30; fee.

Cafés border the grassy **Historic Seville Square** in the center of Historic Pensacola Village (850-595-5985; www.historicpensacola.org). Take a walk around

MORENO COTTAGE IN HISTORIC
PENSACOLA VILLAGE

the neighboring blocks to see furnished period homes spanning from the earliest Spanish settlements to the heyday of the 1920s. Guided tours are available through 18th- and 19th-century homes, featuring the Julee Cottage built in 1804, home to Julee Panton, a free woman of color during the era of slavery. Open Mon–Sat 10–4, with tours at 11, 1, and 2:30 PM; fee.

& Exhibits of the navy's role in the nation's defense are found at **National Museum of Naval Aviation** (850-452-2311), 750 Radford Blvd, Pensacola, with more than 140 beautifully restored aircraft from U.S. Navy, Marine Corps, and Coast Guard aviation. You'll see wood-and-fabric biplanes, an NC-4 flying boat, and a Douglas "Dauntless" bomber in Hangar Bay. Then fly an FA-18 flight simulator on a mission in Desert Storm. See *The Magic of Flight* on the seven-story-high IMAX screen. If the Kennedy Space Center is the place to be on the east coast, then this is the place to be on the west. Open daily. Free.

Pensacola Historical Museum (850-438-1559), 405 S Adams St, Pensacola. Learn about the city of five flags through extensive exhibits on and artifacts from Pensacola's colorful history—from the clay deposits that provided the city's brick streets through the "Gallant capture of a lady's wardrobe" Civil War–era cartoon poking fun at Florida's troops. Open Mon–Sat 9–4:30; fee.

✐ At the **T.T. Wentworth, Jr. Florida State Museum** (www.historicpensa cola.org), Pensacola, you'll discover artifacts collected throughout west Florida by Theodore Thomas Wentworth Jr., for whom the museum is named. The collection of more than 100,000 items is housed in the 1908 City Hall on three floors. You'll find the **Discovery Gallery** children's museum on the third floor. Open Mon–Sat 10–4. Donations appreciated.

WEAVERS COTTAGE IN HISTORIC PEN-
SACOLA VILLAGE

SCENIC DRIVES The city park on the **Pensacola Scenic Bluffs Highway** offers an outstanding view of Escambia Bay. Designated a Scenic Byway in April 1998, the Bluffs takes you amid moss-draped oaks and stately magnolias with scenic vistas along the way. At one point you'll reach the highest point along the entire Florida coastline. Then continue through freshwater and tidal wetlands down to the Escambia River.

SCENIC TOURS Watch dolphins play in the water off Pensacola with **Brown's Inshore Guide Service** (1-877-981-6246; www.brownsinshore.com). Captain David Brown also does fishing trips (see *To Do—Fishing*).

✳ To Do

BICYCLING The **Pensacola Bicycle Path** extends through the commercial district out to the entrance to Fort Pickens, paralleling CR 399. The segment inside the national seashore washed away, but I'd expect to see it rebuilt. Meanwhile, active rebuilding of the connection to the **Navarre Bicycle Trail** is going on at the east end of Pensacola Beach, along the scenic University of West Florida Dunes Preserve.

FAMILY ACTIVITIES ✍ At **Sam's Fun City** (850-505-0800; www.samsfuncity .com), 6709 Pensacola Blvd, Pensacola, you stay dry or get as wet as you like. At Surf City you'll be soaked on four thrilling water slides, two interactive children's pools with mini slides, and a 750-foot winding lazy river, and then dry off at Fun City, which features go-carts, mini golf, and more than a dozen amusement rides. Fun City also has bumper boats, if you want to get a bit of a splash. The only park of its type in the area, it's open daily year-round, 11–10. Rides $3–7; wristband combo passes for rides and water park, $10–40.

✍ For laid-back family fun, head to **Tiki Island Golf and Games** (850-932-1550), 2 Via Del Luna Dr, Pensacola Beach, where you can spread out a picnic and play a round of mini golf at the tropically landscaped entertainment center. The 18-hole course dotted with palm trees and waterfalls will ensure the fun lasts a long time. When your game is over, head into the arcade for a game of Skee-Ball. It's located right on the beach, so you can take a nice stroll with one of their famous ice creams or rent a family-sized bicycle. Open daily year-round 11–10, with later hours on weekends and in summer. A round of mini golf is $6.25 for adults, $5.25 ages 12 and under.

FISHING At **Brown's Inshore Guide Service** (1-877-981-6246; www.brownsinshore.com), Captain David Brown will customize your charter trip, even an excellent fly-fishing trip. Day or night fishing on four- to eight-hour trips include tackle, bait, and fish cleaning. Captain Brown also offers scenic dolphin tours.

Go fishing for the big one with **Captain Wes Rozier** (850-982-7858 or 850-457-7476; www.captwesrozier .com); Captain Wes will regale you with a number of fish tales and local lore. Search out trout hidden in the grass flats or flounder in the mud flats; these are just some of the many species of fish you'll catch. Trips from four to six hours ($255–335).

THE ENTRANCE TO FORT PICKENS

Sandra Friend

Go bottom fishing or trolling with **Livewire Offshore Charters** (850-439-6601 or 850-384-9059; www.fishlivewire.com). Captain Michael Choron will take you out on his 33-foot Blackfin for two- to eight-hour cruises ($300–950 for six people). Rod, reels, bait, tackle, licenses, ice, and water are included; bring your own food.

GOLF Lose yourself at the legendary 18-hole, par 72 Arnold Palmer **Lost Key Golf Club** (1-888-256-7853; www.lostkey.com), 625 Lost Key Dr, Perdido Key. The challenging, heavily wooded course is so much so that golf carts with a GPS yardage system are mandatory.

HIKING The **Florida Trail** (see *What's Where*) is the country's only National Scenic Trail to traverse a beach—and not just any beach, but the sparkling white-sand strands of Santa Rosa Island, up to the trail's northern terminus at Fort Pickens. My pick for a coastal day hike, however, is where the trail scoots across CR 399 and travels for several miles through the undulating bayside dunes of the **University of West Florida Dunes Preserve;** access is from the Pensacola Bicycle Path (see *Bicycling*). You'll also find coastal nature trails at Big Lagoon State Park (see *Green Space—Beaches*) and Tarkiln Bayou State Park (see *Green Space—Wild Place*).

✳ Green Space

BEACHES Big Lagoon State Park (850-492-1595), 12301 Gulf Beach Hwy, Pensacola. Along the edge of Pensacola's Big Lagoon, this 712-acre park provides camping, picnicking, fishing, and a nature trail that leads to a tall observation tower. Fee.

Gulf Islands National Seashore (850-934-2600; www.nps.gov/guis/), 1801 Gulf Breeze Pkwy, Pensacola Beach. Broken into seven segments along Florida's coast, this expansive seaside park includes Pensacola's historic forts, great swimming beaches on Santa Rosa Island and Perdido Key, and the Naval Live Oaks Preserve with its ancient live oak grove culled for shipbuilding over the centuries. Fee.

At **Perdido Key State Park** (850-492-1595), 12301 Gulf Beach Hwy, Pensacola, you're as far west as you can get in the Florida State Parks system; the coastal scrub and beaches preserved here are home to the tiny, federally endangered Santa Rosa beach mouse.

HIKERS ON PENSACOLA BEACH

Sandra Friend

PARK Hawkshaw Lagoon Memorial Park (850-434-1234), located next to Bayfront Parkway, across from Veteran's Memorial Park in downtown Pensacola. Part of a habitat restoration project, this is a perfect location for spotting cormorants, pelicans, and great blue herons. The pedestrian bridge spanning the lagoon serves as a

PERDIDO KEY

platform for the memorial sculpture *The Sanctuary*, the National Memorial for Missing Children.

WILD PLACE ᕟ Walk through wild wet pine flatwoods on a mild paved pathway at **Tarkiln Bayou State Park** (850-492-1595; www.floridastateparks.org/tarkiln bayou), CR 293 south of US 98, or jump off the guided route and explore the woods on old jeep trails. At the end of the paved path, the Emma Claire Board-walk of Hope stretches across a colorful pitcher plant bog and ends at a scenic overlook on the bayou.

✳ Lodging

BED & BREAKFASTS

Pensacola 32501

Located in historic North Hill is the 1905 Tudor Revival **Noble Manor Bed & Breakfast** (850-434-9544; www.noblemanor.com), 110 W Strong St. Each room is nicely appointed with an eclectic mix of antique reproductions. The property also has a heated pool and outdoor hot tub. $79–119.

The Queen Anne Victorian **Pensacola Victorian Bed & Breakfast** (850-434-2818 or 1-800-370-8354; www.pensacolavictorian.com), 203 W Gregory St, was once a ship captain's home. Awaken each morning to fresh

TARKILN BAYOU

fruit, waffles, omelets, or quiche; you'll also be treated to complimentary fresh-baked treats and beverages throughout your stay. $75–110.

CONDO HOTEL RESORT
Perdido Key 32507
Take in the breathtaking view of the emerald green waters at **Eden** (850-492-3336; www.edencondominiums .com), 16821 Perdido Key Dr. The resort features a lush, tropical landscape with heated 176-foot Gulf-side pool complete with waterfalls. On cold or rainy days you'll love the heated indoor solarium with pool and gardens. Other amenities include indoor/outdoor hot tubs, an exercise club, and lighted tennis court for night play. One-, two-, and three-bedroom units come with full kitchens and washer/dryer. Daily $140–570, weekly $840–3,420, monthy $,1680– 4,080 (in fall and winter only).

VACATION HOMES Ocean Reef Resort Properties (850-837-3935; www.oceanreefresorts.com) offers furnished cottages, beach homes, condos, town homes, luxury homes, and resorts by the day, week, or month.

One of the largest suppliers of fully furnished homes, the folks at **Resort-Quest** (www.resortquest.com) can select which will be right for you— from condos in resort-style settings to portfolio homes with private pools, by the day, week, or month.

✳ Where to Eat
DINING OUT
Pensacola
At the seaside restaurant **The Fish House** (850-470-0003), 600 Barracks St, you'll want to be sure to try the Grits à Ya Ya ($13). This appetizer special is a meal in itself—grits are mixed in with spicy jumbo shrimp, spinach, portobello mushrooms, applewood-smoked bacon, garlic, shallots, and cream, and then if those calories weren't enough, the entire bowl is topped with a heaping helping of smoked Gouda cheese. For those wanting something lighter, the cashew-and-vidalia-crusted soft-shelled crab salad ($11), served with mandarin oranges, soy sauce reduction, and Thai red chile vinaigrette, is a good choice. Save room for a piece of Florida Key lime pie, served naturally yellow ($5). Open for lunch and dinner. This is a casual eatery that serves healthy portions, reasonably priced ($9–26).

EATING OUT
Pensacola
You can find places that serve 'gator, frog legs, turtle, crawfish, and other Florida fare throughout the state, but I believe **Ard's Cricket Ranch** (850-433-3838), 827 Lynch St, is the only spot to serve crickets. Yes, you can get them fried with a glass of beer. This is where to pick up your fishing and beach supplies, too—Ard's is also a bait shop and convenience store.

Lively Irish folk music and traditional fare are found at **McGuire's Irish Pub** (850-433-6789; www.mcguires irishpub.com), 600 E Gregory St. Sing-alongs are encouraged; if you don't learn the words, you'll have to kiss the moose, and that's no blarney. The senate bean soup is still only 18¢. You'll find a second location farther east in Destin.

Pensacola Beach
✍ **Flounder's Chowder House** (850-932-2003; www.flounderschowder

house.com), CR 399 at Fort Pickens Rd. Since 1979, this casual beach bar has been a Pensacola favorite, set in a playful tropical atmosphere befitting its setting on Santa Rosa Sound—right down to a lively pirate ship playground for the kids. From the oyster and corn chowder ($4) to Floyd Flounder's Flawless Full-Flavored Florida Flash-Fried Fresh Flounder ($20), you won't go wrong with the fresh seafood cramming the menu. Here for the band? Hoist a "dirty old Mason jar" full of "Diesel Fuel" while you toast your buddies over platters of baked oysters ($6–11) and seafood nachos ($13). Add speedy, friendly service for lunch and dinner daily, and this one's a winner.

A favorite of my hiking buddies, **Peg Leg Pete's** (850-932-4139; www .peglegpetes.com), 1010 Ft. Pickens Rd, survived the 2004–2005 hurricanes and looks as rugged as ever. With a real Florida Cracker atmosphere, a large collection of license plates tacked on walls, and a constant sea breeze from over the dunes, it's a great stop for oysters and a beer, or a plate of crab legs (entrées $10–23). Opens at 11 daily.

Perdido Key

Florabama Lounge (850-492-3048; www.florabama.com), 17401 Perdido Key Dr on the state line, prides itself on being the "last authentic American Roadhouse," where you can stop in for a brew and a stack of oysters and stumble upon Jimmy Buffett playing acoustic out on the porch, unannounced. It's a laid-back, rambling, beachside bar and grill serving burgers, seafood baskets, and fresh seafood platters for lunch and dinner ($5–20); it also hosts the Annual Interstate Mullet Toss, first full week-

Sandra Friend

PEG LEG PETE'S

end of Apr, with prizes for successful tosses across the river from Florida to Alabama (you have to see it to believe it!). Cover charge for bands and special events.

Warrington

Stop for lunch at the colorful **Hip Pocket Deli** (850-455-9321), 4130 Barrancas Ave, featuring world-famous gyros, calzones, sandwiches, and more. Open Mon–Sat 10–2:30.

THE FLORABAMA LOUNGE, HOME TO THE ANNUAL INTERSTATE MULLET TOSS

Rob Smith, Jr.

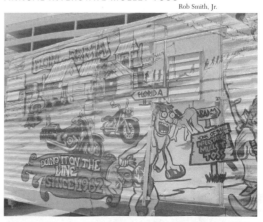

✴ Entertainment

The **Pensacola Little Theater** (850-434-0257; www.pensacolalittletheatre
.com), 400 Jefferson St, Pensacola.
The community theater puts on main-stage and children's shows throughout
the year. Note the remnants of the old
county jail in the courtyard. The 1936
building is also home to the **Pensacola Cultural Center** and **Ballet Pensacola** (850-432-9546; www.ballet
pensacola.com).

✴ Selective Shopping

Pensacola
For the absolute freshest seafood, head
to **Joe Patti's** (850-432-3315; www.joe
pattis.com), South A St and Main.
Since 1931, this world-renowned fish
market has had locals and international
clients picking out freshly cleaned fish
and seafood. They even ship around
the world. It's worth a visit just to see
the frenetic operation.

Look for folksy stuff for your home
at **Shabby Chic Antique Boutique**
(850-457-7537), 2601 Gulf Beach Hwy.

The crowds pack in at **T&W Flea
Market** (850-433-4315), 1717 N T St
at W St, billed as "Pensacola's Largest
Flea Market."

HIP POCKET DELI

Sandra Friend

Rob Smith, Jr.

PENSACOLA CULTURAL CENTER

✴ Special Events

January: Don't miss the popular
Polar Bear Dip at the Florabama
Lounge (see *Eating Out*). This annual
splash in the Gulf of Mexico on New
Year's Day isn't as cold as its New
England counterparts, but it's fun
nonetheless. Afterward, join in the
tradition of eating black-eyed peas.
Whoever finds a dime in their peas
has good luck for the year.

Let's hope they continue the tradition
of the **Big Band Concert Series** at
the National Museum of Naval Aviation (850-453-2389). The museum
hosts five spectacular evenings of the
best in big-band music for only $18
per show.

January–February: **Mardi Gras** (1-
800-874-1234) celebrations continue
in Pensacola throughout January and
February with numerous parades,
where moonpies and beads are tossed
from floats, just like in New Orleans.
Many festival and entertainment events
throughout the city.

March: The Arts Council of Northwest Florida sponsors **Gallery Night**
(850-432-9906) three times a year

(also in April and November). Enjoy touring arts and culture in downtown Pensacola at this quarterly event. The free trolley makes a great way to see the area, while stopping off at various galleries along the way.

April: The **Annual Interstate Mullet Toss** (850-492-6838; www.flora bama.com) at the Florabama Lounge (see *Eating Out*), first weekend, is not to be missed. This wacky tournament is a local tradition, with real mullet tossing, live music, food, and drinks throughout the weekend.

Historic Bartram Park is host to the **Annual Pensacola Crawfish Creole Fiesta** (850-433-6512; www .fiestaoffiveflags.org), celebrating the Cajun influence in northwest Florida. The crawfish boil is one of the largest in the state, with other Cajun fare like spicy chicken, red beans and rice, **Pensacola Beach Air Show** featuring the world famous Blue Angels. The event packs in lots of music, food, and fun.

Gallery Night (see *March*).

October: Visit 50 sites on the **Haunted House Walking and Trolley Tour** (850-433-1559), led by costumed guides, around the historic Seville and North Hill districts.

November: The **Okaloosa County Fair and Fine Arts Show** takes place at the Okaloosa County Fairgrounds (850-862-0211).

The **Blue Angels** (850-452-BLUE; www.blueangels.navy.mil), the navy's precision flying team, perform a spectacular air show when they return to their home base at Pensacola Naval Air Station.

Penascola Bay International Film & Television Festival (1-866-611-9299; www.pensacolafilmandtv.com) takes place over four days. Submissions come from the United States, Britain, France, and Spain and include feature films, series and documentary television, and student shorts.

Gallery Night (see *March*).

THE FLORABAMA LOUNGE

Rob Smith, Jr.

INDEX